Sustainable Management Development in Africa

T0295654

"This book is a window on African management practice and issues that will prove valuable to those interested in doing business in Africa."
—James P. Walsh, *University of Michigan, USA*

Sustainable Management Development in Africa examines how African management and business scholarship can serve African and multinational management and organizations operating in Africa. In a broader sense, this book, within an African context, explores how human capital and intellectual capabilities can be organized at the higher education level; describes the cultural, social, and political influencers impacting management and organization; helps conceptualize African management theories to address organizational effectiveness; addresses the current management and organizational practices in Africa in identifying challenges; and provides guidance for more effective management and organizational operation.

Aimed at researchers, academics, and advanced students alike, this book lays the groundwork for the application of uniquely African theoretical and practical perspectives for sustainable management and organizational operation, as explained from a contemporary African point of view. In addition and most important, this book contains uniquely African content that allows for developing new theories and examining new ways of doing business, thus reaffirming the rise of African scholarship in the fields of management, organization, and business.

Hamid H. Kazeroony is a Professor of Business at Minnesota State Colleges and Universities, Inver Hills, USA.

Yvonne du Plessis is a Full Professor at the Graduate School of Business and Government Leadership at the North-West University, South Africa.

Bill Buenar Puplampu is an Associate Professor of Organizational Behavior, a Chartered Psychologist (BPS), and Dean of the Central Business School of Central University College, Ghana.

Routledge Studies in International Business and the World Economy

For a full list of titles in this series, please visit www.routledge.com

Sustainable Management Development in Africa

Building Capabilities to Serve
African Organizations

Edited by
Hamid H. Kazeroony,
Yvonne du Plessis, and
Bill Buenar Puplampu

Routledge
Taylor & Francis Group

NEW YORK AND LONDON

First published 2016
by Routledge
711 Third Avenue, New York, NY 10017

and by Routledge
2 Park Square, Milton Park, Abingdon, Oxon OX14 4RN

First issued in paperback 2018

Routledge is an imprint of the Taylor and Francis Group, an informa business

© 2016 Taylor and Francis

Library of Congress Cataloging-in-Publication Data
Names: Kazeroony, Hamid H., editor. | Du Plessis, Yvonne, editor. |
    Puplampu, Bill B., editor.
Title: Sustainable management development in Africa : building capabilities to serve
    African organizations / edited by Hamid H. Kazeroony, Yvonne du Plessis, and Bill
    Buenar Puplampu.
Description: New York : Routledge, 2016. | Series: Routledge studies in international
    business and the world economy ; 63 | Includes bibliographical references and index.
Identifiers: LCCN 2015050398 | ISBN 9781138887015 (cloth : alk. paper) |
    ISBN 9781315714424 (ebook)
Subjects: LCSH: Management—Africa. | Management—Study and teaching—Africa. |
    Economic development—Africa.
Classification: LCC HD70.A34 S87 2016 | DDC 658.4/08096—dc23
LC record available at http://lccn.loc.gov/2015050398

ISBN 13: 978-1-138-34011-4 (pbk)
ISBN 13: 978-1-138-88701-5 (hbk)

Typeset in Sabon
by Apex CoVantage, LLC

Contents

PART III
Theorizing African Management and Organization

PART IV
Organizational Practices and Management
Challenges in Africa

Figures

Tables

Foreword

In 2009, our esteemed colleague, James P. Walsh, 65th President of Academy of Management, Professor of Strategy in the Stephen M. Ross School of Business at the University of Michigan, began looking outside North America to expand on the diversity of management scholarship, making the field of management more meaningful, and the application of constructed theories more consistent with the social, political, and cultural realities as practiced in different localities.

Walsh's vision with behind-the-scenes efforts of numerous other colleagues, notably, the distinguished Stella Nkomo, the Academy of Management staff, and Africa Academy of Management (AFAM) was able to hold its inaugural conference in 2011 in San Antonio, Texas, and its first truly African meeting in Johannesburg, South Africa in January 2013. Subsequently, Academy of Management held its African Management–focused meeting in Gaborone, Botswana in January of 2014. This exciting development allowed for institutionalization of examination and exploration of various conceptual and empirical management fields from African perspectives to benefit African organizations' effectiveness and improve multinationals' understanding of the African management context.

To serve the aims of the mission started by Walsh and Nkomo, and much effort was put into it by other equally dedicated colleagues from around the world, Yvonne du Plessis from South Africa, Bill Puplampu from Ghana, and I began with a single question: how can we help African scholarship to serve African management and organizations? Many colleagues of the African diaspora joined us in expressing the same interest, leading us to believe that more work must be done to advance African management scholarship. Our work was framed as the examination of issues in the postcolonial era. The African Continent, since its liberation from colonialists in the 1950s until the overthrow of the apartheid system in the 1990s, has given rise to a social transition impacting organizational development through the entire continent.

Hamid H. Kazeroony

1 Framing Sustainable Management Development in Africa

Hamid H. Kazeroony

BACKGROUND

Despite all the social and political will, there has been an absence of clear relationship between the transition from decolonization and apartheid and economic opportunity for indigenous populations of African countries. As Derrida (1994) would have viewed the situation, "The Time is out of joint. The world is going badly. It is worn but its wear no longer counts" (p. 77). Indeed, transition has created a vacuum in implementation of social justice to connect liberation from economic masters to development of human capital for the indigenous population in feeding the organizational human resource needs. "Following decades of totalitarianism, society is too atomized and demoralized to be able to mobilize for or against economic reforms or yet another change or regime. Instead, atomized individuals try to survive and stay warm" (Tucker, 2005, p. 23). "Between business and society, there exist an implicit social contract whereby basic human rights are mandatory. . . . Furthermore, together with basic non-market freedom, basic human welfare is advanced as a trump to capitalism and any other ideology" (Matwijkiw and Matwijkiw, 2010, p. 146). As argued by Cuéllar (2004), an international legal system to dispense justice, must (a) help local population to build capacity, (b) promote internal reconciliation, and (c) create and institutionalize domestic capacity by nations in transition to enforce the rule of law.

Since the 1940s, the African political, social, and cultural landscape has changed, some of which was prompted by exogenous factors and some by indigenous dynamics, and all accelerated by technological innovation and use throughout the continent. African changes are unique to its continental landscape, reflecting many distinct demographic and topographical shades of ethnicities, motivations for action, and the desire to blend and excel in the global marketplace. Most importantly, changes have given rise to new organizational needs in conducting business within Africa and the way multinationals interact with African consumers, stakeholders, employees, and managers. New approaches require us to examine the current thinking in providing an appropriate context within which we can address sustainable management development in Africa. To fully appreciate the African dynamics, we will explore the academic thinking about the recent developments, the institutional analysis about the needs for the future progress of Africa, and reflect on the continent's needs for the academic theoretical construct and practices that can make managers and organizations effective in meeting their goals and addressing their internal and external constituents' expectations. Therefore, a quick review of policy formulation, organizational behavior and dynamics, as well as approaches to expanding higher education capacities are essential.

First, Ligthelm (2008) argued that policy makers, today, should concern themselves with creating an environment where small entrepreneurs with little business acumen can flourish in places like South Africa. Walwyn (2008) suggested that countries like South Africa should begin investing in research and development to accelerate a knowledge-based economy. Some, like Akinboade and Lalthapersad-Pillay (2009) proposed that developing the African economy through partnerships can originate from South African regions such as Gauteng that must rely on knowledge-based economies requiring investment in innovation (Blankley and Moses, 2009).

Second, as Akande and Banai's (2009) examination of US-South African joint ventures revealed, "South African managers expect US managers to employ decision-making style that avoids uncertainty, expect workers to follow instructions, and provide job security to employees. They expect US managers to consult subordinates, to delegate tasks to subordinates, and to prefer team's work because they believe that better decisions are made by groups rather than by individual . . . In a sharp contrast to their own autocratic, forceful management philosophy, South African managers believe that an ideal US manager in IJVs should be people-oriented." (p. 9). Ouma (2012), reviewing internal and external organizational behavior of multinational agrobusinesses in Ghana and Kamoche et al (2012), raised the question as to how African managerial behavior should be molded to help grow African-based companies (domestic or multinational) and establish appropriate employee behavior to serve organizational growth drawing on African human capital.

Third, De Beer and Mason (2009) showed that graduate and doctoral work can benefit from blended pedagogies in Africa to accelerate the number of required graduates, manage faculty workload better, and produce numbers of qualified candidates to address higher education needs in the management/business fields. Awayiga, Onumah, and Tsameny (2010), examining the Ghana universities' accounting graduates, supported the proposition that there is a need to address pedagogical methods to enhance their acquired competencies to better address the new workplace needs in Africa. In addition to a re-evaluation of approaches in the field of management, De Maria (2010) argued that understanding corruption and ethics should be within an African context when addressing business/management in Africa rather than arbitrarily imposing Western values on African ways of doing things.

A report by African Development Bank (2009) stressed the need to address higher education to build a strong foundation on which economic development can be possible. The report laid out a strategic process based on integration of industrial needs with higher education institutions in achieving economic growth.

Building Capabilities to Serve African Organizations will examine how African management/business scholarship can serve African and multinational management and organizations operating in Africa. In a broader sense, this book, within the African context, will (a) explore how human capital and intellectual capabilities can be organized at the higher-education level, (b) describes the cultural, social, and political influencers impacting management and organization, (c) conceptualizes African management theories to address organizational effectiveness, and (d) addresses the current management and organizational practices in Africa in identifying challenges and providing guidance for more effective management and organizational operation. The book is an intimate exploration of how the juxtaposition of African practices and realties, and Western theories of management can provide the necessary means for effective organizational strategies in Africa.

This book, drawing on the African diaspora's contributions, will provide the contemporary African approach to business in illuminating effective practices in HR, strategy, marketing, and operation as an integrated system thinking, enabling readers to understand the underlying theories and methods; this can make both African and multinational organizational business pursuits in Africa more successful while offering African and other students at the graduate level a familiarity with the fundamentals of conducting business in Africa. Additionally, this book draws on African colleagues who currently live in or outside Africa to explain how we shape the future of African management higher education to better address the future needs of African business. This book is an edited research monograph aimed at postgraduates, researchers and academics,rather than undergraduate students.

CHAPTERS OVERVIEW

The book is divided into four parts. The first part addresses capacity building, focusing on higher education. The second part discusses the role of social, cultural, and political differences in building an African management framework. The third part is an examination of the theoretical construct in creating African management approaches. The fourth and final part reviews the management challenges and differences in their approach (from the Western practices).

Africa, post 2008 global financial crisis, subjected to political and social upheaval in the north, and suffering from declines in commodity prices in the Sub-Saharan countries, is projected to move at a slower economic pace (about 1.5%) for the next few years, while suffering from possible epidemics, negative trade imbalance, and more conflicts (Chuhan-Pole et al, 2015).

Africa envisions itself as **"An integrated, prosperous and peaceful Africa driven by its own citizens and representing a dynamic force in global arena"** (African Development Bank, 2009). Yet, the reality remains mixed: While economic growth indicates a respectable expansion in Sub-Saharan Africa between 2% and 7% ("Regional Economic Outlook: Sub-Saharan Africa," n.d.), Northern Africa, due to the ongoing internal strife since 2012, has no economic outlook data available. Lack of any economic data explaining the infrastructural position of the continent by the African Union (AU) organization also adds to the foundational challenges in determining where to go from here to realize the African vision as articulated by the AU. An International Monetary Fund (IMF) working paper suggests structural transition from agriculture to other sectors in some countries, while the entire continent suffers from inadequate preparation to meet the transition (Thomas, 2015).

Therefore, as economic analysis suggests, numerous structural challenges exist. However, rather than trying to address a wide array of continental challenges that Africa faces, Part I will focus on the topic of higher education and its role in building capacity for growth. Part I will examine the effects of governmental policies, the role of individuals as educators within higher education, the impact of accreditation and quality control in higher education. Part I will include four chapters—three of which are case studies.

Part II will examine African social, cultural, and political influences on organizations. Within this framework, the first chapter will examine the cross-cultural studies as a resource for multinational companies' (MNCs') effective operation. The second chapter will explain how organizational focus on cross-cultural communication will yield effective behavior by expats and indigenous personnel, leading to better organizational performance. In addition, the second chapter will explore partnerships between private and public institutions to learn how such partnerships can be used to enhance organizational capabilities and serving the public in African countries using a Nigerian case. The third chapter will explore the corporate social responsibilities in the context of public governance, reviews the legal framework for public and private partnerships, and provides suggestions about how to avoid constraints to improve organizational capabilities in Africa.

Part III conducts an examination of African management and organizational theory as a conceptual foundation for developing theoretical work that can lead to increasing practical organizational capabilities. The first chapter surveys the broad approaches to theory construction, some of the work already produced by colleagues setting the stage for additional theory construction to conduct African studies, and suggests how various broad theoretical nuances may be exploited for helping African scholars expand on their work from a uniquely African perspective. The second chapter suggests how hermeneutics, interventionist research, and graphic scales can be applied to African studies to conduct management and organizational research. The third chapter presents African management theories such as *burungi bwansi, kirinju,* and *ubuntu,* which demonstrate Africa's strengths based on indigenous theories.

Part IV provides an insight into some of the organizational practices and current management challenges in Africa. The first chapter explains, in light of societal changes, the need for new approaches to human capital management in building organizational capabilities and how changes have created new opportunities for re-examination of the topic. The second chapter proposes connecting apprenticeship and guided entrepreneurship as a way of educating the new management cadre to help organizations build new capabilities. The third and final chapter presents a framework for building African organizational capabilities.

REFERENCES

African Development Bank. (2009). *African development strategy for higher education, science, and technology.* Retrieved June 15, 2014, from African Development Bank Group website: http://www.afdb.org/fileadmin/uploads/afdb/Documents/Policy-Documents/yol%20%C3%A9duc%20eng.pdf

African Union [Fact sheet]. (n.d.). Retrieved September 19, 2015, from http://www.au.int/en/about/vision

Akande, W. A., and Banai, M. M. (2009). Your next boss is American: Attitudes of South African managers towards prospective US-South African joint ventures. *South African Journal of Business Management, 40*(2), 1–13.

Akinboade, O. A., and Lalthapersad-Pillay, P. (2009). The NEPAD initiative and the prospects of business opportunities in the rest of Africa for South African firms based in Gauteng. *Development Southern Africa, 26*(1), 131–155.

Awayiga, J. Y., Onumah, J. M., and Tsamenyi, M. (2010). Knowledge and skills development of accounting graduates: The perceptions of graduates and employers in Ghana. *Accounting Education, 19*(1/2), 139–158. doi:10.1080/09639280902903523

Blankley, W., and Moses, C. (2009). How innovative is South Africa? *South African Journal of Science, 105*(1/2), 15–18.

Chuhan-Pole, P., Ferreira, F. H. G., Calderon, C., Christiaensen, L., Evans, D., Kambou, G., . . . Buitano, M. (2015, April). *Africa's pulse: An analysis of issues shaping Africa's economic future.* Retrieved September 19, 2015, from http://www.worldbank.org/africapulse

Cuéllar, M. (2004). The mismatch between state power and state capacity in transnational law enforcement. *Berkeley Journal of International Law, 22*(1), 15–58.

de Beer, M., and Mason, R. B. (2009). Using a blended approach to facilitate postgraduate supervision. *Innovations in Education and Teaching International, 46*(2), 213–226. doi:10.1080/14703290902843984

De Maria, W. (2010). Why is the president of Malawi angry? Towards an ethnography of corruption. *Culture and Organization, 16*(2), 145–162. doi:10.1080/14759551003769292

Derrida, J. (1994). *Specters of Marx* (B. M. Cullenburg, Ed., and P. Kamuf, Trans.). New York, NY: Routledge.

Kamoche, K., Chizema, A., Mellahi, K., and Newenham-Kahindi, A. (2012). New directions in the management of human resources in Africa. *International Journal of Human Resource Management, 23*(14), 2825–2834. doi:10.1080/095851 92.2012.671504

Ligthelm, A. A. (2008). A targeted approach to informal business development: The entrepreneurial route. *Development Southern Africa, 25*(4), 367–382. doi:10. 1080/03768350802316138

Matwijkiw, A., and Matwijkiw, B. (2010). Stakeholder theory and justice issues: The leap from business management to contemporary international law. *International Criminal Law Review, 10*(2), 143–180. doi:10.1163/157181210X492225

Ouma, S. (2012). Creating and maintaining global connections: Agro-business and the precarious making of fresh-cut markets. *Journal of Development Studies, 48*(3), 322–334. doi:10.1080/00220388.2011.635201

Regional Economic Outlook: Sub-Saharan Africa. (n.d.). Retrieved September 19, 2015, from IMF eLibrary Data website: http://data.imf.org/?sk=5778f645–51fb-4f37-a775-b8fecd6bc69b

Thomas, A. (2015, August 15). *IMF working paper: Sub-Saharan employment developments: The important role of household enterprises with an application to Rwanda* [White paper]. Retrieved September 19, 2015, from http://www.imf.org/external/pubs/ft/wp/2015/wp15185.pdf

Tucker, A. (2005). Restoration and revolution: Understanding post-totalitarianism. *Policy, 21*(4), 22–28.

Walwyn, D. (2008). A target for South Africa's business expenditure on research and development based on industry structure. *South African Journal of Science, 104*(9/10), 340–344.

Part I
Capacity Building in Africa

2 Public Policy and Higher Education
The Case of Botswana

Dorothy Mpabanga

INTRODUCTION

This chapter assesses the sustainability of management development and graduate employability in the context of a developing country in Africa. Management development is a task carried out by various actors including organizations (internal and external) and academics in order to help produce a cadre of graduates with management and business skills for them to effectively manage national and multinational organizations (Kazeroony and Du Plessis, 2014). Public policy makers have a role to play in higher education as they design, implement, monitor and evaluate policy to ensure sustainability in management development. Management development requires a joint or collective effort from all actors in order to translate into concrete societal practices (Gladwin, Kennelly, and Krause, 1995). Kazeroony and Du Plessis (2014) assert sustainability of management development in higher education institutions as based on three elements entailing economic, social and environmental factors, while Gladwin, Kennelly, and Krause (1995) cite challenges of sustainability in management development as including inclusiveness, connectivity, equality, prudence and security.

This chapter therefore seeks to firstly assess employability of graduates and sustainability of management development in the context of an African country regarding resources (financial, human and structures/facilities) required to enhance learning and management development in higher education. Secondly, the role of public policy makers and academia to produce employable graduates who have management and business skills as well as competencies to effectively manage national and international organizations is assessed. Through primary and documentary data analysis the lessons learned from challenges and the discrepancy between implementation, monitoring and outcomes of policy in higher education are assessed, as well as the sustainability in management development in Botswana.

At the end of the colonial era in the 1950s and 1960s, when most countries in Africa attained sovereignty status,- they formulated administrative policies and programs towards attaining socioeconomic development. These countries also invested in educating their citizens in order to develop human capital to serve government and other organizations in their respective countries. Then most African countries used earnings from their natural resources to finance national development policies and programs in health and education, thus expanding their social systems, also invested in infrastructural development as governments agitated to ensure equality of opportunities to all citizens (Akinkugbe, 2000; Wolhuter and Wiseman, 2014). Investment in human capital was one of the national policy priorities that were adopted to facilitate the formulation, implementation and monitoring of national policies and programs as well as to deliver public services to citizens (Wolhuter and Wiseman, 2014). Worthy of note is Moahi's (2012) observation that globalization of higher education has contributed to the increase in demand for higher education in Africa as well as an increase in student mobility and competiveness in students and faculty. However, Akinkugbe (2000) argued that the sustainability of government spending and continued expansion of higher education was affected by various factors including reduced terms of trade, increased deficits and decline in economic growth.

Factors including economic difficulties, political instability, natural disasters, civil conflicts and a high debt burden as well as trade imbalances are known to have affected the development of higher education in the continent (Karras, 2014). Akinkugbe (2000, p. 1075) further argues that as the expansion of higher education and enrollment increased faster than capacity, quality of education and relevance of universities to national needs was compromised. Hence Moahi's (2012) suggestion for African universities to decolonize their programs and develop curricula that reflect indigenous knowledge that is relevant to the African content instead of emulating Western universities. Wolhuter and Wiseman (2014, p. 9) argued that higher education has evolved from elitism to massification where universities are managed like corporate entities, which raises the demand for relevance, a new research agenda and the need for new teaching methods. Michael (2004) points out that entrepreneurialism emerged as alternative ways to generate revenue, leading to reforms such as cost-cutting techniques, strategic planning, marketing strategies, program review and innovative management methods for survival in an increasingly competitive environment. However, Wolhuter and Wiseman (2014) assert that higher education in Africa is plagued by problems including low enrollment rates, unequal access, universities poorly connected to international scholarly networks and the labor market, undeveloped ICT (Information and Communication Technology) infrastructure, poor resources, traditional study programs, high graduate unemployment rate, and brain drain where the most educated Africans opt to work in Western countries.

PUBLIC POLICY AND HIGHER EDUCATION

Higher education is an important development agenda in Africa (Akinkugbe, 2000). The sector, according to Michael (2004) has evolved from elitism, with high returns on investment in higher education leading to liberalization, massification of higher education and later reductionism due to less public funding, accountability for delivery and resources, and reform in order to do more with less. Michael (2004) further purports "it is the education system that offers the best hope for societal transformation, manpower development, and effective participation in an increasingly global market" (p. 118). Bastedo (2000, p. 10) argues for university and college policies in higher education to aim to increase quality and outcomes of programs, particularly enhancing student learning skills necessary for public life, with faculty playing the important role of ensuring students learn public life skills through community service and capstone projects. Corcoran and Koshy (2010) contend that when universities in the Pacific Islands adopted the UNESCO (United Nations Educational, Scientific and Cultural Organization) framework and incorporated sustainable development policy in higher education and regionalism, the result was graduates who led government, businesses and programs on par with those from Western universities. Blanco-Ramirez and Berger (2014) argue that in order to evaluate and improve quality in higher education (HE), the issue of value should be explored as it connects quality with relevance, access and investment, suggesting that quality is not only about accreditation and international rankings; that HE is value-driven, thus leaders, policy makers and scholars should to be concerned with quality of HE in relation to access, relevance and good returns in investment by providing skilled workforce for economic and civil development. Michael (2004, p. 134) asserts that progressive institutions of higher education prioritize issues of quality in pursuit of academic excellence as outlined in Figure 2.1 below.

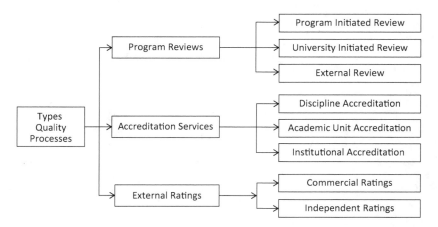

Figure 2.1 Types of Quality Process in Higher Education
Source: Michael (2004, p. 133)

Michael further contends that governments in progressive nations are bound to protect buyers of higher education who in most cases are ill equipped to distinguish quality in an imperfect market.

Berddrow and Evers (2011) argue that competence models are important for managing institutes of higher learning in a constantly changing environment and that lifelong employability "implies having knowledge, the skills to apply that knowledge in a multidisciplinary, team-oriented, dynamic environment, and engaging in lifelong learning" (p. 407). Knowles (1975) argues that (as cited in Berddrow and Evers, 2011, p. 407) competency-based performance models have facilitated for "practitioners and educators to understand the need for and process of identifying skills for effective performance, in this case performance is measured as a lifelong employability." Wright (2002) advocated for universities to teach and practice sustainable development principles and increase environmental knowledge at undergraduate and graduate levels. Environmental literacy could be enhanced through training workshops, seminars and inviting speakers to address students, the community and researchers (Wright, 2002). Moahi (2012) argues for the documentation of indigenous knowledge into databases, recognizing its important role in the modern knowledge economy and that indigenous knowledge should be integrated into educational curricula and be part of learning in African universities. Benefits of learner-centered learning environments identified by Berddrow and Evers (2011, p. 407) include feeling of ownership by students, motivation to learn, promoting genuine exchange of ideas, valuing students experiences and judgments, developing transferable skills, reducing teacher workload and making students think more deeply and learn to criticize constructively.

The following table shows the competence models that identify general skills required by graduates from higher education to support their specific knowledge and skills, and this model is said to be applicable to the public sector and nongovernment institutions. The important component about the model is that students are asked to reflect on these skills required to set goals and assess themselves. According to Berddrow and Evers (2011), self-directed learning, self-reflection, and self-development are the guiding principles of these two models (p. 409). This model was used to guide this study.

The above model was used to guide this study, and the research questions were based on these guiding principles to assess the extent to which higher education institutions build a cadre of students that can effectively manage and lead organizations at national and international levels. The application of capstone courses in program design and delivery would enhance the quality of programs offered by universities in addition to management and business programs and will enhance the development of graduates with skills and competencies required by organizations. The following section highlights experiences from other countries implanting the model in higher education to enhance students' employability and their ability to effectively manage and lead organizations.

Table 2.1   Capstone Course: Connecting Instructional Methods to Competencies

Competency	Group Work	Course Work		Projects
		Participation	Written Assignments	
Managing Self	*	*	*	*
• Learning				
• Personal organization				
• Time management				
• Personal strengths				
• Problem solving/analytical				
Communication	*	*	*	*
• Interpersonal				
• Listening				
• Oral				
• Written				
Managing Self	*	*	*	*
• Coordination				
• Decision making				
• Leadership/Influence				
• Managing conflict				
• Planning and organizing				
Mobilizing Innovation and Change	*	*	*	*
• Ability to conceptualize				
• Creativity/innovation/change				
• Risk taking				
• Visioning				
Specific Skills	*	*	*	*
• Computer expertise in word processing				
• Spread sheets				
• Statistical packages				
• Foreign language				
• Etc.				

Source: Berddrow and Evers (2011, p. 421)

Dolley, Murray, and Crase (2006) state that public policy in higher education has evolved and "transformed from a traditional public service provider to a partly deregulated quasi-commercial enterprise able to use market incentives . . ." (p. 93). The change in higher education policy was also influenced by public service transformation with the advent of a new public management (NPM) concept where, for example, "public services had to be streamlined and customized to meet market requirements through 'market signals' like price" (Dolley et al, 2006, p. 88). Some benefits from this shift in higher education in Australia included reduced dependency on funding from the Commonwealth, increased private sector funding and substantial income from international students. The authors acknowledge that there have been some challenges regarding commercialization of higher education, including quality of programs offered by contemporary Australian universities; for instance, these universities produce less skilled graduates. The Australian government established the National Tertiary Education Union (NTEU) and the Australian University Quality Agency (AUQA) to regulate, monitor, and address quality assurance issues in higher education (Dolley et al, 2006).

As pointed out by Nomura and Abe (2010, p. 121), Japanese higher education was faced by challenges including the reduction in student numbers, global competition in higher education markets and pressures to meet multiple social demands. The two authors posit that some of the significant changes in higher education policy were diversification, the turning of some universities into world-class research and education centers, and internationalization of research and student recruitment. The objective of this policy change, they argued, was to produce students who are ready for the global market and also address the issue of the dwindling number of domestic students. According to Nomura and Abe (2010, p. 124), the government collaborated with the private sector, nongovernmental sector and the international community (e.g., UNESCO) in order to promote policies and programs on education for sustainable development, including substantial funding of research, networking, revision of curriculum at primary and secondary schools to include topics on sustainable development. However, some of the challenges of "internationalization" and "sustainability" include coordinated efforts, university leadership commitment and sustainability of this policy initiative when government funding and support ended (Nomura and Abe, 2010).

Wang, Liu, and Lai (2012) point to many countries including China as experiencing excess education resulting from high investment and the expansion of the sector in the 1990s, which led to many jobless graduates because the economy had not grown adequately to absorb them. China, just like other countries, responded to the unemployment crisis of graduates by designing policies and programs that alleviated the situation. Wang et al (2012, p. 336) argue the unemployment crisis offered the Chinese government an opportunity to develop policies and programs that deviated from the Western model, to a model that aims for job-specific needs of a Chinese society with a policy shift in the 1990s including employment offered only to students majoring in teacher education and those from remote areas in China. The various higher education policy initiatives introduced by the Chinese government were to enhance graduate employability; for instance, between 2003–2007, the government required the higher education system to provide career guidance, planning and counseling services to students including employability skills and courses such as people skills, problem solving and team work (Wang et al, 2012). Table 2.2 below depicts some of the policy changes made in order to make higher education relevant to industry and society needs (Wang et al, 2012, p. 340); these programs recruited an average of 100,000 graduates per year.

Table 2.2 China's Public Policy Changes in Higher Education to Enhance Employability of Graduates

HE Policy Initiative	Year Introduced	Motivation to participate	Policy Outcome/ Impact
Encouraged to work in small-medium sized enterprises and private companies	2005	Enterprises graduates enjoy preferential policy on bank loans at reduced interest rate.	Realignment of curriculum with industry-society needs.
Work in grassroots-level/remote/ rural areas/ under-developed/ poverty-stricken communities for 2–3 years in teaching, medical, health, agricultural technology, youth development, volunteer service, etc.	2005	Guaranteed standard insurance package, refund of higher education tuition and preferential treatment for graduate admission. Salary, allowances.	Contribute to rural development. Alleviates rural-urban brain drain. Employ 20,000 graduates in teacher training in 2006; 75,000 in 2009; 237,000 by 2011. Universities revise curriculum to include society and industry skills.
Participation in national scientific research projects	2005	Guaranteed standard insurance package, refund of higher education tuition and preferential treatment for graduate admission.	
Enlisted into the army	2005	Guaranteed standard insurance package, refund of higher education tuition and preferential treatment for graduate admission.	
Start their own businesses	2005	Enjoy tax breaks and subsidies provide if business is registered within two years of the graduation year.	

(*Continued*)

Table 2.2   (Continued)

HE Policy Initiative	Year Introduced	Motivation to participate	Policy Outcome/ Impact
Universities to offer credit-bearing courses in entrepreneurship, engage part-time successful business people as teachers, entrepreneurship internship.	2010	Entrepreneurship practice, activities. Invite successful business people as motivators.	109,000 graduate students started their own businesses upon graduation in 2010.
Ministry of Education collaborates with industry to plan undergraduate engineering courses.	2010	Collaborative training, attachment and finish final year project in industry.	Some 500 majors in engineering from more than 200 universities joined this initiative. Alignment of university course and industry/job market needs.

Source: Wang et al (2012)

Wang et al (2012) posit that the above innovative policy initiatives have prompted universities to review their curriculum to include courses in communication skills, cultural sensitivity, technical knowledge, problem-solving skills, self-learning capacity, and give early career planning advice, and psycho-social skills to help students cope with the realities of managing organizations in China. There were challenges, particularly the mismatch between graduate courses and skills required by real situations in society and industry.

Sustainable management development policy in higher education is not an easy task for governments, policy makers and implementers—universities and colleges—as demonstrated above. Australia, Japan and China have made increasing efforts to formulate, review and introduce various policies and programs to enhance access, competitiveness and to impart graduates with skills to manage organizations as well as design policies to improve quality and sustainability of higher education. The above case studies have demonstrated that some higher education policies and programs have had positive and unintended outcomes and impact in the cases of Australia and Japan, and multiple benefits in the case of China. They could be good lessons for Botswana in terms of directing and implementing public policy and higher education, monitoring policy outcomes and impact on how policy makers and universities could build capacity in students to help them find jobs and become effective managers and leaders in national and international organizations. As pointed out by Michael (2004), a nation's progress and principles of higher education can be measured by accessibility and participation by different segments of the society, academic freedom, strategic and diverse financing, search for excellence, engage its HR, being able to compete (resources, best students, HR and academics) and being environmentally stable. Berddrow and Evers (2011) asserts that educators' aim should be to effectively prepare students as lifelong learners and to ensure that they are prepared for a smooth transition to the work environment.

The following section reviews policy in higher education in the context of Botswana. It will highlight some of the major policy initiatives in higher education and how they have contributed to guiding and supporting production of employable graduates that can effectively manage organizations in Botswana and elsewhere.

PUBLIC POLICY IN HIGHER EDUCATION OF BOTSWANA

Botswana has been blessed with mineral revenue, which was reinvested into socioeconomic sectors including investment in human capital. The discovery of diamonds after the country gained independence in 1966 from the British colonial government contributed to the country experiencing one of the highest economic growth rates in the world (Salkin, Cowen, and Write, 1998). The government used mineral revenue to establish administrative and legislative structures, processes and systems in order to direct macro-economic policy and program development and implementation. As Botswana was one of the poorest countries in the world, various policies and programs were developed with the aim of guiding the development and growth of economic and social sectors. The Botswana government made education a priority social service to invest in for building local capacity to manage the newly established administrative structures. The Ministry of Education was set up and tasked with directing development, implementation and monitoring the education policy initiatives, the first of which was the 1977 National Policy on Education, and a second, the Botswana Government (1994) Revised National Policy on Education. Both policies came up following consultations with the nation conducted by National Commissions on Education (1976 and 1993) appointed by the president of the country. The national education strategic objectives were later aligned with the 1997 Vision 2016 of an educated and informed nation—a framework for action leading Botswana to 50 years of self-governance—and to the millennium development goals (Botswana Government, 2003).

As shown in Table 2.3 below, various policies were formulated to support human resource development in the country. The main objective of the 1994 revised national policy of education was to increase access, equity and

Table 2.3 Public Policy and Higher Education: Botswana: 1977–2015

Education Policy	Year	Outcomes/Impact/Achievements	Challenges
National Policy on Education	1977	Quantitative expansion of education system.	Undeveloped education infrastructure.
Revised National Policy on Education	1994	To enhance access, equity and improve educational system, reduce class size, abolish automatic progression, introduce assessed progression. Developed of a tertiary education policy.	Limited access especially for those in remote areas. Poor quality of teachers. Large class sizes. Poor results. Poor quality of education.
National Vocational Training Policy. Vocational Training Act	1998	Increased courses/programs in industry specific skills, auto mechanics, service sector like hairdressing, tourism and hotel management. To fund and enhance vocational skills. Upgrading of infrastructure.	Lack of qualified faculty. Construction of vocational education centers.
	2012		
Liberalization on higher education	2006	Increased number of private higher education institutions established in ICT, business, engineering, graphics and design, entrepreneurship.	Problems of quality of programs in tertiary institutions.
Government Sponsorship Policy	1975	100% bursary. Pay back 5% of salary after completion of studies.	Increased demand for tertiary education.
Grant/Loon Scheme	1980s	Sponsor students in local institutions according to priority areas/needs of economy.	High cost of external placement as only 28% of students could be absorbed by local tertiary institutions.
Draft funding model for tertiary education and training development.	2006/7	Increased number of students enrolled in local tertiary education institutions, and increased establishment of local private tertiary institutions from 9,946 in 2006–07 to 48,000 in 2008–09.	Help government monitor and ensure effective use of tertiary funds allocated for teaching, learning and research.
	2008	Reduced expenditure on external education.	
Tertiary Education Policy.	2006	Government sponsorship of students to local and private tertiary institutions. Tertiary Education Council established. Higher education regulatory authority.	Mismatch between opportunities in the labor market and programs offered. High youth unemployment. High fees charged by private universities.

	Year		Issues
Tertiary Education Council (TEC)		Increased number of registrations. Establishment of private tertiary institutions because of positive environment.	High number of unregistered institutions. Poor quality of programs. Lack of facilities, e.g. library. Lack of qualified teachers. Oversupply of programs/fields of study.
Quality Assurance and Relevant Academic Quality Management Framework	2006	Botswana Training Authority (BOTA) established to monitor accreditation of tertiary education institutions. Diversification of programs, home economics, ICT, gender, population/family studies, design and technology, entrepreneurship. Upgrade on teacher qualifications.	
National Credit Qualifications Framework (NCQF). Academic Quality Management Framework (AQMF).	2012	Address problems of quality, accreditation, and management of education. External review of programs, e-learning. New academic programs in engineering, ICT, science. Improved research profile. Botswana International University of Science and Technology (BIUST) established, medical school established, teaching hospital established.	Poor quality of higher education. Poor quality of faculty.
National Human Resource Development Strategy	2010	To match skills with the labor market, realize individual potential. To help Botswana produce qualified, productive and competitive HR that meets national labor market. Priority to health sector, development of HR plan for health.	Continued problem of mismatch of graduates with necessary social and economic needs of nation. Lack of qualified teachers in vocational training institutes.
Life skills and preparing graduates for work.	2012	Produce relevant competencies and skills.	There are concerns of poor monitoring and evaluation of the internship program to assess if interns gain management and business skills to help them find permanent employment.

(Continued)

Table 2.3 (Continued)

Education Policy	Year	Outcomes/Impact/Achievements	Challenges
National Internship Program.			GVS program was introduced without the evaluation of impact of the national internship program.
Graduate Voluntary scheme (GVS)	2015	Research and development to address issues of mismatch.	
Human Resource Development Council (HRDC) (Former TEC)	2013	Relevance, quality of education and training. Focus on employability and skills. Graduates employment opportunities. Develop education innovation hubs. Promote Research and development. Enhance use of ICT. Increase access to early childhood. Learning and tertiary education.	University-industry needs mismatch. Lack of monitoring and evaluation of policy. Unresponsive higher education Institutions.

Source: Botswana Government, 2010; HRDC, 201.

to manage the expanding social structures in the social, health, education and economic sectors, infrastructural projects as well as water, electricity, transport and telecommunication services (Botswana Government, 2003). Botswana has continued to invest in human capital and has been allocating a substantial portion of the national budget to education. For example, during the 2014–15 budget allocations, 29% was reserved for the Ministry of Education and Skills Development (Botswana Government, 2014). The country has recovered from the 2008 global financial crisis and experienced a real GDP growth rate of 5.8% in 2013, while foreign exchange reserves were USD7.8 billion and the lowest inflation rate of 3.6% in December 2014 (Botswana Government, 2015). This recovery has contributed to continued policy direction by government to develop human capital. According to the Botswana Government (2010), the national education strategic goal is to ensure the country has "an adequate supply of qualified, productive and competitive human resources" (p. 92). Thus a vocational training policy was developed in 1998 in order to develop vocational skills and train students in industry skills such as auto-mechanics, hairdressing, tourism, retail and hotel management that were not covered by the then-existing tertiary education institutions (Botswana Government, 2010).

Obasi (2008) recognized the influence of globalization on the emergence of the new 2006 tertiary education policy in Botswana where one of the significant developments arising in policy shift was the registration of private tertiary institutions. As pointed out by Obasi (2008), "higher education flourishes mostly under a policy environment of a free market ideology such as neo-liberal capitalism, where globalization, privatization, cutting government expenditure and educational reforms are orders of the day" (p. 9). Obasi (2008, p. 127) applauds the new tertiary education policy to have contributed to the increase in the number of institutions of higher learning and the new status accorded to these institutions. Table 2.3 below illustrates the evolution and challenges of public policy in higher education in Botswana.

Tertiary Education Policy

One major challenge facing the Botswana government was a tertiary education system that did not produce graduates with management and technical skills to compete in the labor market (Botswana Government, 2010). This prompted the government to develop a tertiary education policy in order to address issues of access to higher education, quality and direct the education system to meet industry needs and produce graduates who could compete in the international labor market. The Tertiary Education Policy was thus developed in 2008 in order "to match skills with national labor market and to promote individual potential to advance and contribute to economic and societal development" (Botswana Government, 2010, p. 92). As Obasi (2008, p. 145) points out, the main concern of government when liberalizing the policy on higher education was for cost reduction and human

Table 2.4   Enrollment in Tertiary Institutions (%)

Institution	2010 % of Enrollment
Colleges of Education	5.6%
Institute of Health Sciences	3.6%
University of Botswana	31.4%
Botswana College of Long Distance and Open Education	2.2%
Botswana College of Agriculture	2.1%
Other Public Tertiary Institutions	9.7%
Tertiary Education Private Providers	45.4%

Source: Botswana Government (2010, p. 97).

resource development through increased enrollment. The cost reduction was obtained by increasing sponsorship of students into local tertiary institutions and reduction of external sponsorship in external universities such as in South Africa, Malaysia, Australia, UK and US (Obasi, 2008). Table 2.4 below shows enrollment in tertiary institutions following the amendment in policy to allow sponsorship for students in other registered local colleges and universities. Increased enrollment, from 20,011 in 2003–04 to 47,889 in 2008–09, was realized in private colleges and universities (Botswana Government, 2010, p. 96).

Nonetheless, the quality of higher education remained a big challenge for Botswana, just as it was a concern at primary and secondary school levels that fed tertiary institutions with prospective students.

Quality Assurance

In order to enhance the quality of higher education in the country, the government established regulatory institutions such as the Botswana Training Authority (BOTA) and the Tertiary Education Council (TEC). The Botswana Training Authority's role was to regulate and oversee the quality of education in the country including accreditation of programs (Botswana Government, 2003). The Tertiary Education Council was established in order to formulate, coordinate, monitor, audit, assess and review the tertiary education system and to advise government on issues affecting tertiary education (Botswana Government, 2003, p. 279). The National Credit Qualifications Framework (NCQF) was also established to further strengthen the higher educational policy and programs in the country and address problems of quality, accreditation, articulation, coordination and management (Botswana Government, 2010, p. 98).

Human Resource Development Policy

The Human Resource Development Policy was developed to develop strategies and polices that address issues of mismatch of university programs with industry or labor market requirements. To address the gap, the National Human Resource Development Council (NHRDC) was established in 2013 in order to guide, advice, monitor and direct higher education policy to produce graduates who are productive and competitive and meet the national human resource needs. In addition, the NHRDC conducts skills audits to identify overproduction and skills shortages as well as to promote research and development in the country (Human Resource Development Council, 2011).

Graduate Management Skills Enhancement

The policy landscape presented in Table 2.3 above indicates the many challenges government is faced with. Despite experiencing high economic development and growth, Botswana is faced with a high rate of unemployment particularly among the youth (Bank of Botswana, 2011). Some of the factors contributing to high unemployment are excess production of graduates in some socioeconomic sectors of the humanities and social sciences, the increase in access to higher education because of government sponsorship into local private institutions, and the inability of the economy to grow and diversify to create jobs (Botswana Government, 2010; Bank of Botswana, 2011). The other challenge is that the programs and curriculum in higher education do not prepare students for the work environment due to their lack in exposing them to management and business skills needed to survive after completing their studies. To this end, government adopted a national internship program (Botswana Government, 2010) and a graduate voluntary scheme enrolling graduates to gain management and business skills (Botswana Government, 2015). A new tertiary education funding model is being explored by the government where programs in short supply such as natural and health sciences, engineering and courses in infrastructure will receive higher sponsorship than programs that are in excess supply (Botswana Government, 2015).

As pointed out by Temtime and Mmereki (2011), "though graduate business education had played an important role in developing corporate leaders, they are currently accused of producing people who cannot effectively understand and act accordingly in a fast changing and turbulent business environment" (p. 111). The two authors further allude that many multinational companies have raised entry qualifications to include management and students have responded to this call by pursuing postgraduate studies with specialization in business and management. However, lack of skills for effective entrepreneurial management, communication, planning, leadership, and negotiation continues to haunt post graduate programs. Temtime and Mmereki (2011, p. 112). A study in Temtime and Mmereki (2011, p. 119) revealed that the skills required by industry were not adequately covered by the MBA program at the University of Botswana and students felt the MBA program lacked or had limited use of case studies, internships, writing, communication and presentation skills. In making a distinction between internationalization and Africanization of higher education, Kamwendo (2014, p. 268) regards the former as remaining Western in terms of philosophies, curricula and epistemological factors and out of touch with African realities. Kamwendo (2014) further asserts that African universities are transforming their curriculum, as well as engaging in research and community, restructuring, international recruitment of students and staff and internationalization of policies and programs to become relevant to the African context. For example, the University of Kwazulu Natal (KZN) in South Africa was transformed in the post-apartheid era to address issues of inequality and imbalances in gender, race and languages, and developed constitutional and national policies, while the University of Botswana transformed differently to pursue an agenda of institutional reform to internationalize and intensify research in order to be globally competitive (Kamwendo, 2014).

Despite various policy interventions and directions to improve the higher education system, Botswana faces protracted challenges in higher education where graduates lack management and business skills and cannot compete in the global labor market graduate and youth unemployment remains the biggest challenge for the government (Botswana Government, 2010, p. 93). Furthermore, the unemployment rate has remained high in the last 20 years, at 17.5%, particularly amongst the youth (approximately 35%), (Bank of Botswana, 2011). The Botswana Gazette (2015a), in criticizing the education system in Botswana, argues that the quality of education continues to be poor despite high budget allocations to the Ministry of Education and Skills and Development. The following section assesses public policy in higher education and its ability to produce employable graduates that have management and business skills and can effectively manage organizations. Empirical data was collected from 92 undergraduate students purposely sampled from three universities in Botswana as explained below.

RESEARCH METHODOLOGY

The objective of this study was to assess the role of public policy and higher education in building a cadre of strong graduates with management and leadership skills to help them find employment and effectively manage and lead national and international organizations. The study identified the problem of discrepancies between public policy directions and implementation outcomes. Botswana has invested heavily in the education system to develop human capital to address knowledge and skills shortages in various socioeconomic sectors. However, there continues to be industry-specific knowledge and skills shortages as public policy intentions to produce students with the necessary management and business skills are not realized by the higher education systems. This study intends to find out the role played by policy makers, academia and other stakeholders in helping government realize the objective of enhancing increasing access and at the same time producing employable graduates with adequate skills to effectively manage and lead nationally and internationally.

This study firstly assessed resources available in higher education to enhance the learning environment, and secondly assessed the role of policy makers and academia in enhancing employability of graduates and identified challenges faced in management development programs. Lastly, the study identified discrepancies between higher education policy direction in capacity building through management development programs and policy implementation, monitoring and evaluation of outcomes for sustainability in management development goals in Botswana and lessons for Africa in general.

The research used purposeful non-random sampling method and survey data was collected through the use of semi-structured questionnaires administered to undergraduate students in three universities in Botswana. Documentary analysis was also used. There were two public institutions surveyed and these were the University of Botswana and the Botswana Accounting College. The private university college surveyed was the Limkokwing University of Creative Technology. The University of Botswana was surveyed because it is a public university owned by government and has the largest student population in the country. The Botswana Accountancy College is also a public university and was surveyed because it specializes in management and business programs including accounting, business, computing and insurance. The Limkokwing University of Creative Technology was surveyed because it is a private tertiary institution and specializes in programs in science and information technology, and art and design as well as business and management programs (Limkokwing, 2015. The reason for surveying Limkokwing was to obtain perceptions of students in a private university regarding the learning environment, management and business development programs and employability after completing their studies. Table 2.5 below shows the population of the three universities and the total number of students surveyed.

The study used the Berddrow and Evers (2011) model of connecting instructional methods to competencies to guide data collection and used dimensions of management and business skills required to equip students

Table 2.5 Surveyed Higher Institutions and Private College Student Population

Institution	Student population	Total Sampled
University of Botswana	18,717	49
Botswana Accountancy College	2,355	20
Limkokwing University of Creative Technology	10,907	23
Total		92

Source: Obasi (2008); Botswana Accountancy College (2009); University of Botswana (2012/13).

become effective managers and leaders in self-management, people management, task management, change management, communication and specific skills. In addition the survey questionnaire had questions on the learning environment including resources, program design and delivery. The Likert's five-point scale was used to measure perceptions of undergraduate students. Lastly documentary analysis of public policy and higher education in Botswana was used. Respondents were also asked to rank in order of importance management and business skills, and through open-ended questions asked to state challenges and to suggest ways to enhance their skills to effectively manage and lead organizations when they graduate. The SPSS software was used to analyze survey data and statistics analysis through Likert's scale structured questions by means of cross-tabulation by university and year of study. Descriptive analysis (content) from open-ended questions of the survey questionnaire and themes were constructed from responses given by undergraduate students. A total of 120 questionnaires were distributed to students in their second, third, fourth and fifth years of study in the three universities. The response rate was good as 92 out of 120 questionnaires were returned. As shown in Table 2.6 below, students were surveyed from Years 2 to 5 in different faculties.

Table 2.6 Respondents' Attributes

Attribute	Frequency (#)	Percent (%)	Cumulative
Gender			
Male	39	42.4	42.4
Female	53	57.6	100
Total	92	100	
Age Group			
18–25	81	88.0	89.0
26–30	8	8.7	97.8
31–40	1	1.1	98.9
41–50	1	1.1	100
Missing	1	1.1	
Total	92	100	
Institute of study			
University of Botswana	49	53.3	53.3
Limkokwing University of Creative Technology	23	25.0	78.3
Botswana Accountancy College	20	21.7	100
Total	92	100	
Year 2	45	49.5	49.5
Year 3	18	19.6	69.2
Year 4	23	26.1	95.6
Year 5	4	4.3	100
Total	92	100	

Attribute	Frequency (#)	Percent (%)	Cumulative
Business	22	23.9	23.9
Humanities	9	9.8	33.7
Social Sciences	20	21.7	55.4
Science	8	8.7	64.1
Education	2	2.2	77.2
Engineering	10	10.9	83.7
Design and Innovation	6	6.5	100
Communication, Media and Broadcasting	15	16.3	

FINDINGS

The following section presents and discusses findings from the survey according to the main research questions.

Teaching and Learning Resources

Students' perceptions were sought to articulate the teaching and learning environment in their university in order to assess the extent to which they have access to resources and facilities to enhance their learning. The teaching environment was viewed by a majority of students (60%) across the three universities as conducive for learning, particularly at Limkokwing (68.1%) and the University of Botswana (67.0%). Students at all years of study felt that the teaching environment was conducive for learning (60.6%) particularly at their final year of study. Regarding access to course material, students were undecided about access to online teaching material though slightly more than half said they are able to access material online, particularly students at Years 3 and 4.

There were indications from the survey that facilities such as access to computers (83.6%) and use of labs (64.7%) to do work were available to enhance learning. A high number of students at the University of Botswana had access to computers (87.5%) and were able to utilize computer labs (79%). An overwhelming number of students (84.5%) at the University of Botswana said they had access to computers to do their work, and the highest number of those students (100.0%) being at fourth- and fifth-year levels. The majority of students (65.2%) said they are not able to access material on line at the three universities, while 69.4% of students at the University of Botswana are able to access material online. Only 52.8% of students are able to access material online across the three universities.

Gaining Knowledge and Skills in a Field of Study

Students' perceptions were sought to articulate the extent to which they have gained knowledge in the field of study. The University of Botswana had the highest number of students who indicated that they were gaining adequate knowledge and skills in their field of study, followed by the Accountancy College. Most of the students (67.4%) felt that their universities gave them adequate skills to get the job once they have completed their studies, and the Accountancy College (90.0%) topped the list of students in this category, followed by Limkokwing.

Interestingly, the majority of students (71.7%) in the three tertiary institutions were happy with the fact that they will be able to perform their duties once they join the world of work. Limkokwing University (82.0%) and the Accountancy College (72.0%) were leading in terms of training students for work compared to the University of Botswana (63.2%).

Program Delivery and Teaching Approach

When asked to indicate program delivery and teaching approach, students said the teaching approach used by lecturers across the three institutions was perceived not to be motivating, as only 51.1% of students agreed that the teaching approach involved diverse teaching styles. However, an overwhelming number of students (83.2%) across the three universities indicated that they wished their lecturers used different methods of course delivery; students at Limkokwing had the highest number (86.4%) and students at the University of Botswana had the lowest number (57.0%). Furthermore, 38.7% of the students were not happy with learning styles expected of them by lecturers; only 39.6% were happy with teaching material provided by lectures and only 34.5% were happy with online course material. More than half of the students surveyed at the University of Botswana were happy with the teaching material (53.2%), while more than half (56.5%) of students at Limkokwing were not happy with online material. It is worth noting that only 17.8% said they did not read course material, and this is an indication that the majority of students in the three universities surveyed consulted course material in order to enhance their learning.

Programs Meeting Students' Expectations

Regarding issues relating to the ability of courses meeting their expectations, only 56.8% agreed their courses meet their expectations, and 63.0% of students at the University of Botswana supported this statement, followed by Limkokwing at 52.2%.

Motivation to Enhance Management and Business Skills

Students in the three universities were asked to indicate the extent to which their lecturers motivated them to improve their management skills in order to enhance their employability. The majority of students (67.8%) said they were motivated by their lecturers to take up an internship or volunteer in industry in order to enhance their employability. Students also indicated that their lecturers motivated them to develop self-management skills (58.4%) and to improve their communication skills (64.7%). Only a few students felt that their lecturers motivated them to improve employability by engaging management people and working on tasks (48.9%) and taking change management courses (44.4%). Students were motivated by their lecturers to acquire specific skills such as computing and other languages as indicated by 56.6% of undergraduate students in the three universities surveyed.

In addition, the majority of students were motivated to learn in the three institutions (63.8%). However, data shows that students at the Accountancy College (73.8%) were more motivated. The majority of students, 83.7% (77 of 92) in the three institutions indicated that the teaching and learning environment motivates them to gain knowledge in their field of study. Students' perceptions by year of study show that 64.5% of students across the three universities were motivated to learn, and the highest motivated to learn were students at the first year level (73.3%).

Students across all years of study indicated that they made an effort (83.4%) and initiative (84.5%) to enhance their studies. This demonstrates an overall high level of enthusiasm of students from Years 2 to 5 in working towards improving their studies at the three universities. The motivation to learn was very high among students across the three institutions, as a high number of students said they take the initiative to enhance their studies (83.6%) and employability (84.7%).

Teaching Management and Business Skills

Students were asked to indicate the extent to which they agree or not with the statement that their lecturers taught students management skills to enhance their employability. The findings were disappointing as only 54.6% of students indicated that their lecturers encouraged them to intern during the long vacation. The highest number was at the Accountancy College (63.2%) and the lowest number of students was at the University of Botswana (50.0%). Regarding lecturers teaching undergraduate students management skills, 57.2% said they were taught self-management skills, 61.9% were taught communication skills, only 50.0% were taught managing people and change, while 54.1% said lecturers taught students to acquire specific skills in computing and foreign languages. Practical skills were encouraged more at the Accountancy College as 63.2% of students said their lecturers encouraged them to intern, while the Accountancy College scored low in developing students in self-management (51.1%), communication (44.4%), people and task management skills (42.1%). On the other hand, lecturers at Limkokwing are leading in teaching students self-management (59.1%), communication (68.1%), people and task management (63.6%) and change management skills (59.1%).

Interestingly, while 69.8% of second-year students in all the three institutions said their lecturers developed their self-management skills, 75% of fifth-year students affirmed this. The same applies to communication skills (64.4%) where mainly second- and fifth-year students felt that their lecturers taught them communication skills. Teaching students people and task management skills scored very low as less than 50% of students said their lecturers developed their management skills.

Knowledge and Skills to Enhance Employability

Students were asked to rank in order of importance areas they would like to improve in order to increase their chances of finding a job when they complete their studies. Interestingly, 74.4% of students said it was extremely and very important to work as interns in order to increase their employability. The majority of students at the Accountancy College were leading (78.9%) followed by students at Limkokwing (73.9%).

In addition, 67.4% of students said it was very important to attend self-management courses to improve time management, problem solving and communication skills through class presentations, listening and reading (77.8%). Furthermore, students said that managing people and tasks including planning, organizing, decision making and conflict management (76.4%) was very important, as much as developing their skills in managing and accepting change, creativity (76.1%), and also acquiring specific skills in computing such as Microsoft Word, Excel and SPSS, and learning foreign languages such as French, Chinese, Spanish and Portuguese (75.3%).

It is worth noting that undergraduate students at the University of Botswana viewed taking internship (72.9%), self-management courses (70.3%), improving communication skills (81.3%), taking courses in managing change (78.7%), and acquiring specific skills in computing and languages (85.4%) as very important in enhancing their employability. Only 45% of students at the Accountancy College viewed attending self-management and managing people and tasks courses as extremely to very important in increasing their employability. This finding is not surprising as the Accountancy College offers and specializes in management and business programs and industrial attachment designed to expose students to practical management and business skills. The highest percentage of students (78.9%) at the Accountancy College said internship was one of the areas that enhanced employability.

It is interesting to observe that an overwhelming number of students (83.6%) across the three universities said they made an effort to enhance their studies; the highest number of students were at the University of Botswana (86.7%) followed by students at the Accountancy College (84.2%).

Knowledge and Skills to Effectively Manage Organizations

Students were asked to indicate their readiness to manage organizations when they completed their studies. More than 50% of students (59.1%) said they would possess adequate knowledge to effectively manage organizations when they completed their studies, with students at Limkokwing University leading in this regard (65.2%), followed by students at the Accountancy College (62.9%) and students at the University of Botswana coming in last (51.7%). In relation to undergraduate students being equipped with skills to effectively manage organizations, an overwhelming 80.4% of students agreed that they were equipped, the highest being Limkokwing (85.7%), followed by students at the University of Botswana (80.0%) and the Accountancy College trailing behind (66.0%).

Surprisingly, only 60.4% of undergraduate students indicated that their degree program prepared them to effectively manage organizations, with the highest number of students from the Accountancy College. Fewer students at the University of Botswana (57.2%) agreed that their degree program prepared them to effectively manage organizations. When asked to indicate if their degree program prepared them to effectively manage organizations, the greatest numbers were at the first-year (65.7%) and fifth-year (100.0%) levels. An overwhelming 80% of students across all years of study said they would possess the skills to effectively manage organizations, while only 58.5% said they will have the knowledge to effectively manage organizations, particularly students in their final year of studies (100.0%). As pointed out by Obasi (2008), students have a variety of certificate, diploma and degree programs to choose from in order to study business management.

Students' Employability

Regarding the three institutions' ability to prepare students for employment once they have completed their studies, slightly more than 50% of students indicated their respective universities prepared them for employment, while 54.4% said they were confident they could find a job after completing their studies. The University of Limkokwing was leading in this respect (60.8%). Overall, based on confidence level among students for finding a job once completing their studies, was slightly higher than 50%. The highest confidence was at Year 1 (62.2%) and students at the fifth-year level (75.0%). Confidence in finding a job decreased at Years 2 and 3 and increased in the final year of study.

The research has revealed that many students take the initiative to enhance employability, as indicated by 84.7% of students surveyed. The highest number of students who indicated this were at Limkokwing (91.3%), followed by the accountancy college (84.2%). Overall, 75% of students were happy to intern in order to enhance their employability, particularly at Years 4 and 5. Some 68.1% said it was very important to improve employability by attending self-management courses especially those doing Years 2 and 4. Students at years 2 to 5 felt that it was extremely and very important to train in communication skills (78.4%), people and task management skills (74.3%), change management (76.5%) and computing and foreign languages (76.2%).

The majority of undergraduate students were happy to be identified with their university as shown by 75.9%, the greatest number at the University of Botswana (81.7%), followed by Limkokwing (69.5%). A good number of students were very happy to be identified with their university (75.6%), particularly at Years 4 (75.0%) and 5 (100.%), the final years of study.

Challenges of Learning and Management Development

As shown in Table 2.7 below, students were asked to write down their comments regarding resources and faculty and identify areas that would increase

Table 2.7 Challenges and Suggestions to Enhance Management Development

Open-Ended Question	Themes constructed from responses by students in open-ended questions of the survey questionnaire (N=92).
Management Development: Suggest ways to improve employability	Industry attachment, volunteer, industry-specific programs, improve curriculum, field work, guest speakers from industry, career fairs, project work, innovativeness, establish own company, job shadowing, improve CV, public speaking, networking, motivational speakers, increase research, part-time work.
The role of faculty: What should lecturers do to enhance learning and improve employability?	Mentor, prepare for class, remove theory, link with industry, instill culture of hard work, search for talent and let them develop products, communication and time management skills, free interaction, one-on-one consultation to find out student problems, don't isolate students, get more serious lecturers, adapt to individual learner, stop spoon-feeding students, more innovative teaching, be punctual for class and help students to be more productive.
Resources: What should the university do to enhance the learning environment?	Have smaller classes, increase learning resources, teach students life skills, get industry-relevant/up-to-date software and equipment, monitor lecturers, get professional management team, improve curriculum, establish relations with industry, motivate lecturers, get qualified lecturers, improve Internet connection, and provide adequate library facilities and books.
Challenges: Challenges and problems you face as a student at your college	Shortage of computers and books, too much workload, too much theory, too many in class, time management, difficult lecturers, no inspiration to study, improve facilities, equipment, software, slow registration process.
Other Issues: Write down any other comments	UB has good learning environment, too much copying, too many in class, respect international students and take care of off-campus students, engage students in class, being chased out of class, teach and don't read to students, where is education money going?

their employability and enhance their management skills. Most of the challenges centered around resources, theoretical approach to program delivery, enhancement of management skills and qualifications of academic staff.

Suggestions to Enhance Learning and Management Skills

A number of themes emerged for lecturers to enhance learning and management development from the student responses to the open-ended questions, which are discussed in the next sub-sections.

1 Merge Theory With Practice

Students were of the view that lecturers should minimize theory and expose them more to industry management and business skills to enhance development and prepare them for the world of employment. Most of the students surveyed would like their employability and ability to manage organizations to be enhanced by introducing practical courses into their degree programs, as well as by intensifying internships and industry attachments. As shown in Table 2.7 above, students across the three universities surveyed suggested integrating theory with practice to enhance their employability through, for example, industry attachment, job shadowing and networking.

2 Industry-Specific Skills Development

Students also felt that industry-specific skills such as management, communication, public speaking, job shadowing, project-based work, networking and a practical approach to teaching in tertiary institutions should be adopted to help graduates effectively manage organizations when they complete their studies. In addition, students felt that tertiary institutions should have career fairs where students and industry can interact in order to identify expectations from each other (see Table 2.7 above).

3 Inspirational Academic Staff

Students suggested that academic staff should also strive to motivate and teach students communication and time management skills. In addition, students suggested that lecturers should be interactive when delivering programs, as well as invite guest speakers from industry. Academic staff should also develop students by mentoring and coaching and instilling a culture of hard work. It emerged in open-ended questions that students at Limkokwing had multiple complaints regarding their lecturers, including some lecturers' habit of coming to class without being prepared for lessons and dictating notes, while other academic staff tended to "spoon-feed" students.

4 Investment in Resources and Facilities Enhancement

When asked to suggest ways the three universities could enhance the learning environment, the majority of students suggested the universities should reduce class sizes, increase facilities and resources, particularly computers, to improve access to online material. Universities should also acquire the latest industry-specific computer software.

5 Enhance Governance Structures

Students suggested that the institutions should improve management and governance structures, particularly improve the relationships between faculty, university management and students. Issues of enhancing governance structures and the university management team were prominent at Limkokwing where students suggested hiring a professional management team and that the university monitor academic staff.

The following section discusses findings regarding the role of public policy makers and academia in management development in higher education, outlines lessons for Botswana, and suggests ways to enhance sustainability in management development in Botswana and Africa in general.

DISCUSSION OF FINDINGS

The following is a discussion of findings according to the main objectives of this study, which is public policy and higher education and the role of policy makers, academics and students in enhancing teaching and learning in management development.

Opportunity of Policy Makers to Build a Strong Cadre of Students as Managers and Leaders

Policy makers have the opportunity, through public policy in higher education, to build a strong cadre of graduates that can find employment. They formulate and develop public policies and pass them to public agencies responsible for implementing, monitoring and evaluating outcomes. In the case of Botswana, the implementation and monitoring agency for policy in education is the Ministry of Education and Skills Development through different public and private providers of higher education. The Ministry, through its agencies, is responsible for the implementation and monitoring of the revised national policy on education including the policy on higher education. The aim of the Revised National Policy on Education is to enhance access and equity, and to improve the educational system in the country (Botswana Government, 1994). The national policy on higher education aims to achieve sustainable socioeconomic development, improve standards and quality of life for citizens, as well as to enhance HR development, promote research and innovation and to develop human capacity through equitable access to quality tertiary education system (Government of Botswana, 2010).

At its inception in 2006, the Tertiary Education Council (TEC) regulated higher education institutions, and accreditation and monitoring was carried out by the Botswana Training Authority (BOTA) (1998). The subsequent development of the tertiary education policy in 2009 increased access to HEs as government sponsorship was extended to students in private local tertiary institutions. The TEC evolved to become the Human Resource Development Council (HRDC) in 2013, and was tasked with assessing relevance and quality of Higher Education Institution (HEI) programs and providing guidance on skills required by various sectors of the economy (HRDC, 2011). All of these structures and systems were established with the objective of increasing equitable access to higher education, structuring the higher education system and directing policy to produce students with relevant knowledge and skills to address shortages in various socioeconomic sectors of the nation. The following are the positive outcomes of the national policy on tertiary education and efforts made by policy makers and implementation agencies to achieve HE policy goals.

There have been noticeable improvements in relation to public policy and higher education in various aspects:

1 Increased Access and Enrollment

The heavy investment in education made by Botswana over the years, as evidenced by the 29% of 2014–15 budget allocation, (Botswana Government, 2015) resulted in increased access at all levels of education. For example, enrollment in tertiary institutions increased from 20,011 in 2003–04 to 47,899 in 2008–09 (Botswana Government, 2010). The investment drive in education was to meet the policy objectives of increasing access to education, enhancing equity and promoting individual potential to advance and contribute to economic and social development.

2 Diversity of Programs

In addition, investing in education has contributed to the increase in the number of HEIs in the public and private sector and an increase in the development of various programs at the certificate, diploma and degree levels. For example, there are 20 public institutions offering programs in business, natural and health sciences, engineering and technology, humanities and education (Tertiary Education Council, 2009). In addition, multiple colleges and universities were established since the national policy on tertiary education was introduced, including five major private universities: Limkokwing University of Creative Technology, Ba Isago University College, ABM (formerly known as Academy of Business Management), GIPS (Gaborone Institute of

Professional Studies) Botswana and Botho College. These universities offer diverse programs in business, science, technology, management and art and design (Obasi, 2008). In addition, the TEC and BOTA made concerted efforts to implement and monitor the development of the tertiary education system through support, guidance, advice and monitoring the quality of tertiary education accreditation, program design and development, advice on improvement of governance structures, and the teaching and learning environment in tertiary institutions in the country. This study revealed that 51.1% of students surveyed felt their program delivery was diverse, even as an overwhelming 86.4% wished their lecturers used diverse teaching delivery methods. In addition, 56.8% of students felt their universities met their expectations. This is a positive outcome, though not very impressive considering the amount of financial resources invested into the education sector by government.

3 Human Capital Development

Investment in education has contributed to the enhancement of training and development of human capital that supplies the socioeconomic development needs of the nation. For example, there are many medium- to short-term management development programs and short courses in management, technical and leadership fields offered by public and private capacity building institutions such as the University of Botswana, National Productivity Center, Institute of Development Management and other private capacity-building organizations. Vocational training centers also build capacity in the artisan fields as well as the service sector in retail and tourism, and manufacturing. The government has developed a policy where short-term training can be conducted for private sector employees through a fund administered by the then-TEC; the fund was established to build capacity in business, leadership and management skills. Students surveyed indicated they would acquire adequate skills to get a job; 67.4% of students agreed and 71% said they would perform their jobs once they have completed their studies. This demonstrated an over human capital overcapacity in the country, though only 56.8% of students surveyed said the programs meet their expectations.

Challenges in Policy and Higher Education

1. University-Industry Mismatch

The results of this study indicate that policy makers and implementing agencies were not able to attain the main objective of management development in HEIs, which was to help build a cadre of strong students who have management and business skills to effectively manage organizations at the national and international levels. For example, one of the major findings of the study was first that public policy in higher education has not influenced the production of graduates who can effectively manage organizations. Undergraduate students surveyed revealed low preparedness for employment (51.1%) and low confidence in finding a job (53.9%). In addition, only 50% of students surveyed will be ready to manage organizations when they complete their studies. Undergraduates were also not equipped with people, task management (50.0%), and change management (50.6%) skills to help them manage organizations, even though 61.4% indicated their degree program prepares them to effectively manage organizations.

This finding is in line with other studies; for example, a study by Temtime and Mmereki (2011) revealed that the MBA program at the University of Botswana lacked communication, problem solving, entrepreneurship, and leadership skills and detected a gap between skills and knowledge most needed in industry, the skills most relevant to employers. This is mainly because the methods of program delivery mainly emphasize theory rather than practical industry-specific management and business skills. The survey and descriptive analysis revealed that students in the three universities were complaining about too much theory in programs and lack of training in management and business skills to help them find employment and enhance their ability to manage and lead organizations. Furthermore, students are interested in learning management and industry-relevant skills as over 70% said so in the three universities surveyed.

2 Poor Implementation, Monitoring and Evaluation of Policy

One of the major weaknesses in public policy in Botswana is poor implementation and monitoring of policies and programs. As stated above, Botswana has developed very good policies and programs to enhance access to higher education and to build capacity of human capital through various management development programs. These goals were achieved through high investment in education systems and structures to implement and monitor outcomes. Lack of capacity to implement and monitor policies in HE have contributed to reduced intended outcomes or impact, such as building a strong cadre of students with adequate management and business skills to find employment and effectively manage and lead organizations nationally and internationally. The Ministry of Education and Skills Development as the parent ministry is supposed to monitor implementation of policies in higher education by overseeing that HEIs design and deliver relevant and quality programs that are responsive to industry and national socioeconomic needs. However, as the results of this study have indicated, national policies on higher education are not able to produce graduates suitable to manage and lead organizations as expected, despite the existence of institutions and agencies established to support and guide HE policy implementation and monitor progress.

Some of the constraints faced by these agencies are lack of capacity to implement policies and lack of financial and human resources to monitor and evaluate policy outcomes and impact. There is a general shortage of the specialized skills required for policy implementation, monitoring and evaluation in these agencies and in the labor market. Other factors contributing to the skills shortage are unresponsiveness of universities to invest in regular program and curriculum design and review, theory-based course delivery, and the general poor working conditions and quality of academia in some universities. For instance, students surveyed in the three universities complained about the poor quality of academic staff, theory-based teaching and learning, and lack of adequate facilities to enhance learning.

Opportunities for Academia to Build Strong Students as Managers and Leaders

One of the major roles played by academia in HE is the ability to effectively train and develop students that are employable because they would have adequate management and business skills to manage and lead organizations anywhere in the global economy. As mentioned earlier, one of the main goals of public policy in higher education are to increase access, design and deliver relevant programs and curricula, be responsive to industry and socioeconomic needs and growth, and give everyone an equal opportunity for employment so that they can improve their socioeconomic standing and their quality of life. The quality of programs is usually reflected in the curriculum design and development and delivery of teaching by qualified academic and staff. Quality programs are also accompanied by good governance structures and learning and teaching environments supported by academic infrastructure and facilities. Access to facilities such as computers and labs to support learning was not a problem in the three institutions studied. However, the major concern was the quality of academic staff, teaching material and teaching styles used in the three institutions. For example, 39.6% of students surveyed were happy with teaching material provided by lecturers, while 83% wished their lecturers used varied styles of teaching. Statements from students asked about enhancement of learning by the lecturers and the university were mainly on issues of quality of academic staff and course delivery methods. Students questioned the commitment and teaching competencies of some of their lecturers, hence suggested close monitoring of lectures by management. Students also need to put in effort to enhance their learning, as Berddrow and Evers (2011, p. 407) found that a student-centered learning environment can be effective if students put significant and meaningful energy into self-assessment assignments since these develop a sense of responsibility for self-learning and skills development.

HEIS' ABILITY TO PRODUCE EFFECTIVE LEADERS

HEIs do not invest adequately in management development programs that would help build strong managers and leaders to serve African and multinational organizations. For example, the Botswana government sponsors students in local HEIs with the policy outcomes of producing graduates who

Table 2.8   Important Skills to Enhance Employability

Skills to enhance employability	% Ranked as important
Time management, class presentation and communication skills	77.8%
Managing people and tasks: planning, decision making and conflict management	76.4%
Managing and accepting change, creativity	76.1%
Acquiring computing and foreign language skills	75.3%
Internship	74.4%
Self-management courses	67.4%

Source: Survey data, Botswana, (March 2015).

can effectively manage and lead organizations, and are equipped with the knowledge and skills to survive on their own after graduation. However, HEIs failed to increase such returns as revealed by the results of this study. By failing to invest in regular reviews of curriculum, course design and program delivery, HEIs are rendered unresponsive to management and organizational needs and requirements. As demonstrated in Table 2.8 below, the demand for management development skills is high across the three universities surveyed. Lecturers also attempt to enhance students' skills. For instance, 54.6% of students said their lecturers encouraged them to intern, and 57.2% said lecturers taught them self-management. This is in contrast with what students ranked as important skills to enhance employability as shown in Table 2.8 below.

Suggestions to Enhance Employability and Management Development in Botswana and Africa in General

1. Enhance Implementation and Monitoring of HEIs

Enhance implementation and monitoring of public policy in higher education to ensure it builds capacity of students to have management and business skills to effectively manage organizations in Botswana, Africa and multinationals. The government has identified project implementation, monitoring and evaluation, and plans to address this weakness to enhance timely delivery of public policy and programs, including in the higher education subsector (Botswana Government, 2015).

2 Enhancing Monitoring and Evaluation of Outcomes in HEIs

Enhancing monitoring and evaluation could be achieved by policy makers paying considerable attention to implementation, devotion to monitoring and evaluation of higher education policy impact and outcomes on graduates, human resources, university program-industry needs and socioeconomic development needs in general. Higher education implementation and monitoring agencies such as the HRDC could increase capacity in this area. Karras (2013) suggests including students in the university administration and evaluation processes.

3 HEIs' Investment in Management Development

Universities should commit to invest in resources to enhance facilities, systems, curriculum design, and program delivery. HEIs should commit adequate financial resources to: improve the quality of academic programs and improve curriculum to include more management and business courses; invest in building the capacity of academic staff through appropriate recruitment and retention policies; invest in human capital by training and developing faculty through mentoring, coaching, course design, integrating research, theory and practice in course delivery; use diverse teaching methods and collaborate with students in course design and delivery. For example, Temtime and Mmereki (2011) suggested that the university program-industry needs gap could be improved by creative teaching that includes case studies, action research, continuous program assessment and review, recruiting transformational leaders for tertiary institutions, market-driven and business-minded deans and heads of departments. Bastedo (2000) posits that public policy should aim to increase quality and outcomes by introducing community service as part of the degree program and capstone projects to enhance students' skills necessary for public life.

4 HEIs as Learning Organizations

Temtime and Mmereki (2011) suggested that business schools operate as learning organizations where there is continuous learning and improvement and that business schools should emphasize programs less and partnerships with stakeholders more, and that faculty should be more concerned with mentoring. Furthermore, universities could also strive to learn from the past and develop value-based leadership, programs, and curricula that strive to produce graduates who can survive in the socioeconomic environment once they have completed their studies.

5 Motivate Faculty

HEIs should enhance their management of academic staff/faculty by enhancing general working conditions and providing a positive teaching environment that recognizes and rewards talent and innovativeness in teaching and research.

6 Recognize and Reward Achievements

Governments should recognize and reward HEIs that are responsive to the policy directions of increasing access, equity in opportunities, delivering management development programs that equip students with business and leadership skills, and reviewing programs and curricula to reflect industry-specific needs and address socioeconomic knowledge and skill shortages. For example, in the case of Botswana, the human resource development council conducted a national skills audit survey and identified knowledge and skills required in socioeconomic sectors. The council has developed a government sponsorship program where students are sponsored according to the skills required in industry. For this policy to have positive outcomes, the Ministry of Education and the HRDC should seriously implement and monitor its progress to ensure sustainability in management development programs delivered by HEIs.

7 Collaborative Approach

A collaborative effort is required between faculty, students, and communities in program and curriculum design and delivery where there is an exchange of ideas, dialogue, and a bottom-up approach to infuse indigenous knowledge and skills into curriculum and management development programs. This could be, for example, a joint effort to identify and explore viability in natural resources and medicinal plant production, processing, and scientific research while exploring collaborative opportunities in the national and international markets. Collaborations between faculty and students will help students come up with innovative ideas for the application of indigenous knowledge and skills in building their own skills and establishing their own businesses once they complete their studies. China developed a policy in management development programs where students were attached to communities at the grassroots level in teaching health and agricultural technology, and thereafter universities revised programs and curricula to include society and industry skills (Wang et al, 2012). This could be a good lesson for Botswana. As pointed out by Karras (2013), internationalization and regional collaboration can be used to improve quality and relevance of the education system and can be used to Africanize higher education through regional and continental bodies like the Southern Africa Development Community, the African Union's commission on education, as well as the Association of African Universities. Karras further posits that Africa can learn from the European Union's educational policies as outlined in the Bologna Process to enhance quality, assurance, accreditation, mobility and joint degrees.

8 Involve Stakeholders

As sustainability in management development is a joint effort involving all stakeholders, the involvement of the private sector, including multinational companies, is important in building the management and business skills of students. Collaboration between HEIs and industry in curriculum design and delivery, internships, mentoring of students in entrepreneurship, involving students in national research projects, as well as using the expertise of businesses owners as guest lecturers would enhance management development in HEIs. The Botswana Accountancy College and the University of Botswana collaborate with partners to develop and offer programs that are short in supply, such as engineering, procurement and taxation courses (*The Botswana Gazette*, 2015b). Blanco-Ramirez and Berger (2014) suggest African universities join efforts to develop their own quality assurance, accreditation, and ranking standards, considering factors peculiar and unique to the continent. The University of South Pacific Islands involved stakeholders in their sustainable development policy endeavors and engaged the national government, NGOs, business sector, the media, and the community (Corcoran and Koshy, 2010).

9 *Document and Celebrate Success*

The documentation and celebration of achievements in management development program outcomes and impact will motivate other HEIs to invest in management development programs. For example, the Botswana Accountancy College celebrated the awarding of its graduates with certificates in public sector procurement, tender process management, and advanced taxation (*The Botswana Gazette*, 2015b). Moahi (2012) suggested incorporating efforts made by institutions such as the New Partnership for Africa's Development (NEPAD) to document and integrate indigenous knowledge into the education system as it is tacit knowledge that resides in the community.

As alluded to by Gladwin, Kennelly, and Krause (1995), the collaborative effort of all stakeholders will enhance the policy direction of increasing access, equity, inclusiveness, and prudence in management development in HEIs, and promote sustainability.

Sustainability in Human Capital Development in Botswana

Sustainability in management development will be enhanced by vigorous implementation of public policy in higher education coupled with close monitoring and evaluation to assess impact and outcomes. The monitoring and evaluation of outcomes should be carried out by the Ministry of Education and Skills Development; agencies established to monitor, implement, and guide HE policy; as well as consumers of capacity-building programs—students, organizations, HR managers, academia, parents, and civil society. As mentioned before, management development is a collaborative undertaking that needs a joint effort by all in the society (Gladwin, Kennelly, and Krause, 1995). Vigorous monitoring and evaluation of management development goals will contribute to sustainability in access, equity, and prudence in developing the capacity of students in management and business skills to manage organizations in Botswana, Africa and beyond. Wright (2002) posits that sustainability could be enhanced by researchers and universities publishing research to create awareness of sustainability development, including intervarsity cooperation on policy measures, and partnering with government, NGOs, and industry. While Corcoran and Koshy (2010) suggest countries can learn from the University of South Pacific Islands, which incorporated the UNESCO framework of higher education system for sustainable development and had positive outcomes including production of graduates with business and education skills to lead government.

RESEARCH CONTRIBUTION

This chapter contributed to debates regarding the role of public policy in higher education and African universities' endeavors to drive a policy of equity, access, inclusiveness, and prudence in management development programs aimed at producing students equipped to effectively manage organizations in Africa and internationally. Berddrow and Evers (2011, p. 407) suggest that there is enough evidence to support the view that "knowing is not enough," but being able to apply that knowledge to analysis, decision making and problem solving is key to succeeding. Reflective learning, self-assessment and learner-centered environments are said to be important in higher education (Berddrow and Evers, 2011, p. 407). Academics, researchers, students, and policy makers who are interested in experiences from other countries in Africa can draw invaluable lessons from the findings of this research. The research also sheds light into areas for future research in the role of public policy and higher education and sustainability in management development.

CONCLUSION

The major objective of public policy in Botswanan higher education is to increase access and build capacity through management development programs to meet the socioeconomic needs of the country. To achieve these goals, government invested in higher education to build a strong cadre of students who can find jobs because they possess management and business skills to manage organizations. However, capacity-building goals were not attained as expected, and this created problems of discrepancy between policy intentions and implementation outcomes. Academia is not responsive to the policy direction of building students who can effectively manage and lead organizations, survive after completing their studies or be employed. Some of the factors contributing to these discrepancies are the poor implementation, monitoring and evaluation of policy outcomes by overseers of HEIs. This has contributed to an increase in the mismatch between students' skills and industry requirements. Government has responded by introducing the national internship program and the graduate voluntary scheme to enhance students' management and leadership skills.

As suggested in the literature and empirical data collected from undergraduate students surveyed at the three universities in Botswana, the policy in higher education can be enhanced by changing the provision approach to include teaching industry-specific management and business skills and increasing the alignment between higher education program design and delivery to job market requirements (Berddrow and Evers, 2011; Temtime and Mmereki, 2011; Wang et al, 2012). The sustainability of government sponsorship will be short-lived if the state continues to pour financial resources into tertiary programs that continue to produce unemployable graduates who cannot meet the human capital needs of industry and the country. A policy shift from aiming at increasing access to focusing on implementation, monitoring, and evaluation of outcomes of the higher education system will enhance sustainability and minimize wastage of limited public financial resources. Universities should aim for sustainability of institutions and programs by improving their governance structures and by investing in promoting a progressive teaching and learning environment. Adoption of alternative methods of raising revenue to cater to a shift in government policy in the tertiary education funding model and sponsorship formula will enhance management development, the employability of graduate students, and sustainability in management development. Suggestions for enhancing sustainability include expanding access but controlling unit cost, improving internal efficiency, cost recovery, mobilizing resources from alumni as well as encouraging the private sector to invest in higher education (Akinkugbe, 2000). Future research should expand the survey sample to include all key players such as academia, the private sector, indigenous communities, parents, industry, as well as policy makers and those who implement and monitor outcomes. In addition, using both qualitative and quantitative methodological approaches will enhance the generalizability of findings.

REFERENCES

Akinkugbe, A. (2000). Higher education financing and equality in Swaziland. *International Journal of Social Economics, 27*(11), 1074–1097. Retrieved August 7, 2015, from http://www.emeraldinsight-library.com

Bank of Botswana. (2011). *Financial statistics.* Gaborone: Bank of Botswana.

Bastedo, M. N. (2000). Students outcome and state policy in public higher education. *On the Horizon: January/February, 8*(1), 10–12. Retrieved March 6, 2015, from http://www.emeraldinsight.com/authors

Berddrow, I., and Evers, F. (2011). Base competence: A framework for facilitating reflective learner centered education environments. *Journal of Management Research, 35*(3), 406–427. Retrieved November 11, 2011, from http://jme.sagepub.com

Blanco-Ramirez, G., and Berger, J. B. (2014). Rankings, accreditation, and the international quest for quality education: organizational approach to value in higher education. *Quality Assurance in Education, 22*(1), 88–104. Retrieved August 7, 2015, from http://www.emeraldinsight.com/0968–4883.htm

Botswana Accountancy College. (2009). *Facts and figures.* Retrieved June 15, 2015, from http://www.bac.ac.bw

The Botswana Gazette. (2015a, March 11–17). *The state in failure: Education crisis.* Special Report: Education.

The Botswana Gazette. (2015b, June 17–23). *PPADB engages World Bank to introduce price guide for works.* Business Report. Botswana Government. (1994). *The revised national policy on education.* Gaborone, Government Printer.

Botswana Government. (2003). *National development plan.* Gaborone, Ministry of Finance and Development Planning.

Botswana Government. (2010). *National development plan.* Gaborone, Ministry of Finance and Development Planning.

Botswana Government. (2014). *Budget speech.* Gaborone, Ministry of Finance and Development Planning.

Botswana Government. (2015). *Budget speech.* Gaborone, Ministry of Finance and Development Planning.

Botswana Training Authority. (1998). Retrieved March 27, 2015, from http://www.bota.co.bw

Corcoran, P. B., and Koshy, K. C. (2010). The pacific way: Sustainability in higher education in the South Pacific Islands. *International Journal of Sustainability, 11*(2), 130–140. Retrieved August 7, 2015, from http://www.emeraldinsight.com/1467–6370.htm

Dolley, B., Murray, D., and Crase, L. (2006). Knaves or knights, pawns or queens? An evaluation of Australian higher education reform policy. *Journal of Education Administration, 44*(1), 86–97. Retrieved August 7, 2015, from http://www.emeraldinsight.com/1467–6370.htm

Gladwin, T. N., Kennelly, J. J., and Krause, T. S. (1995). Shifting paradigms for sustainable development: Implications for management theory and research. *Academy of Management, 20*(4), 874–907. Retrieved June 15, 2015, from http://amr.aom.org/content/20/4/874.full.pdf+html

Human Resource Development Council. (2011). *The beginning.* Retrieved June 15, 2015, from http://www.hrdc.org.bw

Kamwendo, G. H. (2014). Language in higher education transformation: Contrasts and similarities between two African universities. In Wiserman, A. W. and Wolhuter, C. C. (2013). *The Development of Higher Education in Africa: Prospects and Challenges on Education and Society, 21,* 265–283.

Karras, K. G. (2013). European education policies and the unification of higher education in Europe: Some lessons from the Bologna process for education and teacher education in Africa, *21,* 375–399. Retrieved August 7, 2015, from http://www.emeraldinsight.com/

Kazeroony, H., and du Plessis, Y. (2014, January). *Sustainable management development: Overcoming social transition.* Paper presented at the Africa Academy of Management, conference, Gaborone, Botswana.

Knowles, M.S. (1975). *Self-Directed Learning: a guide for learners and teachers.* New York: Associated Press.

Limkokwing University of Creative Technology. (2015). *Academic.* Retrieved June 15, 2015 from http://www.limkokwing.net/boswana

Lunz, M. E., and Culver, S. (2010). The national survey of student engagement: A university-level analysis. *Tertiary Education and Management, 16*(1), 35–44. Retrieved November 11, 2011, from http://www.tandfonline.com/loi/rtem20

Michael, S. O. (2004). In search of universal principles of higher education management and applicability to Maldavian higher education system. *International*

Journal of Higher Education Management, 18(2), 118–137. Retrieved November 11, 2011, from http://jme.sagepub.com

Moahi, K. H. (2012). Promoting African indigenous knowledge in the knowledge economy: Exploring the role of higher education and libraries. *Aslib Proceedings, 64*(5), 540–554. Retrieved August 7, 2015, from http://www.emeraldinsight.com

Nomura, K. O., and Abe, O. (2010). Higher education for sustainable development in Japan: Policy and progress. *International Journal of sustainability in Higher Education, 11*(2), 120–129. Retrieved March 6, 2015, from http://www.emeraldinsight.com

Obasi, I. N. (2008). *Private higher education and public policy: A contrasting case of Nigeria and Botswana.* Göttingen: Cuvillier Verlag.

Salkin, J., Cowen, C., and Write, M. (1998). *Aspects of the Botswana economy: Selected papers.* Gaborone: Lentswe la lesedi.

Temtime, Z. T., and Mmereki, R. N. (2011). Challenges faced by graduate business education in Southern Africa. *Quality Assurance in Education, 19*(2), 110–129. Retrieved March 6, 2015, from http://www.emeraldinsight.com

Tertiary Education Council. (2009). Retrieved March 27, 2015 from http://www.tec.org/bw

University of Botswana. (2012/13). *Annual report.* Gaborone: University of Botswana.

Wang, D., Liu, D., and Lai, D. (2012). Expansion of higher education and the employment crisis: Policy innovations in China. *On the Horizon, 20*(4), 336–344.

Wolhuter, C. C., and Wiseman, A. W. (2014). The incalculable promise of the African continent: Higher education rising to the occasion?, in Alexander W. Wiseman, Charl C. Wolhuter (ed.) *The Development of Higher Education in Africa: Prospects and Challenges (International Perspectives on Education and Society, Volume 21)* Emerald Group Publishing Limited, 3–19.

Wright, T. S. A. (2002). Definitions and frameworks for environmental sustainability in higher education. *International Journal of Sustainability in Higher Education, 3*(3), 203–220. Retrieved August 7, 2015, from http://www.emeraldinsight.com/147-6370.htm

3 Challenges in Developing African Management Scholars

An Auto-Ethnographic Study

Emmanuel Mukwevho and Yvonne du Plessis

INTRODUCTION

The main aim of this chapter is to shed light on typical experiences and present the major challenges that create a chronic shortage of black scholars or academics specifically in South Africa. The story of a black South African male, born in 1977, who passed through the motions and emotions of seeking betterment, education and development despite all the challenges of apartheid and post-apartheid, will inform this study.

Furthermore, this auto-ethnography may serve as an inspiration to others in following the scholarly path as black South Africans, as a glimmer of hope that it is possible to become a scholar despite a poverty-ridden background dominated by hordes of unemployed and uneducated migrant laborers who were home seldom. Although the scholarly road seems to be a road less travelled among black South Africans, it is a promising journey. Many great black South Africans, such as Nelson Mandela, Oliver Tambo, Chris Hani, Desmond Tutu, to mention a few, known for making great exploits, were not born and raised in affluent homes with adequate developmental and educational support, yet their determination to achieve their goals was a critical factor in achieving their dreams. The layout of this chapter starts with a brief background on South African scholarly development and the need for study, then present the research methodology, auto-ethnography and findings, followed by a discussion on current South African challenges in developing African scholars, and ending with conclusions and key recommendations.

BACKGROUND TO SOUTH AFRICA AND AFRICAN SCHOLARLY DEVELOPMENT

South Africa as a developing country presents two sides of a coin: *the head* (whites who are ahead scholarly) and *the tail* (black Africans lagging behind scholarly), as indicated in the statistics of scholars in the country. According to the Organization for Economic Cooperation and Development (OECD, 2008), South Africa post 1994 (post-apartheid) has had a stagnant pace in the production of PhDs par to other world-leading economies. For example, South Africa (SA), with a population of 51 million, has 23 institutions of higher learning, whereas Finland with a population of 5 million, ten times fewer than South Africa, has 46 institutions of higher learning. The production of PhDs is reported to be 28 per every million in SA, whereas Finland has 356 per every million due to their intensive investment in research and development (R&D).

Education is a powerful source in any society and proven to change the fortunes of those who attain it. This was reiterated by former president Nelson Mandela, who said, "Education is the most powerful weapon which you can use to change the world" (Madi, 1993). However, the general lack of education in South Africa and subsequent PhDs, the feeder of academic scholars, resulted in black South Africans lagging behind academically, mainly due to segregation and a lack of developmental opportunities during the apartheid era, compared to previously advantaged whites, who had received opportunities. According to the data provided by the South African Department of Higher Education and Training (DHET, 2011), the percentage of white professors in South African Universities was 75.6%, while that of black professors was a measly 14%. This is a very worrisome number considering that blacks constitute about 80% of the country's population compared to 10% of whites. These statistics show the great need for the development of African scholars in the country. Jo-Anne Vorster of Rhodes University wrote a piece in *The Conversation* entitled, "Professors aren't born: they must be nurtured" (Vorster, 2014). Indeed, there is an urgent need to develop and nurture African scholars to eradicate the historically generated imbalances and repair the impact of previously legislated apartheid.

It is February 2015, and our postgraduate program has just commenced. In front of me (white South African female scholar and professor) are 55 black African MBA learners enrolled in the subject of Organizational Behavior at a Business School in South Africa. I am especially interested in African business managers and their development, and here a class full of them is sitting in front of me with expectations and assumptions of becoming better managers/leaders in their organizations. This is a challenge I thought to get them to comply with all the requirements of doing an MBA. Where are they from? Have they got the will and ability to persevere? Why are they here, to learn and develop their managerial competence or to get a better job? As all these questions shoot through my head, I become nostalgic as very few of these learners, who already made it so far, will enter academia as a career choice. We need these learners to see the scholarly journey as a possible career opportunity and embrace it to uplift our country. Why are there so few black South African scholars? Most of the black scholars in South African universities are foreigners . . . and then I saw the name on the attendance register, Prof. EM. I am amazed, and ask him as a young black South African scholar to join me in this research—developing black South African scholars—as he is one and made it despite odds against him.

The challenges began when he was born in a typical African village called Dididi, which is 4 miles away from the nearest town, Thohoyandou, in Venda (currently the Limpopo Province of South Africa). He was born with very little hope around him, especially of attaining higher education, a fact that epitomizes the lives of millions of black South Africans and Africans alike. He, however, was fortunate and had many blessings and the opportunity to graduate in 2009 with a PhD in biochemistry from a top-rated University in South Africa, The University of Cape Town. He chose the academic career option and received an associate professorship in 2014 at the early age of 37 during post-apartheid; therefore, it is legible to narrate his experiences and challenges in becoming an African scholar.

It is against this background that we are going to present this auto-ethnographic study and discussion on African scholarly development.

RESEARCH METHODOLOGY

Auto-ethnography is a qualitative research approach within the postmodernist paradigm where the researcher "seeks to describe and systematically analyze (graphically) personal experience (auto) in order to understand cultural experience (ethno)" (Ellis et al, 2010). Thus, the writer (researcher) uses tenets of autobiography and ethnography to produce the results of an auto-ethnography. Ellis and Bochner (2000) describe the auto-ethnographic researcher as someone who seeks to produce "meaningful, accessible, and evocative research grounded in personal experience, research that would sensitize readers to issues of identity politics, to experiences shrouded in silence, and to forms of representation that deepen our capacity to empathize with people who are different from us." Auto-ethnography allows for the researcher to influence the research by being subjective and emotional rather than to avoid being human with feelings and not allowing this (Ellis et al, 2010). This is why we have chosen auto-ethnography to write this chapter as it engages the reader (empathically) in the world of black South Africans becoming scholars who have lived in poverty and been deprived of good education and development, to feel their emotions on their journey of desperation, and to hear their voices crying for improved development.

In the process of conducting this auto-ethnography, we retrospectively and selectively wrote about epiphanies (happenings) in the life of a black African scholar who went through the experience of becoming a scholar, being part of a culture (South African) and/or possessing a particular cultural identity (black African village, Tshivenda ethnic person) (Ellis et al, 2010).

A purposive sample with a single participant who has experienced the challenges of becoming a black African scholar was chosen. For the purpose of this chapter, the participant will be referred to as 'Em'. Data were collected through narratives and open interviews with 'Em'. The auto-ethnographic journey was co-constructed by the two researchers.

The core challenges identified in analyzing the data from narratives and transcripts of interview can be divided into two main categories:

1) African Village life and School Education, and
2) Becoming a Scholar, which again can be divided into two subcategories:
    a) Obtaining a Degree, and
    b) Postgraduate studies and PhD: The scholarship key

THE SCHOLARLY JOURNEY OF A BLACK SOUTH AFRICAN

African villages usually comprise clusters of people (villagers) belonging to a traditional tribe under the reign of a traditional leader away from city life, having little education themselves and just striving to make ends meet.

> Em's voice: *Dididi is a small village of about 7,000 people mostly dominated by the unemployed, uneducated and a handful of migrant laborer residents. Traditionally, women would be home looking after children and tilling the fields whilst most of the adult men were working in mines and farms as laborers [migrant workers].*

School is not seen as a priority; however, it is legally required to send children to school. Parents, due to lack of education, cannot explain to their children why education is important. The lack of role models and career insights limited opportunities for children to learn. Working to earn a living was the motivation and valued, not spending endless time on education.

> Em's voice: *School was a place to keep children away from home whilst parents could be able to do their errands without disturbance. We went to school because we had to, not knowing the end goals and benefits of it. It was more of a punishment for us to be in school than to be playing. When I started my primary school in 1983, there was no one who had gone to a University in that village. At that time only a handful few managed to go to teaching colleges and only one being in a nursing college. Matric [end of secondary school] was a prestigious achievement, and going to a college being the most illustrious achievement. A University was seen as a far distant dream to achieve if coming from villages, and only handful few in the former Venda, had managed to pass their grade 12 [matric] and register at a university. As such the prevailing societal perception was when you pass matric, you go to teaching or nursing college; these were the two most chosen options post-matric and to think beyond that was hard. . . . Most people at the time would hardly go through to grade 12 and would rather seek employment as migrant labors in mines and farms in the then-Transvaal cities and*

towns like Johannesburg, Pretoria (now Gauteng Province) and Brits (now North West province). To work as a migrant laborer was more prestigious than going through school grades which seem to be a long route for one to make a living. . . . unskilled labor was available . . . it came at the backdrop of the apartheid system where unskilled laboring was acquired from a majority of Blacks.

Households are big and mostly illiterate mothers or grandparents who look after children while fathers are migrant laborers away from home for extended periods of time.

EM's voice: *My father was a migrant labor too in Pretoria. So we would hardly see him except for Easter and Christmas holidays. I was born with 6 siblings; 4 boys and 2 girls . . .*

The village schools often have little or no facilities and classrooms are few, so teaching under trees is the only option, especially in primary schools. Schools are far from villages and children have to walk there and back every day, making it tough to attend during winter and rainy seasons. High schools are scarce, and children often have to attend school away from the village. Village secondary [high] schools do not offer all the subjects to enter into university. Mathematics and science teachers are scarce and so are the facilities at school to teach these subjects. After school there is little or no time for homework as children have to look after livestock (farm animals) and gardens. School dropout is high due to socioeconomic conditions, and entering into university is hard due to the wrong subjects or a lack of funds or both.

Em's voice: *Fortunately we had a primary school within 1 mile walking distance. I walked to school and daily walked [home] for lunch and back. After school one would go to look after goats or cattle. Within the 7 years of primary education, 3 of those years I attended classes under trees that were in the school yard. Most of the bigger trees within the school yard were usually classrooms due to the shade they provided, in the scratchy heat of Limpopo. Most of my peers drop out of school and get unskilled labor somewhere whilst most of the ladies would get married, which was more valuable than schooling then. Of all I attended primary school with, none of them have made it to University level.*
My secondary [high] school comprised three schools . . . [seeking for a school with the right subjects—Mathematics and Science] . . . my village was 50 miles away from the last school [also in a village and I stayed with an Aunt], where I completed my Matric in 1994, the same year South Africa's Apartheid system was abolished and Mr. Nelson Mandela becoming the first Black president. I could not go to University due to a lack of funds. As such in 1995 I went back to Matric . . . [to improve] took up Physical Science as subject and I was forced to look

for the nearest school, 5 miles away from Dididi [my village]. By this time two [villagers] had gone to University, and few registering which made it easier to take the route less taken by those coming from villages. Of all those that I did high school with . . . no more than five managed to graduate at a university level.

Teachers are very important role models for school children especially those growing up in villages, where parents are often illiterate or not well educated.

Em's voice: *I completed my primary school in 1989. . . . Teachers like Mr X and Mr Y were my main role models in primary school.*

[T]he [high] school principal Mr M . . . was my role model and inspired me to take Mathematics and Physical Science as subject that would give me better prospects at tertiary level [scarcity of skills in mathematics and science in South Africa].

Becoming a Scholar

Drive and resiliency are viewed as key factors in starting the education journey irrespective of your background. Some recognition from others early in your life may give the spark for wanting to improve yourself; that is also why mentors and heroes are important—someone who shows interest and energizes the learner.

EM's voice: *I grew loving school dearly and always dreamt of making it big in life. There was always this self-drive inside, of not wanting to conform nor accept the poverty and hopelessness around me. Most of those who taught me in primary schools quickly noticed the potential, zeal and eager to learn.*

Obtaining a Degree

Career guidance and understanding career choices are often not available in black village schools. If you did well enough at school, the subjects you have might not allow you to enter the necessary courses at university. Many students only realize what is available or what interests them after entering university, which might be too late to change as funding is a problem. The universities are not near villages, and accommodation and travelling present additional challenges. Funding to enter and sustain university life is a major challenge. Special funding schemes were introduced by Mr. Mandela as President of SA in 1996; the then-TEFSA (Tertiary Education Funding Scheme South Africa) and now NFSAS (The National Student Financial Aid Scheme) made it possible for black students to access university. Some students access but have to leave their studies to go and work due to poverty at home. If the community does not assist in the education through special collections, few students will have access to university. There is a saying in Africa: "It takes a village to educate a student."

> Em's Voice: *Mr Nelson Mandela assisted me through special bursaries to complete my 3 year degree. . . . it covered only tuition fees, it was very difficult to get transport and living expenses these 3 years, with mom who was not working and none of my brothers working. The social workers assisted us as a family, in giving my mom a grant of $45 per month from which $6 I could pay transport fees from my village to the university which was 7 miles away. . . . Students opt for work due to the level of poverty at their homes and were compelled to find a job to alleviate dire financial situations in their homes.*
>
> *At University I met a lot of people [professors] who guided me on choosing a career past my degree . . . who advised me to choose wisely. I had wanted to do medicine but their advice made me change routes and I decided to do Postgraduate level in Biochemistry.*

Postgraduate Studies and PhD: The Scholarship Key

Funding is available for postgraduate studies if students do well in their first degree. Universities do not all offer the same postgraduate programs and students might have to enter another university further away from home. This away-from-the-known has its own challenges of adaptation and financial implications. The key to entering postgraduate levels is to study hard and be conscientious. Having passionate postgraduate supervisors who believe in and support their students is vital. Dealing with cultural diversity is a challenge for the village student as postgraduate supervisors in South African universities are from different countries and ethnic groups. Entering into postgraduate studies also brings you into contact with other nationalities and students, who most often had better opportunities than the village student, and this results in changing the existing paradigm of the learner. In the postgraduate program, competition among students is tough and perseverance is pivotal.

> Em's voice: *I got admitted at the University of Cape Town (UCT), under the supervision of Prof H and K [great scholars]. I graduated in June 2003 with a Master's degree in Molecular and Cellular Biology funded by the National Research Foundation (NRF). I fell in love with Biochemistry, the cell and how it makes life, and the interactions of these molecules within the cell. We were very few blacks at UCT and adjusting to the standard and environment dominated by whites was not easy, but with time one started learning new ways in life. I got a lot of exposure in Cape Town, and started seeing life in different ways, with interaction with students from various nations and countries and cultures.*

> *I wanted to be tops in life, and PhD will enable me to reach the heights in my dreams than having a junior degree. That propelled me to register for PhD in 2004 and completed in 2009. [Professor EO, an African scholar] . . . the man who taught me so many things—to be a better scientist, writer and teacher. He had noticed my passion for teaching and gave me opportunities to learn to teach research and write papers. It was through him I managed to travel to U.S.A, UK and Norway in my PhD and attend many conferences where I met expert researchers who inspired me further.*

The findings from the auto-ethnography indicate challenges experienced under apartheid in the village and schooling situation, as well as the post-apartheid situation in becoming a scholar. The core challenges identified and discussed from the above mentioned will be elaborated on in further discussions on the current post-apartheid South African context.

CURRENT SCHOLARLY CHALLENGES IN SOUTH AFRICA: POST-APARTHEID

South Africa is a country with two sides of the coin. Apartheid-legislated governance for about 45 years until 1994 when suppressive legislation was abolished and a new dispensation was born. It is without doubt that the apartheid system robbed many blacks and benefitted many whites under its dominion. As such these have left a huge racial divide in skills, education and inequalities among blacks and whites. The new dawn of an equal society was born when former president Nelson Mandela took office to lead a non-racial, non-sexist and better nation for all who live in it. In his endeavor to bridge the gap left by apartheid, he focused on education as a means by which the divided nation could achieve equity, equality and redress for the destructive nature of apartheid that left blacks with substandard education and skill levels.

Education is a key instrument in developing individuals and societies. The "knowledge economies" build on education as their cornerstone which result in key inventions and technologies that our world depends on for modern living. While most renowned scholars and inventors recognized as instrumental in developing knowledge economies are Western white scholars, black African scholars have remained unrecognized, particularly, in South Africa. In many of South African institutions of higher learning, the academic staff continues to be dominated by whites, highlighting the urgency to find pathways to develop black African scholars to redress this societal imbalance.

Challenges in Accessing Higher Education

In 2011, statistics show that 938,201 students were in higher education, a significant increase from 473,000 in 1994 (CHE, 2013). Despite these improvements, the same year, the Parliamentary Monitoring Group published a briefing by Higher Education South Africa (HESA) indicating some of the challenges still faced by vulnerable groups in accessing higher education such as the poor state of basic education and a lack of funding (PMG, 2011). In line with inadequate basic education, Wilson-Strydom (2015) argues that a new form of social exclusion in dealing with access to higher education in South Africa has emerged, that of increasing access without increasing the success of underprepared undergraduates from poorer backgrounds. This is strengthened by the CHE report that acknowledges that students entering university do so from positions of extreme inequality (CHE, 2013). Thus, while overall numbers are encouraging, they do not necessarily provide the whole picture of the direction of access, especially by marginalized young people living in informal settlements (Alkire, 2010).

Government has endeavored to provide National Student Financial Aid Scheme (NFSAS), which has proven not enough with many youth prospects of being at university doors shut due to lack of funding. As reported by the OECD, countries that heavily invest in education also increase in their economic growth and development. South Africa needs to heavily invest in higher education, so we draw from this larger population in the country and increase African scholars and reduce poverty and unemployment.

Socioeconomic Challenges of Africa: African Scholars' Struggle

A former American president, Benjamin Franklin, said, "If a man empties his purse into his head, no man can take it away from him." An investment in knowledge always pays the best interest" (Chronicling of America, 1903). Although the continent is rich and endowed in many natural resources, it is very weak in developing and raising African scholars of its own, partly due to lack of access to education. This has resulted in a large dependence on first-world countries to manage and refine its very own natural resources like crude oil and precious stones (diamonds, gold and platinum) due to lack of skills and proper training. It is difficult to build a pool of scholars in a continent that is very unstable socially and economically. Civil wars and well-documented poverty in the continent has robbed it of the smooth development of scholars who could possibly be the key solution to its socio-economic problems and unrest. In Africa, many citizens are still battling to feed themselves, which makes education a distant reality.

Africa, a continent known as the "Dark Continent," needs a serious overhaul and investment in the education system, a feeder for the development of quality and enviable scholars who can be the key light in brightening the continent's future and prospects. Lack of resources and schools on the continent has led to impoverished and unstable basic higher and tertiary education development. Poverty and education are intimately linked. Schools and universities are

TOTALS

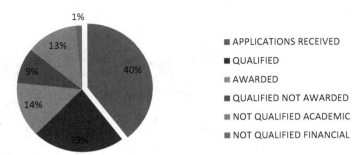

Figure 3.1 NFSAS Graph Depicting 2014 Applicants: Those Who Qualified and Were Awarded Versus Those Whom They Could Not Award

key pillars in the development of academic scholars. As such, there is a great need to the development of academic scholarship culture in Africa.

Funding plays a major role in accessing higher education. It is this that I believe is what increased the pool of what is now called "black diamond," a collective term that is used pejoratively in South Africa to refer to members of the new black middle class. Unfortunately, NFSAS cannot fund every deserving student who wants to enter the tertiary institution although they qualify. Figure 3.1 below shows the number of applications NFSAS received against those that they could fund for the year 2014. The qualifying students NSFAS can't fund end up dropping out of university.

Nico Cloete, director of the Centre for Higher Education Transformation, the world-renowned nongovernmental organization, said the real tragedy was that university dropouts would join about three million youth who are not in education, employment or training (DHET, 2011): "This is where the door of learning is bolted. About 800,000 of these 18-to-24-year-olds [matriculated]." Although the government has allocated increased funds to higher education, these have not kept pace with universities' tuition fees. Cloete said tuition fees had risen from R7.8 billion ($490 million) in 2000 to R15.5 billion ($722 million) in 2012. "Over 12 years, students have had to find R7.7 billion more. NSFAS funds have almost tripled, but they still don't support all the students. Lower middle-class parents, such as police and nurses, who earn more than R150,000 ($9,424) per annum, and whose children don't qualify for NSFAS, can't afford more than one child at a university (DHET, 2011).

Poverty in South Africa

Across a variety of quantitative definitions and methodologies, it is accepted that between 45% and 55% of the South African population are poor and between 20% and 25% are in extreme poverty (Everatt, 2003; Gelb, 2003;

Landman, 2003; van der Berg and Louw, 2003; Bhorat et al, 2004; Meth and Dias, 2004; UNDP, 2004). This means between 18 and 24 million people are in poverty, including between 8 and 10 million in extreme poverty. Unsurprisingly, this poverty has pronounced spatial, racial and gender dimensions (Everatt and Maphai, 2003; Gelb, 2003). South Africa is regarded as one of the most unequal societies in the world. This has divided the nation into two: those who have and those who don't have. It is usually those not plagued by high unemployment rates and lack of access to higher education. Dropout rates are highest in poverty-stricken, rural and township areas where there is high unemployment. Unless these inequalities are addressed, the nation will remain a society of two, which makes social cohesion difficult. It is these areas where crime rate rates are also higher. Education can be a key solution to these social problems.

The Impact of Drop-Outs Among Schools' and Universities' Students

South Africa has one of the highest dropout rates in schools and universities. Of those starting grade 1, only 60% manage to pass grade 12. Education researcher Nic Spaull puts blame on especially poor learning in the foundation phases as the problem in South Africa (Spaull, 2013; 2015). Such numbers are very worrying especially among black Africans, where dropout rates are concentrated compared to other races. This is the pool of young potential black people who should be recruited as future scholars. Currently post-apartheid education is not as appealing as it was under the black youth of "1976," who fought even with their lives to get quality education. One man said if you want to destroy a nation, destroy its youth with alcohol, drugs and immorality. Most of our youth today are fighting for their lives especially with substance abuse and HIV/AIDS. Most of these social problems are results of broken homes, especially in the black communities. Most black families are run by single parents or by children because the parents have passed on from HIV and AIDS-related diseases. These socioeconomic problems have significant impact on potential African scholarliness. The impact of these problems is the increase in crime in the country. Unless one is armed with education or some skills, one is faced with difficult future ahead, which is the picture this country is painted with today. Many youth are unemployed and unemployable due to a serious lack in skills and formal academic training.

Universities: Key Incubators of Talent

Xolela Mangcu wrote on the key nature of tertiary education and its critical importance in any society: "Universities are arguably the most influential institutions in any society. Governments, businesses, newspapers, television and radio networks are run by university graduates. Universities produce the theories, ideas, technologies and products upon which the modern world is built" (Mangcu, 2014). This continent can be rebuilt on the backs of developing African scholars who can become the think tanks and solution providers of its many socioeconomic challenges. Unfortunately, wars and poverty have stolen the precious key driver, which is education, critical in the development of its citizens.

Apart from war, university doors are shut based on lack of quality education from the level of basic education where students are prepared to be ready for university education. Furthermore, as already mentioned elsewhere, funding is a critical issue in accessing tertiary education—the doorway to the development of scholars. The lack of role models from black African communities with regard to education is also playing a deterrent factor in getting masses of blacks into academia. Skill shortages can be directly linked to lack of education, especially post-matric education.

Research and Development (R&D): Key Driver in Economic Development

The quality of education has also decreased post 1994, with South Africa ranked second to the bottom of 141 countries in mathematics. Such poor quality education makes our students not ready for tertiary education. If they make it to tertiary education, many of them are reportedly dropping out in numbers due to many reasons ranging from financial exclusion, academic exclusion and serious lack of discipline fitting tertiary education. This further complicates the scholastic potential of the country and even the future generation (Spaull, 2013). These are some of the challenges one is faced with as a black student. Despite the lack of quality education, some managed to climb the academic ladder, but these some are too few.

South Africa needs to aggressively invest in research and development by increasing PhDs and postgraduate degree holders in order to change its landscapes and fortunes. Unless the country changes its formulas and current disruptive education culture, South Africa will find it too difficult to emerge as a global force to be reckoned with. South Africa has just lost its prestigious lead as the biggest economy in Africa to Nigeria during the past three years. Countries that have declined in academic scholarship, especially in R&D, also show economic decline. Education reduces poverty, lowers crime, and increases the revenue, fortunes, and wealth of the country. It is against this backdrop that the quality of education has to improve and massive investment in R&D is needed if South Africa is to move away from its shackles of crime, diseases and poverty.

AGING SCHOLARS IN UNIVERSITIES

The South Africa Department of Higher Education and Training (DHET) has reported that South African universities professors are aging, at an average age of 60. Therefore, there is an urgency to replenish this aging profession. It is within this backdrop that the development of African scholars can play a critical role, since they make the larger proportion of this country's population. Worldwide, in Africa and in South Africa, the importance of the doctorate has increased disproportionally in relation to its contribution to the overall graduate output over the last decade. This heightened attention has not been predominantly concerned with the traditional role of the PhD, namely the provision of a future supply of academics. Rather, it has focused on the increasingly important role that higher education, particularly high-level skills, is perceived to play in the knowledge economy.

In South Africa, the National Development Plan (2012) has prioritized an increase in doctoral output from 1,400 per year to 6,000 by 2030 (NPC, 2011). At the Africa Convention on the Doctorate in October 2013, sponsored by the National Research Foundation (NRF) and Carnegie Corporation, there was broad agreement that Africa needs tens of thousands more PhDs in order to renew an aging professoriate staff, the rapidly expanding higher education field, boost research, and generate the high-level skills growing economies need (PHDproject.org).

Education a Key Driver of Sustainable Development

Education is critical for promoting sustainable development and improving the capacity of the people to address socioeconomic issues, public participation in decision making, ethical awareness, values and attitudes, skills and behavior and effective development issues [United Nations Conference on Environment and Development (UN Summit for the Adoption, n.d)]. Thus higher education and development of scholars serve a critical role in the development process worldwide. This role is often considered a given in the first-world countries, particularly in the United States. "Nowhere has the connection between higher education and the development of scholars been more clearly drawn than in the United States" (Hodges and Dubb, 2014). Considerations of the newly established global 'knowledge economy' can be found in Asia and Europe alike, where the knowledge produced by universities has significance for all sectors, both private and public (Marginson, 2011). In Sub-Saharan Africa, "International donors and partners regarded universities, for the most part, as institutional enclaves without deep penetration into the development needs of African communities" (Cloete, 2009). Despite the very real capacity challenges many higher education institutions face, a burgeoning body of scholarship demonstrates that tertiary education has positively impacted development (Kimenyi, 2011), particularly traditional economic development indicators, such as per capita income (Gyimah-Brempong et al, 2006). Moreover, growth in the higher education sector has sought to attenuate many of the inequities, those that constrained development, formerly associated with the university in sub-Saharan Africa (Ashcroft and Rayner, 2011).

It is within this backdrop that the development of scholars is vital for the life of any country and all societies to advance, which improves all aspects of life. Within the South African context where scholarly development, especially in the black communities, has been seriously suffering due to many factors including poverty, socioeconomic factors and unemployment, there needs to be special measures to address the chronic shortage of African scholars. If South Africa is to achieve true freedom, equality, equity and social redress, the development of African scholars can be a key solution in nation rebuilding and social cohesion among races within the country. "Education is a better safeguard of liberty than a standing army." —Edward Everett (William, 1852).

Academia as a Career Path for Black South Africans

The two main reasons why academia is not attracting more black scholars are: academia cannot match the private sector's higher salaries and; therefore, qualified black scholars are drawn to other industries due to the pay differences. The private sector as well as top positions in government pay very lucrative remuneration packages. The South Africa Equal Employment Act of 1998 (EEA) makes provision for advancement of previously disadvantaged groups, which allows for payment of premiums with all of the benefits to attract educated black people into high-rank jobs at a very early stage of their career. Second is that many blacks especially in South Africa hardly study further to senior degrees especially doctorates. Producing a doctoral graduate takes longer and most blacks would have preferred going to the market place with junior degrees. It is this very reason that government is increasing efforts to produce more PhDs, but the question remains, will they enter into scholarly engagement?

A degree is now seen by villagers as enough and something to find a better job and get married. In villages success is measured materially such as driving big cars and wearing expensive designer clothes. It is seen as a waste to have a masters or doctorate that does not contribute to the latter. Being a scholar, which does not yield immediate capital and material growth, is not seen as valuable.

CONCLUSION

Many challenges, some due to the past and others due to the current environment, are in our midst, hindering the progression towards developing black African scholars. The need to address these challenges is rife and it needs a whole nation, not just a village, to make this happen.

The pool of black African PhDs needs more attention. The number of PhDs South Africa is producing is lower compared to other developed countries in the world. There is a need for an aggressive and well-coordinated program to increase the number of PhDs. Previous attempts have failed as the NRF has spent millions towards the PhD progression but yielded little success since the number of PhDs in South Africa has remained at 27 per every million people for quite some time now. New strategies are required that can change this landscape. Most South Africans don't seem much interested in full-time postgraduate studies and opt to go find a job after their junior degrees. This also makes it very difficult for those who enroll part-time in postgraduate studies, especially doing a PhD, as the workload just becomes too much to progress.

Creating a culture of education and embracing all the human potential is a necessity in South Africa and the African continent in developing effective scholars who will take on the challenges of being excellent mentors, researchers and teachers, and laying the foundation for the future of higher education strategy.

REFERENCES

Alkire, S. (2010). Development: A misconceived theory can kill. In C. W. Morris (Ed.), *Amartya Sen*. New York: Cambridge University Press, pp. 191–224.

Ashcroft, K., and Rayner, P. (2011). *Higher education in development: Lessons from Sub- Saharan Africa*. Charlotte, NC: Information Age Publishers.

Bhorat, H., Poswell, L., and Naidoo, P. (2004). *Dimensions of poverty in post-apartheid South Africa, 1996–2001*. South Africa: Development Policy Research Unit, University of Cape Town.

Chronicling America. (1858, November 10). *The Raftsman's Journal* (Clearfield, PA), p. 3, col. 2.

ChroniclingofAmerica.(1902,August25).*TheProgressiveFarmer.*p.7,img.7.Retrieved February 10, 2016. http://chroniclingamerica.loc.gov/lccn/sn92073049/1903-08-25/ed-1/seq-7/#date1=1836&index=3&rows=20&words=always+best+interest+investment+knowledge+pays&searchType=basic&sequence=0&state=&date2=1922&proxtext=An+investment+in+knowledge+always+pays+the+best+interest&y=17&x=14&dateFilterType=yearRange&page=1

Cloete, N. (Ed.). (2009). *Responding to the educational needs of post-school youth: Determining the scope of the problem and developing a capacity-building model*. Cape Town: Centre for Higher Education Transformation.

Council on Higher Education (CHE). (2013). *2011/2012 Annual Report of the Council on Higher Education South Africa*. Pretoria: Council on Higher Education.

Department of Higher Education and Training (DHET). (2011). *Green paper for post-school education and training*. Pretoria: Department of Higher Education and Training.

Ellis, C., Adams, T. E., and Bochner, A. P. (2010). Autoethnography: An overview [40 paragraphs]. *Forum Qualitative Sozialforschung/ Forum: Qualitative Social Research, 12*(1), Art. 10. Retrieved from http://nbn-resolving.de/urn:nbn:de:0114-fqs1101108

Ellis, C., and Bochner, A. P. (2000). Autoethnography, personal narrative, reflexivity. In Norman K. Denzin and Yvonna S. Lincoln (Eds.), *Handbook of qualitative research* (2nd ed., pp. 733–768). Thousand Oaks, CA: Sage.

62   *Emmanuel Mukwevho and Yvonne du Plessis*

Everatt, D. (2003). The politics of poverty. In Everatt, D., and Maphai, V. (Eds.), *The real state of the nation*. Johannesburg: Interfund.

Gelb, S. (2003). *Inequality in South Africa*. Johannesburg: The Edge Institute.

Gyimah-Brempong, K., Paddison, O., and Mituku, W. (2006). Higher education and economic growth in Africa. *Journal of Development Studies, 42*(3), pp. 509–529.

Hodges, R. A., and Dubb, S. (2014). Road half travelled: University engagement at a crossroads. *Oxford University Press and Community Development Journal*, 49, 495–503.

Kimenyi, M. (2011). Contribution of higher education to economic development: A survey of international evidence. *Journal of African Economy*, 20(Suppl. 3), 14–49.

Landman, J. P., Bhorat, H., Van der Berg, S., and Van Aardt, C. (2003). Breaking the grip of poverty and inequality in South Africa 2004–2014: Current trends, issues and future policy options. Ecumenical Foundation of South Africa (EFSA). Stellenbosch.

Madi, P. M. (1993). *Affirmative action in corporate South Africa*. 1st edition. Kenwyn: Juta and Co.

Mangcu, X. (2014). 10 steps to develop black professors. *News24*. Retrieved from http://www.news24.com/Archives/City-Press/10-steps-to-develop-black-professors-20150429

Marginson, S. (2011). The new world order in higher education: Research rankings, outcomes measures, and institutional classifications. In M. Rostan and M. Vaira (Eds.), *Questioning excellence in higher education: Policies, experiences and challenges in national and comparative perspective* (pp. 3–20). Rotterdam, The Netherlands: Sense Publishers.

Meth, C., and Dias, R. (2004). Increases in poverty in South Africa, 1999–2002. *Development Southern Africa, 21*(1), 59–85.

OECD (2008). Economic Surveys, South Africa Economic Assessment, Vol. 2008/15, July 2008

Parliamentary Monitoring Group (PMG). (2011). *Access to higher education. Challenges: higher education briefing*. Meeting Report Information. Date of Meeting: 07 February 2011. Retrieved July 1, 2015, from http://www.pmg.org.za/node/25042

South Africa National Planning Commission (NPC). (2011). *Annual Report 2010-2011*. Jounasburg: S. Africa NPC. Retrieved from http://www.npconline.co.za/medialib/downloads/home/NPC %20 National %20 Development %20Plan %20Vision %202030 %20-lo-res.pdf.

Spaull, N. (2013). *South Africa's education crisis: The quality of education in South Africa 1994–2011*. Report Commissioned by CDE in October 2013. Retrieved from http://www.section27.org.za/wp-content/uploads/2013/10/Spaull-2013-CDE-report-South-Africas-Education-Crisis.pdf

Spaull, N. (2015). A significant number of pupils drop out of school before they reach Matric. *eNCA*. Retrieved from https://www.enca.com/south-africa/high-dropout-rate-sas-school-system

The Ph.D. project: Business Doctoral Programs for minorities. (2015). Retrieved August 1, 2015, from www.phdproject.org

United Nations Conference on Environment and Development (UNCED). (2015). *Encyclopædia Britannica Online*. Retrieved September 1, 2015, from http://www.britannica.com/event/United-Nations-Conference-on Environment-and-Development

United Nations Development Programme. (2004). *South Africa: Human development report 2003*. Pretoria: UNDP.

UN Summit for the Adoption of the Post-2015 Development Agenda. (n.d.). In *International Institute for Sustainable Development*.

van der Berg, S., and Louw, M. (2003, September). *Changing patterns of SA income distribution: Towards time series estimates of distribution and poverty*. Paper delivered to the Conference of the Economic Society of South Africa, Stellenbosch.

Vorster, J. (2014). Professors aren't born: They must be nurtured. *The Conversation*. Retrieved from https://theconversation.com/professors-arent-born-they-must-be-nurtured-43670

William, B. (1852). *The Common School Journal and Educational Reformer*, 28. Retrieved August 25, 2015.

Wilson-Strydom, M. (2015). *University access and success: Capabilities, diversity and social justice*. London: Routledge.

4 The Role of Accreditation in Overcoming the Challenges of Graduate Management Programs in Africa

Enase Okonedo and Timothy Aluko

INTRODUCTION

In recent years, Africa—once described as the Hopeless Continent—is beginning to show signs of hope (August, 2013; Dowden, 2000). Its economic growth averaged 4.0% and 4.7% in 2013 and 2014, respectively (UNCTAD, 2014). In 2013, 11 of the top 20 fastest-growing economies in the world (August, 2013; Kawa, 2013) were countries in Africa. The World Bank projects that average GDP growth in Sub-Saharan Africa will be 4.6% and 5.0% in 2016 and 2017, respectively. Despite this renewed hope, the growth potential may be threatened if the requisite human capital is lacking. A major challenge facing businesses in Africa is the perceived lack of managerial talent (African Management Initiative, 2012). Increasingly, there is a growing recognition of the need for competent managers not only to drive, but also to sustain economic growth across Africa.

Across the continent, there are sometimes changing policies, weak institutions and feeble enforcement of regulations (Birdsball, 2007; Herbst and Greg, 2003; and Noman and Stiglitz, 2014). Skills deemed to be in short supply include problem solving, creativity, adaptability and the ability to manage under uncertainty (African Management Initiative, 2012). Various suggestions have been offered to meet the skill gap, and businesses look to a large number of business schools, universities and other training institutions across the region to provide graduates with the required skills. However, the limited number of business schools in the region compared to its population of 1.033 billion people as at 2013 (World Population Statistics, 2013) lead one to conclude that the number of business schools is insufficient for impact. According to the Table of African Business Schools, the number of business schools in Africa is 58 (TIA, 2012). However, the African Management Initiative (AMI) in its report published in 2013 estimates that there are 90 business schools on the continent. India, with a population of 1.252 billion people, has an estimate of 4,000 business schools (Shah, 2012; World Bank, 2013). The business schools in Africa may be insufficient to provide the education, skills and training required. However, the ability of business schools and universities to meet the requirements for qualified managers on the continent go beyond the number of available schools. It is in large part also dependent on the quality of management education offered in the region. In assessing quality, various measures could be employed. One way by which an institution's quality can be adjudged locally and globally is by the accreditation it has obtained.

A study of the MBA curriculum of ten business schools across Africa reveals that only two offer courses specific to doing business in Africa. Other business schools may take the peculiarities of Africa into consideration in courses offered but this is not explicitly stated in their curricula. In the respective countries where management education institutions operate, there are requirements for accreditation from local/domestic accrediting bodies. Across the region therefore, one would find that almost all higher education institutions have local accreditations. There is however a growing awareness of the need for, and interest in seeking global accreditation depending on the mission and objectives of particular institutions.

The chapter addresses the following questions:

1. What are the challenges of graduate management programs in Africa?
2. Are management programs offered in Africa relevant to the realities of global management practices?
3. Can accreditation standards improve the quality of management and business education in Africa?

The chapter is structured as follows. The first section examines the challenges of graduate management education in Africa from a broad perspective. The second section describes the accreditation bodies and assesses their standards. The third section discusses the role of accreditation in overcoming the challenges of graduate management education in Africa.

APPROACH

The study relied on secondary data including journal articles, official publications, newspaper articles, unpublished thesis and magazines. Relevant articles regarding challenges of graduate management education in Africa and the importance of accreditation to business schools were identified using tools like Google Scholar, EBSCO and JSTOR. The custom range feature in Google Scholar was used to limit the search to the desired time frame (2000–2015). An extensive search was conducted using broad search terms including: challenges of higher education in Africa; AACSB International accreditation criteria; AMBA accreditation criteria; EQUIS accreditation criteria; ACBSP accreditation; importance of business school accreditation and pros and cons of accreditation including as many relevant articles as possible. The articles were examined in detail and selection was based on quality of content, relevance and date of publication.

CHALLENGES OF MANAGEMENT EDUCATION IN AFRICA

Various challenges bedevil graduate management education in Africa. These challenges include poor funding, poor research capabilities, outdated curriculum, inadequate infrastructure and high student-faculty ratio (Yizengaw, 2008; Jegede, 2012; McKinsey and Company, 2014). These challenges impact the quality of management programs in Africa.

Funding

Many management institutions in Africa are government-owned and these institutions lack sufficient government funding as a major consequence of poor economic conditions and the diverse government priorities competing for a share of the budget (Yizengaw, 2008). On a general note, budgetary allocation to higher education is considered inadequate. And within the institutions, priority is given to science and technology–based courses, leaving very little for management and other related faculties. The upshot of poor funding of higher education in Africa is that, amongst other consequences, it limits research and the ability of African universities to retain quality faculty (Yizengaw, 2008). Ultimately, it doesn't allow for adequate and fully functional facilities. The poor state of infrastructure is also a direct consequence of poor funding (Montanini, 2013)

On the average, African countries allocate around 0.7% of their GDP and around 20% of public current expenditure on education to higher education ("Financing Higher Education in Africa," 2010). As at 2013, few African countries met the UNESCO's recommendation of 26% budget allocation for education. Table 4.1 below shows the annual percentage budget to education for selected countries across Africa.

Table 4.1 Annual Percentage Budget to Education in Selected African Countries in 2013

Country	Budget %
Botswana	19.0
Burkina Faso	16.8
Cote d'Ivoire	30.0
Ghana	31.0
Kenya	23.0
Lesotho	19.0
Morocco	17.7
Nigeria	8.0
South Africa	25.8
Swaziland	24.6
Tunisia	17.0
Uganda	27.0

Note: From Kupoluyi (2012, November 26).

Furthermore, a peculiar problem facing business schools all over the world that perhaps is more heightened in Africa is the structure of business schools within the university. There is usually a conflict between business schools and their parent universities for independence in decision making. In several instances, particularly amongst the middle-tier and standard schools, these business schools function more like departments within the university, and decision making does not rest with the business school but with the university, thus limiting the power of the business school to make independent decisions. Also, some business schools regarded as 'cash cows' within the university may not be at liberty to utilize a substantial part of the income generated by the schools for their benefit. The relationship between the schools and the university under such circumstances may be ill defined and too rigid.

Inadequate Research

Management research is a critical factor in management schools. Research output in higher institutions in Africa is considered largely deficient for some reasons. A key factor is the insufficiency of funding for research. Africa allocates less than 0.5% of its GDP to research (Oyango-Obbo, 2015). Poor funding, lack of research grants and the poor state of infrastructure pose a great limitation to research capabilities (Yizengaw, 2008; "Financing Higher Education in Africa," 2010). Thus, hindering the ability of management schools, especially state-funded schools, to conduct meaningful management research. In addition to this, there may be some deficiency in research skills. Given the paucity of doctorally qualified faculty in many institutions, the required research skills may be lacking in institutions. Furthermore there is usually a conflict in what research agenda to pursue. Top-tier management schools are eager to attain international prestige and push to have publications by faculty in top A-rated journals. Nevertheless, theory-oriented research brought into the classroom hardly meets the objective of contributing to the development of the community. Rather, to meet this objective, the research agenda has to focus on the practical problems and needs of businesses in the community.

Relevance and Currency of Curriculum

There is a serious concern about the relevance of management education curriculum to current business needs in Africa and on the global scene. On a general note, the curricula on offer in higher institutions in emerging economies including African countries are gradually becoming outdated (Deverajan, Monga, and Zongo, 2011). Those on offer in many management schools across Africa do not promote the development of skills such as critical thinking and analytical ability (Mooko, Tabulawa, Maruatona and Koosimile, 2009). The importance of regular curriculum review to ensure relevance and currency so as to keep abreast of contemporary issues and development in business and management need emphasis. Also, poor funding is a challenge for curriculum development in Africa as it has an impact on curriculum implementation. Without a doubt, it is difficult to implement a curriculum successfully without adequate funding. Furthermore, many management teachers find it difficult to translate the curriculum into meaningful and participatory teaching (Badugela, 2012).

The successful implementation of management curriculum depends largely on management teachers. It is therefore pertinent to have management teachers trained in curriculum implementation. But, the poor conditions of service have forced many management teachers to focus valuable time and energy in private money-making ventures while channeling very little effort into improving and implementing the curriculum. There are also insufficient resources like books, industry reports, case studies, journals, etc. to support the implementation of the curriculum.

Inadequate Infrastructure

There is a huge infrastructure deficit in African higher institutions largely due to very limited funds and huge reliance on government funding (Yizengaw, 2008). Most institutions still grapple with poor Internet access, outdated books, archaic equipment and laboratories and inadequate lecture rooms (Sifuna and Sawamura, 2011). The student population is increasing without any corresponding increase in infrastructure thereby compromising on the quality of the programs on offer ("Financing Higher Education in Africa," 2010). Student enrollment grew at the rate of 16% per annum while current expenditure grew at the rate of 6% per annum between 1991 and 2006 ("Financing Higher Education in Africa," 2010). The declining per-student expenditure impacts negatively on the quality and relevance of programs in African higher institutions ("Financing Higher Education in Africa," 2010). Insufficient lecture halls have resulted in overcrowding, and this has led to the deterioration of the existing facilities. The problem is made worse by the fact that public institutions allocate the bulk of their budget to personnel and other running costs, leaving very little for infrastructural development.

High Student-Faculty Ratio

The demand for higher education is increasing in Africa ("Financing Higher Education in Africa," 2010). With the increasing number of students leaving secondary school each year, universities are gradually increasing their admission quota without any corresponding increase in infrastructure and staff strength (Sifuna and Sawamura, 2011). Enrollment into tertiary institutions in Africa has grown from 3.53 million in 1999 to 9.54 million in 2012 (ICEF Monitor, 2015). This increase poses a challenge to sustainable financing of higher education ("Financing Higher Education in Africa,"

2010). The World Bank projects that the number of students in Africa's higher institutions could rise to about 20 million in 2015. And the number of academics, which stood at 456,000 in 2006, would have to double to about 908,000 in order to meet the required standards ("Financing Higher Education in Africa," 2010).

A major challenge facing management schools in Africa is high student-faculty ratio. There is a drought of qualified and talented teachers due to poor incentives and lack of motivation. The few teachers retained in these institutions are over-burdened and cannot operate effectively nor pay adequate attention to the needs of each student (Montanini, 2013).

ACCREDITATION

There are four widely acclaimed international accreditation bodies for business schools. These are: Association to Advance Collegiate Schools of Business (AACSB International); Association of MBAs (AMBA); European Foundation for Management Development (EFMD) and Accreditation Council for Business Schools and Programs (ACBSP). However, several African countries also have national accrediting bodies who have defined what is regarded as quality standards across several dimensions and ensure that universities and the programs they offer conform to these predefined standards (see Table 4.2).

Some business schools in Africa that do not seek to attract students from outside their countries or collaboration with international institutions focus all their effort on fulfilling the requirements for national accreditation solely. In addition, funding international accreditation, which has substantial costs, may be an added constraint given the paucity of funds in African institutions. Adherence to national accreditation and striving to meet the required standards ultimately improves the quality of graduate management

Table 4.2 National Accrediting Bodies of Selected African Countries

S/N	Country	Accrediting Body
1	Nigeria	National Universities Commission
2	South Africa	Council for Higher Education
3	Ghana	National Accreditation Board
4	Egypt	National Authority for Quality Assurance and Accreditation of Education
5	Ethiopia	Higher Education Relevance and Quality Agency
6	Kenya	Commission for University Education
7	Uganda	Uganda National Council for Higher Education
8	Tanzania	Tanzania Commission for Universities
9	Namibia	Namibia Qualifications Authority
10	Rwanda	Higher Education Council

education in Africa. However, these national accrediting bodies are sometimes constrained by factors such as bureaucracy, a narrow perspective and understanding of the management of business schools, amongst others (Montanini, 2013). These issues question the effectiveness of the national accrediting bodies. Sometimes, the standards prescribed stifle innovation and limit the ability of schools to offer relevant and current content. Also, the delegates who come to evaluate business schools on behalf of these bodies are usually subject-matter experts who may be very astute in their subject matter but not necessarily knowledgeable about management education. This therefore leads to suggestions and recommendations following the evaluation, which may not be particularly relevant nor useful to business schools. If, however, properly conducted by a pool or selection of persons with a combination of skills and expertise in both their subject areas as well as the management education field, national accreditations could be quite beneficial in improving the quality of graduate management education in Africa. Therefore, accrediting bodies should constantly review their standards and methods to ensure the requisite parameters for ensuring high quality of the institutions as well as the development of talent relevant to Africa and meet the demands of organizations operating in Africa. Table 4.2 shows the national accrediting bodies of selected countries across Africa.

Association to Advance Collegiate of Business (AACSB International)

Founded in 1916, AACSB International, which originated in the United States, first formulated standards for business administration degree programs in 1919. The underlying objective of AACSB International is "to encourage business schools to hold themselves accountable for improving business practice through scholarly education and impactful intellectual contribution." To achieve this objective, AACSB International has a predefined set of standards that business schools must meet to earn its accreditation. The scope of its accreditation is the institution as a whole and it defines the institution as "an organization through which business programs are authorized, resourced and overseen." AACSB International acknowledges the fact that institutions can differ in terms of their organizational structure; therefore, it identifies uniqueness in various institutions prior to accreditation. It also conducts regular peer review and identifies and recognizes business schools that maintain high-quality standards. Its accreditation process is in three stages, namely, eligibility, pre-accreditation, and initial accreditation. It has reviewed its standards several times since they were first adopted in 1919 to stay abreast of current business trends and sustain its relevance. The last review was held in 2013 after an in-depth study in conjunction with management institutions and employers across the world. There are only three schools (5%) with AACSB International accreditation in Africa as of December 2014.

In general, only in recent years have the major accrediting bodies such as AACSB International and EFMD expanded their scope outside their regions to other emerging countries. The major limitation prior to this, in schools in emerging countries seeking accreditation from these bodies, is a limited understanding of the region and its peculiarities as well as the stage of development of the management education sector. Schools being assessed using standards developed for schools in more developed countries face a major hindrance in their quest for accreditation.

Accreditation Council for Business Schools and Programs (ACBSP)

Accreditation Council for Business Schools and Programs (ACBSP) originated in the United States in 1988. ACBSP offers accreditation to business programs with emphasis on teaching excellence. It accredits undergraduate and graduate business programs. Its mission is to "promote continuous improvement and recognize excellence in the accreditation of business education programs around the world." ACBSP's review process focuses on the following areas: leadership; strategic planning; student and stakeholder focus; student learning and performance; faculty and staff focus; and educational and business process management. ACSBP insists on institutions developing innovative programs and regular review and enhancement of the curriculum. It also prescribes that institutions must have a formal structure for developing courses with the aim of enhancing student learning experience (Kline, 1994). There were two schools with ACBSP accreditation in Africa as at March 2015.

Association of MBAs (AMBA)

AMBA established in 1967 accredits Masters of Business Administration (MBA), Doctor of Business Administration (DBA), and Master of Business and Management (MBM) programs. Its core objective is "to advance business education at postgraduate level." AMBA accredits the various programs independently in contrast to AACSB International and EFMD who accredit the institution as a whole. AMBA places particular emphasis on mission and strategy, curriculum, and student and faculty qualification. There are only nine schools with AMBA accreditation in Africa as of March 2015, which amounts to about 15% of African business schools listed in the TIA (2012) special report on business education.

European Foundation for Management Development (EFMD)

European Quality Improvement System (EQUIS) is an international accreditation managed by the European Foundation for Management Development (EFMD) with headquarters in Brussels. Founded in 1972, EFMD began awarding the EQUIS accreditation in 1997 and similar to AACSB International, EFMD focuses on the institution as a whole. It defines the institution as "the organizational unit providing business and management education." The institution may be a stand-alone business school or part of a larger institution. In whichever case, the school must satisfy 10 criteria to earn its accreditation. Schools seeking EQUIS accreditation must demonstrate high quality in all aspects of its activities while exhibiting a high level of internationalization. EFMD revised its standards in (AACSB, 2013) placing more emphasis on ethics, responsibility and sustainability, thus ensuring that institutions focus and become advocates of sustainable and ethical behavior. As of December 2014, three business schools have attained EQUIS accreditation in Africa. That is about 5% of African business schools listed in the special report on business education (TIA, 2012).

ACCREDITATION ROLE IN GRADUATE IN AFRICAN MANAGEMENT PROGRAMS

Management education is a relatively new development in Africa. Prior to 1990, only about thirteen business schools had been established in Africa (TIA, 2012). In the aftermath of the global financial crises in 2007, one observed an increased influx of multinational corporations into Africa. This phenomenon further highlighted the absence of sufficient numbers of suitably qualified managers across the continent and a number of corporations turned to business schools on the continent to meet their needs. This influx meant that managerial skills were required within the continent and organizations turned to business schools in Africa to meet those needs. This development spurred business schools in Africa to consider the relevance of their programs in order to satisfy the growing needs of not only multinational but also local corporations. It more significantly led to a renewed interest in global accreditations by business schools seeking to improve quality and standards.

The schools in the region can be classified into three categories—Tier 1, Tier 2, and Tier 3 (see Table 4.3). AMI (2012) identified nine schools in Tier 1, 41 in Tier 2 and 42 in Tier 3 (see Figure 4.1).

The Tier 1 schools are very similar to business schools in the Western world in terms of their program offering. The programs include courses in executive education, degree programs, open enrollment programs as well as custom or specially designed programs for individual organizations. Such schools are usually autonomous or semi-autonomous and have decision-making and financial autonomy from parent institutions. The faculty profile here is typically a mix of doctoral qualified as well as practitioners from industry in varying proportions. Some of these schools run courses outside their home countries and are more advanced in the use of technology in delivering courses and have students from other countries. The teaching of

Table 4.3   Describing the Business School Categories

	Tier 1 Schools	Tier 2 Schools	Tier 3 Schools
Academic	MBA, EMBA, Diplomas	MBA, (sometimes EMBA), BA/Bsc/Com, Masters, Diploma	MBA, Undergrad, Masters, Diplomas
Business Links	Extensive executive education (open and customized, Sponsorship, Thought Leadership	Executive education short courses and certificates	Little executive education, some certificate courses
Faculty	Mix of academics and practitioners; international lecturers	Largely traditional academics	Mostly academics, fewer doctorates
Research	Some offer PhD/DBA. Research matters but rarely a top priority	Some offer PhD/DBA. Research but rarely international	Limited research
Teaching Methods	Action learning, case studies, simulation, role-plays, experimental, internships, exchange	Case studies, lectures	Traditional lectures, occasional case studies
International Links	Faculty, research, partnerships, exchanges, rankings	Limited, sometimes foreign degree-awarding body	Very few
Structure	At least some level of independence from parent institutions	Often embedded in a public or private university	Usually part of universities
Financial Model	Often NPO but self-sustaining; High fees	Part of university funding structure, High fees, but generally lower than Tier 1	Part of university funding structure

Note: From African Management Initiative (2012)

management is largely practice-oriented to equip managers with practical skills useful in day-to-day as well as strategic management.

The schools described as Tier 2 business schools are business schools that are not financially or otherwise autonomous and function within a centralized structure in the universities. Their main offerings are degrees in business and few open enrollment courses. Their faculty profile is almost entirely academic with a good number having doctorate degrees. The student population is drawn from the home country. In these schools, the teaching of management could be a combination of theory and practice.

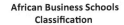

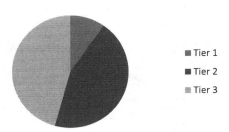

Figure 4.1   African Business Schools Classification (AMI, 2012)

The Tier 3 business schools also predominantly offer degrees in business, but their faculty is largely made up of individuals without doctoral qualification who have no decision-making authority, this being fully vested in the university. Students typically are from the home country in which the school is located. The teaching of management is typically theoretical and offers little practical applicability.

In general, Tier 1 schools are most likely in the process of pursuing global accreditation or have attained at least one global accreditation in addition to the local accreditation. Such schools aspire to be global players in the management education field and accreditation by any of the global accreditation bodies confers a status of being world class. Tier 2 schools have local accreditation but aspire to pursue global accreditation in the medium to long-term future. Tier 3 business schools both have no aspiration to pursue global accreditation and may find attainment of local accreditation challenging.

Benefits of Accreditation

The major benefit of accreditation is that it improves the overall quality of the institutions and the graduates of such institutions through assessing various aspects of the institution's processes and measuring these against defined standards. The process of accreditation assists business schools in defining the essential attributes that the graduates of the institution should have, fostering connection with industry, and depending on the accreditation body and its requirements. The accreditation body helps in ensuring currency and relevance of the curriculum and introduces rigor in the processes in place in the management development institutions and business schools.

A consideration of obtaining accreditation entails revealing varying standards and measures of quality. However, the key measures include: student and faculty qualification, curriculum, research output and corporate connections amongst others. In the process of assessing business schools' preparedness for accreditation, global accrediting bodies evaluate the quality of faculty, programs, students and research, amongst others. In doing so, accreditation introduces structure and rigor into the processes of business school, which assists in making these more focused with objectives clearly defined. Business schools in a bid to achieve accreditation have to consider carefully their mission and objectives and make sure that across all dimensions, certain standards of quality excel.

As part of the accreditation process, accrediting bodies typically send a team of inspectors to evaluate certain aspects of the business school to ensure they meet set standards. Hence, accreditation helps to maintain minimum internationally acknowledged standards across several dimensions. The accrediting bodies specify certain criteria like skill acquisition, program delivery, program evaluation, the minimum number of case studies adopted in the curriculum and internationalization, amongst others. Strict adherence to these standards ultimately improves the overall quality of graduate management programs in Africa and beyond.

Implications of Accreditation for Business Schools in Africa

The quest for global accreditation is considered to be of immense value to business schools in Africa. It is potentially beneficial in helping business schools address most of the problems facing Africa's educational system. For instance, to ensure the quality of intake, AACSB International, ACBSP, AMBA and EQUIS emphasize a robust selection process. Most business schools in Africa require a minimum of second-class lower or a postgraduate diploma to get admission into the MBA program. Some of the schools, in line with AMBA's specification require a minimum of three years' work experience. And many of them including the Lagos Business School, Strathmore Business School, the American University in Cairo, School of Business; Gordon Institute of Business Science, South Africa; and University of Witwatersrand Business School, South Africa; amongst others require standard entrance examination such as Graduate Management Admission Test (GMAT). The Financial Times Limited states that 14 out of 58 schools surveyed required GMAT as the standard entry test. (TIA, 2012).

Also, the international accrediting bodies place emphasis on the evaluation process and the assurance of learning. The programs must have clear teaching objectives and a standard way to measure the learning outcomes. Other areas that accreditation may have a positive impact on are here discussed below.

Faculty

The faculty is essential to the development of management schools but in general, it is believed that there is a dearth of qualified doctoral faculty

across the world. Business schools need suitably qualified faculty as speci-
fied by the accrediting bodies. The ideal business school faculty should
show scholarship and also be conversant with industry. They should have
an acceptable wealth of professional experience in the industry and be able
to bring this experience to the classroom; indeed there is a limit to what a
faculty whose knowledge of business and workplace practices limited to
books can pass on to the students. These qualities are particularly scarce in
a lot of business schools in Africa. Collectively speaking, several schools are
making a spirited effort to engage well-qualified faculty. African business
schools have not fared badly in terms of the number of full-time faculty.
TIA (2012) special report on business education revealed that only 34% of
faculty in African business schools have doctorate degrees and 15 out of 58
schools surveyed had 10 or more international faculty.

Research

EFMD defines research (EFMD, 2015b, p. 42) as:

> A broad spectrum of intellectual endeavor ranging from scholarly pub-
> lication aimed primarily at the academic community, through profes-
> sionally relevant publications and activities aimed at organizations and
> business practitioners, to educationally relevant productions aimed at
> learners and teachers in universities, schools and companies.

The quality of scholarship is one of the ways to increase institutional
prestige. An important role of business schools in Africa is to conduct
research that can strengthen economic development and contribute to the
development of the society. One important question that business schools
should be asking is what kind of research should they be doing. Should the
focus be on research that leads to publications in top-rate journals earning
the school institutional prestige? Or impactful research focused on the needs
of the region, which may not be readily published in top journals but find a
space in practitioner journals? However, as prescribed by the three international accrediting bodies, the research should be of high quality, impactful,
exhibit an international dimension and be in line with the school's mission.
Research contributes to institutional reputation, attracts funding, attracts
high-quality faculty and students, and enhances interface with industry and
international relations.

Collaboration With Industry

It is important for business schools to build and maintain strong corporate
connection to enhance quality and meet accreditation standards. It is useful
not only for funding but also for career placements, research opportunities,
and shapes the curriculum and executive education. Therefore, across these

five dimensions and more, the corporate connection is necessary without which the progress of any business school will be grossly impeded. Business schools do not necessarily generate the kind of funds that will enhance their development from core programs. Therefore, they have to rely on what support they get from the corporate bodies. Again, this is an area where accreditation is helpful.

Ethics, Responsibility and Sustainability

Accreditation may help business schools deepen the teaching and practice of ethics, responsibility and sustainability assessed by at least one of the major accrediting bodies. It is required and important in the African context given the challenges of leadership and resource management across the continent and considering the stage of Africa's development. The issues of sustainability have only recently been implemented across the continent. Therefore, it is the role of business schools to educate the nation about sustainability and responsible leadership. At Lagos Business School, Nigeria, the teaching and activities of all programs emphasize the point that management is a service to society and not an end in itself. The school encourages its students to inculcate these values during and after their studies. Therefore, accreditation helps the business schools play a pivotal role in the society in this regard.

Control and Autonomy

With regards to the conflict in matters of control between the parent university and the business school, the process of accreditation may help in resolving this. Accreditation specifies that business schools should exert a "significant degree of control over their destiny." It is important for business schools to be autonomous or semi-autonomous to allow for independent decision making and invest in areas that improve overall quality.

Constraints to Accreditation

There are, however, constraints to seeking global accreditation. Some of the problems highlighted in the previous paragraphs are also constraints. Cost is another strong limiting factor. Outside of the explicit costs for accreditation that vary, depending on the body from $20,000 to $50,000, there are other costs associated with putting in place the processes, funding research and attracting high-quality faculty. In a continent where the cost of tuition for an MBA program range from of $10,000 with top-tier schools not charging more than $25,000 for the program, the costs of seeking accreditation from one of the foremost accrediting bodies is prohibitive. As discussed earlier in this chapter, in situations where the business school is not autonomous and control is centralized, there are limits on spending or a reluctance to commit to a process deemed costly given the competing needs of the university.

Other constraints include the availability of qualified faculty within the school, which is an essential part of the standards required by all accrediting bodies.

The attainment of global accreditation by African business schools has numerous benefits and should be encouraged. Apart from the overarching benefit of improvement in quality of the school across several dimensions, other benefits likely to add to such institutions include: an increased ability to attract highly qualified and perhaps international faculty, an increased likelihood of research collaboration with academics from other regions, and collaboration on programs with other accredited schools.

Table 4.4   Accredited Business Schools in Africa

SN	SCHOOL	COUNTRY	AACSB International	EQUIS	AMBA	ACBSP
1	American University of Leadership	Morocco				✓
2	AUC—The American University in Cairo	Egypt	✓	✓	✓	
3	Ecole Hassania des Travaux Publics	Morocco			✓	
4	Gordon Institute of Business Science, University of Pretoria	South Africa			✓	
5	Maastricht School of Management—School of Finance and Banking SFB	Rwanda				✓
6	Mediterranean School of Business	Tunisia			✓	
7	Potchefstroom Business School, North West University	South Africa			✓	
8	Rhodes Business School	South Africa			✓	
9	University of Cape Town Graduate School of Business	South Africa	✓	✓	✓	
10	University of Stellenbosch Graduate School of Business	South Africa	✓	✓	✓	
11	Wits Business School, University of Witwatersrand	South Africa			✓	

Note: From AACSB International (2013); AMBA (2013b); Accredited Programs by Main (2015); and EFMD (2015a).

Overall this would lead to increased attractiveness for students—both local and foreign.

The Future Role of Accreditation in African Business Schools

Given the increasing number of business schools across the continent, it is essential that there is a system by which high-quality schools are distinguished. Accreditation by recognized bodies—regional or global—that have established themselves in the management education sectors as being of high standards can promote high quality within schools in the region who seek such accreditation. As at March 2015, only very few African business schools have attained accreditation. Nevertheless, the accreditation process for international/global accreditation could have the desired effect of improving standards in African business schools. There are eleven business schools in Africa who have at least one of these accreditations and six of these in South Africa as at March 2015. Table 4.4 below list these schools and their accreditation.

When properly administered, accreditation will encourage business schools to aspire to improved, higher standards comparable to top global business schools. Overall the effect would be higher-quality graduates who can contribute to the economic and social development of the region. The quest and achievement of accreditation will enhance the standard of business schools in the region. Nevertheless, perhaps a regional accreditation that focuses on the peculiarities of the continent and takes into cognizance the stage of development of the management education sector may better serve the needs of management development institutions in Africa.

CONCLUSION

This chapter discussed the challenges of graduate management education in Africa. It explores the relevance of the programs offered by business schools in Africa to the realities of global management practice and suggests ways by which accreditation can enhance the quality of graduate management programs in African business schools.

REFERENCES

AACSB International. (2013a). *Accredited institutions*. Retrieved January 15, 2015, from http://www.aacsb.edu/en/accreditation/accredited-members/global-listing. aspx

AACSB International. (2013b). *Eligibility procedures and accreditation standards for business accreditation*. Retrieved January 15, 2015, from http://www.aacsb. edu/en/accreditation/standards/2013-business/

African Management Initiative. (2012). *Catalyzing management development in Africa: Identifying areas of impact.* Retrieved from http://c.ymcdn.com/sites/www.gbsnonline.org/resource/collection/C7F63EF4–0CDC-4A6F-9805-DA0680C0FD88/AMI_interim_report_.pdf

AMBA. (2013a). *AMBA accreditation guide for business schools.* Retrieved January 14, 2015, from http://www.mbaworld.com/~/media/Files/Accreditation/Accreditation%20Guidance%20for%20Business%20Schools.ashx

AMBA. (2013b). *AMBA accredited schools.* Retrieved January 14, 2015, from www.ambaguide.com/find-an-accredited-programme/schools/

AMBA. (2013c). *Criteria for the Accreditation of MBA programs.* Retrieved January 14, 2015, from www.mbaworld.com/en/Accreditation.aspx

August, O. (2013, May 13). Emerging Africa: A hopeful continent. *The Economist,* 2. Retrieved from www.economist.com/node/21541015

Badugela, T. M. (2012). *Problems facing educators implementing the national curriculum statement: The case of Tshifhena Secondary School.* Vhembe District, Limpopo Province, South Africa (Unpublished master's thesis). The University of South Africa. Retrieved from http://uir.unisa.ac.za/xmlui/bitstream/handle/10500/7642/dissertation_badugela_tm.pdf?sequence=1

Birdsball, N. (2007). Do not harm: Aid, weak institutions and the missing middle in Africa. *Development Policy Review, 25*(5), 575–598.

Deverajan, S., Monga, C., and Zongo, T. (2011). Making higher education finance work for Africa. *Journal of African Economies, 20*(3), 133–154. Retrieved arch 26, 2015, from http://ent.arp.harvard.edu/AfricaHigherEducation/Economics.html

Dowden, R. (2000, March 2). The hopeless continent. *The Economist,* 19. Retrieved from www.economist.com/node/21519234

EFMD. (2015a). *EQUIS accredited schools.* Retrieved January 15, 2015, from https://www.efmd.org/accreditation-main/equis/accredited-schools

EFMD. (2015b). *EQUIS standards and criteria: European foundation for management development.* Retrieved January 15, 2015, from https://www.efmd.org/accreditation-main/equis/equis-guides

Financing Higher Education in Africa. (2010). Retrieved February 12, 2016, from https://openknowledge.worldbank.org/handle/10986/2448

Herbst, J., and Greg, M. (2003). The future of Africa: A new order in sight. *Adelphi Paper, 361*(1), 1–86.

ICEF Monitor. (2015). *African summit calls for a major expansion of higher education.* Retrieved from http://monitor.icef.com/2015/03/african-summit-calls-for-major-expansion-of-higher-education/

Janjua, P. Z. (2011). Upgrading the standard of higher education in developing countries through international cooperation. *International Journal of Education Administration and Policy Studies, 3*(7), 103–111.

Jegede, O. (2012, February 1). *The status of higher education in Africa.* Paper for panel discussion in the launch of *Weaving Success: Voices of Change in African Higher Education*-A project of the Partnership for Higher Education in Africa (PHEA) held at the Institute of International Education, New York.

Kawa, L. (2013, January 29). The 20 fastest growing countries in the world. Retrieved February 12, 2016, from http://www.businessinsider.com/fastest-growing-economies-through-2015-2013-1?op=1

Kline, D. S. (1994). Strange bedfellows: Competency models and ACBSP accreditation standards. *Developments in Business Simulation and Experiential Learning, 21.* pp. 87–89.

Kupoluyi, A. (2012, November 26). 2013 budget: Rescuing education. *Vanguard News*. Retrieved from http://www.vanguardngr.com/2012/11/2013-budget-rescuing-eduction/

McKinsey & Company. (2014). *Africa is forecast to be the 2nd fastest growing market over the next 10–12 years. Lions on the move: The Japan-Africa Business Forum 2014*. Retrieved from http://cdn.mg.co.za/content/documents/2015/03/06/african-higher-education-summit.pdf

Montanini, M. (2013). *Supporting terry education, enhancing economic development, strategies for effective higher education funding in sub-Saharan Africa*. ISPI Working Paper, Fondazione *Edu*, No. 49, 1–37.

Mooko, T., Tabulawa, R., Maruatona, T., and Koosimile, A. (2009). *Revitalizing higher education in sub-Saharan Africa*. The United Nations University Project Report, 5–33.

Noman, A., and Stiglitz, J. E. (2014). Economics and policy: Some lessons from Africa's experience. In *The Oxford Handbook of Africa and Economics: Policies and Practices*. London: Oxford University Press, pp. 1–16.

Oyango-Obbo, C. (2015). The state of higher education in Africa. *Mail and Guardian*, 6. Retrieved from http://cdn.mg.co.za/content/documents/2015/03/06/african-higher-education-summit.pdf

Shah, A. (2012). India's business schools get a tough lesson in supply and demand. *Reuters*. Retrieved from http://in.Reuters.com/article/2012/09/10/india-education-mba-business-schools-idINDEE88900W20120910

Sifuna, D. N., and Sawamura, N. (2011, March). *Challenges of quality education in sub-Saharan Africa-Some key issues*. In CICE Africa-Asia University Dialogue for Educational Development Report of the International Experience Sharing Seminar (1) Effort Towards Improving the Quality of Education, 1–12. Hiroshima.

TIA. (2012). *Table of African business schools*. TIA: A Global Perspective Special Report. June/July Edition, 6–7.

UNCTAD. (2014). *Economic development in Africa Report 2014: Catalyzing investment for transformative growth in Africa*. Retrieved from http://unctad.org/en/PublicationsLibrary/aldcafrica2014_en.pdf

World Bank. (2013). *India*. Retrieved from http://data.worldbank.org/country/india

World Bank. (2015). *India data*. Retrieved February 3, 2015, from http:data.world bank.org/country/india].

World Population Statistics. (2013). *Africa Population 2013*. Retrieved March 20, 2015, from www.worldpopulationstatistics.com/africa-population-2013/

Yizengaw, T. (2008). Challenges of higher education in Africa and lessons of experience for the Africa-US higher education collaboration initiative. A Synthesis Report, based on Consultations between March–April.

5 Meeting the Graduate Management Program Challenges in Nigeria

Olusegun Matanmi

INTRODUCTION AND BACKGROUND

In general, training delivery systems that propagate knowledge and applications of business organization and management are critical institutional requirements for sustainable organizational development of the African nations. Some additional specific demands of effective graduate training and research programs in business administration include imparting practical competencies in critical thinking, emotional intelligence, interpersonal relations, and research administration, among others. The required professional competencies in the embedded subject-matter specializations within the management discipline also include: human resources and industrial relations; organizational behavior; productivity and performance management; accounting and finance; information and communications system management, and more. However, strategic investments in human capital development and the achievement of wholesome workforce engagement are two other salient managerial requirements of the modern-sector organizations that robust graduate management educational systems can further serve well. Unfortunately, the political and economic circumstances of many of these organizations, including the management development institutions, in the developing African countries have generally also tended to encumber the prospects of the wider organizational benefits that are derivable from human capital development investments and the expected functioning of the management development institutions. For example, in Nigeria, the political and economic circumstances since the 1990s have recurrently generated serious funding restrictions and tensions, endemic labor crisis in the educational sector, consequent instability of the academic calendar of educational institutions in general, the adverse impact of asymmetrical as well as highly politicized institutional authority structures, and so forth—thus, also demonstrating the underlying connectivity between purely macroeconomic phenomena and the regime of organizational and managerial activities at the microeconomic level of the specific African nations (Falola, 2014).

Besides, the major challenges facing the African continent in the 21st century have also been reported in the organization and management literature. In this connection, Farah, Kiamba and Mazongo (2011) have reported that many socio-political and economic challenges persist in the economic subsectors of health, social equity, energy, sustainability and general development balance. The same challenges are said to be amenable to a combination of development policies and practices, which essentially draw from classical organization and management thought as well as aim to resolve these challenges. Similarly, Collier and Gunning (1999) have aggregated empirical evidence to show that African economic performance has been comparatively markedly worse than that of the other world regions, having exhibited slow growth since the economic recession of the 1980s. They further noted that neither households nor firms have as yet successfully created the desired social institutions that promote growth—thereby extolling the virtue of institution-building as one of the potent catalysts of sustainable economic growth and national development.

In the same vein, Court and Kinyanjui (1986) have reported that Africa's grave development crisis—also typically characterized by rising demographics and declining productivity—has continued to deepen as a result of the consistently exhibited adverse metrics and soaring foreign debts that inhibit economic growth. They, therefore, recommended that African governments and the international development partners must evolve longitudinal and sustainable strategies for the pursuit of both the immediate and long-term national needs. One of these strategies is related to the need to embrace the promotion of high levels of investment in human resources so as to break the vicious cycle of pervasive economic stagnation and decline in the continent. The two authors have asserted that the low level of human resource development in Africa, compared to other resource inputs, has accounted for the poor economic predicaments in most of the continent—and which has generally tended to render African institutions and projects to "languish or become inoperable" due to the dearth or total lack of human capital for their effective management. The above predicaments, as captured by the various authors, have also further highlighted the primary essence of management training and executive development for the continuous enhancement of professional competencies in favor of the required organization and management of the increasingly complex modern-sector organizations in Africa. Further still, Cheru (2002) has challenged the African governments to tackle the myriad obstacles and crisis-enabling triggers in the way of economic development, also specifically attributing the way forward to: the acceleration of democratic acculturation; dedicated investments in education; re-invigoration of agricultural productivity; poverty reduction; strengthening of regional economic partnerships and integration; management of the emergent patterns and trends of urbanization; and, the prevention of volatile conflicts. The bottom line is that the attention to the foregoing development subsectors must precede any exploration of the wider benefits that are also derivable from the international political and economic system.

In light of this backdrop, it is also insightful to further note the existing thrust and framework of management thought, as applicable to the African context. The work by Nzelibe (1986) espoused the perspective that African management thought, both in terms of conceptualization and research by the management scholars, has advanced only marginally in its theoretical and practical applications. In that sense, much of the work on African management has tended to rely on the earlier theories, which affirmed universals in human behavior as well as organizational structures and processes, thereby undermining or underestimating the wider impact of the often peculiar and extenuating work environments in the developing African nations. Consequently, Nzelibe (1986) suggested that theory construction for African management should ideally recognize the peculiar organizational and managerial contingencies of the African environment—often with characteristic (and incredible) infrastructural deficits that sometimes adversely impact organizational behavior as well as impede robust aggregate performance and productivity. Similarly, Hofstede (1999) submitted that the thrust of management thought in the 21st century is not necessarily different from management in the 20th century; but rather that in the contemporary times, the direction of theory construction in management will tend more towards adaptation to the national cultural value systems in the various parts of the world. Consequently, all of the foregoing thoughts are noteworthy for the holistic comprehension of the needs, challenges and ideal thrusts of the generality of graduate management development programs in the African countries whose political leaderships continually interface and grapple with the challenges and pangs of socioeconomic development.

Therefore, the purpose of this chapter is to present a Nigerian case study that, more specifically, will address the contingent challenges of graduate management educational programming, while initially situating the trajectory of tertiary (i.e., polytechnic and university-level) educational delivery in general, and the development of graduate programs in particular, in Nigeria. Thus, the Nigerian experience of the associated challenges of graduate management development within the educational industry and subsector of the economy, as elaborated in the following segments, should serve as a compass for the appropriate guidance or direction of public policies, programming and practices that are involved in the national processes of graduate management development in the rest of Africa. The chapter then particularly describes the genesis of tertiary educational delivery and graduate programs in Nigeria. Further attention is also devoted to an account of the status and output of graduate management development programs as well as the manifested challenges of their delivery. Suggestions for realistically getting around those challenges are proffered, and the future of graduate management development programs in Nigeria is projected.

GENESIS OF TERTIARY EDUCATIONAL DELIVERY IN NIGERIA

The remote origin of tertiary educational delivery in Nigeria is traceable to the formative efforts of the Sir Eric Ashby Commission, which was set up in 1959 by the colonial government on the eve of independence from British tutelage on October 1, 1960 (Ade-Ajayi, 1975). The Commission was established to identify the high-level human resource needs of the then-anticipated new nation-state. The Commission's report specifically recommended that education should be accorded appropriate policy and administrative attention because of its perceived instrumental role in the pursuit and possible attainment of national economic development. In addition, the same report recommended the establishment of four federal universities, and with the prescription of selected course areas for early concentration. The policy outcomes of the Ashby Report naturally also influenced the ebb and flow of the following early (so-called 'first-generation') universities in Nigeria, namely: University of Ibadan, Ibadan, which had evolved from its original status as University College, Ibadan (established in 1948 and affiliated with the University of London); University of Nigeria, Nsukka, in 1960; Ahmadu Bello University, Zaria, in 1962; University of Ife, Ile-Ife, in 1962 (later re-named Obafemi Awolowo University); and University of Lagos, Lagos, also in 1962 (Ade-Ajayi, 1975; Mkpa, 2015).

During the post-independence years, various other tertiary educational institutions were also established in Nigeria, catalyzed by the Ashby Report. These included: colleges of education, polytechnics, and colleges of technology (Mkpa, 2015). It is further noteworthy that the National Universities Commission was established in 1962 by the federal government of Nigeria. The vision of this Commission was and is to be a dynamic regulatory agency acting as a catalyst for positive change and innovation for the delivery of quality university education in Nigeria. Furthermore, its mission is to ensure the orderly development of a well-coordinated and productive university system that will guarantee quality and relevant education for national development and global competitiveness. Correspondingly, the goals (functions) of the Commission encompass the following developmental and institution-building ideals, namely:

- Attainment of a stable and crisis-free university system;
- Working with Nigerian universities to achieve full accreditation status for at least 80% of the academic programs;
- Initiating and promoting proficiency in the use of ICT for service delivery within the Commission and the Nigerian university system;
- Upgrading and maintaining physical facilities in the Nigerian university system for delivery of quality university education;
- Matching university graduate output with national human capital needs; and
- Fostering partnership between the Nigerian university system and the private sector (Okebukola, 2002; Mafiana, 2014; National Universities Commission, 2014; Adedipe, 2015).

Within the same general timeframe in Nigeria, various policy-capturing and institution-building reform initiatives were taken by the federal government also generally in favor of strengthening the existing apparatuses of tertiary or higher educational delivery, most especially the graduate pro-grams within the university system. The battery of higher education policy reforms was aimed at necessarily harmonizing practices within the national university system with international best practices. The generality of these reforms were targeted at addressing the specific issues of institutional autonomy, the necessary achievement of greater system differentiation, the strengthening of governance of the educational system, and the accultura-tion of tenets and tools of quality assurance. The ultimate justification was to practically build and longitudinally sustain a flexible and functional aca-demic tradition in the university system—which could promote innovation and creativity as well as catalyze organizational performance and produc-tivity towards sustainable growth and economic development (Saint, Hart-nett, and Strassner, 2003: 259–281). Thus, and as part of this proactive endeavor, the Joint Admission and Matriculation Board was also created in 1977 to regulate the admission of students into the universities, in tandem with the exigencies of available operating capacity at the institutional level and the compounded demands of managing educational inequalities that have arisen from the vast structural diversity of the country's demography (Adeleye, Atewologun, and Matanmi, 2014, pp. 200–203).

STATUS AND OUTPUT OF GRADUATE MANAGEMENT PROGRAMS

Currently, there are about 145 approved universities operating educational programs in Nigeria (by reckoning, till date; presented in Table 5.1 below). This figure is further broken down into some 44 federal universities, 41 state universities, and some 60 private universities. But, out of this gross number, only about 58 universities are specifically approved to run graduate programs—variously at the postgraduate diploma (PGD) level, master's degree level, and doctor of philosophy (PhD) level. The figure of 58 can be further broken down into 26 federal universities, 21 state universities, and

Table 5.1　Nigerian Universities at Mid-June 2015

CATEGORY	NUMBER	%
Federal Government-Owned	44	30.3%
State Government-Owned	41	28.3%
Privately Owned	60	41.4%
TOTAL	**145**	**100.0%**

Source: National Universities Commission (2015), Abuja, FCT, Nigeria; (http://universitiesof nigeria.com/national-universities-commission-nuc/), accessed 8/20/2015; also, from personal cumulative reckoning of figures as regularly periodically announced in the public media by the National Universities Commission up until August 2015.

11 private universities that are currently officially approved to run post-graduate programs of any kind.

Furthermore, the universities that are approved to run postgraduate programs in Nigeria can also be categorized on the basis of ownership status (i.e., whether federal, state-government, or private ownership). These comprise 26 federal universities, 21 state universities, and 11 private universities (from statistical data and information collated variously from the NUC, the CDPGS, and in the author's capacity as a former member and dean of a postgraduate school). In terms of their periodic graduation output, each of these institutional graduate programs—which also practically run specific varieties of management degree programs—turns out an average of between 100 and 300 business and management graduates within one calendar year or an academic session. Significantly, this status again basically throws up the issue of representation and adequacy of student access to quite a large number of those graduate management programs. But, of course, with proper harmonization and strengthening of the existing operational capacity of several of these programs, they should become better positioned to provide enhanced access to the programs as may be dictated by the volume of aggregate demand for the same, and without undermining quality and standard of training delivery. It needs no gainsaying the fact that qualitative outputs of the increasing numbers of graduate management development institutions in Nigeria should ideally and continuously add to, or replenish, the vanguard of managerial human capital that are also required to drive the critical research and development (R&D) function in the modern-sector organizations, R&D being the formative engine of entrepreneurship and business/market development as well as innovation and technology management. The successful creation and operation of a robust graduate management training/development apparatus and system provides an ideal institutional mechanism for the generation of the longitudinal fruits of thematic graduate management research and training for the necessary achievement of sustainable national development.

CHALLENGES OF GRADUATE MANAGEMENT PROGRAMS

The proper instrumentation of graduate management development and related educational programs in Nigeria has historically been encumbered by horrendous challenges, which can be categorized into some seven broad types as will be outlined and elaborated below. The same general types are discernible for both conceptual and cognitive purposes as follows:

1 Funding and Liquidity-Related Challenges

In this category, there is the challenge of poor funding/finance that is often directly manifested in gross resource and operational tool inadequacies or scarcities (Ogu, 2008).

2 The Prevalence of Sheer Structural Odds and Ends

This specifically refers to the serious dearth or total lack of appropriate facilities, such as classrooms, libraries and learning-support resource centers, and laboratories (e.g., management development centers or laboratories for the necessary demonstration of the applicability of management software and analytics to aid student learning and tool knowledge assimilation).

3 Operational and Process-Induced Deficits

The variables under this caption generally include: the dearth or scarcity of uniform academic standards for the purpose of symmetrical practices across graduate management programs, and the sometimes indirect but implicit disincentive of low or poor attraction of the foreign student population to quite a number of the existing graduate management development programs—which otherwise could have tipped the multiplier scale in favor of mutual benefits that are desirable and derivable, if the right opportunities and market scenarios were prudently harnessed (Daramola, 2013).

4 Strategic Resource-Based Gaps

This cluster of variables encompasses the shortage or total lack of academic/research human capital, by way of supervision expertise for the appropriate and effective coaching and supervision of the same graduate management training programs.

5 Pangs Induced by Contextual Externalities

This category of factors situates (or recognizes) the periodic and situational disruption to a necessarily stable operating calendar by the often high frequency of labor action, induced especially by militant and powerful industrial unions that operate within the university system—which often also truncate and frustrate well-planned academic calendars in postgraduate school subsystems (Matanmi, 2012).

6 Consequential Factors

This latter category embodies the knock-on effects of combinations or all of the foregoing challenges with concomitant impact on the overall quality of graduate-level research and evaluation outputs, including the processing of thematic project reports, theses, and dissertations (Salako, 2014; Abbey, 2015; Ajienka, 2015).

7 Linkage Gaps Attributed to the Lack of Synergies

This variable refers to the spill-over adversity of the resultant effect of the often low or poor utilization of graduate management research output by relevant business and/or industry—thereby frustrating or outrightly blocking the ideals of research and development (R&D) synergies (Saad, 2010; Ajienka, 2015).

OVERCOMING THE CHALLENGES

The following requirements are outlined and prescribed for the strengthening and sustenance of graduate management programs in Nigeria and towards strategically overcoming the albatross of challenges that currently encumber the programs. They are:

1. The devise and implementation of a robust institutional graduate management development and educational delivery system—which is imbued with the benefit of appropriate and adequate staffing, in terms of the required numbers, quality, and profile (i.e., staff variety and mix).
2. The urgent need for incremental investments in the creation of better graduate student overall experience and program immersion (or bonding)—in ways that the required learning support infrastructure (e.g., facilities including classrooms, libraries, laboratories, equipment, apparatuses and ICT alike, management development software and accessories for the purposes of professional counseling, career guidance, and related advisory services and mentoring roles, etc.) is guaranteed as provided.
3. Promotion and assurance of the achievement of value for money, especially at the individual beneficiary level, and in ways that the graduate management programs are generally perceived as being instrumental in meeting the career development and enhancement expectations of the students or patrons of these programs.
4. The need for continuous review and upgrading/updating of training/educational content of the curricula of graduate management development programs to increasingly encompass the intermittently required reorientations of thoughts and thrusts of management principles, methods and procedures, which may be periodically necessitated by the peculiarities and idiosyncrasies of organizational contingencies. For example, some emergent challenges and needs of firms and other corporate organizations may require a special re-orientation of training emphasis (or stress) on the development of managerial skills and competencies, purely at the psychological or psychometric level. The increasingly emergent trends in organizational behavior and organizational learning have continued to suggest that management behavior, and employment behavior in general, are often also functions of highly dynamic and complex multilateral phenomena—hence, the need for painstaking flexibility and dynamism in the general packaging and running of graduate management development programs.

5. The continuous re-engineering of graduate business administration and management curricula to incorporate and keep abreast of trends in macroeconomic and microeconomic metrics or aggregates. For example, incidences of microeconomic and macroeconomic decline during periods of recession (or outright depression) should be factored into, or reflected in, the structure and content of programs' curricula scope and coverage in order to enhance robustness and longitudinally contribute to improvements in the appraised deficits associated with the overall status of such critical economic aggregates.

6. The additional and, perhaps, overriding stimuli of the enforcement of high accreditation standards cannot be overemphasized in the wider reckoning of things. It is evident and logical that quality assurance could and should provide the required checks and balances for driving the process of sustainable development of graduate management development programs in Nigeria, and also in the African countries generally (Abbey, 2015; Ajienka, 2015). Through a credible and functional system of quality assurance, program services delivery can be streamlined and standardized, variously for the achievement of operational symmetry, customer satisfaction, resource optimization for performance and productivity enhancement as well as the possible achievement of competitive advantages as an additional corporate objective.

7. In the foregoing regards, the activities of the National Universities Commission of Nigeria have been germane and insightful. The terms of reference of this Commission have typically encompassed the following specific gamut:

   a. The approval, monitoring and periodic review of graduate programs (in this context), but also generally of university-wide educational programs;
   b. Evaluation of the totality of students in the programs, with the aid of a set of public criteria, regulations, and procedures that are consistently applied;
   c. A similar deployment of the means of quality assurance for the assessment of teaching faculty and associated other support staff of the university (including graduate management) programs;
   d. The verification and assessment of availability, adequacy, and appropriateness of learning resources and student support in the university programs;
   e. Assurance of the availability of appropriate information systems for the necessary collection, analysis, and usage of relevant information also generally in favor of the effective operation and management of university educational/training programs and other activities;
   f. Assurance of the availability of continuous generation of public information and the regular publishing of such comprehensive

information (both quantitative and qualitative—e.g., on success/ graduation rates, student satisfaction, attrition rates, the variety or diversity of degrees or qualifications awarded, specific nature of teaching and learning imparted, opportunities for graduation— generally in the tradition of public accountability and social responsibility) across university programs (Mafiana, 2014; National Universities Commission, 2014).

8. A further recent intervention by the National Universities Commission that began in 2014 has been the commencement of the extension of the accreditation function to the realm of graduate programs, starting with management or administration-related graduate training programs (Mafiana, 2014). Hitherto, the traditional accreditation of educational programs in Nigerian universities had been restricted to undergraduate programs only. As a regulatory measure, the National Universities Commission has conceived this as an innovative and strategic move in the direction of holistic assurance of the quality of educational administration across the entire subject matter disciplines, from undergraduate to postgraduate (Mafiana, 2014). Future systematic evaluation of the impact of this measure should affirm the validity and efficacy, or not, of that innovation.

9. Further still, the role and activities of the existing Committee of Deans of Postgraduate Schools (CDPGS) in Nigerian universities have also been complementary to those of the National Universities Commission and other stakeholders in the educational industry. This has demonstrated the need for collaboration and proactive synergy among stakeholders. It is particularly additionally noteworthy that the CDPGS—which was officially inaugurated in 1987—has represented a thought platform that unifies all deans of graduate schools for purposes of academic and professional discourse, as well as strategic act   ion and productive peer-review synergies that have incrementally enhanced educational practices at the level of the inclusive graduate programs and positively promoted the acculturation of international best practices within the industry (CDPGS- Communique, 2013, p. 39; Abbey, 2015; Ajienka, 2015). This is an appealing demonstration of the power of institutional stakeholdership and multilateral action in the effective pursuit of public good.

FUTURE OF GRADUATE MANAGEMENT DEVELOPMENT PROGRAMS IN NIGERIA

In the final analysis, the future of graduate management development programs in Nigeria appears to be largely dependent on the extent to and rapidity with which the perceived and enumerated associated challenges can generally be overcome. Towards that end-view, the following mentions are made:

One, the serious funding crisis must be urgently mitigated with dedicated action by university or institutional proprietors to commit adequate funds as well as provide the required support infrastructure for the ideals of teaching, research and institutional learning.

Two, as the number of universities in the country has lately markedly increased, and continues to increase—in spite of the seemingly constant national labor market system from where all the existing universities also continue to source for human capital supply—there is an equally critical need for universities and tertiary institutions to generally invest massively in strategic human capital development for the appropriate staffing of existing universities and graduate management training programs.

Three, given a 2014 survey report finding on sub-Saharan Africa that Nigeria—Africa's largest economy—was ranked second in occupational fraud and abuse, and next to South Africa that was credited with the region's highest (Okojie, 2014), there is also a need to expand the curriculum content of the graduate management programs across-board, to continually enhance management capacity to uphold and promote enduring core values of integrity as well as acculturate tenets of corporate governance, probity, transparency and accountability, through purposive leadership training and management development as well as the re-orientation of organizational values ultimately also for sustainable institution-building, organizational learning and holistic development— a possible derivative of robust and effective graduate management program exposure of the students and prospective top corporate managers.

Four, the existing graduate management programs in the country must be further revamped to additionally embody specialized training on the specific uses of such versatile skill areas as emotional intelligence and human capital accounting as catalysts of employee performance and productivity—which managerial function remains the potent driver of a work organization's strategic human resource management model or cycle.

Following from the above, therefore, the lesson for the rest of Africa from the Nigerian experience is definitely of the essence. For purposes of wider regional and African development, the successful engineering and installation of a robust graduate management training/development apparatus and operating system, on a national basis, will provide the required basic institutional infrastructure for the continuous generation of longitudinal fruits of graduate management research and training—ultimately in favor of the necessary achievement of sustainable development. It is increasingly important that graduate management research and training as well as their associated delivery systems in the African countries should primarily reflect national development priorities and social needs. In this way, graduate management development institutions should particularly also seek to positively impact upon the aggregate macroeconomic metrics and trends manifested in the African nations—for example, in ways that such organization, management, and development dilemmas like low productivity, acute unemployment, excessive foreign indebtedness, the lack of sustainability and development balance, widespread social impoverishment, squalor and filth, and others, can be tackled headlong as well as necessarily reduced or checkmated, for the enhancement of the quality of life of the larger populace of the component nations. These are some direct social developmental correlates of the general applications of thematic outputs of graduate management research and training, as evident in Nigeria and across the developing African nations.

By and large, in summation, one critical lesson from the Nigerian case for the rest of Africa is that the need to realistically commit adequate funds as well as provide the required support infrastructure for the fulfillment of ideals of graduate management development programming and practices cannot be overemphasized. Besides, there is an equally critical need for the African nations to generally invest heavily in strategic human capital development for the appropriate staffing of the existing and future graduate management development delivery systems. Similarly, there is also a need for the creative design and constant revision (or expansion) of the curriculum of the graduate management development programs operated in the African nations, in favor of continually enhancing management's performance and productive capacity as well as competency mix across the board. Also, towards this end goal, the horrendous challenges of the work-lives and career trajectories in the modern sector of the Nigerian and, indeed, other economies on the African continent can be effectively managed.

Furthermore, the Nigerian experience has also been quite insightful for the purpose of tackling the global challenge of graduate management development. The following few but specific notes are additionally made towards the embrace and support of proactive policy initiatives as well as positive orientations that prioritize dedicated investments in strategic human capital development for the continuous support and logical enhancement of professional graduate management development, within the context of an increasingly integrating international political and economic system.

First, the increasing number of complex work organizations of the 21st century, across the globe, will benefit from greater institution-building and capacity-expansion processes that could leverage highly professional human capital (indeed, the totality of specialized competencies) that are products of robust and solid graduate management development delivery systems. The multitude of managerial and organizational challenges in the contemporary world of work is generally amenable to a similar battery of managerial and organizational solutions—which only well thought-out and highly competitive graduate management development programs can provide.

Second, such ideal and desirable graduate management development programs are (among other imperatives) the functions of exceptional foresight, ingenious proactivity, prudent investment of scarce resources in asset development (including human assets), the required institution-building, and logistics and general resource management. Where these variables are lacking, the goals of sustainable graduate management development become far-fetched and practically difficult to attain, even in the long run.

Third, the observable trends in political and economic growth across regions of the globe, or the lack of such appreciable growth in the less developed regions of the globe, are also quite amenable to corporate governance and leadership competencies that are often borne out of well-crafted and well-administered professional graduate management development programs—hence, another universal challenge of graduate management development.

Fourth, a continuing global challenge for management development also relates to the issue of relevance of specific forms, types, and scopes of graduate management development. In this connection, it becomes highly imperative that management development programs should have general and wider social and developmental relevance—in ways that the particular socioeconomic and development aggregates of a nation-state are factored into the packaging of such graduate management development programs, for the purpose of positively moderating or regulating the unfavorable metrics that are often conveyed by social aggregate data. In particular, the developing African countries should endeavor to promote the socioeconomic relevance of graduate management development programs by ensuring that critical socioeconomic metrics or analytics, such as economic growth and development parameters, the poverty regime, aggregate unemployment, social criminality trends, and composite indices of general socioeconomic well being, are targeted for possible gradual amelioration of any existing or pervasive adverse trends.

SUMMARY AND CONCLUSION

By and large, this chapter's contribution has focused on the situational challenges of the existing graduate management programs within the Nigerian industrial and operational context. The enumerated challenges range from the purely economic and physical or structural to the organizational and managerial as well as various others that were totally human-centered or behavioral in nature. Some of the latter have essentially emanated from sheer existential or systemic gaps and asymmetries in the framework of the formulation and implementation of public educational policies. Specific suggestions were made towards surmounting the various challenges, including the necessary catalytic role of accreditation regimes that are anchored by centralized authorities to promote and uphold tenets of quality assurance in educational services delivery as well as the utility of concerted action, collective partnerships, stakeholder collaboration and synergetic interorganizational relations. The chapter is concluded by drawing attention to some imperatives of successful future graduate management programs in Nigeria, but also with possible wider applications to similar situations and practices across the African continent.

REFERENCES

Abbey, B. W. (2015). Research, postgraduate training and national development. *A Lecture Paper presented at the 49th meeting of the Committee of Deans of Postgraduate Schools (CDPGS) in the Nigerian Universities*, held at the University of Port Harcourt, 6 May.

Ade-Ajayi, J. F. (1975). Higher education in Nigeria. *African Affairs, 74*(297), 420–426.

Adedipe, N. O. (2015). Strains and stresses in the Nigerian University System: Sustainable quality assurance prospects by private universities. *Text of the Third Convocation Lecture* of the Al-Hikmah University, Ilorin, Nigeria.

Adeleye, I., Atewologun, D., and Matanmi, O. (2014). Equality, diversity and inclusion in Nigeria: Historical context and emerging issues. In A. Klarsfeld, L. A. E. Booysen, E. Ng, I. Roper and A. Tatli (Eds.), *International handbook on diversity management at work: Country perspectives on diversity and equal treatment* (pp. 195–216). Cheltenham, UK: Edward Edgar.

Ajienka, J. A. (2015). *Research, Graduate Training and National Development: A Keynote Address at the 49th Meeting of the Committee of Deans of Postgraduate Schools (CDPGS) in the Nigerian Universities* held at the University of Port Harcourt, 6 May.

Cheru, F. (2002). *African renaissance: Roadmaps to the challenge of globalization.* London: Zed Books, p. 253.

Collier, P., and Gunning, J. W. (1999). Explaining African economic performance. *Journal of Economic Literature, 37*(1), 64–111.

Committee of Deans of Postgraduate Schools (CDPGS) in Nigerian Universities. (2013, July 11). Communique. *Punch International Business, 39.*

Court, D., and Kinyanjui, K. (1986). African education: Problems in a high-growth sector. In R. J. Berg and J. S. Whitaker (Eds.), *Strategies for African development: A study for the committee on African development strategies (U.S.).* Council on Foreign Relations, Inc., Overseas Development Council. Berkeley, USA: University of California Press. [HJML] pp. 361–392. Retrieved August 20, 2015, from google.com

Daramola, O. (2013). Postgraduate studies in Nigeria: The journey so far. *46th Meeting of the Committee of Deans of Postgraduate Schools in Nigeria Universities.* September 25–27, pp. 14–15.

Falola, T. (2014). Public universities vision and knowledge economies. *Text of the Third Convocation Lecture*, Osun State University. Osogbo, Nigeria: Osun State University.

Farah, I., Kiamba, S., and Mazongo, K. (2011). Major challenges facing Africa in the 21st century: A few provocative remarks' at the International Symposium on Cultural Diplomacy in Africa—*Strategies to confront the challenges of the 21st century: Does Africa have what is required?* Berlin, July 14–17.

Hofstede, G. (1999). Problems remain, but theories will change: The universal and the specific in 21st-century global management. *Organizational Dynamics, 28*(1), 34–44.

Mafiana, C. F. (2014). Perspectives and imperatives of quality assurance in the Nigerian university system. *Keynote Presented at the 48th Meeting of Deans of Postgraduate Schools of Nigerian Universities*, Imo State University, Owerri. December 2.

Matanmi, O. (2012). Consensus-building in the context of minimum wage determination: Issues and challenges. In *Consensus building, conflict management and social transformation in Nigeria: An industrial relations perspective*. Ilorin, Nigeria: Michael Imoudu National Institute for Labor Studies, pp. 59–88.

Mkpa, M. A. (2015). Overview of educational development: Pre-colonial to present day. *Online Nigeria (Community Portal)*. Friday, March 27.

National Universities Commission. (2014a). *Top 100 universities in Nigeria.* Retrieved from http://universitiesofnigeria.com/top-nigeria-universities/

National Universities Commission. (2014b). *List of universities with approved postgraduate programmes in Nigeria.* Retrieved from http://www.nigeriaembassygermany.org/

National Universities Commission. (2015a). *List of universities in Nigeria.* Abuja, FCT, Nigeria. Retrieved August 20, 2015, from https://en.wikipedia.org/wiki/List_of_universities_in_Nigeria

National Universities Commission. (2015b). *Online portal.* Retrieved February, March, April, May.

Nzelibe, C. O. (1986). The evolution of African management thought. *International Studies of Management and Organization, 16*(2), 6–16.

Ogu, E. (2008). Challenges facing Nigerian universities. *Nigeriaworld.* Retrieved from nigeriaworld.com/articles/2008/sep/300.html

Okebukola, P. (2002). *The state of university education in Nigeria.* Abuja, FCT: National Universities Commission.

Okojie, J. (2014). Nigeria ranks second in occupational fraud, abuse in sub-Saharan Africa. *BusinessDay,* p. 61, 13 October. Retrieved August 20, 2015, from http://www.businessdayonline.com

Saad, A. (2010). Nigerian universities in crisis. *Universities in Crisis.* Blog of the Sociological Association, 26 January. Retrieved from www.isa-sociology.org/universities-in-crisis/?p=248

Saint, W., Hartnett, T. A., and Strassner, E. (2003). Higher education in Nigeria: A status report. *Higher Education Policy, 16*(3), 259–281. doi:10.1057/palgrave.hep.8300021

Salako, C. T. (2014). Challenges facing university education in Nigeria: The way forward. *Journal of Educational Foundations, 4,* 93–98.

Part II
African Social, Cultural, and Political Influences

6   Cross-Cultural Studies as a Resource for Management Development in Africa

Mariya Bobina and Mikhail Grachev

CROSS-CULTURAL MANAGEMENT: A RESOURCE FOR MANAGEMENT DEVELOPMENT

While still "at a crossroads" and with known economic gaps among its countries, Africa has nevertheless been moving towards integration into the global economy, with visible acceleration in the 21st century evidenced in strong growth, foreign direct investment, differentiation of trade, and interaction with Western partners in poverty reduction and export performance.

These advancements, however, depend to a great extent on the quality of management and effective organizational practices in the business sector. The development of local management talent is crucial, and the following questions prove particularly pertinent: How to prepare African managers and organizational leaders to interact effectively with their partners and competitors from around the world? How to build cross-cultural skills and acquire international management know-how to respond to international business expectations and comply with modern educational standards to serve African and multinational management and organizations operating in Africa?

The urgency of these tasks stems from the unique situation defined by the African Management Initiative as a "management gap" between competent senior executives with foreign education and exposure and middle- and lower-level managers who lack basic work readiness skills and have experienced little or substandard training and development. Large companies face fierce competition for rare management talent and are forced to export expats. Small companies become overly dependent on a small group of senior managers. The majority of local African managers often "lack practical experience" and exhibit a "lack of international exposure." Only a small group of managers is knowledgeable about the best practices overseas, or has been exposed to the same breadth of different projects, markets, and business scenarios as their counterparts in more developed economies (Catalyzing Management Development in Africa, 2013). The urgency of building cross-cultural competencies also responds to the unique African cultural landscape and the differences between norms, values, and behaviors in that environment and those in the West; if not addressed appropriately, such differences may create additional frictions and serve as impediments to effective cross-border business communication, trade, and investment.

Building cross-cultural competencies in the African managerial community has for a long time been on the periphery of attention in the region's business education and management development, with the exception of a few tier 1 business schools that meet international standards or selective management training programs of large Western multinational firms operating in the region. Research on cross-cultural diversity in the region has also been in an "embryonic" state (Horwitz and Jain, 2008, p. 97).

Hence, understanding the cultural attributes of African management in a cross-cultural space and helping managers to successfully overcome cultural frictions in cross-border interactions become critical for international success. This chapter addresses these needs by highlighting the practical value of modern cross-cultural theories in management development in Africa. It responds to known methodological difficulties of multidisciplinary research (behavioral, anthropological, management, and economic studies) as well as to the lack of reliable empirical data about the cultural distinctions of African managers. In particular, the authors summarize the major contributions of the cross-cultural school of thought, apply those theories to attributes of African management in four geographically clustered countries in the southern part of the continent—Namibia, South Africa, Zambia and Zimbabwe—and offer insights about the instrumentality of cross-cultural theories and data to practical areas such as international trade and leadership development.

SUB-SAHARAN AFRICA IN ADVANCED CROSS-CULTURAL STUDIES

The key areas that should be addressed in Africa's business education and management development in response to globalization combine managers' understanding of culture and cultural differences and their sense of the instrumentality of that knowledge in business and organizational practices. While these complex competencies are traditionally included in the domain of Western general management background, this is not the case in Africa. Because of shortcomings in this area, cultural know-how needs to be delivered to individuals who may lack a general management background. Before exploring culture's effects in African business and management, it is important to explain what we mean by culture and how to compare African countries in a cross-cultural space.

CULTURE: DEFINITIONS AND ATTRIBUTES

Culture is a set of attributes that distinguishes social groupings from one another in a meaningful way (Kroeber and Kluckhohn, 1952, p. 181;

Hofstede, 1980, pp. 25, 48). It is manifested in norms, values, and beliefs that are shared by all or most of all members of a social group and transferred from older to younger generations; and which shapes the behaviors of people (House et al, 2004, p. 15). Huntington (1993) distinguished eight major human civilizations, conditionally naming the African civilization as one of those, and he explained that fault lines separating civilizations from one another are evidenced in different views about the relations between God and man, individual and group, husband and wife, parents and children as well as about the relative importance of rights and duties, liberty and authority, equality and hierarchy.

Culture plays an important economic role in a society and shapes its management and organizational practices. Fukuyama (1995) emphasized the role of cultural attributes, trust, and moral principles in post-industrial societies, explaining that law, contracts, and economic rationality provide a necessary but not sufficient basis for prosperity. Developmental economics literature argues that in African countries, on the one hand, income outcomes, collective actions, and contribution to the public good respond to social control on norm observance, family support, and benefits through extra-familiar networks; on the other hand, powerful, tightly knit social groups not accountable to society as evidenced in corruption or cronyism in political institutions, serve as impediments to effective development (Narayan and Cassidy, 2001). Interest in these cultural factors stems from their relevance not only to the structure of networks or social relations but also to behavioral dispositions such as trust, honesty, or reciprocity along with the institutional quality of the rule of law, contract enforceability, and civil liberties (Woolcock, 2001).

Cultural distinctions are shaped by a country's history. Jackson (2004; 2015) claimed that without a question, thorough interpretation of the realities in African countries by cross-cultural theories should be supplemented and complemented by a deep exploration of underlying factors in precolonial and colonial histories (colonialism, imperialism, apartheid). These include Western influences on local business practices, social anthropology's findings on the evolution of values in African societies, cultural heterogeneity of societies, the importance of ethnic or social groups' dominance in organizations, complex stakeholder perspective as well as the emergence of hybrid forms of management in the region. For example, cultural distinctions may have been influenced by colonial history such as traces of German heritage in Namibia, British and Portuguese influences in Zambia, and remnants of Dutch and British colonization in South Africa, or British influences in Zimbabwe.

Several key cultural manifestations make African management distinctive. First, there is the importance of *ubuntu*—an African paradigm that interprets the quality of people or a person in a social setting. A broader interpretation of *ubuntu* involves humanistic philosophy, ethics, and worldview while a more focused approach relates it to humanistic and community values and humane, kind, and generous behaviors in a society (Mangaliso,

2001; Littrell et al, 2013). Second, African society is rooted in a tribal system, which influences the perception and interpretation of power. This is manifested in highly centralized organizations: an unwillingness to delegate authority or share information, the minimization of autonomy at lower levels of hierarchies, or the prioritizing of organizational relations over strong performance orientation (Blunt and Jones, 1997). Overall, these unique cultural attributes distinguish African management practices from those in other parts of the world.

Cultural distinctions become instrumental when they are compared, especially at a country level of analysis. Hence, the transition from cultural stereotypes to comparative analysis may enhance management development in Africa. This transition, however, faces challenging issues stemming from the lack of comprehensive cross-cultural data on many or most African societies beyond single-criterion studies of history, colonial past, religion, or language differences, and from the historically late inclusion of African countries into the Western mainstream behaviorist and anthropological research.

In modern cross-cultural literature, different comparative patterns coexist, shifting research from single-criterion comparisons towards the search for complex, multivariable composite measures of cultural profiles of managerial population further generalized to societal levels. Table 6.1 displays influential multi-criteria in comparative studies of cultures. This stream of research can be traced in an earlier work by Douglas (1973), where she offered a two-dimensional grid to analyze and compare patterns of social control among societies, namely group bonds and members' roles (homogeneity vs. diversity). The follow-up studies offered different combinations of universal dimensions for comparative purposes. The contribution by Hofstede's (1980) four-dimensional model was originally based on managers' responses about their perceptions of cultures along criteria such as Individualism-Collectivism, Masculinity-Femininity, Uncertainty Avoidance, and Power Distance (with Long-Term Orientation and Indulgence added later to the original framework). Ingelhart (1997) designed a two-dimensional model known as the World Values Survey and applied it to over 80 countries to compare societies along traditional versus secular values and along survival values versus self-expression. Hampden-Turner and Trompenaars (2000) offered a seven-dimensional model to compare culturally endorsed communication patterns in over 40 countries so as to explain how people control time and environment, express emotions, or relate to others in a group. Schwartz (1992; 1999; 2004) developed a three-dimensional model of universal human values measured along Embeddedness vs. Autonomy, Mastery vs. Harmony, and Hierarchy vs. Egalitarianism. And House with associates (Schwartz, 2004) offered a nine-dimensional model that extended Hofstede's tradition and enriched it with contributions from McClelland (1961; 1985) and Kluckhohn (1961).

While these researchers built a solid foundation for a multidimensional cross-cultural analysis, the representation of African countries—and in particular those from the southern geographic cluster—in those studies was

Table 6.1 Advanced Multidimensional Cross-Cultural Studies and Sub-Saharan African Countries

Author	Number of dimensions	Dimensions	African societies (southern geographic cluster) included/not included in the original study
M. Douglas (1973)	2	Group bonds, Members' roles (homogeneity vs. diversity)	NO
G. Hofstede (1980; 1993)	4 (original version) later added 2 more	Power Distance, Individualism vs. Collectivism, Masculinity vs. Femininity, Uncertainty Avoidance + Long-term Orientation vs. Short-term Orientation, Indulgence vs. Restraint	ZAF
S. Schwartz (1992)	3	Embeddedness vs. Autonomy, Mastery vs. Harmony, Hierarchy vs. Egalitarianism	ZBW
R. Inglehart (1997)	2	Traditional values vs. Secular values, Survival values vs. Self-expression values	ZAF, ZAM, ZWE
Ch. Hampden-Turner and F. Trompenaars (2000)	7	Universalism vs. Particularism, Analyzing vs. Integrating, Individualism vs. Communitarianism, Inner-directed vs. Outer-directed, Time as sequence vs. Time as synchronization, Achieved status vs. Ascribed status, Equality vs. Hierarchy	NO
R. House and associates (2004)	9	Uncertainty Avoidance, Institutional Collectivism, In-group Collectivist, Power Distance, Gender Egalitarianism, Assertiveness, Future Orientation, Performance Orientation, Humane Orientation	ZAM, ZAF, NAM, ZWE

Note: The authors use ICO country codes for Namibia (NAM), South Africa (ZAF), Zambia (ZAM) and Zimbabwe (ZWE).

either nonexistent or limited. For example, neither Douglas nor Trompenaars included them in their original studies, Hofstede addressed only a white sample in South Africa, Schwarz interviewed respondents only in Zimbabwe, Ingelhart conducted surveys in South Africa, Zambia and Zimbabwe; and House and associates analyzed empirical data from Zambia, Namibia, Zimbabwe, and two samples—white and black—in South Africa. Some countries were added to the research at a later time; for example, Hofstede analyzed societal cultures of Zambia and Zimbabwe in his follow-up work (Hofstede, 1993).

While reactions to these multidimensional studies range from exaggerations to "blunt tool" statements, there is significant knowledge and practical value stemming from a combination of cross-cultural data collection and relevant theoretical constructs. Similar to Western management practices, these identifiable patterns need to be included in development programs in Africa, with a focus on data on African cultures and cultural differences.

The GLOBE research[1] (House et al, 2004; Chhokar et al, 2007) sets a powerful example of defining the cultural attributes of African management by accessing local respondents' perceptions about values and practices in those countries, and processing empirical data with advanced analytic tools. His study grouped Namibia, South Africa, Zambia, and Zimbabwe into the Sub-Saharan African cultural cluster (House et al, 2004, pp. 187–188). In this aggregation, not only empirical data but also scholarly literature, archival data, and statistical sources (UN, IMF, etc.) have been used. The countries of this cluster shared historical roots and attributes in humaneness that individuals and groups display for one another, such as norms of reciprocity, suppression of self-interest, and human interdependence (Mangaliso, 2001).

As a part of the GLOBE project, local managers from four countries in the southern part of the African continent were surveyed, and the data was processed with the nine-dimensional analytic instrument at two levels that responded to anthropological and behaviorist traditions in cross-cultural studies, namely practices ("as is") and values ("should be"). Cultures of Namibia, South Africa (separately black and white samples), Zambia, and Zimbabwe were measured on a seven-point response scale. Tables 6.2 and 6.3 summarize those scores relative to all countries' averages, and Figures 6.1–6.4 display behavior-tied and value-tied profiles of each country's societal culture based on generalized managers' responses[2]. These profiles illustrate distinctions in cultural profiles of Namibia, South Africa, Zambia, and Zimbabwe on nine universal dimensions, permit further cross-cultural comparisons on a unified scale, and lead to the following conclusions.

First, all four African countries' profiles displayed gaps between practices and values scores—most visible on Power Distance, Gender Egalitarianism, Future Orientation, and Performance Orientation dimensions. The data supports arguments about the divides in organizational practices and the need to address those frictions through improved motivation and management development.

Table 6.2   Behavior-Tied GLOBE Scores for Sub-Saharan African Countries (practices "as is")

	Namibia (NAM)	South Africa (ZAF)			Zambia (ZMB)	Zimbabwe (ZWE)	All-countries' average scores
		Average	White	Black			
Performance Orientation (PO)	3.67	4.39	4.11	4.66	4.16	4.24	4.07
Future Orientation (FO)	3.49	4.39	4.13	4.64	3.62	2.77	3.81
Uncertainty Avoidance (UA)	4.20	4.34	4.09	4.59	4.10	4.15	4.10
Humane Orientation (HO)	3.96	3.91	3.39	4.34	5.23	4.45	4.10
Power Distance (PD)	5.29	4.63	5.16	4.11	5.31	5.67	5.19
Institutional Collectivism (IC)	4.13	4.51	4.62	4.39	4.61	4.12	4.24
Group Collectivism (GC)	4.52	4.70	4.50	5.09	5.84	5.57	5.17
Gender Egalitarianism (GE)	3.88	3.46	3.27	3.66	2.86	3.04	3.40
Assertiveness (AS)	3.91	4.48	4.60	4.36	4.07	4.06	4.11

Source: (House et al, 2004) and authors' computations

Second, behavior-tied results on Future Orientation, with the exception of South Africa's white sample, displayed scores below all countries' average (62 societies). All African countries scored above all countries' averages on Power Distance and Uncertainty Avoidance, and on Performance Orientation (with the exception of Namibia). Results on other cultural dimensions were mixed. On Gender Egalitarianism, Zimbabwe, Zambia, and South Africa (white sample) scored below all countries' average, and Namibia and South Africa's black sample scored above average. On Humane Orientation, Zimbabwe, Zambia, and South Africa's black sample displayed higher scores, whereas Namibia and South Africa's white sample's scores were below average. On Assertiveness, both samples of South Africa scored above average while the other three countries scored below average. On Assertiveness, both South Africa's samples scored above average while the other three countries scored below average; and on Group Collectivism, the same two samples scored below average while the other three countries

Table 6.3   Value-Tied GLOBE Scores for Sub-Saharan African Countries ("should be")

| | Namibia (NAM) | South Africa (ZAF) | | | Zambia (ZMB) | Zimbabwe (ZWE) | All-countries' average scores |
		Average	White	Black			
Performance Orientation (PO)	6.40	5.57	6.23	4.92	6.24	6.45	5.95
Future Orientation (FO)	6.12	5.43	5.66	5.20	5.90	6.07	5.51
Uncertainty Avoidance (UA)	5.30	4.73	4.67	4.79	4.67	4.73	4.66
Humane Orientation (HO)	5.40	5.36	5.56	5.07	5.53	5.19	5.42
Power Distance (PD)	2.86	3.14	2.64	3.65	2.43	2.67	2.74
Institutional Collectivism (IC)	4.38	4.34	4.38	4.30	4.74	4.87	4.73
Group Collectivism (GC)	6.07	5.45	5.91	4.99	5.77	5.85	5.69
Gender Egalitarianism (GE)	4.25	4.43	4.60	4.26	4.31	4.46	4.51
Assertiveness (AS)	3.91	3.75	3.69	3.82	4.38	4.60	3.86

Source: (House et al, 2004) and authors' computations

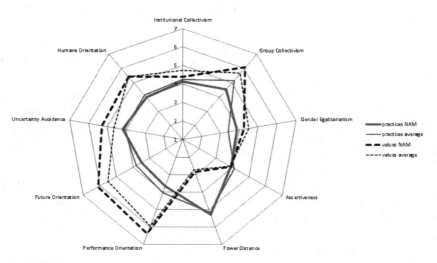

Figure 6.1   Cultural Profile of Namibia

Source: Data for the chart retrieved from (House et al, 2004)

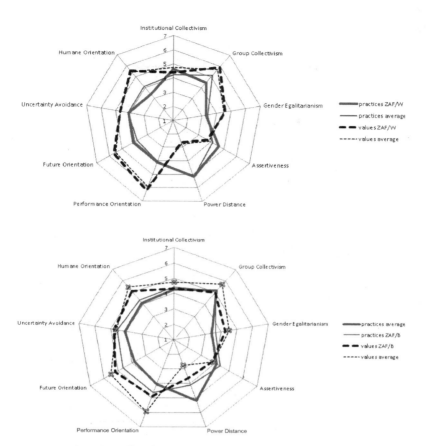

Figure 6.2 Cultural Profile of South Africa (white and black samples)

Source: Data for the charts retrieved from (House et al, 2004)

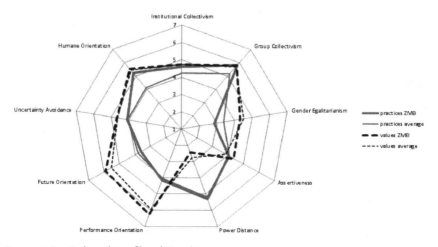

Figure 6.3 Cultural Profile of Zambia

Source: Data for the charts retrieved from (House et al, 2004)

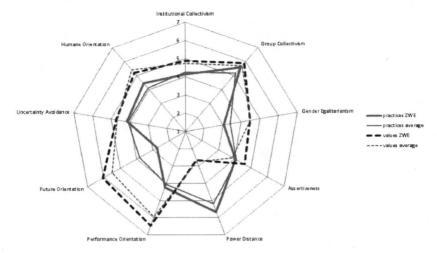

Figure 6.4 Cultural Profile of Zimbabwe
Source: Data for the charts retrieved from (House et al, 2004)

displayed high scores on that dimension. And on Institutional Collectivism, all countries were either on par or higher than all countries' averages. Overall, these data support the profile of African management as centralized and hierarchical, with preference for institutional authority, structured processes, and risk-averse behaviors not oriented into the future.

Third, values-tied results for African countries were consistent on Uncertainty Avoidance—they all scored above all countries' average. This may be seen as a motivational impediment from risk-driven entrepreneurial and innovative activities. African countries with the exception of South Africa's black sample scored higher than all countries' average on Performance and on Future Orientation. These scores may add support to arguments about the motivational potential of African managerial corps. On Gender Egalitarianism, all African countries in the study with the exception of South Africa's white sample leaned to lower results when compared to the all countries' average. On the other dimensions, the findings were mixed, highlighting higher or about average scores on Humane Orientation and on Assertiveness, and lower or average scores on Power Distance (with the exception of South Africa's black sample). These data support arguments about African managers' search for stronger performance and future outreach, but in an environment with lower risk and uncertainty, and with traditional gaps in organizational gender roles.

Fourth, in the case of South Africa, there was a notable contrast between the scores derived from white and black samples. The black sample displayed higher behavioral scores on Performance, Humane, and Future Orientation and on Gender Egalitarianism and Group Collectivism; and at the same time lower scores on Uncertainty Avoidance, Power Distance, Assertiveness, and Institutional Collectivism. On values-tied scores, managers from the black sample were relatively lower on Performance Orientation, Group Collectivism, and Humane Orientation, but higher on Power Distance scale. The analysis of those gaps may provide a valuable resource for management development and lead to a deeper understanding and interpretation of relative strengths and weaknesses of management practices in African countries.

Overall, advanced cross-cultural studies permit the creation of complex multidimensional behavior-tied and values-tied profiles of four Sub-Saharan African countries and enrich our interpretation of those cultures through the eyes of local managers. These findings may assist local managers in understanding their own cultures and, hence, the strengths and weaknesses of those cultures when interacting with the other countries.

CULTURE: FROM DIFFERENCES TO DISTANCE MEASURES

Clustering international environments and management practices based on cultural similarities may offer valuable solutions in international business— such as the formation of effective cross-border teams and expatriate assignments, the standardization of human resources activities and motivational patterns—as well as in strategic decision making about entry modes or regional growth patterns. The inclusion of African data may further enrich choice options and offer solutions for cross-border collaboration not only to multinational firms but also to local managers in African countries, hence supporting the need to understand and apply the advances in comparative studies in management development.

The measurements of cultural differences, however, have long been a serious problem in social studies. While the mainstream cross-cultural literature explores qualitative differences between and among societies, scholars face serious problems with quantitative comparisons due to the nature of, and the ambiguities in cultural metrics, asymmetries, and conflicting levels of analyses, contextual inappropriateness, ambiguous aggregations, and insufficient validity and reliability of constructs. Furthermore, cultural distance has traditionally been viewed as negative "friction" in business relations (Neal, 1998; Shenkar, 2001) with limited attention to multinational companies who capitalize on cultural differences when conducting business internationally (Gratchev, 2001) or seek "arbitrage" factors that derive from differences between home and host countries' environments (Ghemawat, 2003).

Each of the above-mentioned multidimensional paradigmatic studies (Hofstede, GLOBE, etc.) generated quantitative data for different countries, thus permitting comparisons and the inclusion of those data into predictive models. In simpler cases, cultural differences may be displayed in a two-dimensional space, thus grouping countries on attitudinal dimensions on cross-cultural maps. For example, Inglehart and colleagues (2004; 2005) clustered African countries around Traditional Values (less Secular-Rational Values) and Survival Values (less Self-Expression Values) on an Ingelhart-Welzel Map. In the case of studies involving more than two dimensions, researchers offer complex distance measures of cultural differences, such as Euclidian distance (Tadesse and White, 2010) or measures adjusted by variance averaged squared distances known as the Kogut-Singh index (Kogut and Singh, 1988), with recommendations that "future studies should incorporate more than one distance measure, or opt for a composite index" (Ambos and Hakanson, 2014, pp. 5–6).

While data on African cultures is available from a number of sources, it has not been processed towards distance measures for academic purposes or combined and interpreted with a pedagogical intent. The application of composite measures may help position African countries in a cross-cultural space, and the GLOBE database permits computation of such cultural distance matrixes (nine dimensions, Kogut-Singh indexes for country pairs), sorting countries that are culturally more or less compatible with Namibia, South Africa, Zambia, and Zimbabwe.

Figure 6.5 displays distance matrixes in the form of a cross-cultural map for 62 societies formatted with a multidimensional scaling procedure

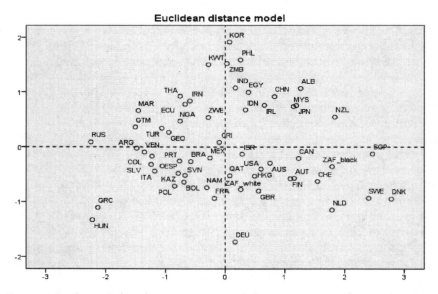

Figure 6.5 Cross-Cultural Distance Maps (behaviors, "as is") for 57 Countries Including ZAF, NAM, ZWE, and ZMB, Based on Multidimensional Scaling of Cultural Distance Matrixes

Source: Data for cultural distance computations and visualization with MDS map retrieved from (House et al, 2004)

(behavior-tied, $R^2 = 0.852$) where Euclidian distances between cultures on the map best correlate with distance scores in the cultural distance matrix. The analysis of 62 societies' positioning in the cross-cultural space suggests that four Sub-Saharan African countries studied within the GLOBE project were not that different or marginal in terms of composite measures of cultural distance.

Country-tied distance measures permit distinguishing between cultures that are more or less "compatible" with each of the four African countries. In the case of South Africa's white sample, the close distance results for Israel, United Kingdom, United States, Australia, or Austria were natural due to historic colonial ties and grouping with the Anglo cluster. South Africa's black sample also clustered with North American and European countries. Among countries closer to Namibia, one could find representatives of Mediterranean Europe (Portugal, France, Italy) and Latin America (Costa Rica, Venezuela, Brazil, Mexico). Zambia's behavioral distance scores leaned to Asian clusters (Indonesia, India, Thailand, Malaysia, China). And Zimbabwe was closer to African countries (Zambia, Nigeria), Asian (India, Thailand) and Middle-Eastern clusters (Morocco, Turkey, Egypt).

These findings may be useful in considering multinational firms' entry modes into each of four Sub-Saharan African countries. The research states that differences in cultures among countries influence the perception of managers regarding the costs and uncertainty of alternative modes of entry into foreign markets, and a large-sample multiple regression test supported the hypothesis that the greater the cultural distance between the country of the investing firm and the country of entry, the more likely a firm was to choose a joint venture or wholly owned greenfield over an acquisition (Kogut and Singh, 1988).

Overall, cross-cultural studies provide African managers and their foreign partners analytic instruments in their search for effective trade, cross-border strategic collaboration and foreign direct investment; additionally, they help provide more comprehensive interpretation of the complex factors that influence those decisions. The important implication of cultural distance research is the departure from traditional stereotypes about high frictions and low compatibility with African managers when conducting business internationally.

ECONOMIC APPLICATIONS OF CROSS-CULTURAL STUDIES

The analysis of culture's effects in Sub-Saharan African (SSA) countries' economic developments is one of the powerful examples of the cross-pollination of economics and social studies. To what extent do cultural differences moderate effective trade flows? Which product groups are influenced by cultural frictions? Does cultural distance serve as a contributor or impediment to effective trade flows? Answers to these questions may have important policy implications to African countries rich in natural resources and agricultural products, and displaying accelerated differentiation of product lines. The answers may also respond to the efforts to overcome various disadvantages of colonial history such as inefficient human capital, deep social problems, poor education and health care, and a lack of balanced investment in the economy.

Economic trends in the region attest to accelerating diversification of exports and an increase in intra-African trade (in nominal and real terms), yet with a declining share of inter-Africa trade. All four countries—Namibia, South Africa, Zambia, and Zimbabwe—participate in regional economic integration through the Southern African Development Community. In the past decade Namibia's foreign trade increased from $4.64 billion (2004) to $13.9 billion USD (2013) with primary exports in diamonds, uranium or thorium ores, and fish and fish products with top destinations of South Africa, the UK, and Angola, and with primary imports in petroleum oils, motor vehicles, copper, and medicine, with South Africa, Switzerland and China as top partners. South Africa's foreign trade increased from $106.5 bln USD (2004) to $198.7 bln USD (2013) with primary exports in platinum, iron ores, gold, coal, and motor vehicles mainly to China and the US, and with primary imports in petroleum oils, commodities, motor vehicles, electrical and data processing machines, and medicine, mostly from China, Germany, and the US. Zambia's foreign trade increased from $4.4 billion USD (2004) to $20.8 billion USD (2013) with primary exports in copper, corn (maize), tobacco, sugar, and gold, with top destinations in Switzerland, China, and South Africa, and with primary imports in copper ores, petroleum, motor vehicles, and construction machinery, from South Africa, DR Congo, and China as import sources. Zimbabwe's foreign trade increased from $4.2 billion USD (2004) to $11.2 billion USD (2013) with primary exports in gold, nickel, and diamonds as well as tobacco and cotton mainly to South Africa, United Arab Emirates, and Mozambique, and with primary imports in petroleum, fertilizers, motor vehicles, and medicaments, mostly from South Africa, the UK and the US. However, the region still yields a relatively low diversity of trade, with the major share in exporting national resources and agricultural products, and low importance of manufacturing. The impact of informal economies is substantial, and the relatively small size of enterprises impedes the boosting of international trade (Olofin, 2002; Nicita and Rollo, 2015).

Economists use complex economic models to estimate the role of different factors in trade flows. The mainstream instruments in the economic analysis of distance effects in international trade have traditionally been associated with so-called gravity models[3] that consider trade as a dependent variable and distance measures as independent variables, thus permitting predictions of cross-border interaction patterns. Classical gravity models interpreted the effects of geographic distances on trade (for example, geographic proximity, transportation, etc.) between countries defined by their

GDPs, and in multiple studies export and import flows, with multiple studies confirming that on average a 10% increase in physical distance lowers bilateral trade by about 9% (Disdier and Head, 2008, p. 37). The most recent scientific inquiries, however, extended the scope of distance measures towards a broader set of variables beyond geographic, namely trade barriers, migration, administrative and legal differences, and cultural distance (Ghemawat, 2001; 2003; 2007). For example, scholars at Tinbergen Institute distinguished machinery, transport equipment, food and live animals, and beverages and tobacco among product groups where Hofstede-tied cultural distance measures computed with the Kogut-Singh index and displayed positive effects on trade (Mohlmann et al, 2010).

In order to further explore the impact of cultural distance on the bilateral trade flows of South Africa, Namibia, Zambia, and Zimbabwe with the other countries, the authors applied the augmented gravity model for international trade with GLOBE-based cultural distance measures. In this model, trade serves as a dependent variable, and economy (GDP), geographic distance, cultural distance, language commonality, and colony ties serve as independent variables. The logarithmic form of the augmented gravity model with cultural distance variables is as follows (1):

$$\log X_{ij} = \alpha_1 + \alpha_2 \log Y_{it} + \alpha_3 \log Y_{jt} + \alpha_4 \log D_{ij}$$
$$+ a_s index_{ij} A + \sum c_k z_{ij}^m + e_{ij} \tag{1}$$

Y_{it}—GDP for country i (i = 1, 2, 3, 4 for SSA country);
Y_{jt}—GDP for country j; (j—1, 2 ... 57 for GLOBE countries, including SSA
    countries);
D_{ij}—measure of geographic distance from i country to j country;
$\log D_{ij}$—time invariant (in km);
A_{ij}—time invariant cultural distance index for GLOBE-tied countries i and
    j (Kogut–Singh index)
z_{ij}—represent m control variables (comlang_off, comlang_ethno, comcol,
    colony);
e_{ij} is a random error term.

The computations cover 57 countries that participated in the GLOBE study, with economic data derived from the United Nations' Statistics Division (COMTRADE), and geographic data from the CEPII database (Mayer and Zignano, 2011). The composite cultural distance index was computed on behavior-tied and values-tied GLOBE data, with averaged squared distances adjusted by variance. Regression coefficients were estimated and R^2 ranged between 0.63 and 0.76, which was consistent with published literature. Tables 6.4 and 6.5 summarize model estimates.

As expected, in all cases involving South Africa, Namibia, Zambia, and Zimbabwe, the size of partners' economies (GDP) displayed statistically

Table 6.4 Regression Coefficients (with standard error) and R² for Independent Variables Associated With Trade Flows for Namibia, South Africa, Zambia, and Zimbabwe (composite culture distance measures derived from GLOBE practice-tied scores)

Category	Namibia (NAM)	South Africa (ZAF)	Zambia (ZMB)	Zimbabwe (ZWE)
Cultural Distance (cultural_distance_practices)	0.015 (0.392)	−0.228 (0.253)	0.220 (0.485)	0.602 (0.480)
Geographic Distance (Ln_geo)	−3.560** (0.772)	−3.215** (0.575)	−4.558** (1.030)	−4.760** (0.876)
Economy size, GDP (Ln_gdp_2004)	1.574** (0.212)	1.385** (0.127)	2.365** (0.333)	1.981** (0.276)
Language dummy 1 (comlang_off)	−1.157 (0.625)*	−0.059 (0.420)	0.192 (1.114)	0.953 (0.928)
Language dummy 2 (comlang_ethno)	0.214 (0.626)	0.954* (0.441)	2.464* (1.312)	1.286 (1.078)
Colonization dummy 1 (colony)	−0.352 (1.670)	−0.299 (0.936)	−0.747 (4.021)	−0.752 (3.367)
Colonization dummy 2 (comcol)			−0.014 (1.626)	−0.093 (1.362)
R²	0.630	0.757	0.682	0.670

Source: authors' computations

Note: *– Significant at < 0.05 level; **—Significant at < 0.01 level

Table 6.5 Regression Coefficients (with standard error) and R² for Independent Variables Associated With Trade Flows for Namibia, South Africa, Zambia, and Zimbabwe (composite culture distance measures derived from GLOBE value-tied scores)

Category	Namibia (NAM)	South Africa (ZAF)	Zambia (ZMB)	Zimbabwe (ZWE)
Cultural Distance (cultural_distance_practices)	0.406 (0.549)	−0.204 (0.272)	0.549 (0.700)	0.830* (0.488)
Geographic Distance (Ln_geo)	−6.451** (1.168)	−3.191** (0.575)	−4.699** (1.029)	−4.760** (0.865)
Economy size (Ln_gdp_2004)	2.470** (0.320)	1.398** (0.126)	2.370** (0.327)	1.857** (0.287)
Language dummy 1 (comlang_off)	−1.755 (1.006)*	10.170 (0.412)	0.342 (1.124)	1.219 (0.927)
Language dummy 2 (comlang_ethno)	1.176 (1.019)	0.992* (0.435)	2.335* (1.267)	1.385 (1.067)
Colonization dummy 1 (colony)	−3.545 (2.728)	−0.170 (0.923)	−0.476 (3.988)	−0.47 (3.325)
Colonization dummy 2 (comcol)			0.068 (1.618)	−0.009 (1.346)
R²	0.696	0.873	0.643	0.678

Source: authors' computations

Note: *– Significant at < 0.05 level; **—Significant at < 0.01 level

significant positive effects on trade (at the level < 0.01) and geographic distance displayed a statistically significant negative effect (at the level < 0.01) on trade. While consistent with the previous research on negative effects, the impact of geographic distance evidenced in regression coefficients was much higher for Sub- Saharan African countries (between −3.215 and −4.760 for practices-tied set, and between −3.191 and −6.451 for values-tied set) when compared to the average effects for multiple countries reported in the literature as −0.6 (Learner and Levinson, 1995), −0.87 (Disdier and Head, 2008) or ranging between −0.9 and −1.5 (Redding and Venables, 2003). This data attests both to the critical role of intra-Africa trade for the target countries and to the importance of geographic location factors associated with communication, transportation costs, and logistics.

Cultural effects on trade were reported with regression coefficients for cultural distance and for dummy variables in common language and common colonial history. While the magnitude of regression coefficients was relatively small and in most cases statistically insignificant, some effects may be considered. In three cases (with the exception of South Africa) cultural distance served as a contributor to trade flows (significant in the case of Zimbabwe, at the level < 0.05), and results were consistent for behavior-tied and for values-tied data. There was not much difference between the two sets of equations (with practices-tied distance and values-tied distance) in terms of the coefficient values, thus confirming the consistency of findings along two dimensions and supporting the importance of complex tests beyond a single cultural distance measure. These results supported the arguments about the impact of culture-sensitive specialization in trade and international firms' preference for trade over foreign direct investment in higher-friction environments; such results were compatible with similar findings in the literature (Dunning, 1993; Mohlmann et al, 2010).

Overall, cross-cultural studies provide valuable patterns for interpreting economic processes in Sub-Saharan Africa. The models based on those theories support arguments against a one-sided view of cultural distance as a negative factor in international trade and, when transferred to a management development system, these results may add to the value and appreciation of cultural distinctions and the self-awareness of local managers in cross-border activities.

BEHAVIORAL APPLICATIONS OF CROSS-CULTURAL STUDIES

The other potential area of cross-cultural theories' instrumentality is the relevance of theoretical constructs to predictions of behavior patterns in a country's organizational context. What makes African organizational leaders effective? How different are their leadership attributes when compared to managers in other countries? These questions are not simply theoretical. They target important intangible resources and address practical situations in multinational functional groups, expatriate assignments, and interactions with international strategic partners. The answers may balance globalization and localization patterns in management development systems and in business organizations in Africa.

Organizational leaders in Sub-Saharan African countries are motivated by one or more business philosophies that stem from their history and culture: *bureaucratic* behaviors linked to patriarchal and patrimonial hierarchies in organizations with high power distance; *predatory* behaviors, which stem from the corruption and suppression of rivals by any means; *pragmatic* behaviors for survival and growth, connected to a colonial heritage and Western practices as well as to in-group and tribal traditions; and *socially responsible* behaviors that are rooted in humane orientations of *Ubuntu*, spirituality, tolerance, and the religious foundations of the African society. Additionally, African organizational leaders' thinking patterns are known to involve a consideration of interpersonal relations, hierarchies, obligations to ethnic affiliates, and paternalism (Blunt and Jones, 1997).

Considerable research has been conducted to better understand the distinctive leadership behaviors in Africa (Literell and Ramburuth, 2007; Muchiri, 2011; Nkomo and Kriek, 2011; Walumbwa et al, 2011; Littrell et al, 2013). Most of these studies emphasize context and cultural environment; connect relations between leaders and followers to family and tribal traditions, patrimonial behaviors, clan responsibilities and obligations; highlight tolerance and forgiveness; and suggest paternalistic actions in age-tied egalitarian yet hierarchical environments. And while perceptions of effective leadership in African organization stem from *Ubuntu*, hierarchies and power structures, as well as patrimonial traditions and loyalty to rulers also matter.

Muchini (2011) explained the importance of cultural context in leadership effectiveness in Sub- Saharan Africa and offered the following arguments. First, individualistic behaviors are not encouraged in a tight and cohesive African in-group environment. Second, strong family, ethnic, and religious networks expect leaders' protection, which emphasizes group-tied leadership behaviors. Third, cultures in Sub-Saharan Africa are known for the expression of generosity and compassion, for sacrificing personal interests to helping others, and for altruism and benevolence in relations. And finally, these cultures are known for paternalistic structures and patrimonial behaviors, and also for the importance of status and authority.

GLOBE research provides an example of how cross-cultural studies may help in predicting effective leadership behaviors in a societal context. It confirmed that attributes and entities that distinguish a given culture from other cultures are predictive of the practices of organizations of that culture, and also predictive of leader attributes and behavior that are most frequently enacted, acceptable, and effective in that culture (House et al, 2004, p. 19). In other words, when applied to an African context, the study permits predictions of leadership behaviors that are perceived and interpreted as effective in those societies. It creates a causal link between a nine-dimensional configuration of a national culture and six-dimensional profiles of effective leadership in that culture[4].

Values-tied cultural profiles for South Africa, Namibia, Zambia, and Zimbabwe lead to the following predictions. With the exception of South Africa's black sample, the predictions highlight the importance of Charismatic and Value-Based Leadership (visionary, inspirational, self-sacrifice, integrity, decisive, performance-oriented). Predictions for Team-Oriented Leadership (collaborative, integrated, diplomatic, benevolent, administratively competent) are modest, with stronger effects for Namibia. Support for Participative Leadership (participative, non-autocratic) is modest for all but South Africa's black sample, which is negative. Support for Humane-Oriented Leadership (modesty, humane orientation) is also moderate—more visible in the case of Namibia. African countries' profiles, with the exception of South Africa's black sample, suggest a search for less Autonomous (individualistic, independent, unique, autonomous) and less Self-Protected (self-centered, status-conscious, conflict-inducing, face-saving, procedural) Leadership.

The analysis of questionnaires completed by local managers in four countries, as well as responses about organizational leadership effectiveness, support these predictions. Figure 6.6 displays the results of managerial surveys in Zambia, Namibia and Zimbabwe, and in South Africa's white and black samples. All four countries displayed a stronger endorsement of Charismatic and Value-Based Leadership, and Namibia and Zambia displayed an endorsement of Team-Oriented Leadership. Participative Leadership only slightly contributed to outstanding leadership in all countries. All but South Africa's black sample endorsed a visible Humane Orientation. Zambia and Zimbabwe's leadership profiles tended to be less Autonomous, and Zimbabwe and South Africa's white sample was less Self-Protective.

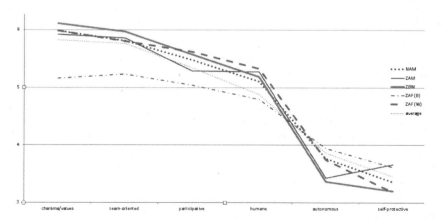

Figure 6.6 Comparison of Culturally Endorsed Leadership Attributes in Sub-Saharan Africa

Source: Data for the chart retrieved from (House et al, 2004)

These findings are consistent with similar aggregations (Wanasika et al, 2011; Littrell et al, 2013), which highlighted African managers' charismatic and value-based behaviors with skills of oratory, tribal traditions that impact team-oriented behaviors, connection of humane behaviors to *Ubuntu* (humaneness) philosophy, and rejections for heavy-handed behaviors. Also, outstanding leadership was personified in charismatic examples like South Africa's Nelson Mandela, Zambia's Kenneth Kaunda, Namibia's Sam Nujoma, and Zimbabwe's Robert Mugabe.

It is important to emphasize a balanced approach to qualitative and quantitative methods in researching leadership behaviors, or "mixed-method approaches" (Muchiri, 2011, p. 449; Walumbwa et al, 2011), hence positioning cross-cultural studies as an important but not a unique source for understanding African organizational and cultural realities. In sum, a multidisciplinary manner of thinking is the most critical approach in addressing complex issues of management development in Sub-Saharan Africa.

CONCLUSIONS

The continued regional and international integration of the Sub-Saharan region of Africa requires management education. Management development must include cultural awareness, as well as instrumental application of cultural measures. This chapter provided basic patterns that may enhance the integration of cross-cultural studies into management development activities in Africa.

The discussion sheds light on the link between the lessons learned from cross-cultural studies and management development activities in Africa. While the authors did not intend to propose curricula or practical educational or training tools, they emphasized the instrumentality of cross-cultural studies in the analysis and understanding of management and business practices in Namibia, South Africa, Zambia, and Zimbabwe. This chapter displayed the content and value of cross-cultural comparisons and offered applications to economic and behavioral issues in the African countries.

These patterns and examples may serve African organizations in developing a unique perspective for sustainable management and organizational operation. They combine information from local managers, integrate distinctive African attributes such as *Ubuntu* and the role of power structures, and refer to internationally recognized theoretical constructs that reveal universal dimensions of culture. Finally, the chapter makes a strong appeal to a comprehensive quantitative analysis of cultural distinctions, which may help generate sound predictions in managerial decisions. The cumulative information contained in cross-cultural studies will enlarge the domain of awareness of differences and similarities—especially for those African mid-level and lower-level managers who lack the experience and exposure to international business interactions.

The following lessons result from this discussion:

- Cross-cultural theories and empirical findings can contribute to management development in Africa, especially, in areas related to international business activities.
- Comparative studies help to both better understand home cultures in African countries and to compare them with the culture of international partners.
- Cross-cultural studies reveal distinctive attributes of each of the four countries' management corps, emphasizing gaps between behaviors and values, the role of centralized and hierarchical structures, traditional gaps in gender roles, low-risk behaviors not oriented into the future, and at the same time, value orientation towards higher performance.
- Typically, in Sub-Saharan African countries, cultural distance serves as a predictor of and contributor to effective cross-border trade flows with other countries.
- Cultural predictors of effective organizational leadership highlight the importance of charismatic and value-based attributes in the perception of effective African organizational leadership.
- Cross-cultural studies may further contribute to management development in Africa not in isolation but as one part of a multidisciplinary effort to advance the competencies and effectiveness of the local management talent in the region.

ACKNOWLEDGEMENTS

The authors acknowledge the valuable contribution by Prof. Emeric Solymossy (Western Illinois University, USA) and Prof. Lars Isaksson (Bond University, Australia) to the development of this chapter and thank anonymous reviewer(s) for thoughtful and critical comments that helped finalize the chapter.

NOTES

1. GLOBE research applied the following nine cultural dimensions to the analyses. *Institutional Collectivism (IC)*, the degree to which organizational and societal norms and practices encourage and reward the collective distribution of resources and collective action; *Group Collectivism (GC)*, the degree to which individuals express pride, loyalty, and cohesiveness in their organizations or families; *Gender Egalitarianism (GE)*, the extent to which an organization or society minimize gender role differences; *Assertiveness (AS)*, the degree to which individuals in organizations or societies are assertive, confrontational, and aggressive in social relationships; *Power Distance (PD)*, the degree to which members of an organization or society expect and agree that power should be unequally shared; it relates to society's acceptance and

endorsement of authority along with status privileges; **Future Orientation (FO)**, the degree to which individuals in organizations or society engage in future-oriented behaviors such as planning, investing in the future, and delaying gratification; **Uncertainty Orientation (UO)**, the extent to which members of the organization or society strive to avoid uncertainty by relying on social norms, rituals, and bureaucratic practices to alleviate the unpredictability of future events; **Humane Orientation (HO)**, the degree to which individuals in organizations or societies encourage and reward individuals for being fair, friendly, generous, caring, and kind to others; and **Performance Orientation (PO)**, the extent to which a society encourages or rewards group members for performance involvement and excellence.

2. In case of South Africa, for the purpose of a follow-up country-level economic analysis, the authors computed additional set of averaged scores from white and black samples.
3. It is known for its association with the Newtonian Law of Gravity.
4. The GLOBE study distinguished between *universal* leadership contributors and impediments to effective leadership applicable to cross-country comparisons (Charismatic and Value-Based Leadership, Team-Oriented Leadership, Humane-Oriented Leadership, Participative Leadership plus inverse Autonomous Leadership and Self-Protective Leadership), on the one hand, and *culture-contingent* leadership attributes on the other.

REFERENCES

Ambos, B., and Hakanson, L. (2014). The concept of distance in international management research. *Journal of International Management, 20,* 1–7.

Blunt, P., and Jones, M. (1997). Exploring the limits of Western leadership theory in East Asia and Africa. *Personnel Review, 26*(1/2), 6–23.

Catalyzing management development in Africa. (2013). Interim report. Nairobi: African Management Initiative.

Chhokar, J., Brodbeck, F., and House, R. (Eds.). (2007). *Culture and leadership across the world. The GLOBE book of in-depth studies of 25 societies.* Mahwah, NJ: Lawrence Erlbaum.

Disdier, A., and Head, K. (2008). The puzzling persistence of the distance effect on bilateral trade. *The Review of Economics and Statistics, 90*(1), 37–48.

Douglas, M. (1973). *Natural symbols: Explorations in cosmology.* London: Barrie and Rockliff.

Dunning, J. (1993). *Multinational enterprises and the global economy.* Workingham, UK: Addison-Westley Publishing Company.

Fukuyama, F. (1995). *Trust: The social virtues and the creation of prosperity.* New York: Free Press.

Ghemawat, P. (2001, September). Distance still matters. The hard reality of global expansion. *Harvard Business Review,* 137–147.

Ghemawat, P. (2003, November). The forgotten strategy. *Harvard Business Review,* 77–84.

Ghemawat, P. (2007). *Redefining global strategy: Crossing borders in a world where differences still matter.* Boston: Harvard Business School Press.

Gratchev M. (2001, November). Making the most of cultural differences. *Harvard Business Review,* 28–30.

Hampden-Turner, Ch., and Trompenaars, F. (2000). *Building cross-cultural competence: How to create wealth from conflicting values*. New Haven: Yale University Press.

Hofstede, G. (1980). *Culture's consequences: International differences in work-related values*. Beverly Hills: Sage Publications.

Hofstede, G. (1993). Cultural constraints in management theories. *Academy of Management Executive, 7*(1), 81–94.

Horwitz, F., and Jain, H. (2008). Managing human resources in South Africa: A multinational firm focus. *The Global Diffusion of Human Resources Practices: Institutional and Cultural Limits. Advances in International Management, 21*, 89–123.

House, R. J., Hanges, P. J., Javidan, M., Dorfman, P. W., and Gupta, V. (Eds). (2004). *Culture, leadership, and organizations: The GLOBE study of 62 societies*. Thousand Oaks: Sage Publications.

Huntington, S. (1993, Summer). The clash of civilizations? *Foreign Affairs, 72*(3), 22–49.

Inglehart, R. (1997). *Modernization and post-modernization: Cultural, economic, and political change in 43 societies*. Princeton, NJ: Princeton University Press.

Inglehart, R., and Welzel, C. (2005). *Modernization, cultural change and democracy*. New York and Cambridge: Cambridge University Press.

Inglehart, R., Basanez, M., Jaime, H., Loek, L., and Luijkx, R. (Eds.). (2004). *Human beliefs and values: A cross-cultural sourcebook based on the 1999–2002 values surveys*. Mexico: Siglo XXI.

Jackson, T. (2004). *Management and change in Africa*. London: Routledge.

Jackson, T. (2015). Management studies from Africa: A cross-cultural critique. *Africa Journal of Management, 1*(1), 78–88. doi:10.1080/23322373.2015.994425

Kluckhohn, F., and Strodtbeck, F. (1961). *Variations in value orientation*. New York: HarperCollins.

Kogut, B., and Singh, H. (1988). The effect of national culture on the choice of entry mode. *Journal of International Business Studies, 19*(3), 411–432.

Kroeber., C. and Kluckhohn., W. U. (1952) *Culture: A Critical Review of Concepts and Definitions*. New York, NY: Vintage Books

Learner, E., and Levinson, J. (1995). International trade theory: The evidence. In G. Grossman and K. Rogoff (Eds.), *Handbook of international economics* (Vol. 3, pp. 1339–1394). North Holland, New York.

Literell, R., and Ramburuth, P. (2007). *Leadership and management in Sub-Sahara Africa*. Vol. 1. San Diego, CSA: University Readers.

Littrell, P., Wu, N., Nkomo, S., Howel, J., and Dorefman, P. (2013). Pan-Sub-Saharan African leadership and the values of Ubuntu. In P. Lituchi, B. Punnett, and B. Puplampu (Eds.), *Management in Africa: Macro and micro perspectives* (pp. 210–231). New York: Routledge.

Mangaliso, M. (2001). Building competitive advantage from Ubuntu: Management lessons from South Africa. *Academy of Management Executive, 15*, 23–35.

Mayer, T., and Zignago, S. (2011). *Notes on CEPII distance measures: The GeoDist database*. CEPII Working Paper 2011–25. Paris: CEPII.

McClelland, D. (1961). *The achieving society*. Princeton, NJ: Van Nostrand.

McClelland, D. (1985). *Human motivation*. Glenview: Scott, Foresman.

Mohlmann, L., Ederveen, H., de Groot, H., and Linders, G. -J. (2010). Intangible barriers to international trade. In P. Bergeijk and S. Brakman (Eds.), *The gravity model in international trade* (pp. 224–251). Cambridge: Cambridge University Press.

Muchiri, M. (2011). Leadership in context: a review and research agenda for sub-Saharan Africa. *Journal of Occupational and Organizational Psychology, 84,* 440–452.

Narayan, D., and Cassidy, M. (2001). A dimensional approach to measuring and validation of a social capital inventory. *Current Sociology, 49*(2), 59–102.

Neal, M. (1998). *The culture factor: Cross-cultural management and the foreign venture.* Houndmills, UK: MacMillan.

Nicita, A., and Rollo, V. (2015). Market conditions and Sub-Sahara Africa's exports diversification. *World Development, 68,* 254–263.

Nkomo, S., and Kriek, D. (2011). Leading organizational change in the "new" South Africa. *Journal of Organizational and Occupational Psychology, 84,* 435–470.

Olofin, S. (2002). Trade and competitiveness in African economies in the 21st century. *African Development Bank, 14*(2), 298–321.

Redding, S., and Venables, A. (2003). *Geography and export performance: External market access and internal supply capacity.* NBER Working Paper, w9637.

Schwartz, S. (1992). Universals in the content and structure of values: Theory and empirical tests in 20 countries. In M. Zanna (Ed.), *Advances in experimental social psychology* (Vol. 25, pp. 1–65). New York: Academic Press.

Schwartz, S. (1999). A theory of cultural values and some implications for work. *Applied Psychology: An International Review, 48,* 23–47.

Schwartz, S. (2004). Mapping and interpreting cultural differences around the world. In H. Vinken, P. Soeters, and P. Ester (Eds.), *Comparing cultures: Dimensions of culture in a comparative perspective.* Leiden: Brill Academic Publishing, pp. 43–73.

Shenkar, O. (2001). Cultural distance revisited: Towards a more rigorous conceptualization and measurement of cultural differences. *Journal of International Business Studies, 32,* 519–535.

Tadesse, B., and White, R. (2010). Cultural distance as a determinant of bilateral trade flows: Do immigrants counter the effect of cultural differences? *Applied Economics* Letters, v. 17, pp. 147–172.

Walumbwa, F., Avolio, B., and Aryee, S. (2011). Leadership and management research in Africa: A synthesis and suggestions for future research. *Journal of Occupational and Organizational Psychology, 84,* 425–439.

Wanasika, I., Howell, J., Littrell, R., and Dorfman, P. (2011). Managerial leadership and culture in Sub-Sahara Africa. *Journal of World Business, 46,* 234–241.

Woolcock, M. (2001). The place of Social capital in understanding social and economic outcomes. *ISUMA,* Spring, 10–17.

7 The Role of Cross-Cultural Communication in Management Practices of Multinational Corporations (MNCs) in Sub-Saharan Africa

James Baba Abugre

INTRODUCTION

It has been argued by researchers (Lustig and Koester, 2006; Thomas, 2008; Moran, Harris, and Moran, 2011; Abugre, 2013a) that knowledge in cross-cultural communication helps to strengthen multinational corporations' (MNCs) capabilities and successes in the global markets. Indeed, the importance of cross-cultural communication in the African context cannot be over-emphasized. The reason is that, to understand African management practices successfully, there is the need for expatriates to identify and appreciate the cultural challenges of diverse African views. Appreciating African cultural diversity would enable expatriates to communicate effectively in new markets such as Sub-Saharan Africa (SSA) with its diverse people and ethnic pluralism. Hence, cross-cultural communication competence would enhance shared interpretations between local workers and expatriates, which would further improve predictability and stability in African management practices.

Communication pervades all aspects of organizational activity (Konopaske and Ivancevich, 2004; Abugre, 2012), and it is the process whereby multinational practices and activities are accomplished. Expatriates and local employees of MNC subsidiaries in SSA are constantly involved in and affected by the process of communication. Therefore, the ability of these groups to be culturally sensitive to each other depends on their knowledge and abilities to interact cross-culturally. In particularly, expatriates from other parts of the globe coming to Africa must learn to understand the cultural rules, conventions, and codes of the African people, and to be sensitive to African cultural differences in terms of communication styles. Cross-cultural communication is the process of interaction between individuals who are culturally different from each other on such important attributes as their value orientations, preferred communication codes, role expectations, and perceived rules of social relations (Moran et al, 2011). It involves the communication between different people with different cultural backgrounds in a particular context (Lustig and Koester, 2006), especially within the subsidiaries of MNCs in SSA. An essential aspect of cross-cultural communication

is its ability to help academics and practitioners to understand the differences in context-related communication styles (Hall, 1959) given the heterogeneity of African societies affected by global mobility of managers, the
increasingly cross-cultural nature of business negotiations, and the interactions of different people throughout the African continent.

Increasing investment in African markets by multinational companies is
fast growing, and this interest is partly due to the globalization of markets
and therefore the exploration of newer and more resources, and partly due
to the current improved investment climate in Africa (UNCTAD, 2007).
Many multinational organizations see globalization as a frame-breaking
change that will undoubtedly have a significant impact on their transnational
communication process because communication facilitates relationship
development (Jeannet, 2000), and facilitates the acquisition of contextual
knowledge that requires direct interactions between senders and recipients
in order to adapt the sender's knowledge to the recipient's context clearly
and unambiguously (Riusala and Suutari, 2004). Therefore, and increasingly, global managers and expatriates have to be able to operate smoothly
within Sub-Saharan African cultures, and this can be possible by encouraging expatriates to interact freely and actively with local African workers in
order to obtain as much information as possible about the communicative
behaviors of African people. Continuous interaction between expatriates
and indigenous workers both outside and within the various MNCs' subsidiaries would unravel the perceived paradoxes of the African continent.
According to Jackson (2004), these perceived paradoxes (conflicts in policies and practices) that constitute the nature of African organizations and
the need to develop African capacity can only be understood by learning the
intercontinental level of cultural analysis. Analyzing and appreciating the
diverse cultural composition of the Sub-Saharan African countries is a step
to understanding the management systems in Africa. Therefore, it appears
competent cross-cultural communication would become progressively
more valued to these MNCs as an approach to effectively respond to the
dynamic global competitive African markets. For example, the management
of MNCs in Africa requires the transfer of knowledge to local employees in the various subsidiaries. Similarly, the control and coordination of
headquarters-subsidiary relationships all call for successful communication
and understanding of management practices. However, Sub-Saharan Africa
presents a wide range of differences in beliefs, values, norms, and social
practices of its people. It is also the subcontinent that displays the most
linguistic diversity of any region in the world (Bowden, 2007). This makes
it difficult for outsiders to appreciate the value of African management practices. Moreover, the need to understand and appreciate the diversity and
complexity of Sub-Saharan Africa is greatly hampered by an apparent and
constant pejorative view of Africa (Jackson, 2004). Therefore, the quality of
management knowledge generated in Africa can transform the developmental state of most countries in Africa (Nkomo, 2011) by providing alternative

management knowledge through the influential role of cross-cultural communication in African management practices, which is the core aim of this chapter. Similarly, cross-cultural management theory has been criticized for its lack of theory connecting cultural values to management and work practices at the behavioral level (Cray and Mallory, 1998). Given that cross-cultural management knowledge that effectively builds capabilities is vital to high-quality management education on the continent, it is important that this chapter provide the significant role of cross-cultural communication in management practices of MNCs in Sub-Saharan Africa.

Using empirical research, this chapter therefore equips the reader with knowledge of the importance of cross-cross-cultural communication in management development in Africa. First, it defines and presents a multi-discourse perspective of cross-cultural communication and its importance in headquarters (HQ) and subsidiary relations. Second, it presents an evidenced-based picture of the cross-cultural context of MNCs in Sub-Saharan Africa through interviews of very senior expatriate executives of MNCs in Ghana, as explained in the section on method.

THE NATURE OF CROSS-CULTURAL COMMUNICATION

There is a need for global managers or expatriates to understand the context of communication and interpersonal behaviors of local employees in the African landscape. This is because cross-cultural communication is a basic form of human behavior derived from the need to connect and interact with people in different places and cultures (Samovar and Porter, 1997). It is a process that reveals the inseparability of human communication theory and its application (Tannen, 1984). The practical significance of cross-cultural communication is its ability to help us to understand differences in context-related communication styles (Hall, 1959) given the heterogeneous nature of the world's social order affected by global migration, the increasingly cross-cultural nature of business negotiations, and the interactions of different people throughout the world. The ability to effectively communicate with people from other cultures has become an increasingly important skill in international management. Therefore, if MNCs are to remain competitive in today's business environment, then they must rely more on their employees' competency in cross-cultural communication (Adler and Graham, 1989). Cultural nuances impacts communication when translating words from one language to another (Tannen, 1984); that is why communication is a complex process comprising much more than the linguistic component. It requires the interpretation of speech, tone, facial expressions, body language, gestures, and assumptions shared between the communicants about the context and purpose of the exchange (Bradby, 2001). The Sub-Saharan African business environment is comprised of 48 diverse countries stretching from the savannas south of the Sahara Desert to the coastal mountains of the valleys of the cape, with cultures that are varied, manifold, and containing many ethnic languages (Abdul-Raheem, 1996). It is thus obvious that the indigenous people manifest different communication styles and values based on their social context, which without doubt affects communication and management practices in the various MNC subsidiaries in Africa. This is shown in Table 7.1 below, which provides a catalog of some of the major and diverse languages spoken by the various ethnic

Table 7.1   Taxonomy of Ethnic Groups and Languages Spoken in Sub-Saharan Africa

Ethnic Group/ Language	Sub-Saharan African Country
Afar	Ethiopia, Djibouti and Eritrea
Afrikaner	South Africa and Namibia
Akan	Ghana and Ivory Coast
Alur	Uganda and DR Congo
Anuak	South Sudan and Ethiopia
Baka	Southeastern Cameroon, Northern Congo, Northern Gabon
Beti-Pahuin	Cameroon, Republic of the Congo, Equatorial Guinea, Gabon, Sao Tome and Principe
Biafada	Senegal, Gambia and Guinea-Bissau
Efik	Nigeria and Cameroon
Ewe	Ghana, Togo, Benin, Nigeria and Togo
Fulani	Guinea, Nigeria, Cameroon, Senegal, Mali, Sierra Leone, Central African Republic, Burkina Faso, Benin, Niger, Gambia, Guinea Bissau, Chad, Mauritania, Sudan, Togo and Ivory Coast
Ga	Ghana and Togo
Great Lakes Twa (Batwa)	Rwanda, Burundi, Uganda and DR Congo
Hausa	Nigeria, Niger, Ghana, Benin, Chad, Cameroon and Sudan
Herero	Namibia, Botswana and Angola
Hutu	Rwanda, Burundi and DR Congo
Lugbara People	Uganda and DR Congo
Makonde	Tanzania and Mozambique
Mole-Dagbani	Ghana, Burkina Faso and Northern Togo
Oromo	Ethiopia, Sudan and Kenya
San (Bushmen)	South Africa, Zimbabwe, Lesotho, Mozambique, Swaziland, Botswana, Namibia and Angola
Shona	Mozambique and Zimbabwe
Somali	Somalia, Ethiopia, Djibouti and Kenya
Sotho	Lesotho, South Africa and Zimbabwe
Swahili	Tanzania, Kenya and Mozambique
Swazi	Swaziland, South Africa and Mozambique
Tigray-Tigrinya	Ethiopia and Eritrea
Tsonga	Swaziland, South Africa and Mozambique (Chiredzi and Mwenezi)
Tutsi	Rwanda, Burundi and DR Congo
Wayeyi	Namibia, Botswana and Angola
Zulu	South Africa

Source: Author Research

groups in the SSA region. From Table 7.1, most of the major languages in the subregion are spoken across many African nations, which explains the ethnic pluralism in the subregion. The pluralism of traditions also explains the reason why most indigenous people use multiple languages as a means of communication across the subcontinent.

Whereas some of these major languages are further divided into smaller linguistic groups, what makes them even more complex is the fact that SSA countries were partitioned and colonized by different colonial masters from Europe who imposed their languages like English, French, Spanish and Portuguese on the African continent. These foreign languages became the official lingua franca used in both work organizations and schools. The dilemma of the African is how these foreign languages have impacted their indigenous languages and cultural values. It is thus not surprising that an educated African in a typical MNC workplace would be confronted with different linguistic styles as he or she communicates with an expatriate from the West. While the expatriate or foreigner is only used to his or her maternal language that is either English, French or Portuguese, the local African worker is confronted with the multiple languages including the 'imposed' official language at work. This makes communication and understanding quite difficult when interacting with foreigners at work since the African is obliged to shift between the communicative styles of his/her maternal language and that of the official language at work or school. Consequently, the complex cross-cultural dynamics in SSA countries call for appreciation and acceptance of the different dimensions of communicative behaviors in the subsidiaries of MNCs in Africa. Global managers can only be culturally sensitive to the local African worker if they are able to acknowledge the diverse cultural dimensions of the SSA environment.

Many researchers in cross-cultural management have described the different dimensions in which people fail to communicate appropriately during cross-cultural interaction; for example, when to communicate or talk (Tannen, 1984), what to say (Eades, 1982; Scollon, 1982; Tannen, 1984), pacing and pausing (Tannen, 1984), listenership through steady eye contact (Erickson and Shultz, 1982), intonation (Gumperz, 1982), and directedness and indirectedness (Tannen, 1982). These levels of differences also describe the ways that meanings are communicated during interactions (Tannen, 1984), and the ways of communicating meanings are learned in a particular speech community or culture, especially by communicating with people with whom one identifies socially. This is why Hall (1959) says culture is communication. To that extent, all aspects of communication are culture-bound, and in a cross-cultural environment understanding cross-cultural communication is a means to understanding language; this facilitates the resolution of problems and tasks facing the world and the people in it (Tannen, 1984).

Differences in communication styles and values are augmented by differences in management practices, since culture has a significant impact on managerial practices particularly between vastly different countries (Hofstede, 1980). Thus, the quest to go global and capture higher synergies from distant operations has called attention to the communication network and internal knowledge flow within the MNC (Govingarajan and Gupta, 2001), and understanding the cultural myths and cross-cultural communication can help to sharpen and motivate global leaders' competence (Wong-Mingji and Kessler, 2012).

As MNCs consist of diverse and geographically dispersed subunits, they definitely encounter language barriers when communicating with their local business communities as well as within their networks (Triandis, 1982; Adler, 1983; Ronen and Shenkar, 1985; Hofstede, 2001; Branine, 2011). Consequently, cross-cultural communication competence is a key ingredient in this direction, which can shape organizational change processes, information exchange, competitive activities, global coordination, and intra-corporate value creation. It is through effective communication that expatriate executives develop their strategies and policies, disseminate and implement them. Hence, the famous Deborah Tannen's (1986) dictum that, "the fate of the Earth depends on cross-cultural communication." The cross-cultural communication barriers of expatriates in international assignments can be an impediment to effective negotiations and alliance evolution, and can have an impact on conflict management in cross-cultural teams (Von Glinow, Shapiro, and Bret, 2004), headquarters-subsidiary relations (Gupta, 1987), training effectiveness (Tung, 1982), knowledge transfer and diffusion (Ghoshal and Nohira, 1989), and the efficiency of the global value chain (Govingarajan and Gupta, 2001). Therefore, the SSA business environment communication competence indicates the ability of MNCs from the West, East and other sections of the globe to properly identify and realize messages from the African environment in different situations of interaction. These include knowledge of the African languages and knowledge of African non-verbal behaviors.

CROSS-CULTURAL COMMUNICATION AND MNCs IN SUB-SAHARAN AFRICA

Market-seeking and foreign direct investment (FDI) processes of the MNCs rely on global expansion, thus the ability to create an effective knowledge-sharing culture within the multinational teams in Africa rests on the maintenance of intra-team respect, mutual trust, reciprocity, and positive individual and group relationships, which can only be facilitated through cross-cultural communication competence. The importance of cross-cultural communication is thus an impetus for greater globalization, FDI, and MNCs, in the cultural flexibility of global managers working in SSA. Cultural flexibility enhances the global manager's self-esteem and self-confidence (Mendenhall and Oddou, 1985), and these qualities are associated with achievement, since flexible expatriates will be able to respond more effectively to ambiguous situations (Hogan and Holland, 2003) in the SSA business environment.

Through globalization, the MNC has become a multilingual community with the various subunits dispersed across a variety of national locales, each with a workforce having its own native language, form of discourse, and cultural environment (Adler, 1983; Babcock and Babcock, 2001; Phillips, Lawrence, and Hardy, 2004). The Sub-Saharan African business environment, which comprises diverse cultures, has depended very much on FDI inflows since their independence. The FDIs are mostly in the form of greenfields investments, and acquisition and merging with the existing firms in the Sub region. These foreign investments (MNCs) come with their foreign expertise and technical staff who must work with local African staff by implementing common Human Resource Management (HRM) practices in response to the receptiveness of the Sub-Saharan African institutional environment. As language boundaries are not clear cut, multiple languages are often and concurrently used within a subunit, between subunits, and between subunits and headquarters (Luo and Shenkar, 2006). This reality produces a multitude of linguistic cultures within the MNC enclave, as reflected in the various idiosyncratic communicative behaviors and actions of the workforce (Heracleous and Barrett, 2001; Zaidman, 2001). Consequently, within the MNC, communication behaviors appropriate to a set of local African staff may be seen as inappropriate to expatriate staff. This may be due to the fact that the expatriates are not considered 'in-group' members (non-Africans), and for that matter may not enjoy the same rights and privileges as the group members (Francis, 1991; Abugre, 2013b). Extant literature points to the pervasive tendency of individuals always wanting to identify with their own group members, the 'in-group'. This 'in-group' identification typically leads to differences in the treatment and perception of 'out-group' members relative to 'in-group' members (Lustig and Koester, 2006). To avoid the seeming differences between expatriates and local staff during work, the influential role of cross-cultural communication will certainly be an impetus for a greater globalization of the MNC enhanced by the cultural flexibility of the global manager. The cultural flexibility of the global manager leads to greater adaptation and accommodation of the perceived 'foreignness' of the indigenous African workers when the global manager alters his or her communication styles in order to adjust to the seeming differences in attitudes and beliefs (Ellingswworth, 1988) of the African. Communication between an expatriate staff and a local staff involves two different voices and persuasions. On one instance, the voice of an expatriate from a different culture with a different frame of reference; on the other hand, the voice of a local staff with a different voice and a different frame of reference. This is what makes cross-cultural communication a difficult process. The possibility of 'Western' perceptions highlights an important difference between expatriates and host Sub-Saharan employees' approaches to work when communicating with each other, and this underscores the importance of cross-cultural

Table 7.2   A Framework of Cross-Cultural Communication in Diffuse
Management Practices in MNC Subsidiaries in Africa

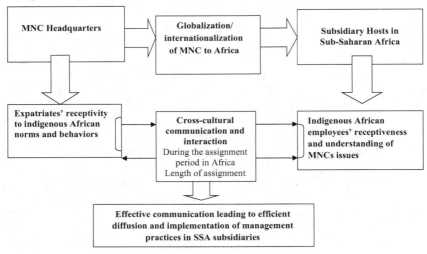

Source: Author

communication in the management of MNCs in the African environment.
Table 7.2 below illustrates the role cross-cultural communication can play
between expatriates and local African employees in harmonizing MNC HQ
and the MNC subsidiary HRM practices.

The framework in Table 7.2 above explains the role of cross-cultural
communication as a key factor in the effective transmission and diffusion of
management practices in the SSA business environment. It reveals the relationship between MNCs headquarters (HQ) and their subsidiaries in the
SSA business environment. For effective diffusion of management practices
(for example, knowledge, skills and technical abilities) in the SSA MNCs,
expatriates or global managers who are sent by the MNCs' HQ to SSA
subsidiaries must be receptive to host cultural norms and behaviors that
can affect the efficient delivery of work practices through cross-cultural
communication and interaction with local employees. Table 7.2 equally
highlights the role of host African country nationals (HCNs) and their perceptions of understanding MNCs' issues disseminated by expatriates in the
course of work.

Thus using empirical data, this chapter has explored the extent to which
cross-cultural communication plays an essential role in the management
practices of MNCs in the SSA business environment through the lens of
senior expatriates' oral narratives. In the following section, this chapter will
briefly discuss a hermeneutic approach that includes the interpretation of
narratives and collecting empirical data for this project. Hermeneutics refers

to the theory and practice of interpretation and understanding in different kinds of human contexts (Odman, 1988).

METHOD

As stated earlier, empirical data was used to situate the thematic position of this project. It involved in-depth, open-ended, and mostly unstructured one-on-one interviews with 21 senior executive expatriates from different countries of origin and different MNCs operating in Ghana. Out of the 21 participants, four were females while 17 were males. The respondents were various regional HR managers and in some cases the managing directors of the MNCs. (Regional managers here means the managers were overseeing other subsidiaries within the subcontinent and not only those in Ghana.) The interview data, which was tape-recorded, took into account a wide array of contextual factors inherent in the cross-cultural communication of expatriates in MNCs in the Sub-Saharan African business environment. Through thorough reading and thematic analysis, and categorizing the themes according to the different roles of cross-cultural communication as the focus of this work, the following thematic findings were arrived at.

THE IMPORTANCE OF MNCs' CROSS-CULTURAL COMMUNICATION PRACTICES IN AFRICA

As MNCs' headquarters (HQ) and their subsidiaries in Sub-Saharan Africa (SSA) continue to coordinate, cross-cultural communication is very important to expatriate work because it is the basis of expatriate work life. The findings indicated that cross-cultural communication is indispensable to the work of MNCs in the SSA environment. The emphasis is on expatriates' communication, which is mostly conducted orally with local staff (Africans) because they work together at all times whether in the office or in the field. Fundamentally, communication is critical as both Africans and Western expatriates must understand what is being asked or requested. The need to communicate and understand the verbal and behavioral cues in African MNCs' subsidiaries require building organizational training capacities to help employees (expatriates and local staff) arrive at the same meaning for words used and the behaviors revealed to avoid unnecessary work conflicts. Competence in cross-cultural communication is critically important to effective work in the SSA business environment, without which organizations cannot exist (Keyton, 2005). Cross-cultural management is basically the interaction of culturally diverse workers in the context of multinational companies (Thomas, 2008). For example, the findings showed that the goal of every expatriate is to train him/herself to impart knowledge, skills, and competencies, and if he/she is not communicating well with the local staff, it may be difficult to perform this role. Hence, global managers should understand the influential role of cross-cultural interactions on MNCs operations in Africa. This is eloquently demonstrated by the following excerpts from the interviews:

> Cross-cultural communication is critical, and oral communication is essential for common understanding. Because the English that is spoken in one country is not necessarily the same that is spoken in another country and different phrases could have different meanings. So in South Africa, if I say just now, it could be anything say in the next three weeks. If I say just now in Zambia, it means immediately, and if I say just now in Ghana, it might mean immediately but not mean just exactly immediately, so they would all have different meanings if one doesn't understand the nuances of language in a particular culture. If one doesn't clarify the meaning and understanding, it's very easy to get into miscommunication.

Thus, it is very important that expatriates working in SSA understand the individual local employees working with them since the quality of expatriates' work in the subregion would depend very much on the ability to achieve their goals by interacting competently with the African people. The fact that indigenous African workers speak multiple languages with different value systems that are at variance with those of the expatriates presupposes that there are obvious consequences to working in a multicultural organization in SSA. In order to avoid the continuous doubt, misunderstanding, and expectations resulting from the differences between expatriates and local African workers, competence in cross-cultural communication is more necessary than ever. Expatriates can share and learn better from the way Africans behave if they engage interpersonally with local workers in continuous communication since meanings are created and shared as people participate in common activities. Engaging in common activities through continuous interaction with local Africans would enable expatriates to make sense of the common experiences derived from indigenous workers in the various MNCs' subsidiaries in SSA. Consequently, cross-cultural communication is critically vital in the management practices of MNCs in Africa. Acquiring skills in cross-cultural communication in SSA would facilitate expatriates' transfer of knowledge and technical skills to host African employees, thereby improving the overall management practices of the SSA organizations. Similarly, skills in cross-cultural communication would assist expatriates' interpretative process within the SSA social and political environments. This would further enhance understanding and how to reach agreement on any negotiation process between expatriates and local African workers.

DIFFERENCES IN COMMUNICATIVE BEHAVIORS OF INDIGENOUS AFRICAN STAFF AND EXPATRIATES

It is widely acknowledged that there is the need to recognize cultural diversity and differences of people, and develop intercultural sensitivity toward such differences within and across nations. The merging of two or more cultures will definitely affect the manner of communication in the host country. This is particularly so when expatriates from the West come to Africa to work. African cultural and environmental differences make possible the varied and distinctive communicative behaviors of the indigenous people in work organizations. This stems from the fact that there are appropriate and inappropriate kinds of communicative behaviors in various countries associated with national cultural beliefs, attitudes, values, expectations, and norms. Thus in particularly, the diverse ethnic background of the African continent suggests a clear study and understanding of the social and communicative behaviors of the indigenes. Differences in people's communicative behaviors between the West and Africa can sometimes cause people to erroneously conclude that they differ on substantive issues, hence negatively influencing their behavior in the MNC work context. Consequently, global managers or expatriates ought to understand these observable and symbolic manifestations of the pattern of ideas and actions of the local African people when they are working together in the various subsidiaries of MNCs. These differences in communicative behaviors arising from differences in expectations certainly impact on the work behaviors of expatriates, which they will have to address and adapt for successful work outcomes in the subsidiary MNC. The study findings demonstrate that the differences in work attitude and behaviors of expatriates and indigenous Africans are rooted in the social backgrounds of the individuals. For example, Americans are time-conscious and therefore depend on getting things done in a timelier manner. This is different from Africans who may mostly take a couple of hours or days to get things done. This attitudinal difference in work would certainly create frustrations for one group within the subsidiary MNCs in SSA. However, both groups would have to learn to manage their expectations through interpersonal interaction and understanding of the differences between them as emanating from the differences in culture, business, and the amount of bureaucracy that one has to deal with in the African business terrain.

Similarly, cross-cultural difference in communicative behaviors between local staff and expatriates in MNCs involve varied and distinctive styles of actions including directness and indirectness and formality and informality emanating from the diversity of value systems. These can affect the interactional approaches of expatriates and local African workers, which may eventually affect the outcome of the work in the MNCs' subsidiary. The basis for what is an acceptable and an unacceptable attitude for the two groups working together will always be a contentious issue because of the spread of nationalities and the way of doing things in one's culture. Thus, learning to understand the African culture through cross-cultural communication is very important to those expatriates who work in Africa. It is the diverse African cultures and value orientations of its people that explain the seeming differences in communicative behaviors of Africans. Expatriates working in SSA must therefore appreciate the multiplicity of the African traditions and cultural differences through cross-cultural communication in order to successfully achieve their full objectives in the African continent. Africans, just like Europeans or other Westerners, have been socialized in their indigenous and native behaviors. People grow, albeit through Western education, and still maintain or indulge in their traditional behaviors. MNCs in SSA must thus go beyond just recognizing the differences between some Africans' behaviors at work and those of expatriates, and learn to accept and coexist with them.

CROSS-CULTURAL COMMUNICATION AS A SOLUTION TO EFFECTIVE GLOBALIZATION OF MNCs IN SSA

Globalization has made it possible for expatriate workers to be sent to any part of the world for business. As multinational businesses keep growing as a result of seeking natural resources and markets, the number of expatriate workers will always grow because their knowledge, skills, and abilities are needed in the new markets. Global communication takes place because of the contacts of many different people from diverse cultures in the area of business, yet there is no one single standard of global communication. For example, in heavily Muslim countries, one needs to understand the religion to understand how to treat people, the staff, and how important religion plays into that culture. Particularly in Africa, there is the presence of a vast multiculturalism, and each country not far off from the other has different ethnic groups with different behaviors and customs. Africa is the new 21st-century market where all the industrial powers are moving in to do business. Hence, expatriates have to understand the diversity of the national conditions in the various SSA countries; not only do they have to appreciate that they are guests and abide by traditions, cultures, and customs. They also need to understand the mindset of African people. Therefore, appropriate cross-cultural skills that facilitate more effective interaction between foreign expatriates and local African workers in the subsidiary companies are needed to avoid high levels of expatriate failure (Debrah and Rees, 2011). This is highlighted in the following words of a respondent:

> We've got expatriates from Canada, the US, the UK, Australia, New Zealand, and Brazil. Different cultures have their own style, and so if you have turn over and you've got an employee who is used to a South

African style and a South African accent and idioms or idiosyncrasies with language, then you get an Australian or a Canadian, it might be confusing for the staff, so that will hinder things. People again have different styles and that can be a hindrance to communication or certainly language barriers to effective communication. Just in my dealings here, I'll use a word or my HR managers will use a word that I don't read the same meaning to it, and this will mean that we aren't communicating well because, of course, we tap [attach] different meaning to different people.

Therefore, for expatriates working in SSA to be competent and effectively transmit their knowledge and skills as part of the management practices of MNCs to indigenous Africans working with them, they (expatriates) have to fully understand the backgrounds and cultures of the local workers, which are likely to hinder communication at work. The different African cultures have different ways of getting messages across and understanding issues. So, as globalization brings different economic cultures into an integrated network of common communication, there should also be an increasing embrace of MNC management for the multicultural dimensions of their workers in multiple locations within the Sub-Saharan African business environment. Culture, society, and the organization of people can influence the effectiveness of MNCs' operations based on the beliefs of the people. Information collected from participants for this work shows that the polarity between two opposing ideologies, especially the East/West dichotomy and their differing perceptions of life, must be given a compromise if MNCs want to succeed in their businesses in Africa. This is echoed by a respondent in the following words:

> Cross-cultural communication competence is therefore critical for any expatriate coming to Ghana to understand the cultural dynamics of the people, I call it capitalist working in a socialist environment. I am not saying Ghanaian are socialist, but they are social people, they support the social norm and they don't support the capitalist norm, and you got to understand that to operate successfully in Ghana. If you don't understand this, you would not succeed.

Certainly, Africa and the rest of the world are not the same. To appreciate Africa as a cradle of human civilization, Westerners and foreigners must learn to accept the African value systems in order to communicate effectively and facilitate their businesses with Africans. Being socialist means being a communalist. Africans are mostly collectivist in nature. They socialize with their extended family members both at home and at work, and thus, it is normal to the African to receive a family member or friend as a visitor even at work. This is what may not be tolerated by an expatriate manager especially during working hours. Hence a conflict can set in because of the differing views of the expatriate and the African. The main difficulty in cross-cultural communication results from conflict in the different value systems. For example, while indigenous African business people and their foreign counterparts may agree on the general goals of a business proposal, conflict in how to achieve such goals especially, with respect to time management, location and other factors, might be anticipated. The lack of openness of expatriates and foreign business executives to consider SSA values would lead to disagreement and failure in business.

STRATEGIC DRIVERS OF CROSS-CULTURAL COMMUNICATION IN MNCs

The fourth thematic finding of this work revolves around the strategies that expatriate managers might employ to deal with cross-cultural communication problems in MNCs in Sub-Saharan Africa. From the organizational point of view, this work emphasizes that it is necessary for an expatriate going into an African country for the first time to have the basic training around the culture and the environment of the host country in which he/she will work. Acquiring knowledge about African value systems as part of preparation before departure would help expatriates to fit in better as new entrants to the African environment. The reality is that the benefits of cross-cultural experience are enjoyed by both the MNC and its staff. As the expatriate acquires a common understanding and agreement on the work culture, interaction, and communication in the organization, it benefits the expatriate, the local staff, and the MNC as a whole. Table 7.3 below summarizes the views of respondents in this study, which demonstrate the various administrative strategies that can facilitate expatriates' cross-cultural communication in MNCs in the SSA business environment.

CONCLUSION

This chapter has indicated the preponderant role cross-cultural communication plays in management practices of multinational and international businesses in Africa. For successful globalization of trade MNCs' search for natural resources and markets in Africa, the critical role of cross-cultural communication in management practices of the various MNCs in the African business terrain is worthy of study. The SSA region is vast and multifaceted; MNCs operating in Africa must understand the complex cross-cultural dynamics of the SSA environment. For example, when comparing cultures, such as the West and Africa, and how they affect the business environment, the expatriate or foreigner must understand that Africa is a high-context culture. As a result, Africans place emphasis on collectivism, group participation, and tend to be more people-oriented and value their extended family system. In much of their (Africans') communication processes, a greater

Table 7.3   Strategic Portfolio of Effective Cross-Cultural Communication in MNCs in Sub-Saharan Africa

---

Strategic Behavior Competencies of Expatriates in Cross-Cultural Communication in SSA

Direct communication is always the best; management of MNCs must try to facilitate discussions between expatriates and local African workers in order to clear any misunderstanding.

Expatriates should stick to cultural commitments by understanding the nonverbal signals of local African employees.

Expatriates should encourage face-to-face communication with local African workers and adopt proactive approach to issues in the SSA work environment.

Expatriates should try to engage on a one-on-one basis by getting to know what local African employees look at as a norm in order to avoid generalizations.

Expatriates should do more follow-ups in oral and written communications in order to be familiar with the invisible differences that exist between themselves and local African workers.

Communication is always important; expatriates must give time to ask questions and make sure they understand the issues in the SSA landscape.

Expatriates must learn as they go and put their ears on the ground by respecting individual African workers.

Expatriates must adapt to the system of doing things in Africa and open up by being sensitive to the nonverbal cues of Africans.

Expatriates should learn to dialogue with local Africans to see why people are doing what they are doing so that they (expatriates) can adopt a middle ground for communication.

Expatriates should speak through the next person who understands them better, and also learn things in the SSA environment as they go.

Expatriates must show a lot of patience and understand the needs of indigenous African staff by doing more listening as they work in the SSA environment.

---

aspect of the meaning comes from not only the words, but is internalized in the individual. This means the significance of any communication is tied to the environment and also linked to the relationships between the ideas expressed in the communication process. Therefore, Africans utilize much nonverbal communication and interpret more of the unspoken words as a significant understanding of messages than merely relying on the verbal words—hence, the significance of symbols, emblems, and gestures in communicating messages in the SSA social context. Expatriates' behaviors towards Africans are thus interpreted not only by the words they (expatriates) speak, but the nonverbal behavior and attitudes towards the Africans. Thus, seeking to understand and accepting the actions and behaviors of Africans in a nonbiased atmosphere is what cross-cultural communication is about. Gudykunst and Kim (1992) stress that when strangers violate the nonverbal behaviors of people, the latter interprets the violation negatively, resulting in ineffective communication.

For international business scholars, reading this chapter will help organizations understand variations in exchanges and relationships they develop with foreigners. As more international firms expand into Africa, the global manager would have to understand the exigencies in their cooperative relationships with indigenous African employees. The multiplicity of African cultures and the communicative behaviors of the local staff certainly impact Sub-Saharan business operations, and global managers have to appreciate the possibilities of the African people. This can be done by embracing respect and sensitivity to the local African workers in the various MNCs. This is what the outside world and global managers must appreciate in order to give back to Africa its enormous contribution to the world (Moran et al, 2011). The empirical insights from this chapter will enable MNCs to improve on their operational efficiencies through effective cross-cultural behavior and management within the SSA region. Similarly, this chapter opens a window of opportunity for both African and international scholars to acquire cross-cultural knowledge and skills, as there is increasing scholarly and practitioner interest in African management due to the prospective changes in many economies.

REFERENCES

Abdul-Raheem, T. (1996). *Pan Africanism: Politics, economy and social change in the twenty first century.* London: Pluto Press.

Abugre, J. B. (2012). How managerial interactions affect employees' work output in Ghanaian organizations. *African Journal of Economic and Management Studies,* 3(2), 204–226.

Abugre, J. B. (2013a). *The role of training in facilitating expatriates' cross-cultural communication in multinational companies in Ghana,* unpublished Ph.D. thesis, University of Wales, Swansea.

Abugre, J. B. (2013b). Current and desired employee communication patterns in Sub-Saharan Africa: Empirical evidence on four Ghanaian organizations. *Journal of African Business,* 14(1), 33–46.

Adler, N. J. (1983). Cross-cultural management research: The ostrich and the trend. *Academy of Management Review,* 8(2), 226–232.

Adler, N. J., and Graham, J. (1989). Cross-cultural interaction: The international comparison fallacy? *Journal of International Business Studies,* 20(3), 515–537.

Babcock, R. D., and Du-Babcock, B. (2001). Language-based communication zones in international business communication. *Journal of Business Communication,* 38, 372–412.Bowden, R. (2007). *Africa South of the Sahara.* Coughlan Publishing.

Bradby, H. (2001). Communication, interpretation and translation. In L. Culley and S. Dyson (Eds.), *Ethnicity and nursing practice* (pp. 129–148). Basingstoke: Palgrave.

Branine, M. (2011). *Managing across cultures: Concept, policies and practices.* London: Sage Publications.

Cray, D., and Mallory, G. R. (1998). *Making sense of managing culture.* London: Thomson.

Debrah, Y., and Rees, C. (2011). The development of global leaders and expatriates. In Anne-Wil Harzing and Ashly Pinnington (Ed.), *International human resource management* (3rd ed., pp. 378–414). Sage Publications, London.

Eades, D. (1982). *"Where You Going?" Reasons and privacy in Southeast Queensland aboriginal society*. Ms. Department of Anthropology and Sociology, University of Queensland.

Ellingswworth, H. W. (1988). A theory of adaptation in intercultural dyads. In Y. Y. Kim and W. H. Gudykunst (Eds.), *Theories in intercultural communication*. Newbury Park, CA: Sage.

Erickson, F., and Shultz, J. (1982). *The counselor as gatekeeper: Social interaction in interviews*. New York: Academic Press.

Francis, J. N. P. (1991). When in Rome? The effects of cultural adaptation on intercultural business negotiations. *Journal of International Business Studies, 22*(3), 403–428.

Ghoshal, S., and Nohira, N. (1989). Internal differentiation within multinational companies. *Strategic Management Journal, 4,* 96–102.

Govingarajan, V., and Gupta, A. K. (2001). *The quest for global dominance: Transforming global presence into global competitive advantage*. San Francisco, CA: Jossey- Bass.

Gudykunst, W. B., and Kim, Y. Y. (1992). *Reading and communicating with strangers*. New York: McGraw-Hill.

Gumperz, J. J. (1982). *Discourse strategies*. Cambridge: Cambridge University Press.

Gupta, A. K. (1987). SBU strategies, corporate-SBU relations, and SBU effectiveness in strategy Implementation. *Academy of Management Journal, 30*(3), 477–500.

Hall, E. (1959). *The silent language*. New York: Doubleday.

Heracleous, L., and Barrett, M. (2001). Organizational change as discourse: Communicative actions and deep structures in the context of information technology implementation. *Academy of Management Journal, 44*(4), 755–778.

Hofstede, G. (1980). *Culture's consequences: International differences in work-related values*. London: Sage.

Hofstede, G. (2001). *Culture's consequences: Comparing values, behaviors, institutions, and organizations across nations*. London: Sage Publications.

Hogan, J., and Holland, B. (2003). Using theory to evaluate personality and job performance relations: A socioanalytic perspective. *Journal of Applied Psychology, 88,* 100–112.

Jackson, T. (2004). *Management and change in Africa; across-cultural perspective*. London: Routledge.

Jeannet, J.-P. (2000). *Managing with a global mindset, Financial Times*. New York: Prentice.

Keyton, J. (2005). *Communication and organizational culture*. Thousand Oaks: Sage.

Konopaske, R., and Ivancevich, J. M. (2004). *Global management and organizational behavior: Text, readings, cases, and exercises*. Irwin: McGraw-Hill.

Luo, Y., and Shenkar, O. (2006). The multinational corporation as a multilingual community: Language and organization in a global context. *Journal of International Business Studies, 37*(3), 321–339.

Lustig, M. W., and Koester, J. (2006). *Intercultural competence: Interpersonal communication across cultures* (5th ed.). Boston: Pearson Education Inc.

Mendenhall, M., and Oddou, G. (1985). The dimensions of expatriate acculturation. *The Academy of Management Review, 10*(1), 39–47.

Moran, T. R., Harris, P. R., and Moran, S. V. (2011). *Managing cultural differences: Leadership skills and strategies for working in a global world.* Oxford: Butterworth-Heinemann.

Nkomo, S. M. (2011). Leading organizational change in "New" South Africa. *Journal of Occupational and Organizational Psychology, 84*(3), 453-470.

Odman, P. J. (1988). Hermeneutics. In J. P. Keeves (Ed.), *Educational research methodology and measurement: An international handbook* (pp. 6370). New York, NY: Pergamon Press.

Phillips, N., Lawrence, T. B., and Hardy, C. (2004). Discourse and institutions. *Academy of Management Review, 29*(4), 635–652.

Riusala, K., and Suutari, V. (2004). International knowledge transfers through expatriates. *Thunderbird International Business Review, 46*(6), 743–770.

Ronen, S., and Shenkar, O. (1985). Clustering countries on attitudinal dimensions: A review and synthesis. *The Academy of Management Review, 10*(3), 435–454.

Samovar, L. A., and Porter, R. E (1997). *Intercultural communication: A reader* (8th ed.). Wadsworth Publishing Company.

Scollon, S. B. (1982). *Socialization to non-intervention and its relation to linguistic structure.* Doctoral dissertation, University of Hawaii.

Tannen, D. (1982). Ethnic style in male-female conversation. In John J. Gumperz (Ed.), *Language and social identity.* Cambridge: Cambridge University Press, pp. 217–231.

Tannen, D. (1984). The pragmatics of cross-cultural communication. *Applied Linguistics, 5*(3), 189–195.

Tannen, D. (1986). *That's Not What I Meant! How Conversational Style Makes or Breaks Relationships.* New York: Ballantine.

Thomas, D. C. (2008). *Cross-cultural management: Essential concepts.* Thousand Oaks, CA: Sage.

Triandis, H. C. (1982). Dimensions of cultural variation as parameters of organizational theories. *International Studies of Management and Organization, 12*(4), 139–169.

Tung, R. (1982). Selecting and training procedures of U.S., European, and Japanese multinational corporations. *California Management Review, 25*(1), 57–71.

UNCTAD. (2007). *World investment report 2007: Transnational corporations, extractive industries and development.* New York and Geneva: United Nations.

Von Glinow, M. A., Shapiro, D. L., and Brett, J. M. (2004). Can we talk, and should we? Managing emotional conflict in multicultural teams. *Academy of Management Review, 29*(4), 578–592.

Wong-Mingji, J. D., and Kessler, E. H. (2012). Motivation of global leaders from cultural mythologies. In E. Christopher (Ed.), *Communicating across cultures* (pp. 10–19). London: Palgrave-Macmillan.

Zaidman, N. (2001). Cultural codes and language strategies in business communication. *Management Communication Quarterly, 14*(3), 408–441.

8 Surviving in Africa
MNCs' Response to Institutional Deficiencies and Moral Implications

Adeyinka A. Adewale and
Sharif M. Khalid

INTRODUCTION

Nigeria has a population of over 177 million people, out of which 13 million live in Lagos ("Africa: Nigeria," 2016). Lagos state is also the busiest commercial center of the nation where most multinationals across all industries are headquartered. The potential for economic prosperity in Nigeria has been particularly celebrated globally as Africa's largest economy (Robinson, 2015). Yet amidst this huge prospect, Nigeria's business landscape still faces many challenges. The purpose of this paper is to uncover these contextual challenges, how multinationals claim to respond to them as well as the likely moral ramifications of their responses. This focus is essential in the light of an increasing necessity to combat systemic deficiencies, especially corruption at all levels of society, in which multinationals are major stakeholders whose activities can either make or mar this course. More interesting is the critical role multinationals can play in shaping the moral consciousness of their employees, who can become useful beyond the walls of these firms. For this, we adopt two American firms as a case study.

RESEARCH METHODOLOGY

A case study research design was adopted in this study. A crucial advantage of this approach is the closeness it offers the researchers to both the context of the study and participants who tell their stories. The Nigerian pharmaceutical industry offered the context within which this study investigated the phenomenon of corruption and the strategies employed by multinationals in responding to issues arising from the context. The choice of the Nigerian pharmaceutical industry as the context of this study was predicated on its well-documented, recurrent history of scandals and corruption (NAFDAC, 2015) alongside a proven long-term operational presence of foreign multinationals in the industry (UNIDO, 2012).

Three broad categories of players make the Nigerian pharmaceutical industry, namely: Western, Eastern and indigenous firms (IMS Health,

2012). Amongst these, Western firms, comprising firms from Europe and America, have the longest historical presence in the Nigerian pharmaceutical landscape dating over 50 years (UNIDO, 2012) and were therefore the focus of this study. More specifically, this study focused on American multinationals amongst the possible array of Western firms for two reasons: First, they granted the researchers easy access, which others did not give, and second, they met the ethical standards employed in this study. Due to the sensitive nature of the pharmaceutical industry, anonymity of all participating firms and their employees was crucial at the design stage. Given that only British and American firms have an excess of three major players within the context, they were the only subsets for which anonymizing data was more realistic since data containing specific sensitive information might be easily traceable to its source. All British firms approached denied participation in this study, while two American firms granted access to conduct the study with the assistance of internal leads (employees of these firms within the professional network of the researchers).

Upon gaining access, a mix of stratified and random sampling methods was employed. First, potential participants within the internal lead's network were assigned to a group called 'lead's network,' from which simple random sampling followed in selecting part of the final sample. To control bias and ensure greater data reliability, participants from outside this network were also randomly selected. Overall, 11 employees across low, middle and senior management took part in the study. Six of these were within the lead's network and five were outside this network to control bias.

In-depth semi-structured interviews were conducted with all participants, each lasting an average of 90 minutes. Questions were structured to facilitate rich discussion on internal firm contexts as well as the broader industry and societal contexts in which the firm operated. Using clever 'how' and 'why' questions, further issues surrounding the responses of the firms to the challenges identified were discussed from which interesting insights into likely moral ramifications ensued. Gathered data were manually transcribed using a combination of software, namely Dragon speech dictator and InqScribed, lasting an average of four hours per interview. Generated texts were imported into NVivo, within which data was analyzed using thematic analysis. Thematic analysis (TA) is "a method of identifying, analysing and reporting patterns (themes) within data" (Braun and Clarke, 2006, p. 6). Hammersley and Atkinson (1995) describe TA as aiming to generate descriptions of behaviors through identifiable themes and patterns in living and talk. Themes depicting both internal firm cultures, broader industry context, and ensuing challenges were first observed. Then, other themes showing participants' opinions of how their firms are responding to these contextual issues were also observed, followed by indications of broader impacts on the employees themselves. All these were coded into NVivo nodes and explored critically in generating relevant themes and subthemes. Results and findings from this exercise are presented below.

FINDINGS AND DISCUSSIONS

The core findings from this study showed that Nigeria has been plagued by weak institutions and a culture of corruption as defined by five critical features that emerged as central to the opinions of all participants in this study, as follows:

Illegal Processes

Nothing gets done unless the process is 'helped' or 'fast-tracked,' and following proper procedures is tantamount to a waste of time. Hence, to get things done, such as securing a major contract, registering a company, clearing an import, and as many other activities as are covered in the gamut of the industry's value chain, people expect to bribe their way through processes to get a speedy response. Garuba, Kohler, and Huisman (2009) in a study of the Nigerian pharmaceutical industry reported that every aspect of the industry—registration, procurement, distribution and so on are susceptible to corruption 89% of the time. As a respondent also retorted, "In Nigeria, things are never straightforward." This has been accepted as the norm and the way business is done; hence, different firms have their own ways of coping within such a context.

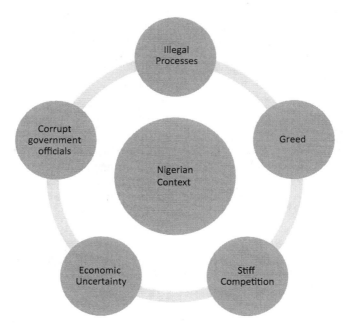

Figure 8.1   Features of the Nigerian Context

Source: Fieldwork

Corrupt Government Officials

An average government official has a feeling of entitlement and the widespread belief is that "everyone has a price," and hence can be bought. For instance, labor officials are sent by the federal government's Ministry of Labor to check on employee welfare in organizations around the country to ensure employers comply with minimum labor conditions as stipulated by law. But this is hardly done. As an employee reported in her interview, "I know of companies where government labor officials get hosted by their bosses, who give them branded goods and other gifts. Then they just ask the staff simple questions and never do anything about their real complaints." Yet, economic uncertainties in the country mean employees' choices are limited in securing other jobs; hence, they remain at their jobs regardless.

Greed

There is also a widespread belief that an average citizen is never content and as such is always seeking quick money-making means, even illegal ones as the case may be. For instance, pharmaceutical representatives complain that many doctors will not prescribe drugs unless they are compensated in some way, and this pressures them into different unethical practices. A medical representative explained, "Doctors are greedy. They put us under a lot of pressure. They demand money, sponsorship to international conferences, promotional materials, and some even ask that we equip their private clinics with satellite television." As a result, it is common knowledge that some firms buckle under the pressure by putting some doctors on paychecks for prescribing a certain volume of drugs monthly, while also obliging them in other ways.

Cutthroat Competition

A lot of generic drugs have flooded the Nigerian market from different parts of the world. This is besides the already stiff competition amongst local and foreign pharmaceuticals currently doing business in Nigeria. A manager in one of the firms explained: "The industry is flooded. For malaria alone, there are over 200 drugs that claim to be very effective in malaria curative and preventive treatment and other categories of ailments likewise have a lot of competing brands from established pharmaceuticals and generic brands." All these force a lot of pharmaceutical representatives to engage outside ethical norms to meet their sales targets. The height of this is revealed when doctors pit pharmaceutical representatives against one another to see who will pay them the highest for drug prescriptions without necessarily basing their judgment on the quality of the drug or the circumstances of their patients. Only multinationals with patented drugs enjoy a lot of immunity in this regard as doctors are forced to prescribe their drugs. Competition forces the game to be played outside of set rules as implied throughout this study.

High Economic Uncertainty

In spite of anticipated prosperity, a large percentage of Nigerians still live below the poverty line while the fears of economic dividends not trickling to the bottom abounds. This creates constant fear in the middle class, who feels the pressing need to survive. Most participants expressed their fears about the economic uncertainty in Nigeria. In the words of one of the participants: "The job market it tough. Things are tight out there and we really don't have a lot of choices so we have to hang on to what we have now and not lose out eventually." With rising living costs as well as few jobs to match this pressing demand, the sense of insecurity has gripped many and kept them glued to whatever jobs they currently have for the fear of losing out altogether.

The prevalence of these features makes the thought of doing ethical business almost impossible, yet several multinationals claim to successfully operate in this context. It would therefore be interesting to critically explore how these multinationals strategize to survive in Africa.

CASE: AMERICAN FIRMS: HISTORY, CULTURE, PRACTICES, AND SCANDALS

American pharmaceuticals are amongst the strongest players in the Nigerian pharmaceutical industry in terms of size, market share, profit, and historical presence (UNIDO, 2012). With over 50 years of well-documented presence in Nigeria, American pharmaceutical companies have generally been largely successful (IMS Health, 2012). They have at different times owned different drug production and manufacturing assets locally, diversified into veterinary medicine, livestock feed production, and so on (Livestock Feed, 2014). Such success in a corrupt environment may be commendable from a business perspective; however, it also raises curiosity about how these American firms have been able to handle the obvious institutional deficiencies identified within the context.

In this section, we examine the internal firm culture and practices of American pharmaceuticals within this context. It is expected that external contexts should strongly influence firm culture and also leave clues as to the likely response of firms to the challenges of such contexts. Further, we argue that some of the current practices observed in most Western multinationals within the region may not be entirely isolated from some historical antecedents; hence, we attempt to link some of these practices with major scandals—for instance, Pfizer's Trovan scandal in Nigeria—before exploring the broader implications of these.

Firm Culture and Practices

A few factors were observed as common threads in the cultural fabric of the studied American multinationals. First, there is a very strong customary culture of compliance to set procedures. In fact, all studied firms consider compliance and strict adherence to set standard operating procedures (SOPs) as the strongest ethic any employee must have to survive in them. So regimented are internal processes that there is hardly any activity without written procedures to them and as such, employees are expected to follow these procedures in all executions. The strict compliance environment also implies that employees caught transgressing any set procedure could lose their jobs depending on the level of atrocity committed. These features of the firms reveal the bureaucratic tendencies that exist in internal structures for the purposes of ensuring employees' activities are regulated and controlled by set standards as multinational enterprises desire to protect their brand reputations.

In practice, this culture of compliance is instilled through frequent rigorous trainings, with a view to exposing employees to case studies that test their ability to effectively apply SOPs to real-life scenarios. We are left, however, to question whether rules can sufficiently cater to all possible challenges employees face in reality, and also, whether explicitly dictating moral reactions to employees who are meant to be fully mature in their cognitive moral reasoning (Kohlberg, 1971) does more good to them than harm in the long run. From another critical perspective is the issue of the effectiveness of written codes, which has been reported severally in literature, could help moderate ethical behavior—yet, could also be cleverly employed as a cover to hide unwholesome practices.

Secondly, internal work environments are very structured yet very flexible, cordial, and free. It was a common expression throughout this investigation in one of the American firms that "change is the only constant thing" and therefore, change agility is a crucial skill to have on the job. One could occupy a position today, and the next it is gone, leaving such persons to apply for other internal positions or leave the firm. Such is the flexibility of internal structures that it seems to create an environment of uncertainties and insecurities in some sense. Nevertheless, employees described their work environment as 'family', 'cordial' and 'open' with all employees encouraged to "say it as it is" with "zero tolerance" for disrespect of colleagues and any breach of compliance. Punishments for such are extreme and very harsh; hence as an employee, focus is on doing things right. Reviewing this seemingly friendly environment from a critical perspective, it can be argued that this kind of environment could create informal mechanisms for normalizing unethical practices and even distracting employees from the moral consequences of their actions since their focus would be on pleasing their bosses and other employees. In addition, these firms have some of the best welfare packages in the industry, with employees receiving all possible incentives—new cars and high salaries, among others, to give security and discourage any unethical practices in the field. However, these welfare packages could easily make employees feel indebted to the firms and cause them to go all out to meet their sales target to justify such welfare packages.

Thirdly, in engaging doctors in the field, American MNCs adopt a common practice of sponsoring a select few doctors to international conferences and subscribing to medical journals on their behalf as contributions towards increasing awareness of global medical trends. However, concerns were raised as to the influence these gestures have on doctors who may feel indebted to the firms and respond by continually prescribing their sponsor's drugs. But the American firms claim they insist all doctors sign an agreement that their accepting to be sponsored for a trip abroad is not in any way an inducement to make the doctors prescribe company products. They go as far making them declare that these gestures are for their professional development only and that they still maintain full discretion to prescribe drugs they feel will help their patients the most. The documentation and processes involved are also quite long and tedious for obvious reasons, and many doctors have been reported to complain bitterly about the processes involved, thinking it is almost an insult to their pride. Thus, only a few are able to wade through the maze to get the prize. The effectiveness of signing agreements for such favors remains contestable especially since the favor is expected to have induced the doctors in ways beyond any written document, yet many claim not to be involved in any form of inducements. But as a participant explained, it is an unwritten rule that after doctors benefit from such sponsorship, they will go ahead to prescribe such company's product more. This then raises tension about the difference between gift-giving as opposed to bribery.

Finally, in contrast to the above, there is an acclaimed zero tolerance to all forms of bribery and corruption by these firms. However, it is interesting to note that in spite of these norms and practices, a lot of emphasis is still placed on meeting set financial and sales targets as performance is largely based on meeting these figures. As profit-making entities, the motive is quite clear, and running at a loss is not an option in Africa's largest market. This therefore gives rise to the question of how MNCs can achieve the delicate balance of pressing employees for financial performance in a highly competitive and corrupt market while expecting them to be completely ethical in the process. Also, whereas the strict rule adherence culture may look great on paper, it also raises a few practicality issues: Can employees always follow set rules in the face of harsh realities in the field? More importantly, are the strict rules really aimed at ethical conduct or are they clever alibis put forth by the firms to exonerate themselves from any scandal, while still allowing for some dirty play in the field by their employees? Looking back at history, we argue that regardless of the ploy by these firms either to really want to do ethical business or just to cover up their tracks while doing business as usual, a few factors may be responsible for this culture. One of these is a historic scandal that rocked Pfizer in 1996 in the northern part of the country and has since left the company trying to recover. After years of legal battle, it can be argued that part of the response of Western multinationals to the scandal in addition to foreign regulations governing their activities was the tightening of internal processes through rigorous standard operating procedures (SOPs). Yet the full motives and effectiveness of this practice are highly debatable.

Pfizer Kano Scandal

In 1996, following the outbreak of cerebral meningitis in Kano, a northern city in Nigeria, Pfizer reportedly moved in within a few weeks of the outbreak to administer a drug, Trovan, on infected children. Trovan was in its last stages of development, and a test on human specimens would validate its potency as a potential 'blockbuster' drug as had been predicted on Wall Street (Stephens, 2000). However, the clinical trial was soon riddled with lots of controversies including the death of many children and the deformity of several others. Arguments surrounding Pfizer's actions have generally been categorized as either a genuine move to save lives or a greedy drive to make profit, with evidence skewing more towards the latter than the former. First, Trovan had been predicted to generate $1 billion in revenue (Brichacek, 2001). Given the huge sums that go into drug development, often spanning 10 years or more, a real-time epidemic offered the perfect platform to test the drug, get final approvals for global deployment, and make predicted profits. Further investigations soon also revealed that Pfizer had falsified consent letters to carry out the trial, that they had administered lesser doses than required by law, and that the parents of the victims were not properly informed before their children were administered the unregistered drugs (Abdullahi, 2002). A parent famously retorted, "The Americans and some local doctors gave Anas this evil drug" (Murray, 2007).

Furthermore, a World Bank report in 2002 ascribed the scandal to the repressive and corrupt military regime of the era, which had weakened all institutions, including the drug regulatory agency in Nigeria, rendering it incapable of carrying out its statutory duties of protecting lives. This made it possible for Pfizer to obtain 'quick' permissions from the authorities without any delays, although it can be argued that the urgency of the matter could have contributed to this. Initial response to the epidemic by a charity medical organization in the region was administering another antibiotic, which, it was reported, had some success (Murray, 2007). But it was the allegation that Pfizer kept the children on their drugs even when improvements were not observed that further accentuated their motive in the trial. Pfizer (2007a) in response to accusations claimed Trovan reduced mortality rates from 20% to 10% and that they sought oral consents due to low literacy in the region using interpreters to communicate their intentions to parents. Pfizer also claimed to have sought appropriate consent from regulatory authorities and insisted that "Trovan helped save lives" (Pfizer, 2007b:1). Finally, Pfizer denied that Trovan was responsible for the death of the children in question but that the disease killed them, and said that they had supported the state government with 18 million naira in contributions and support towards the epidemic.

While Pfizer would not claim responsibility for the children's deaths and insisted their actions were "ethically justifiable," the company suppressed every attempt to allow the fair hearing of a lawsuit leveled against them in the US until 2008 when a $7 billion lawsuit filed by the Nigerian government led to Pfizer's indictment (Goldacre, 2013). Pfizer's actions and responses opened up several debates, but what is of more interest in this study is the real motive of the firm and whether opportunistic behaviors have been at the foundation of their success in Nigeria in the past. In retrospect, had the trial gone smoothly, the firm would still look great on paper as an ethical firm doing good business in the region, yet this one scandal brought to light the real issues. Interestingly, Pfizer also diversified all its investments in Nigeria in 1997 and reduced its activities to merely marketing and distribution in the region. The coincidence of this divestment with the Kano scandal must not be ignored, because in 1997, the scandal was about to gain global attention and as such it can be argued that the divestment was a move by Pfizer to play safe, knowing fully well the consequences of the drug trial on its reputation when it gained global attention. Yet, completely pulling out from the region was not an option, knowing fully well the potential impact of the Nigerian market on the firm's profitability. Thus, if survival in Africa included such opportunistic behaviors, the use of brand power to buy corrupt government officials amongst other unwholesome practices, it can be argued that every other firm culture in place today, as discussed earlier, may just be mere facades masking the real issues or may simply be defense mechanisms aimed at protecting the firm from any legal troubles but do not position the firm for consistent ethical behavior within the Nigerian context.

Therefore, given the capricious business environment previously described and the cultural traits, practices, and scandal explored in this section, we are able to further appreciate the nature of the complex relationships that exist between multinationals and the corrupt contexts of host countries. While there may not be a singular potent tactic able to help firms make decent profit ethically from a highly profitable market, the adoption of the dominant stringent SOP tactic still does not completely protect them from falling prey to the traps of the system, at least for firms willing to do business ethically. Yet, on another note is the reality that, contrary to the claims of several multinationals in the industry that they conduct business ethically, their acclaimed response strategies may simply be mere propaganda.

RESPONSES TO THE INSTITUTIONAL LANDSCAPE AND BROADER MORAL IMPLICATIONS

Following from the previous section, there are five major ways American firms claim to respond to the aforementioned institutional challenges in Nigeria based on their strong culture of compliance as follows:

Avoidance

Employees are instructed to select the people and places where they profitably do their business to meet their targets with little or no effort. As a result, representatives are expected to know hospitals and clinics that are loyal to their brand and will prescribe company brands with little or no persuasion. Through this they are expected to know and avoid problematic and corrupt doctors in their territories.

Firmness

Even when probed for bribery, many employees have said they have stood their grounds on the fact that they don't in any way feel the doctors are doing them a favor but vice versa. The doctors have a primary objective—to save lives and when this is achieved, it is great for their image. That objective is what the pharmaceutical companies are also out to help them achieve.

Brand Power

With patented drugs in the market, American pharmaceuticals have a strong bargaining power when they have the only drug in the market able to cure particular diseases in certain ways. With this, the doctors have no power to ask for bribes and representatives are asked to leverage this in doing business. However there is a possibility of firms leveraging this power excessively as has been experienced in South Africa, where pharmaceutical giants have been accused of suppressing bills that would grant local manufacturers the right to produce generic versions of cancer drugs, thereby making them affordable for the masses (Rutter, 2014). Similarly, in the Trovan case earlier described, Pfizer leveraged its power to gain quick access to the disease-ravaged part of a country for the clinical trial and also leveraged the same for the subsequent suppression of lawsuits brought against it. However, the critical issue is how firms choose to use their brand power in any given context.

Creativity

With lots of competing generics, employees in American MNCs are rewarded for ingenuity and innovativeness in approaching the market to do clean business. Some of the ways they have done this include developing special screening schemes in partnership with state governments after which the treatment of infected persons are paid for. Through sponsorship of conferences both local and international, and supplying medical journals to doctors and hospitals, they are essentially exploiting the gift-giving culture of the country with loyal clients with the claims of adding value to the knowledge of medical professionals.

Relationships

Medical representatives thrive a lot on long-standing relationships with medical professionals over the years such that they keep recycling business as a result. Even when such representatives change jobs to other companies, they attempt to leverage those relationships to sell their new company's products.

Thus, in adopting relational strategies, firms feel safe navigating through the difficult business terrain, yet there are some broader moral implications these strategies raise. While the primary firms' purpose of making profit in the regions is obvious, corruptive practices that are socially acceptable places companies and their employees in a precarious moral position when attempting to follow right ethical practices in Nigeria. Therefore, when companies attempt to enforce strict ethical standards, they may actually create more ethical vulnerability confusing employees about the ethics of their decision-making (Ferrell and Skinner, 1988; Weber, 1990). We explore this further in the next section.

IMPACT ON EMPLOYEE MORALITY

Organizational rules including a code of ethics are a part of the formal structure in organizations. They could help define relationships and guide activities thereby creating sets of mutual expectations as well as reducing uncertainties (Zhou, 1993). Organizational researchers have highlighted the tendency of huge multinationals to avoid and reduce uncertainty, especially those operating in heterogeneous task environments (Ghoshal and Nohria, 1989; Henisz and Delios, 2002) and environments with uncertainties (Das, 1983) by using formalized rules, as is the case in this study. They could also be used as tools in creating compliant employees enforced by rewarding obedience and punishing violations. From an ethics perspective for instance, rules could be very useful in shaping moral capacity in employees and have often been argued to grant organizations more control over the ethical behaviors of their employees (Ferrell and Skinner, 1988). Ferrell and Skinner (1988) in their study concluded that formalization explained the most variance in ethical behavior with the existence of an ethical code as the major factor explaining the variation. In affirmation, corporate policies, usually codes of ethical conduct, have also been linked to increased ethical conduct (Ferrell and Weaver, 1978; Fritzsche and Becker, 1983; Hunt, Chonko, and Wilcox, 1984). Also, Tsalikis and Fritzche (1989); Murphy, Smith, and Daley (1992) concluded in their studies that corporate ethics inhibits unethical behavior and that employees in these organizations were less aware of unethical or illegal activity in their organizations. But while this could be a positive, the fact that moral awareness is reduced is a major point of criticism, whereby employees' individual moral agency is replaced by rules thereby limiting their capacity to recognize moral issues and ability to make sound judgments. Therefore, this has often raised concerns about the presence of a code of ethics being a mere façade to mask the real ethical issues and struggles in organizations.

However, in practice, formalized rules have also been reported to activate role conflict among professionals because of the discrepancy that exists between their personal norms and the organization's (Organ and Greene, 1981). This is also known to create a moral tension between employees and their organization. Merton (1968) further explained that often times the presence of formalized rules implies the need to strictly adhere to those rules, a behavior called compliance. He then argued that the impact of compliance on employees is that following the rules becomes an end in itself and could cause them to lose focus of the bigger goals of the organization or the moral consequences of their actions especially where such rules are used by firms towards unethical ends.

Furthermore, Kohlberg's cognitive moral development theory offers key insights into the moral ramifications of the rule-based morality. According to Kohlberg's (1971) typology of cognitive moral development, rule-based morality places individuals at the pre-conventional level of moral reasoning. At this basic level of moral reasoning, morality is defined in terms of avoiding to break the rules (Colby and Kohlberg, 1971), beyond which every other concern is obliterated. Employee orientation would be on reward, punishments, and obedience only. However, Kohlberg's categorizations suggest higher levels of moral development, that is, the conventional and post-conventional stages are more adequate in resolving significant moral dilemmas (Kohlberg, 1975) than the lower pre-conventional level. Therefore, Kohlberg's theory argues that at the pre-conventional level firms with strict rules expect employees' orientation to be towards keeping set rules, a reasoning level that renders them incapable of making critical moral judgments; whereas anyone reasoning at the higher stages could, for example, recognize a moral issue and make a decision to leave a job based on the violation of some higher moral principle they hold in high regard. As such Kohlberg's theory would presume from a moral standpoint that strict rule compliance in organizations creates a false conscience and a rule- based moral code that keeps employees bound at a lower level of cognitive moral maturity. Hence, moral capacity to see moral issues and make autonomous moral judgment is significantly curtailed.

This position has been substantiated by some empirical studies. For instance, Weber (1990) in his study of moral reasoning among managers in response to three distinct moral dilemmas discovered that managers typically reasoned at the conventional level, implying that their thinking is done at the level of conformity to organization norms without consideration for broader moral implications. Weber (1990) also discovered in his study that managers who worked in large organizations reasoned at a considerably lower level than those working in small self-employed firms, thereby validating the role rules play in limiting moral capacity of employees. Also in a review of ethical decision making literature by Loe, Ferrell, and Mansfield (2000), 17 studies were found to have studied the role of code of ethics in decision-making. The Results varied from those who found a code of ethics useful to the improvement of ethical behavior (Weaver and Ferrell, 1977), to those who discovered it increased a sense of awareness and subsequent reporting of unethical incidents (Trevino and Youngblood, 1990; Valentine and Barnett, 2002), and to those who concluded it was less effective in helping ethical behaviors (Glenn and Van Loo, 1993; Bruce, 1994). However, Beneish and Chatov (1993) opined the contents of codes vary according to industries and this could explain the variations in the findings. Ultimately, the ends for which rules are created is the critical factor in determining their success in organizations.

SUMMARY AND CONCLUSION

This study has explored the difficult business terrain of Nigeria and the response of firms to the context in different forms. Whereas it was clearly established in the course of this study that the nature of business environment makes it almost impossible to do ethical business, it was also quickly established that most firms might be playing to the gallery by claiming to have the best practices of doing business in the country. Exploring this further, the Pfizer scandal shed more light into the likely unethical practices that may be happening behind the scenes within the organizations, and we argued that the prevalent firm practices might simply be clever strategies to mask the moral lapses of these firms. While there may not be clear-cut solutions to doing clean business in Africa given the difficult terrain, a few critical thoughts come to mind: Are multinational firms actually exploiting contextual weaknesses to fatten their bottom lines and if not, is it possible to do business in such an environment without getting involved in the corruption at all levels? While we may not be able to exhaustively answer these questions in this study, yet another interesting point is the thin line between the gift-giving culture in Africa and bribery. At what point can a gift be termed a bribe?

Though within the pharmaceutical industry, the ethical problem of "inducing" doctors and other potential business sources has been a bone of contention, some multinationals believe in securing their businesses first before any exchange of gifts takes place. Any form of gift-giving to doctors by the multinationals in the form of subscription to medical journals, sponsorship to international conferences, giving free drug samples, etc., can be argued already secures the goodwill of that firm with the doctors such that it takes perhaps a far greater treat from another company to convince the doctors otherwise. So prescription of drugs may no longer be based on the science of such drugs. And if financial muscle is anything to go by, multinationals stand the better chance of winning doctors with their already established brand name amongst other key factors. These are some of the grey issues that also typify the Nigerian business landscape. However as also discovered, corporations could endeavor to make raising morally responsible citizens a priority by shifting the focus of their response strategies especially using strict rules not only to cater for their profit needs but also in deliberately molding morally responsible citizens able to think independently and respond properly to moral issues. Also, barring greed, which is yet another major issue in capitalist economies, Western pharmaceuticals can and should leverage their brand power to set positive examples for how ethical business can be done in the region.

REFERENCES

Abdullahi. (2002). *Abdullahi v. Pfizer, Inc*, U.S. Dist. LEXIS 17436 at *1 (S.D.N.Y. September 17, 2002).

Africa: Nigeria. (2016, February 10). Retrieved February 12, 2016, from Central Intelligence Agency: World Fact Book website: https://www.cia.gov/library/publications/the-world-factbook/geos/ni.html

Beneish, M. D., and Chatov, R. (1993). Corporate codes of conduct: Economic determinants and legal implications for independent auditors. *Journal of Accounting and Public Policy*, 12(e.g. 2), 3–35.

Braun, V., and Clarke, V. (2006). Using thematic analysis in psychology. *Qualitative Research in Psychology*, 3(2), 77–101.

Brichacek, Andra. (2001). What price corruption? *Pharmaceutical Executive*, 21(11), 94.

Bruce, W. (1994). Ethical people are productive people. *Public Productivity and Management Review*, 17(3), 241–252.

CIA. (2013). *Central Intelligence Agency*. Retrieved March 22, 2015, fromhttps://www.cia.gov/redirects/ciaredirect.html

Das, S. P. (1983). Multinational enterprise under uncertainty. *Canadian Journal of Economics,* 16(3), 420–428.

Ferrell, O. C. and Weaver, K. M. (1978), Ethical Beliefs of Marketing Managers, *Journal of Marketing*, 42(3), 69–73.

Ferrell, O. C., and Skinner, S. J. (1988). Ethical behavior and bureaucratic structure in marketing research organizations. *Journal of Marketing Research, 25*(1), 103–109.

Fritzsche, D.J. and Becker, H., 1983, Ethical behavior of marketing managers, *Journal of Business Ethics*. Vol. 2, pp. 291–299

Garuba, H. A., Kohler, J. C., and Huisman, A. M. (2009). Transparency in Nigeria's public pharmaceutical sector: Perceptions from policy makers. *Global Health*, 5, 14.

Ghoshal, S., and Nohria, N. (1989). Internal differentiation within multinational corporations. *Strategic Management Journal*, 10(4), 323–337.

Glenn, Jr, J. R., and Van Loo, M. F. (1993). Business students' and practitioners' ethical decisions over time. *Journal of Business Ethics*, 12(11), 835–847.

Goldacre, B. (2013). *Bad pharma: How drug companies mislead doctors and harm patients*. United States: Faber and Faber.

Hammersley, M., and Atkinson, P. (1995). "Research design." In *Ethnography: Principles in Practice*, 2nd ed. London: Routledge, pp. 23–53.

Henisz, W. J., and Delios, A. (2002). Learning about the institutional environment. *Advances in strategic management, 19*, 339–372.

Hunt, S.D., Chonko, L.B., and Wilcox, J.B. (1984), Ethical Probles of Marketing Researchers, *Journal of Marketing Research, 21*(3), pp. 309–324

IMS Health. (2012). *Africa: A ripe opportunity. Understanding the pharmaceutical market opportunity and developing sustainable business models in Africa*. Retrieved May 14, 2015, from http://www.imshealth.com/deployedfiles/imshealth/ Global/Content/Home%20Page%20Content/High-Growth%20Markets/ Content%20Modules/IMS-Africa_WP_101212final.pdf

Kohlberg, L. (1971). Stages of moral development. *Moral Education*, 23–92.

Kohlberg, L. (1975). The cognitive-developmental approach to moral education. *Phi Delta Kappan, 56*(10), 670–677.

Livestock Feed. (2014). *Our history*. Retrieved February 12, 2015, from http:// www.livestockfeedsplc.com/aboutus.php

Loe, T. W., Ferrell, L., and Mansfield, P. (2000). A review of empirical studies assessing ethical decision making in business. *Journal of Business Ethics, 25*(3), 185–204.

Merton, R. K. (Ed.). (1968). *Social theory and social structure*. New York: Simon and Schuster.

Murphy, P. R., Smith, J. E., and Daley, J. M. (1992). Executive attitudes, organizational size and ethical issues: Perspectives on a service industry. *Journal of Business Ethics, 11*(1), 11–19.

Murray, S. (2007). *Anger at deadly Nigerian drug trials*. Retrieved March 1, 2015, from http://news.bbc.co.uk/1/hi/world/africa/6768799.stm

National Agency for Food and Drug, Administration and Control (NAFDAC). (2015). *About us*. Retrieved from March 1, 2015, http://www.nafdac.gov.ng/ about-nafdac/nafdac-act

Organ, D. W., and Greene, C. N. (1981). The effects of formalization on professional involvement: A compensatory process approach. *Administrative Science Quarterly, 26*, 237–252.

Pfizer. (2007a). *Trovan* [Fact sheet]. Retrieved March 1, 2015, from http://www. pfizer.com/files/news/trovan_fact_sheet_final.pdf

Pfizer. (2007b). *Trovan statement*. Retrieved March 1, 2015, from http://www.pfizer. com/files/news/trovan_statement_may292007.pdf

Robinson, J. (2015). *The 20 fastest-growing economies this year*. Retrieved March 25, 2015, from http://www.bloomberg.com/news/articles/2015–02–25/ the-20-fastest-growing-economies-this-year

Rutter, Lotti. (2014). *MSD and others must be held accountable for Pharmagate plot*. Retrieved February 12, 2015, from http://www.tac.org.za/news/ msd-and-others-must-be-held-accountable-pharmagate-plot

Stephens, J. (2000). The Body hunters: As Drug Testing Spreads, Profits and Lives Hang in Balance. *The Washington Post,* December 17, A1.

Trevino, L. K., and Youngblood, S. A. (1990). Bad apples in bad barrels: A causal analysis of ethical decision-making behavior. *Journal of Applied psychology, 75*(4), 378.

Tsalikis, J., and Fritzsche, D. J. (1989). Business ethics: A literature review with a focus on marketing ethics. *Journal of Business Ethics, 8*(9), 695–743.

United National International Development Organisation. (UNIDO). (2012). *Pharmaceutical sector profile: Nigeria*. Retrieved May 14, 2015, from https:// www.unido.org/fileadmin/user_media/Services/PSD/BEP/Nigeria_Pharma%20 Sector%20Profile_032011_Ebook.pdf

Valentine, S., and Barnett, T. (2002). Ethics codes and sales professionals' perceptions of their organizations' ethical values. *Journal of Business Ethics*, 40(3), 191–200.

Weaver, K. M., and Ferrell, O. C. (1977). The impact of corpo-rate policy on reported ethical beliefs and behavior of marketing practitioners. *American Marketing Association Proceedings, 41*, 477–481.

Weber, J. (1990). Measuring the impact of teaching ethics to future managers: A review, assessment, and recommendations. *Journal of Business Ethics*, 9(3), 183–190.

Zhou, X. (1993). The dynamics of organizational rules. *American Journal of Sociology*, 98, 1134–1166.

Part III

Theorizing African Management and Organization

9 Theory Construction to Serve African Management and Organizational Practices

Hamid H. Kazeroony

INTRODUCTION

Explaining ideas scientifically with rigor, creating a body of knowledge, is predicated on sound theoretical construct (Reynolds, 1986). Theoretical construct can be rooted in conceptualization of an idea inductively, generalizing a 'set of laws' into one coherent reasoning and explanation or through deductive reasoning, connecting a set of definitions, axioms, and mathematical data in creating an 'axiomatic theory' (Reynolds, 1986).

Before proceeding to explain the African theoretical construct for management and organization, the current state of thinking, the framework within which a scientist approaches theory building must be briefly explained and the point of departure between Western and the African points of view must be addressed. Within this framework, first, briefly, the purpose of management theoretical construct, its reality, and its evolution to its current stage will be addressed. Second, an overview of the existing work on the African diaspora will be provided to acknowledge the work others have already completed as well as presenting other possible pathways to constructing theories in addressing the management and organizational issues in Africa. Third, nuances of various approaches to theory construction in creating new models and theories to serve management and organizational studies for application to the African context will be discussed.

CURRENT THINKING AND FRAMEWORK

Management and organizational theory construction should investigate and explain (a) how it relates, differs, or is similar to others' contribution, (b) how it contributes to the field, (c) how it provides a different way of investigating, collecting data, and informing its constituents of its findings, (d) how is interpreted, (e) what are its practical applications, and (f) how it connects management and organization to society at large, within which they operate (Easterby-Smith, Thorpe, and Lowe, 2002). To start one's investigation, *reality* should be contextualized and have relevance to the researched topic.

Essentially, reality is a social construction and it is only within that context that one can start unfolding the meaning of any theoretical construct. Therefore, the researcher's cognition, the human element of the research, the interaction of the researcher and her/his environment require a mechanism to objectively assess the validity and reliability of a new theoretical construct as well as giving credence to its relevance to management and organization in the context of human element (Anderson, 1990). Current reality presents a post-industrial view of management and organization.

As Hage and Powers (1992) explained, post-Weber's world reflects new realities where mental activities, informational gathering, fluid roles, flexible time and location of positions, ownership of production and performance by employees, and service orientation of jobs have replaced the highly bureaucratic nature of organizations and the role of managers in controlling activities. In addition, irrespective of an inductive or a deductive approach, an author relates thinking to writing, giving existential credence to his/her own cognitive process, creating new theory or testing a theory's validity and applicability (Creswell, 1994). An author's cognitive process can be based on his/her epistemological construction of reality (Easterby-Smith, Thorpe, and Lowe, 2002).

Further review of the research reveals the need for examination of epistemology, which includes, conversation, narration, language, and its rhetorical and oratory forms (Kvale, 1996; Shank, 2002). Language contains symbolism which can lead to ambiguities based on the interpretation of the receiver; hence, creating another layer of challenge when communicating research (Smith, 1989; Tyson, 1999). This perspective of epistemology can pose severe limitations on quantitative research when it attempts to drive explanations from the statements where the underlying perceptions of the respondent of whom the questions are asked and of the researcher asking the questions are fundamentally different (Reynolds, 1986). Lincoln and Guba (1985) divided forms of reality into four categories: *objective reality* where physical and temporal attributes create tangible existence, perceived reality where its existence depends on one's vantage point, *constructed reality* where one can assemble number of possibilities as to what exists, and *created reality*, which is simply manifested at the point of perception when it comes into existence based on the immediate realization by a perceiver of it. The challenge of *what is* and *what may be* and their distinctions, resulting in possible eschewed results, can originate even in quantitative approaches where there might be a titanic gap between the inquirer's use of language in phrasing the questions and the respondent's understanding the questions when answering them (Lincoln and Guba, 1985). Therefore, the research leads us to re-examine the role of epistemology and reality from the perception of the researcher and the researched. Before the researcher can explore any new theories or validate existing theories in management and organization, the changes in these fields should be reviewed.

The transformation of managers' roles and organizational structure, as explained by Hage and Powers (1992), demonstrates crossing into the post-industrial era. In addition, the nature of changes in the roles of the individual and individuals' interactions within an organization has led to a new form of alienation, "most emphatically through deconstruction" where the tradition of the past, language, meaning, and social contexts are questioned and re-examined (Smith, 1989). Therefore, crossing postmodernism has offered us three tangible social and economic characteristics of global society: 'information processing', 'flexible specialization', and 'informed cooperation' (Borgmann, 1992). The current state, beyond postmodernism, as described (Smith, 1989; Borgmann, 1992) provides the context within which a researcher begins her/his examination of management and organization in creating new theories. Operating within this reality, a small number of writings have emerged re-examining the African context of theory construction and utilization. The changes in management and organizational fields, although global in nature, can have characteristics attributed to specific geographical areas such as Africa based on history, symbolism, cultural factors and artifacts, and ideological lens conducting the research.

Tyson (1999), detailing the historical, symbolism, cultural factors, and ideological lens, explained that in contrast to many claims, we live in a *neo* rather than *post*colonial era where colonialism is manifested by economic domination subjecting the developing countries such as the ones in Africa to cultural imperialism, which can be observed through symbolism. Tyson (1999) defined symbolism as identification and interpretation of text and artifacts. Finally, Tyson (1999) adds that beyond any lens and orientation, producing knowledge involves psychological and community-based interpretation of researcher-researched perception of what is asked and what is being stated.

THE AFRICAN DIASPORA'S WORK

As African scholars rightly claim, precolonial Africa was not knowledge-deficient, yet the market-based colonial system interrupted its trajectory, leading to postcolonial imbalances and complexities. Therefore, African scholars must deconstruct the colonial perspective, overcome postcolonial paradoxes, and build capacities to produce new knowledge from indigenous African perspectives (Nkomo, Zoogah, and Acquaah, 2015).

In response to calls such as those by Nkomo, Zoogah, and Acquaah (2015) and Bagire and Namada (2015), colleagues like Zoogah (2014) began compiling methods that could be applied specifically to African management and organizational studies. Zoogah (2014) advanced a number of key points in designing and conceptualizing the methods necessary for management and organizational strategy, studies among which are:

- Content analysis;
- Experimental analysis in strategic human resource management;

- Examining structured behavior where a set of selected behavior will be analyzed;
- Examining events that can explain the results produced by an organization;
- Conducting dynamic analysis where systematic changes between variables take place;
- Hermeneutics to unfold implicit meanings;
- Action research to provide context for the geographical and environmental factors unique to a particular location;
- Bibliographic examination of topic (i.e., socioeconomics, politics, etc.) is completed to seek out the origin, evolution, and current state of a phenomenon; and
- The truncated Levy Flight (TLF) model when examining organizational equity worth.

Zoogah (2014) provided a comprehensive attempt at creating a conceptual design for conducting research in the African context, yet his edited work presented unique challenges. For example, when reviewing the wider management and organizational content beyond strategy, strictly African-written content for analysis is scant; and hence, any content analysis would lead to inadequate theory construction. At the other extreme, following a mathematical formula such as TLF, due to lack of inadequate and inaccurate data leading to distortions, may not be as useful in creating a new theoretical construct. The view does not dismiss or diminish the value of the Zoogah's (2014) work but rather points out how to build in creating a new African theoretical constructs. Perhaps, to help or entice other colleagues to start examining the topic more closely, the nuances of various theoretical constructs and their possible relevance to African management and organizational context should be briefly examined.

THEORETICAL NUANCES

Management and organizational theories possess two basic attributes: (a) they are socially relevant and (b) they are applied (Bickman and Rog, 1998). Within this framework, in qualitative approaches, when creating new theoretical constructs, conceptual work, or re-examining any phenomenon, sociopolitical, economic, and cultural factors and artifacts as well as other factors should be reviewed for possible explanations as to why the new way of unfolding the examined reality makes sense and how it can be applied (Maxwell, 1998; Foot, 2014; Smith, 2005). In quantitative approaches, when attempting to understand patterns and behavior, eligibility of appropriate respondents within a given sample, distortions in respondents' answers based on their understanding of the questions' context, discerning what constitute a 'normal' subject, and level of societal maturity in relation to the topic and behavior discussed should be carefully examined (Lipsey, 1998).

Corley and Gioia (2011) argued that we should reframe our approach when theorizing in reorienting ourselves towards application of what we construct and adopt as *prescience orientation*, described as "the process of discerning or anticipating what we need to know and, equally important, of influencing the intellectual framing and dialogue about what we need to know" (p. 18).

Theoretical nuances, specific to a domain may allow for use or use with some modification of existing theoretical Western approaches as Zoogah (2014) discussed in the strategic management domain. In other domains, such as operation management, due to their high level of globalized and technical character, dealing with issues such as throughput, inventory, and operating expenses, theory is contracted with the end application in mind to create certain mental models for achieving particular results (Naor, Bernardes, and Coman, 2013).

Both qualitative and quantitative methods can present unique challenges in ensuring the validity and reliability of data and findings. Geography, political turmoil in many parts of Africa (e.g., Libya and Sudan), lack of central power, and suspicion of any data gathering can evoke the basic objections as discussed by Maxwell (1998) and Lipsey (1998). In light of the current thinking, as we discussed at the beginning, disconnection between academia and practitioners, insufficient attention to social justice of or lack of it, conducting research in the context of native views, the role of ethics and politics, and institutional capabilities and resources to carry out research (Bishop, 2005; Christians, 2005; Fine and Weis, 2005; Greenwood and Levin, 2005; Lincoln, 2005) lead us to provide an alternative pathway. Creating new pathways most often leads us to move from one paradigm to another (Kuhn, 1996). Therefore, the following discussions are simply intended to encourage further discussions among colleagues, particularly among dissertation mentors in Africa and researchers addressing African management and organization.

MOVING TO A NEW THEORY CONSTRUCTION PARADIGM

No longer can African management and organizational theories simply be constructed based on its postcolonial approach. As already discussed, social realities and globalization in the postmodern, post-industrial, deconstructionist era pose unique challenges in both qualitative and quantitative methods. Moving away from the existing paradigm to a new one requires concentrated effort and collaboration among colleagues to provide new ways of examining the same issues. Here, we will simply suggest the pathway for constructing the way, but we encourage colleagues to review the process, offer constructive critique, and help move the African diaspora towards the new paradigm. Therefore, building on the research in the first part of this chapter, we now turn our attention to building new approaches. In outlining new approaches, we will thematically address the qualitative and quantitative pathways to new African management and organizational theory construction paradigms by examining the use of various theoretical lenses.

POST-DECONSTRUCTIONISM VIEWS AND BEYOND

Irrespective of research method, African studies examining management and organization domains necessitate a worldview (a lens for examining and explaining *what it is*). Due to changes in management practices compelled by socioeconomic and political pressures after the end of colonial rules and changes in culture and technology impacting management and organization as external factors within the African system, theory construction in the African management and organizational context should be subject to examination of changes in the continental nature of values, historical determinism, and mode of production that impact the researchers' findings (Kazeroony, 2005). Each of the three dimensions of change impacts the research method used to construct new theories or validate the existing ones.

Morality, virtue, values, and ethics, collectively defined as 'values' are fluid and interrelated to the changing social norm within a given environment (Kazeroony, 2005). Therefore, when examining African management and organization, the researcher should be mindful of values in the African context that may be prevalent today rather than the assumptions made in the Western literature about Africa. Congruent with this reasoning, "historical determinism emanates in a form of knowledge of itself in itself where the individuals' judgment and the concept finds unity that explains the phenomena of reality" (Kazeroony, 2005, p. 45). Historical determinism paves a unique dialectical pathway for African management and organizational theory based on its own perpetual dialectical processes, which is distinct from Western-dominated management and organizational literature. The third dimension of change, the mode of production, manifested by the relationship between the means of production and consumption creates a symbiotic relationship that impacts management and organization in its particular environment (Kazeroony, 2005). Therefore, values, historical determinism, and mode of production provide a distinct set of circumstances unique to Africa, requiring its own theoretical approach.

When embarking on research in African management or organization, in addition to the contextual dimensions, the researcher must be mindful of the lenses that may muddy the nature of research and has an extensive range of *para-reality*. There are numerous such constructions from "*de*" to "*post*" concepts, each offering a new way of thinking. For example, postmodernism is a worldview built on perception of pieces of observation rather than logical presentation of whole (Linstead, 2004). Postmodernism is an intellectual curiosity bending time-space continuum to interpret reality *as could be presented* rather than *what we are told*, giving rise to polemics arguing its nature and validity (Tsoukas, 1992; Hassard, 2009; Calas and Smricich, 2009; Child and McGrath, 2009; Boje, Oswick and Ford, 2004; Fineman, 2009; Sherer and Plazzo, 2009) while attempting to address the digital age organizations (Borgman, 1992). Other lenses such as post-industrial, postcolonial, deconstructionist, etc., pose similar challenges and may lead one to abstractions without any purposeful impact on unfolding new relevant knowledge that can be practiced and applied to management and organization in the African context. However, the point should not be perceived as a dismissal of the entire body of knowledge concerning various lenses. There are ample opportunities for a researcher to construct new theories applicable to African management and organization based on the existing work explaining the range of "*de*" to "*post*" concepts.

A number of perspectives can be suggested for a researcher dissecting the range of "*de*" to "*post*" concepts to move towards a new lens required for examination of the management and organization domains. For example, a researcher may conceivably use precolonial African history to determine the way people may think when conducting research in a given country in Africa rather than the Marxist notion of production mode, which simply explains the capitalist impact (Reid, 2011). This view may help elucidate the current events for the researcher in terms of African issues rather than the immediate past interferences by colonialists whose influence in African management and organization has become irrelevant. Yet, the researcher must be mindful of the overarching landscape where the research is taking place and how different approaches may be more feasible than others.

Taking a broad perspective where the researcher works, Neumann (2010) suggested that when examining political ecology, one can begin theorizing about a particular geographical location by

> (1) work employing theorizations of the social production of space and the co-constitution of nature, space, and society; (2) engagements with the political economy of natural resources literature, especially resource conflict; and (3) work linking historical materialist-oriented 'new' regional geography with discourse theory (p. 368).

In addition, the culture of the researcher and the researched, adding complexity to the objectivity of research, are also produced by symbolic elements as results of a range of social processes such as dispensation of justice, legal structure, regulations, nature of work, etc. (Peterson and Anand, 2004). These processes also impact production and organizational processes and interactions created by the nature of production. Moving from the landscape within which a researcher operates to specific approach that a researcher may pursue to conduct an inquiry, some specific suggestions can be made.

When conducting research in African management and organization, some approaches may yield more meaningful results than others. As suggested by some African scholars, one must be careful in the use of networking theories and rely more on ethnographical approaches as would an anthropologist to better unfold the meaning of relationships prompted by management or as a result of organizational processes (de Bruijn and van Dijk, 2012). Within such approach, a researcher can use in-depth interpretive interviewing to grasp the motivation for action and the results of processes on individual interactions and their relationship in organizational context (Pugh, 2013).

Perhaps, as suggested by sociologists in their field (Camic and Gross, 1998) to organize theoretical approaches, the Africa Academy of Management should become a singular body working with various academic affiliations around Africa and beyond to organize theoretical framework for research; and hence, become an enabler for comprehensive undertakings to better direct African management and organizational research.

QUALITATIVE AND QUANTITATIVE RESEARCH PATHWAYS FOR AFRICA: PARTING THOUGHTS

Research method design by its innate nature is constructed to discriminate data collection, interpretation, and application while objectively stating its components for the data context, collection, and analysis (Maxwell, 1996; Locke, Silverman, and Spirduso, 1998). The purpose of such discrimination would be to provide clarity while avoiding subjectivity. Therefore, either qualitative or quantitative methods may be considered for any research in African management and organizational studies. However, a few limitations should be considered when using each method.

Qualitative research methods allow decision makers to objectively understand a subject, unfold everyday experiences' meanings to arrive at an objective understating of social phenomena in their natural setting (Borland, 2001; Poggenpoel, Myburgh, and Van Der Linde, 2001; Meadows, 2003). Qualitative method helps understand the individuals' philosophical underpinnings while maintaining an evaluative position (Drisko, 1997; Maggs-Rapport, 2001). The researcher's lens (whether postcolonial or any other perspective), the instrument used in revealing new meaning in the African management and organizational context, can pose limitations on the nature of work's validity and reliability. Therefore, the researcher who uses qualitative method when attempting to construct new meaning/theory, should be mindful of a few challenges. When conducting qualitative research in African management and organization, consistency, communicability, interpretation of meanings, trustworthiness of the researched in respect to shared meanings generated should be carefully scrutinized (Creswell, 1994; Rubin and Rubin, 1995) because this method does not allow for control of the outcome, yet the researcher must provide a succinct description of the results and possible alternatives (Maxwell, 1996) in uncovering the meaning of experiences (Moustakas, 1994), hence providing validly for the study. Finally, instrumentation and the motivation of the researched for providing a particular response within peculiarities of a social setting, based on his/her sociopolitical lens can create extreme abnormalities in proving a study's reliability (Lincoln and Guba, 1985; Bickman and Rog, 1998).

Quantitative method isolates and examines individual variables in a controlled environment for objectively measuring a controlled element of human behavior (Poggenpoel, Myburgh, and Van Der Linde, 2001; Meadows, 2003). The challenge in conducting quantitative research for examination of management and organization domains in the African context is multifold: (a) as stated earlier, the language, metaphors, and artifacts can skew the hypothesis statement, the questions asked, and interpretation of data due to language ambiguities, (b) Africa has been subject to cultural fluidity due to rapid decolonization combined with drastic technological changes inconsistent with gradual change, creating an inconsistent disparity between culture and technology, making a data analysis framework contextually challenging, (c) and individuals as researchers and the researched may have different understandings of the same question as a research is conducted, based on their sociopolitical lens, variations in understanding of the same words due to unparalleled cultural developments even within the same community based on outside interference, technologically or otherwise.

When theorizing or testing a theory to expand the African management and organization domains, the researcher must carefully and mindfully examine the relevance and actionability of the results (Pearce and Huang, 2012) to serve African management and organization while clearly delineating the common understanding and interpretation of each step by both the researcher and the researched, overcoming the differences in lenses, perspectives, linguistic, cultural, and other factors to arrive at a shared meaning.

REFERENCES

Anderson, W. T. (1990). *Reality isn't what it used to be: Theatrical politics, ready-to-wear religion, global myths*. United States: HarperCollins (PA).

Bagire, V., and Namada, J. (2015). Management theory, research, and practice for sustainable development in Africa: A commentary from a practitioner's perspective. *Africa Journal of Management, 1*(1), 99–108.

Bickman, L., and Rog, D. J. (1998). *Handbook of applied social research methods*. Thousand Oaks, CA: Sage.

Bishop, R. (2005). *The SAGE handbook of qualitative research* (Denzin, N. K., and Lincoln, Y. S. Ed.). (3rd ed.). Thousand Oaks, CA: Sage.

Boje, D., Oswick, C., and Ford, J. (2004). Language and organization: The doing of discourse. *Academy of Management Review, 29*(4), 571–577.

Borgmann, A. (1992). *Crossing the postmodern divide.* Chicago: University of Chicago Press.

Borland, K. W., Jr. (2001). Qualitative and quantitative research: A complimentary balance. *New Directions for Institutional Research, 112,* 5–14.

Calas, M., and Smricich, L. (2009). Past modernism? Reflections and tentative directions. *Academy of Management Review, 24*(4), 649–671.

Camic, C., and Gross, N. (1998). Contemporary Developments in Sociological Theory: Current Projects and Conditions of Possibility. *Annual Review of Sociology, 24,* 453–476. Retrieved from http://search.proquest.com/docview/199621543?accountid=35812.

Child, J., and McGrath, R. (2009). Organizations unfettered: Organizational form in an information-intensive economy. *Academy of Management, 44*(6), 1135–1148. Retrieved from AOM Archive Database

Christians, C. G. (2005). *The SAGE handbook of qualitative research* (Denzin, N. K., and Lincoln, Y. S. Ed.). (3rd ed.). Thousand Oaks, CA: Sage.

Corley, K. G., and Gioia, D. A. (2011). Building theory about theory building: What constitutes a theoretical contribution? *Academy of Management Review, 36*(1), 12–32. doi:10.5465/AMR.2011.55662499

Creswell, J. W. (1994). *Research design: Qualitative and quantitative approaches.* Thousand Oaks, CA: Sage.

de Bruijn, M., and van Dijk, R. (2012). Connecting and change in African societies: Examples of "ethnographies of linking" in anthropology1. *Anthropologica, 54*(1), 45–59. Retrieved from http://search.proquest.com/docview/1022053569?accountid=35812

Denzin, N. K., and Lincoln, Y. S. (2005). *The SAGE handbook of qualitative research* (3rd ed.). Thousand Oaks, CA: Sage.

Drisko, J. W. (1997). Strengthening qualitative studies and reports: Standards to promote academic integrity. *Journal of Social Work Education, 33*(1), 185–198.

Easterby-Smith, M., Thorpe, R., and Lowe, A. (2002). *Management research: An introduction* (2nd ed.). London: SAGE.

Fine, M., and Weis, L. (2005). *The SAGE handbook of qualitative research* (Denzin, N. K., and Lincoln, Y. S. Ed.). (3rd ed.). Thousand Oaks, CA: Sage.

Fineman, S. (2009). Being Positive: Concerns and Counterpoints. *Academy of Management Review, 31*(2), 270–291.

Foot, K. A. (2014). Cultural-Historical Activity Theory: Exploring a Theory to Inform Practice and Research. *Journal of Human Behavior in the Social Environment, 24*(3), 329–347. doi:10.1080/10911359.2013.831011

Greenwood, D. J., and Levin, M. (2005). *The SAGE handbook of qualitative research* (Denzin, N. K., and Lincoln, Y. S. Ed.). (3rd ed.). Thousand Oaks, CA: Sage.

Hage, J., and Powers, C. H. (1992). *Post-industrial lives: Roles and relationship in the 21st century.* Newbury Park: Sage.

Hassard, J. (2009). Postmodern Organizational Analysis: Toward A Conceptual Framework. *Journal of Management Studies, 31*(3), 303–324.

Kazeroony, H. H. (2005). *Leaders' perception of organizational change* [dissertation]. ProQuest Dissertations Publishing.

Kuhn, T. S. (1996). *The structure of scientific revolution* (3rd ed.). Chicago: University of Chicago Press.

Kvale, S. (1996). *Interviews: An introduction to qualitative research interviewing.* Thousand Oaks, CA: Sage.

Lincoln, Y. S. (2005). *The SAGE handbook of qualitative research* (Denzin, N. K., and Lincoln, Y. S. Ed.). (3rd ed.). Thousand Oaks, CA: Sage.

Lincoln, Y. S., and Guba, E. G. (1985). *Naturalistic inquiry*. Beverly Hills, CA: Sage.

Linstead, S. (2004). *Organization theory and postmodern thought*. London: SAGE.

Lipsey, M. W. (1998). *Handbook of applied social research methods* (Bickman L., & Rog, D. J. Eds.). Thousand Oaks, CA: Sage.

Locke, L. F., Silverman, S. J., and Spirduso, W. W. (1998). *Reading and understanding research*. Thousand Oaks, CA: Sage.

Maggs-Rapport, F. (2001). Best research practice: In pursuit of methodological rigor. *Journal of Advanced Nursing, 35*(3), 373–384.

Maxwell, J. A. (1996). *Qualitative research design: An interactive approach*. Thousand Oaks, CA: Sage.

Maxwell, J. A. (1998). *Handbook of applied social research methods* (Bickman, L., and Rog, D. J. Eds.). Thousand Oaks, CA: Sage.

Meadows, K. A. (2003). So you want to do research?: An introduction to quantitative methods. *British Journal of Community Nursing, 8*(11), 1249–1274.

Moustakas, C. E. (1994). *Phenomenological research methods*. Thousand Oaks, CA: Sage.

Naor, M., Bernardes, E., and Coman, A. (2013). Theory of Constraints: Is it a Theory and a Good One? *International Journal of Production Research, 51*(2), 542–554. doi:10.1080/00207543.2011.654137

Neumann, R. P. (2010). Political Ecology II: Theorizing Region. *Progress in Human Geography, 34*(3), 368–374. doi:http://dx.doi.org/10.1177/0309132509343045

Nkomo, S. M., Zoogah, D., and Acquaah, M. (2015). Why Africa journal of management and why now? *Africa Journal of Management, 1*(1), 4–26.

Pearce, J. L., and Huang, L. (June 2012). The decreasing value of our research to management education. *Academy of Management Learning and Education, 11*(2), 247–262. doi:10.5465/amle.2011.0554

Peterson, R. A., and Anand, N. (2004). The Production of Culture Perspective. *Annual Review of Sociology, 30*, 311–334. Retrieved from http://search.proquest.com/docview/199610098?accountid=35812

Poggenpoel, M., Myburgh, C. P. H., and Van Der Linde, C. (2001). Qualitative Research Strategies as Prerequisite for Quantitative Strategies. *Education, 122*(2), 208–414.

Pugh, A. J. (2013). What good are interviews for thinking about culture? Demystifying interpretive analysis. *American Journal of Cultural Sociology, 1*(1), 42–68. doi:http://dx.doi.org/10.1057/ajcs.2012.4

Reid, R. (2011). Past and presentism: The 'Precolonial' and the foreshortening of African history. *Journal of African History, 52*(2), 135–155. doi:http://dx.doi.org/10.1017/S0021853711000223

Reynolds, P. D. (1986). *A primer in theory construction*. New York: Macmillan.

Rubin, H. J., and Rubin, I. (1995). *Qualitative interviewing: The art of hearing data*. Thousand Oaks: Sage.

Shank, G. D. (2002). *Qualitative research: A personal skills approach*. Upper Saddle River, NJ: Prentice Hall.

Sherer, A., and Plazzo, G. (2009). Towards a political conception of corporate responsibility: Business and society seen from a Habermasian perspective. *Academy of Management Review, 32*(4), 1096–1120.

Smith, H. (1989). *Beyond the post-modern mind* (2nd ed.). Wheaton, IL: Theosophical Publication House.

Smith, L. T. (2005). *The SAGE handbook of qualitative research* (Denzin, N. K., and Lincoln, Y. S. Ed.). (3rd ed.). Thousand Oaks, CA: Sage.

Tsoukas, H. (1992). Postmodernism, reflexive, rationalism and organizational studies: A reply to Martin Parker. *Organizational Studies, 13*(4), 643.

Tyson, L. (1999). *Critical theory today: A user-friendly guide*. New York: Garland.

Zoogah, D. B. (2014). *Advancing research methodology in the African context: Techniques, methods, and designs*. Bingley, UK: Emerald Group Publishing.

10 Alternative Approaches to Management Research in Africa
Hermeneutics, Graphic Scales, and Applied Interventions

Bill Buenar Puplampu

INTRODUCTION

Africa is a continent with many nuances, challenges, opportunities, diversities, histories, and cultures. It has over a billion people, covers about 14% of the earth's available land surface, has over 50 different independent nations, four main regions (North, South, East, West)—each with peculiar peoples and histories—and over 1,000 known large language groupings. Africa has a history of major kingdoms with relics, values, cultural artifacts, symbols, and realities that still dominate many African peoples through the traditional chieftaincy system. No other continent has suffered such a sustained period of pillage and emaciation as Africa through some 300 years of slavery perpetuated by Europe and perhaps 1,000 years of slavery through the Sahara and East African routes (Arnold, 2006; Reader, 1998). It is perhaps the only continent where for much of the modern era its economy has been dominated by business and political interests that are foreign to its people. In recent times, scholars are increasingly waking up to the reality that Africa is insufficiently researched and poorly understood (Kamoche, 2011). What is interesting though is that despite the recognition, scholars are as yet to tackle the equally difficult problem of the lens through which we frame the difficult research agendas and the methods with which we operationalize and carry out research in Africa. Without compromising or taking away from the established principle of rigor—that the research questions and the theory behind said questions must direct researchers' design and methods—we argue in this paper that the sheer range of issues, nuances, and diversities call for out-of-the-box approaches to research. We argue that the dominant positivist traditions, valuable as they are, must not necessarily be the starting point of our research; neither must they necessarily constrain our judgment as to what is acceptable. We argue that researchers interested in Africa must show methodological reflexivity (Johnson and Cassell, 2001) and a willingness to challenge the status quo. To this end, this paper suggests four research approaches that scholars may consider as viable tools for researching management and organizations in Africa.

In offering these approaches, a dominant ethic is the work of Boyer (1990). Boyer sets out the scholarship of engagement, composed of four types of scholarship, which he suggests should define and redefine the scholarly enterprise. These four are: the scholarship of discovery, teaching, integration, and application. The pursuit of these types of scholarship invariably requires the academic to examine the pillars of the knowledge generation and application enterprise. The principal question of such examination is perhaps: How can my theory, research, and scholarship assist in the resolution of present and pressing social, community, and societal problems? To quote Boyer (1996):

> Many years ago Oscar Handlin put the challenge this way: 'A troubled universe can no longer afford the luxury of pursuits confined to an ivory tower . . . scholarship has to prove its worth, not on its own terms but my service to the nation and the world'. This in the end is what the scholarship of engagement is all about" (p. 20).

We argue that the resolution to this conundrum has to involve rethinking the means and methods by which we mine, analyze and synthesize data, and the modes and vehicles through which we enable our results to affect practice. In pursuance of such rethinking, this paper discusses three approaches to research that facilitate closer attention to the reflective scholarship that Boyer espouses. These three are: the use of interventionist research, which involves significant attention to application; the use of the hermeneutic principle, which involves clearer statement of what one's own theoretical or philosophical position is testing against successive iterations of data collection till data stabilization is achieved; and the use of single graphic scales; which involves capturing an issue in a pictorial form thus allowing respondents greater scope for their own subjective interpretation of phenomena. This paper suggests that greater and more regular use should be made of these methods as they have potential for assisting scholars to conduct relevant, locally grounded, context-rich research that is also internationally connected.

This chapter proceeds by setting out each of the research approaches. In each case, the approach is described, its challenges explored, and the possible advantages considered. The first approach to be examined is Interventionist Research.

WHAT IS AND WHY INTERVENTIONIST RESEARCH?

Intervention Research has been characterized as research that is not unobtrusive (Jonsson and Lukka, 2005) because the researcher deliberately sets out to achieve certain impacts. While seeking direct impact in organizations and communities/societies, the researcher also expects that the knowledge and understanding gained from the research would feed back into theory building and offer empirical tests of models, concepts, hypotheses, and propositions. In recent times, many scholars active in various fields of management as well as the social and human sciences that deal with work and organizational issues have pointed out that there seems to be a schism between research and practice. Researchers seem to be engaged in esoteric preoccupations with outputs that appear increasingly irrelevant to practice. Management practitioners on the other hand appear to carry on without recourse to the body of knowledge generated by painstaking research. Anderson, Herriot, and Hodgkinson (2001) in a paper that examined the practitioner-researcher divide in I/O (Industrial/Organizational) Psychology describe the pressures in the field that are pushing researchers towards what they describe as 'puerile science': a form of scientific endeavor that is low in practical relevance and low in method and theoretical rigor. Similar arguments are advanced by Jukkula, Lyly- Yrjänäinen, and Suomala (2006) and Jonsson and Lukka (2005), who write from the perspective of management accounting. They also suggest that increasingly scholars are becoming unsettled by the apparent failure of management accounting research to address 'real'-world problems.

All these lead to the simple argument that management researchers should endeavor to reconstruct their dominant ethos and perhaps abandon the artificial dichotomy between the so-called 'Mode 1' (pure science) and 'Mode 2' (problem-solving science) approaches (Anderson et al, 2001, referring to Gibbons et al, 1994 and Tranfield and Starkey, 1998).

In the African setting, Puplampu (2009) has argued that academics and scholars have a duty towards their communities and societies to ensure that their concepts, theories, models, and research do solve problems, rather than *(simply or only)* earn the researcher accolades in obscure scientific meetings/outlets with little applicability to the locale. Africa has many problems. These are manifest in organizations, in management, in politics, in food security, etc. It seems reasonable to argue that in considering innovative approaches to management research, we should pay some attention to those methods and scholarly stances that would enable the management researcher to both tackle critical problems and issues while at the same time contributing to knowledge generation. Puplampu (2009) notes that there are many challenges that confront organizational researchers in Africa. These include difficulties of access to organizations and respondents, data weariness of organization officials (who have to contend with hundreds of students (under- and postgraduates) in their final year looking for organizations in which to carry out projects required for graduation, and researchers and policy analysts seeking data for research that do not seem to address critical challenges such as access to capital, poor infrastructures, employee motivation, etc.).

We argue therefore that for us in Africa, we do not have the luxury of subscribing to Mode 1 research, nomothetic or etic approaches per se.

We argue that management research in Africa needs to innovate towards both theory building as well as problem solving. We suggest that there may well be many issues and difficulties that cannot be adequately explored if researchers take the position of the disinterested bystander.

INTERVENTIONIST RESEARCH APPLICATION

Noting the pressure towards puerile science identified by Anderson et al (2001), it is suggested that management researchers in Africa who wish for greater use of intervention research should establish a number of principles that act as the basis for using interventionist approaches as well as offering checks on scholarly efforts. These principles include the following:

1. Epistemological Reflexivity (Johnson and Cassell (2001). This means that to do interventionist research, scholars need to interrogate their preferred methods and modes of research and subject these to critical questions of relevance and applicability—rather than simply defaulting to an established tradition.
2. Careful design of research to address and include both client- or society-based problem solving as well as efforts at feeding into theory and concept development.
3. Apply the principles of methodological rigor as well as 'inquisitive theoretical integrity' (defined as staying close or true to a particular theoretical frame but doing so with a sufficiently inquiring mind so as to see alternative explanations when they do arise). This is particularly important as interventionist research always starts with problem solution in mind.
4. Apply the principles of verification and replication. Interventionist research cannot offer theoretical insights if researchers retreat or default to the esoteric argument that the phenomena being studied are so unique as to defy systematic recording of process, data, and outcomes.
5. Adoption of what has been called 'scholarly consulting' (Argyris, 1999)—this is research that works with propositions that are valid, actionable, applicable, and generalizable (Anderson, Herriot, and Hodgkinson, 2001). Africa is perhaps a huge consumer of consulting services, particularly those services targeted at public sector organizations, state institutions, and development policy-oriented processes and governance arrangements. It seems a waste of valuable information to note that much of the processes, data, issues, and resolutions that are arrived at through consulting and other advisory services (which do inform public and economic policy) do not find their way into the theoretical discourse. In Ghana, there is evidence that the program known as the National Institutional Renewal Program (1996–2000)

employed the services of many consultants (both local and foreign) as did the Ministry of Public Sector Reform (2005–2008).

6. Deliberate broadening of the research agenda to include contributions and concerns of multiple disciplines, interdisciplinary views, practitioner views, and scholarly views.
7. Greater or more use of exploratory propositions.

ADVANTAGES OF INTERVENTIONIST RESEARCH

There are a number of advantages that may accrue to management research, theory, and practice as well as national socioeconomic development efforts from interventionist research. These advantages are briefly noted below.

African managerial practice is often westernized in the name of best practice and international benchmarking. With interventionist research, scholarly consulting can begin to address lapses in managerial practice while at the same time using the findings to build credible evidence upon which skill development may take place. This should enable a localized set of standards to emerge. This should also help the directors and senior executives of African organizations to see some near-direct benefits emanating from management research. Thus, reducing the sense of disconnect that currently characterizes the relationship between scholarship and management practice in Africa.

Another advantage is that the politics of access and research relevance is perhaps better negotiated in interventionist research. This is because the basis for the research is in the first place grounded in a need. This need may be perceived or real. Either way, the need offers the researcher a better opportunity to gain access to executive thinking, time, or documentary evidences that may otherwise have been inaccessible to the standard research mode. This advantage leads to another: overcoming the pressure of social desirability. Some of the nuances, political consideration, and collectivist tendencies that may result in social desirability pressure (making it difficult for researchers to obtain credible, real-time data and freely elicited views) may be overcome because the intervention is based on accessing credible information, and the senior management of the organization would often have committed itself and employees to providing information. This is demonstrated to some degree by Puplampu's (2005) research interventions in Ghanaian organizations, which led him to propose a continuum of health and ill health for Ghanaian organizations.

Finally, the multidisciplinary and multi-perspectival nature of interventionist research often allows a cross-fertilization with other specialists and professionals, thus enhancing the potential for generating knowledge that is rounded, relevant, and more representative of the mosaic of life (Drenth and Heller, 2004).

OBJECTIONS AND CHALLENGES TO INTERVENTIONIST RESEARCH

It seems that there are three prominent objections and challenges to interventionist research. These are firstly the cost and design challenges inherent in crafting interventionist research that addresses client problems while at the same time fitting established scholarly traditions of knowledge generation. For example, for a researcher to generalize from his or her work, certain levels of sampling rigor may be required. Interventions may not lend themselves to such sampling. Secondly, the politics of academic gatekeeping by dominant coalitions of journal editors, peer reviewers, and academic institutional assessors of scholarly productivity often present a formidable barrier to reporting applied work. This creates a real disincentive for scholars to engage in work that may not be considered scholarly productivity. Finally, the ownership of data derived from interventions is a major area of concern.

WAY FORWARD

There is no doubt that methodological innovation in the direction of interventionist research poses challenges. It took almost 20 years of 'near pitch battles' in a field such as psychology for the debate around the relative merits of qualitative and quantitative approaches to simmer down. However, African management researchers need to accept that the challenges of the continent and the challenges of research on the continent call for a dedication to applicable knowledge generation and solution-oriented practice. To this end, researchers interested in the interventionist mode need to commit to rigor, research integrity, sound design, appropriate negotiation of ownership of data, and potential uses to which research findings may be put. It seems also important that African management researchers who pursue this approach develop skills in how to report their findings in recognized outlets where scholarly peers are more likely to access and use such findings in the development of theory. More collaboration is needed between researchers in different parts of the continent working closely with practitioners in order that fully rounded stories and findings emerge that ultimately facilitate the development of an indigenous management literature. The next approach to be considered is the use of Single Graphic Scales.

SINGLE GRAPHIC SCALES

A graphic scale is a research or therapeutic tool designed to elicit information from respondents using pictorial, diagrammatic, or symbolic representations. Psychometricians, psychotherapists, and personality psychologists have long used graphic and pictorial scales to study individual differences and abnormality or deviations. Their use, however, in organizational behavior and management research is rather limited. For example, Foil and Huff (1992) wrote about the use of cognitive maps in management research. Mapping techniques often seek to capture the mental representations of managers and leaders in respect to decisions, assessment of situations, options, and strategies. However, as indicated by Shamir and Kark (2004), cognitive mapping has normally been used to capture mental representations (which may have been elicited via other means) rather than as tools to elicit responses. What is needed now are more theoretically derived graphic scales that are used to elicit responses rather than as a record of cognitive maps.

GRAPHIC SCALE: A PICTORIAL REPRESENTATION

A single graphic scale would typically have a pictorial or diagrammatic representation of an issue depicted on a single sheet. It is likely to have a set of instructions that explain the diagram and then offer a response format requiring respondents to select options on various parts of the diagram, or select specific symbols, or choose amongst successively different forms of the diagram or picture/s that refer to, agree with, or mirror their view on a matter at hand. In the case of Shamir and Kark, using seven images of two circles that are progressively superimposed on each other, respondents are asked to choose which of the seven depict or indicate the level of their felt identification with their organization.

The graphic scale shown in this paper (Fig. 1) is based on the work of Puplampu (2005). It is designed to explore Organizational Health. Apart from a graphic representation, it also offers explanations and descriptions on different parts of the diagram relating to organizational health or ill health. Respondents are given a series of options, which include: providing open-ended descriptions or explanations, providing a list of characteristics, and circling a number in a box that corresponds to a point on the graphic continuum.

Organizational Health Questionnaire

1. This is a questionnaire designed to assess your sense of the state of health or ill health of the organization in which you work. Try to be as objective as possible. Think of real/factual reasons (rather than hearsay) that lend some support to your view as to the health or otherwise of the organization in which you work. Please read the contents of the diagram below carefully. Then circle the box/number related to the description that best fits your view of the current situation of your organization.

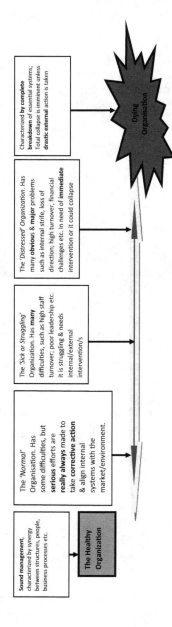

Sound management, characterized by synergy between structures, people, business processes etc.

The Healthy Organization

The *'Normal'* Organisation. Has some difficulties, but **serious** efforts are **really always** made to take **corrective action** & align internal systems with the market/environment.

The *'Sick or Struggling'* Organization. Has **many** difficulties, such as high staff turnover; poor leadership etc. It is struggling & needs internal/external intervention/s

The *'Distressed' Organization*. Has many **obvious & major** problems such as internal strife, loss of direction; high turnover, financial challenges etc. In need of **immediate** intervention or it could collapse

Characterized **by complete breakdown** of essential systems; Total collapse is imminent unless **drastic external** action is taken

Dying Organisation

Figure 10.1   Single Graphic Scale to Explore Organizational Health (After Puplampu, 2005)

Now, please circle any one of the numbers/boxes below in response to the statement—My organization is:

'Healthy'		'Normal'		'Sick and Struggling'		'Seriously Distressed'		'Dying'	
1	2	3	4	5	6	7	8	9	10

2. Please use this space to write out any explanations/views/thoughts you may have:
3. Please list below any behaviors and situations that characterize your organization at the present time:

DIFFERENCES AND ADVANTAGES OF GRAPHIC SCALES

There are several differences between graphic scales and the more commonly used survey questionnaires and Likert scales that tend to be used in management research. Firstly, survey instruments use several questions or items that are largely directional. For example, in developing an instrument to explore organizational health, Miles and others use scales with over 60 items. Graphic scales on the other hand often have just one item—the main pictorial representation. Thus a major advantage is that they offer the possibility of data or response elicitation with fewer items and potentially fewer pages of questionnaires to fill out. This is of particular importance as in the African context, Puplampu (2009) notes that often, many organizations, their managers, and employees can become data-weary due to the numerous surveys undertaken by graduate and undergraduate students, often with little in return by way of feedback to the participating organizations. Secondly, graphic scales offer less room for the investigator to include items that may be redundant to the issue. This is because graphic scales must be constructed in a very parsimonious way so as to maximize the value of pictorial representation while minimizing the complexity of the same. Thirdly, graphic scales offer respondents the opportunity to respond subjectively to the representation. Their response is thus guided by their own felt needs, reaction to, and interpretation of the representation rather than prior questions structured by the investigator. Fourth, graphic scales may well offer a faster mode of administering a data instrument because: instructions tend to be kept to a minimum, they do not involve reading several items that respondents have to understand and seek to make sense of before answering, and they avoid situations where respondents cross-check how they responded to earlier parts of a standard survey in order to be consistent with later responses. Another major potential advantage of graphic scales is their use in organizational interventions. A graphic representation of an organizational situation enables the deployment of metaphors and imagery (Morgan, 1986). This facilitates managerial as well as employee identification and conceptualization of the issues at hand. This should also enable faster data gathering in the applied situation since graphic scales tend to be simpler, shorter, and do not need multiple items as in the case of survey questionnaires.

GRAPHIC SCALES' CHALLENGES

There are two main challenges with the use of graphic scales. The first is that they may suffer from a 'projective technique' character. This may well be a challenge more from the scientific community than from respondents. Secondly, graphic scales need to be designed and constructed from a clear theoretical position or from a clearly articulated construct. This is because the researcher needs to be able to indicate very clearly which part of a theory or construct the pictorial representation or diagram seeks to symbolize. This is important, as anything less would expose the research enterprise to bogus claims and spurious data. For this reason, graphic scales may not easily be amenable to a priori research. In other words, graphic scales in management research would need previously defined concepts, constructs, or some measure of experience as basis for their construction.

These challenges notwithstanding, graphic scales offer the possibility for significant face validity, easier data gathering as well as potential managerial applications by offering ready characterizations of ongoing phenomena—such as the state of an organization, interactions, and interrelations within the organization, etc. Whenever graphic scales are developed, it is necessary for evidence to be obtained over many iterations of use to support the scale's validity and reliability. It also seems necessary that alternative evidence or triangulated data are necessary for correlation or comparison with the results obtained from a graphic scale. The next approach to consider is the use of the Hermeneutic Principle.

HERMENEUTICS

Gabriel (1990) notes that 'hermeneutics' is a system by which interpretation is arrived at by the interplay between the subject matter and the interpreter's original positions (p. 514). The hermeneutic philosophy holds that we understand what we study only when we consider the object of our study—the researched—within the appropriate context and deliberately seek out factors that contextualize the experience of the researched. To do this, we employ an interpretive methodology that involves critical comparisons between a) what is observed, written, or said and b) what we find elsewhere within the sociocultural, historical, institutional, spiritual, mythological, and experiential frame of what we are studying. This requires a commitment to what in recent times has been variously called 'rolling hypotheses', 'constant comparison', and finding the 'referent'. These require a preparedness on the part of the researcher to modify assumptions based on emergent data and understandings. The Collins English Dictionary defines 'hermeneutics' as a science of interpretation, especially of scripture. It outlines two representations of hermeneutics:

1. the study and interpretation of human behavior and social institutions, and
2. the discussion of the purpose of life.

Hermeneutics is thus an interpretive method with a philosophical commitment to achieving empathic understanding and an appropriate meaning frame. It is firstly a philosophy or way of thinking and secondly a procedural framework. It has its origins in classical Greek mythology. The priest of the Delphic oracle was known as Hermeios, the human being working with Hermes, the Greek messenger god. Hermes had the responsibility to transmute the obscure, cosmic, and unknowable—that which belonged to the realm of the gods—"into a form amenable to human comprehension" (Thompson, Pllio, and Locander, 1994; Wilson and Hutchinson, 1991). In this tradition, hermeneutics has become a way of achieving meaning, making sense of and understanding human experience by interpreting that experience. It holds that until 'lived experience' (human phenomena—whether observed, textual or discursive) is interpreted, critically examined in the light of culture, history, social institutions, spirituality, and mythology, an empathic understanding will not be achieved. Such understanding assists the appreciation of the purposes of that lived experience.

The researcher gains an appreciation of the lives, experiences, and purpose of the researched by allowing those experiences to mould the researcher's perceptions and understandings. Such a moulding is nearly impossible without a 'seeing together with' the researched. This does not mean that the researcher effectively abandons their own beliefs or cultural frames of exercise; assumptions are critically tested and allowed to change to reflect or mirror the reality of the researched. It involves a commitment to understanding the lives of others by interpreting their reality through their own eyes, words, and actions.

Hermeneutics was traditionally an old philosophical and procedural framework by which scholars interested in discovering the underlying meaning and cultural significance of texts (both old and current) arrived at stable interpretations. The old usage arose from the attempts of theologians to understand biblical/scriptural and other religious texts given the fact that often such texts were written or discovered after the death of key protagonists. Such literature also described in great detail spiritual experiences, prophecies, and symbolisms. The main purpose of hermeneutics in this tradition was to discover the truths and values of those scriptures.

The process of discovery resulted in what came to be known as the 'hermeneutic principle'. This principle has two key elements: first, it describes the theoretical, philosophical, metaphysical, subjective, or other basis for a person's interpretive stance. For example, does the scholar take a literal view of all spiritual texts? Such a view represents the readers' 'hermeneutic' and affects the type of understanding and meaning derived from the text. Secondly, the hermeneutic principle refers to the particular exegetical methods by which a particular 'hermeneutic' is engaged to achieve interpretive action. Exegesis here refers to the processes by which the researcher or scholar examines the text to gain understanding. These two components underlie the status of hermeneutics as the science of interpretive principles. They determine what is seen and how what is seen is seen.

Much of management research data comes from a variety of sources and in a variety of forms such as textual (e.g., company documents), observations (e.g., observations of the behaviors and interactions of others) and primary data mechanisms or dialogues (e.g., interviews, conversations, etc. in which the researcher participates). The hermeneutic principles to be outlined below can be applied to all these types of data primarily because the methodology gives center stage to the actors, their words, and their subjective experience. We now turn attention to detailing the hermeneutic process in research.

THE CYCLICAL HERMENEUTIC PROCESS

The process of using hermeneutics in management research incorporates questions of design, data gathering, analysis, and inferential conclusions. The hermeneutic approach uses rich description, specific case references, context-specific examples, and thematic analyses to unearth meaning and achieve understanding from data. There is no real attempt during the immediacy of the research process to achieve abstractions. Themes, fully described and validated to ensure location in the lived experience of the researched, are the central focus.

Research Design and the Researcher's Hermeneutic

Research design involves the overall conceptualization of an investigation. Hermeneutic investigations arise from the epistemological tradition of constructionism. This means that we acknowledge the import of socio-cultural software in the creation and interpretation of people's experience. The first point to be noted in outlining the design of a hermeneutic study is the clear statement of the researcher's starting premise. For example, the literal hermeneutics of biblical exegesis produces the premise: the bible is God speaking to His people. Ringma and Brown (1991) started their study of disability with the following premise: "the social world of persons with disabilities is one of disadvantage." This reflects a position that should now be tested. These premises do not occupy the same status as positivist-empiricist hypotheses, which can be rejected or accepted based on the significance levels of statistical tests. They are rather expressions of the epistemological position of the researcher, based on philosophy, theory, and so on. They may also be drawn from prior knowledge about the experience of the researched. Critically, however, their usefulness in research comes from the fact that they connect sampling and data gathering. They determine the type of data that occupies the attention of the researcher. They are not an imposition on the data so much as a test of the 'reality' of the researched.

Focused and Purposive Sampling

Representativeness in the empiricist tradition is not the primary focus. In the quantitative tradition, representativeness is often achieved through random sampling. This is because the aim is to achieve richness, depth, relevance, interpretive understanding, and a deep and clear picture of the situation of the researched. Sampling here refers to respondents, textual information, and/or any items of observation. Importantly, the principle of conceptually driven sequential sampling kicks in after the initial sets of data are collected. This means that the initial sample would be selected on the basis of the researcher's hermeneutic. Subsequent sampling, however, depends on what data emerge and what gaps need to be filled.

Iterative Data Gathering

The process of data gathering in hermeneutics is iterative, reactive, and phased. It is reactive because the subsequent progress of the research depends on reacting to key points in the data. This reactivity is operationalized by a return to the field following preliminary analysis to collect more data. These constitute the phased and iterative elements. Each phase of data gathering reacts to or builds on analytical conclusions from the previous phase. This approach is unique to hermeneutics. Other qualitative methods may make use of it, but the philosophical and epistemological traditions of hermeneutics require that there should not be a deviation from phased reactivity. Between-phase analysis is an opportunity to react to the data. It provides the researcher with an essential test of the starting hermeneutic as well as the exercise of the procedural-exegetical elements of the interpretive paradigm. Hermeneutic analysis here asks one key question: What are the data saying? This question is both context- and hermeneutic-specific, but very much focused on the text or observations that have been unearthed by the researcher. The progress to a next phase of data collection is determined by the gaps identified in the data, the extent to which the starting hermeneutic is being borne out or rebutted, and the emergence of relevant new leads. Below, we graphically present what happens in the case of a hermeneutic research.

This process builds the 'Hermeneutic Circle' depicted by Figure 10.2 above. The more phases are needed, the wider the circle. As can be seen from Figure 10.2, between-phase analyses are informed by a consideration

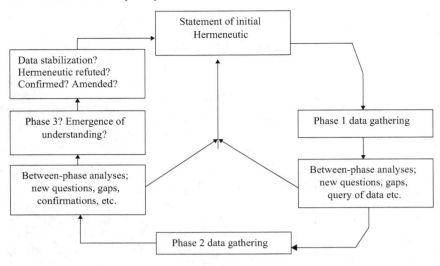

Figure 10.2   Cyclical, Iterative, and Reactive Process of Hermeneutic Research

of what the researcher's original position, aims, and premises were. This is indicated by the arrows from the starting framework to the analyses' stages after each phase. The researcher teases out themes by looking at the data, the premise, and all other available contextual information. Analogies are drawn between concrete data, exemplars (examples, specimens, criteria, etc.), and context. Critical to this process is a consideration of the interaction between researcher and researched, to check out what subjectivities are apparent and why. This toggling back and forth (also known as constant comparison method) between the concrete observation in the field and conjectural explanations is what general semanticists call finding the 'referent'. The process asks whether the data or information obtained are adequate confirmations or rebuttals of initial premises. Answers to the various questions the researcher asks of the data indicate whether the researcher needs to build new premises, rework old ones, seek different theoretical guidelines, or collect more data.

Hermeneutic Data Stabilization—Drawing Inferences From the Iterative Process

Following the various phases of data gathering, the researcher makes inferences and arrives at a decision of cessation of data gathering based on what is known as data stabilization. This means at this point the data suggest that a fairly sturdy comprehension of the issue at stake has been gained by the researcher/s. It also means that successive iterations of data are no longer productive and repetition has set in—despite the data sources, variations in questions, or indeed relevant samples. The hermeneutic circle may be considered to be complete and valid when no new insights are surfacing from the phased reactive data gathering and analyses process, when the starting framework of the researcher becomes mirrored, is refuted, or clearly requires modification based on the holistic data picture that has emerged. The notion of a complete circle can be likened to the principle of 'pragnanz,' in essence, a 'whole' to which nothing new—at that point in time—can be added.

CHALLENGES OF HERMENEUTICS IN MANAGEMENT RESEARCH

The main challenge that confronts hermeneutic research when used in the field of management is that it is painstaking, potentially time consuming, and requires considerable logico-temporal openness. Also, the researcher cannot stop after one cross-sectional pass at data gathering. It is also necessary to ensure respondent availability since sample attrition may compromise between-phase analyses if the data require deeper exploration of the views of respondents from a previous phase. Finally, the difficulty of getting people in organizations to commit to detailed, deep, and (potentially) emotionally involving process of data gathering is real.

These challenges notwithstanding, hermeneutics offers an approach that may enable rich and context-relevant data to be mined in management research in Africa. Further, researchers who are culturally and philosophically alien to Africa may use the notion of a starting hermeneutic to clearly state their positions without apology and through logico-temporal openness, subject their starting hermeneutic/s to amendment and/or abolishment once the data stabilize and point in a certain direction.

RELEVANCE FOR AFRICA

This paper has described three methods of research that may assist management researchers in Africa carry out more relevant and context-sensitive research. In setting the agenda, reference was made to Boyer's work. In this regard, we suggest that the use of interventions as a tool for research is perhaps central to the scholarship of application. Interventionist research should compel the researcher and management scholar to become conscious of the need to make an impact in alleviating poverty, in tackling organizational dysfunctions, and in facilitating leader development, improved corporate governance, etc. When carried out with the necessary attention to research rigor, such work can also usefully impact theory development and build the literature. Hermeneutics can usefully contribute to both the scholarship of discovery and of teaching. Too often, African organizational, management, and economic issues are treated from foreign disinterested perspectives, leading to shallow knowledge, discontinuous concepts, and generally, discovery that is inadequate. Hermeneutics demands depth, concern for the researched, intellectual openness towards the subject of investigation, and a recognition that discovery that celebrates and mirrors the reality of the researched is perhaps most fulfilling. African management research can only conclude context-relevant understandings when scholars commit to respecting the locale. In the same way, graphic scales can assist discovery by simplifying and enhancing the data-gathering process. It can also facilitate teaching by providing pictorial and graphic images to enquiring minds as well as offer a means of simplifying difficult theoretical concepts when scholars attempt to use the same in the context of interventions of management development.

In conclusion, we refer to Whetten's (1989) highly relevant paper, which suggests that researchers and scholars need to ask a number of questions when conceiving of their potential contributions. We believe those questions are directly applicable to the quest for innovative research methods: What factors or variables are we examining with our research? How are the variables related—especially in terms of relationships that lead us to understand the problems at hand? Why should other researchers and practitioners give ear to our representation of extant reality derived from innovative research? This paper does not call for the use of innovative or different research approaches for their own sake. Change is required in order to improve understanding of real, emergent societal and organizational difficulties, and this call sits well within a growing global call for change in research methods in the management and organizational sciences (Symon, Cassell, and Dickson, 2000).

REFERENCES

Anderson, N., Herriot, P., and Hodgkinson, G. (2001). The practitioner-researcher divide in industrial, work and organisational psychology: Where are we now and where do we go from here? *Journal of Occupational and Organizational Psychology, 74,* 4, 391–411.

Argyris, C. (1999). *On organizational learning.* Oxford: Blackwell.

Arnold, G. (2006). *Africa: A modern history.* London: Atlantic Books.

Boyer, E. (1990). *Scholarship reconsidered—priorities of the professoriate.* Carnegie Foundation for the Advancement of Teaching, NY.

Boyer, E. (1996). The scholarship of engagement. *Journal of Public Service and Outreach, 1*(1), 11–20.

Drenth, P., and Heller, F. (2004). The dangers of resource myopia in work and organisational psychology: A plea for broadening and integration. *Applied Psychology—An International Review, 53*(4), 599–613.

Foil, C., and Huff, A. (1992). Maps for managers: Where are we? Where do we go from here? *Journal of Management Studies, 29,* 267–285.

Gabriel, C. (1990). The validity of qualitative market research. *Journal of Market Research Society, 32*(4), 507–519.

Gibbons, M., Limoges, C., Nowotny, H., Schwartzman, S., Scott, P., and Trow, M. (1994). *The new production of knowledge: The dynamics of science and research in contemporary societies.* London: Sage.

Johnson, P., and Cassell, C. (2001). Epistemology and work psychology: New agendas. *Journal of Occupational and Organisational Psychology, 74*(2), 125–144.

Jonsson, S., and Lukka, K. (2005). *Doing interventionist research in management accounting.* GRI-rapport 2005, 6. Retrieved October 15, 2010, from http://gupee.ub.gu.se/dspace/bitstream/2077/2987/1/2005–6_for_web.pdf

Jukkula, V., Lyly- Yrjänäinen, J., and Suomala, P. (2006). *Challenges of practically relevant management accounting research—the scope and intensity of interventionist research.* Retrieved October 15, 2010, from http://webhotel2.tnt.fi/cmc/pdf/ChallengesOfPracticallyRelevantManagementAccountingResearch.pdf

Kamoche, K. (2011). Contemporary developments in the management of human resources in Africa. *Journal of World Business, 46*(1), 1–4.

Morgan, G. (1986). *Images of organisation.* Beverly Hills: Sage.

Puplampu, B. (2005). Toward a framework for understanding the distressed organization—insights from practitioner-based organisational interventions in an emerging economy. *Consulting Psychology Journal—Practice and Research, 57*(4), 246–258.

Puplampu, B. (2009). Our conundrums: Researching, writing and publishing in Africa. *Management and Organisation—A Multidisciplinary Journal of Business, 1*(1), 1–12.

Reader, J. (1998). *Africa. A biography of the continent.* London: Penguin Books.

Ringma, C. and Brown, C. (1991). Hermeneutics and the social sciences: An evaluation of the function of hermeneutics in a consumer disability study. *Journal of Sociology and Social Welfare, 18*(2), 57–74.

Shamir, B., and Kark, R. (2004). A single-item graphic scale for the measurement of organizational identification. *Journal of Occupational and Organizational Psychology, 77*(1), 115–123.

Symon, G., Cassell, C., and Dickson, R. (2000). Expanding our research and practice through innovative research methods. *European Journal of Work and Organisational Psychology, 9*(4), 457–462.

Thompson, C., Pllio, H., and Locander, W. (1994). The spoken and the unspoken: A hermeneutic approach to understanding the cultural view points that underlie consumers' expressed meanings. *Journal of Consumer Research, 21*(3), 432–452.

Tranfield, D., and Starkey, K. (1998). The nature, social organization and promotion of management research: Towards policy. *British Journal of Management, 9,* 341–353.

Whetten, D. (1989). What constitutes a theoretical contribution? *Academy of Management Review, 14*(4), 490–495.

Wilson, H., and Hutchinson, S. (1991). Triangulation of qualitative methods. Heideggerian hermeneutics and grounded theory. *Qualitative Health Research, 1*(2), 263–276.

11 Management Theories
The Relegated Strengths-Based African Practices

Shiphrah Mutungi, Emmanuel Mutungi, and Rose Fuentes

INTRODUCTION

The Western management theories introduced in Africa at the time of colonialism plus the new ones that are imported on a regular basis have continued to discard and cripple the evolution and development of the indigenous management theories that sustained Africa for centuries Oghojafor and Chinyere (2013). Oblivious to Africa's strengths-based practices, the colonial administrators introduced Western management theories that were hinged on Western cultures, values, ideals, and economic setup, with an assumption that this would steer development in Africa to the same level as Western countries, which has not happened until now (Hofstede, 1991). Consequently, communities were turned into observers of development interventions rather than architects of their own destiny. Western discourses have continued to relegate indigenous management of Africa, which is not only community-owned but also embedded with many strengths by replacing them with ones that are foreign to African norms (Oghojafor and Chinyere, 2013). The importance of African-based management theories was recognized and promoted by a few individuals such as Julius Nyerere, the first president of Tanzania, when he tasked people to live and work together to achieve collective development. Although Nyerere's *Ujama* (villagization) did not entirely succeed (Kamugisha, 2011; Itika, de Ridder, and Tollenaar, 2011), Nyerere demonstrated that Africa could depend on its indigenous systems (Ajei, 2007). The African way of management is practical, grounded in local wisdom, and based on the traditional African values that serve the same functions as Western management theories.

Characterized by diverse cultures, Africa has several indigenous management practices embedded in various community responsibilities that each member observes and that guide the functions of every community (Ajei, 2007; Oghojafor and Chinyere, 2013; Mendelek, April, and Blass, 2015). Management of African society was organized through community organizing, family systems, clans, tribes, villages, age groups, philosophies, doctrines, rituals, and beliefs (Ajei, 2007). The selected concepts of *burungi bwansi*, *kirinju*, and *ubuntu* were part of the African strengths-based theories that underpinned Africa's management success but are now replaced with Western management theories and practices. These management practices were community initiatives through which communities were organized. Although Western management knowledge and practices were essential elements in modernization of Africa, this chapter argues that traditional practices were appropriate management theories and practices in Africa that could still be promoted for sustainable development. The aim of this chapter is not to discredit the management theories promoted by Western ideologies but to highlight the strengths embedded in certain relegated African management practices that could be integrated into modern management systems. These strengths would not only benefit management practice in Africa but the entire field throughout the world. The chapter explains three African management practices that would greatly influence the current management theories and discusses the possible ways to integrate them into organization management in Africa.

Background

When we talk of management theories in Africa, we tend to think just of the famous historical and contemporary theories by the Western scholars such as Frederick Taylor (1890–1940), Max Weber (1930–1950), and the behavioral scientists (1930–today) as captured by McNamara (2013). However, management theory is a combination of the concepts and principles that help us to understand human behavior in organization and help increase organizational productivity. Hence, a theory is simply a logical grouping of related ideologies and serves as a way of categorizing relevant knowledge (Nwachukwu, 1992; Oghojafor and Chinyere, 2013). Theories and concepts are selected depending on the workplace, purpose, and workforce; but when it comes to organizations based in Africa, traditional management practices and knowledge are not only ignored but also relegated. Researchers and management scholars worldwide promote management theories with less or no attention at all to the African practices. Organizations practice theories such as scientific, bureaucratic, and human relations or the contemporary theories (McNamara, 2013) without considering the African contexts in which they operate. All efforts concentrate on the application of Western management theories by organizations based in Africa and led by Africans.

Africa's narrative is based on the interpretation of the developed world as Jackson (2012) refers to the work of Said (1978/1995) and argues that Western domination through Western culture developed a logical form of theory and practice that represents the position of Africa. In colonial times and even today, everything from the West is regarded as logical while everything from African and perhaps other parts of the developing world are regarded degenerate, primitive, mystic, and suspicious (Jackson, 2012). Elsewhere Xaba (2008) argues that the collision of African culture with modern civilization suppressed and marginalized African political, economic, social, religious, and cultural practices. Contact with external approaches to societal systems such as political, economic, social, religious, and cultural practices led to the abandoning of indigenous management systems such as *burungi bwansi*, *ubuntu* and *kirinju*.

African indigenous communities from the time of cave life to fruit gathering and later organized societies depended on the strength of indigenous knowledge including management theories (Adegboye, 2013). Such management theories can be explained by precolonial construction of the great pyramids in Egypt; some studies such as Bartol and Martin (1991) who described these early management work in Africa as "pre-scientific" and uncivilized management practices. Without necessarily refuting this assertion, limiting our understanding of management theory to only scientific methods denies us the chance to explore the strengths of African theories and beliefs. Rather than dismissing the pre-scientific practices, researchers and implementers should bridge the gap by documenting them. The construction of the Egyptian pyramids was a unique management practice that needed to have been allowed to grow gradually without interference from the Western management theories. The present study postulates that modern management theories should look at indigenous African management theories as community-grounded theories that can ignite appropriate management practices for development.

Approach

The researchers chose to analyze the African strengths-based management practices with an intention to highlight their strengths in contemporary management practices. This was because available literature reveals that Western management practices are simply destroying local management practices that sustained African institutions for centuries (Inyang, 2008). We hypothesized that this could bring on board the already relegated and infringed-on African management practices such as the communal way of life in preference to the Western individualistic approach to life and organization. There is an assumption that Western ideas steer development, yet we know that Africa is not the nearest in philosophy to the Western world (Hofstede, 1991). The assumption could be based on the fact that the West is already developed, but it could also be based on other socioeconomic conditions (Inyang, 2008). Both Africans and Western managers have continuously failed to identify and explore certain strengths-based African values that would enhance management in Africa.

Ethnography was used to gather data for this study. We employed in-depth semi-structured interviews and Focus Group Discussions (FDGs). We purposively selected five elderly people of Banyankore descent who were knowledgeable about the Banyankore tradition. We used chain referral method to access them. The researchers organized two FDGs of five people each among communities of Banyankore ethnicity. The FGDs brainstormed some of the important practices that carried a lot of strengths and yet have been neglected.

The collected ideas were transcribed and later triangulated with information gotten from in-depth interviews. A word cloud was developed to map the merging patterns for the data. This was helpful because the study wanted to see correlations between individual and group perceptions. Later, the outcomes from the in-depth interviews and FGDs were discussed among researchers to discern emerging patterns that generated ideas on what African traditional management practices meant in modern management theories. FGDs were highly participatory and received a lot of enthusiasm; participants could go on and on mentioning one point after another. Together we came up with a list of more than 50 idea cards with rituals, proverbs, beliefs, and practices closely related to theories of management.

Findings

Data were analyzed using content analysis, and outcomes were discussed among the researchers. The researcher's discussion was based on all of the ideas generated from the FGDs and triangulated with in-depth interviews. The discussion was mainly focused on the strengths of each of these rituals and the value added to organization management theory in African contexts. It was observed that African management concepts were creative, and hence ideas, concepts, phrases, proverbs, and arguments were all at play. The general themes that emerged from the FGDs and in-depth interviews were the fact that most of the African management practices were strength-based in nature. Whereas many ideas emerged from the field ethnography, the study focused mainly on the strengths embedded in *burungi bwansi, kirinju* and *ubuntu*, which could be added to management theories in African-based organizations. We noted that there are a lot of conflicting values when it comes to management in organizations based in Africa because unique African practices such as *burungi bwansi, kirinju* and *ubuntu* are not given any place in modern management. Yet as Africans, this is important not only as social responsibilities but also as a path to success cherished in the related social support. This argument fits well in Adegboye's (2013, p. 205) findings towards the applicability of management theories in Nigeria, in which he notes that

> Nigerian culture does limit the usefulness of western management practices in the workplace. In reality, these conflicts can be minimized or avoided if the local cultural norms and practices are recognized and considered in the application of contemporary management principles.

In modern management practices, it is almost impossible to maintain unique responsibilities while at the same meet the demands of Western management practices.

Whereas all ideas that emerged from the process were captured, the final discussion is more focused on African strength-based practices as management theories. We anticipate the struggle by someone reading this chapter in an effort to pronounce some of the words captured; we want to assure you that for many people in Africa, reading certain words such as 'theory' or 'bureaucratic' is not as natural as it is with people from which cultures these words originated. What this brings out is the fact that organizations in Africa are not only struggling with borrowed concepts but also with the ability to understand them due to language limitations. One can argue that organizations are managed by the educated class; while that is true, we all know how diluted a concept gets in an effort to explain it more and more. Information can be diluted as it moves from the author to another person; the familiar exercise in communication trainings about passing on a message from one person to another explains this metaphor. For example, the original message could be "I eat fish" and the final message could be "I don't eat fish." That said, we will endeavor to explain the meaning of each of the beliefs or practices captured in this paper.

The Selected Strengths-Based African Management Practices

Africa is not a single unified nation but an entire continent characterized by diverse cultures. As such, the beliefs and practices discussed here may not necessarily apply to other parts of Africa but are representational and mainly extracted from the Ugandan knowledge base. Despite these differences, Africans have much in common in their beliefs, cultures, values, and social structures. Africans share many things in their overall behavior and ways of life, such as family ties, respect for elders, community work, etc. Therefore, the majority of the management practices discussed may as well apply elsewhere in Africa. For example, whereas the theory of "*Ubuntu*" stems from South Africa, in Uganda and in other Bantu-speaking communities, it is called "*Ubuntu*," meaning exactly the same. It is hard to envision a traditional African organization without thinking about a village, community, a family, and groups, etc. Even Western management theorists sometimes compare organizations to family, so when the present study talks of beliefs and practices at the family level, the study wants the reader to envision these at organizational level because of their applicability. There is a wealth of meaningful practices on the African soil that many people might consider in managing organizations. We are discussing below three particular practices of *Burungi bwansi*, *Kirinju*, and *Ubuntu*, which are all strengths-based management theories and yet relegated.

Management Through *Burungi Bwansi*

Achievements within the African traditional culture were usually attributed to group efforts (Osarumwense, 2014). *Burungi bwansi* means coming together to address community needs. The practice was common in Uganda but similar practices exist elsewhere such as the successful practice of *Umuganda* in Rwanda, built on that same doctrine. *Burungi bwansi* was effective in mobilizing the people to respond to a community agenda. It was very effective in organizing communities, cities, cleaning up, road and bridge construction, maintenance, etc. In modern management, we talk about teamwork; *burungi bwansi* is driven on teamwork principles in which members are not only team members but can cause the team to form and function. At the sound of a drum or a trumpet, each community member would turn up for a community action. Management based on *burungi bwansi* made each member of the community responsible and accountable to one another.

In traditional community management, emphasis was put on the collective interest of the people and not on competition. *Burungi bwansi* meant that you were in a community with and for the people; whenever a neighbor died, nobody went to the garden or did any other form of work. In modern management practices, failure to work because a neighbor of family member has died is not understood and not provided for. For many colleagues and bosses from the West do not understand the fact that you can be absent from work because of a burial or seeing a patient in the hospital. What is happening is that in situations like this, most African employees juggle between two worlds without meeting the needs of either. In Africa, the welfare of each African was and in most cases a concern of every member of his or her community. Africans do not stop living and being influenced by the larger community; in fact the more educated and exposed Africans become, the closer they get and develop the desire to maintain their traditional ties. The challenge most Africans face is to learn and understand the Western ways of work life while maintaining their cultural dimensions. Despite the challenges of copying and pasting Western management theories as they are into Africa, the perception that indigenous management knowledge is vague and backwards prevails. The value of *burungi bwansi* was to promote the welfare of all without making exceptions. However, present organization management in Africa is overlooking this value.

This traditional practice could be adapted in today's organization management by encouraging all employees of the organization to feel that they belong to a community and that a community is theirs. In Rwanda, for example, *umuganda*, a village community service, has always been used to improve community infrastructure. Bonnier et al (2014) postulates that although *umaganda* was politicized and used to carry out the 1994 genocide, it had been beneficial to the community for a long time. Bonnier et al (2014) argue that despite the negative effect of *umuganda* in promoting genocide in Rwanda, there are positive outcomes of community meetings in increasing social capital because community meetings provide arenas for people to attend collectively to community needs. *Umuganda* has been revived in Rwanda and President Kagame participates in it.

Unlike in situations where employees work just for pay, we see the spirit of volunteerism and a management principle of ownership in its real meaning in *burungi bwansi* practice. The ownership promoted by foreign management principles is based on Western guidelines; hence in most cases it does not necessarily create ownership but a cosmetic one. For example, Kampala City has for a long time been operating on the principles of Western management practices to keep the city clean and orderly. This did not work at all, but instead the situation was getting out of hand until, like in Rwanda, the Kampala Capital City Authority (KCCA) started *burungi bwansi* and communities were supportive. The KCCA and the residents took part in cleaning the city and a tremendous improvement was realized. In *burungi bwansi* model, the principles of leading by example are exhibited. The participation of leaders such as the President of Rwanda and the Executive Director of Kampala City Council Authority increases community participation because people want to support their leader and they feel their leader understands their concerns. In paid work, people tag their efforts to how much they are paid, and this leads to poor results.

In *burungi bwansi*, participation was based on the spirit of ownership, which is lacking in modern management systems where everything is monetized. Inyang (2008) cites the work of Ahiauzu (1999), arguing that wage employment in African communities introduced by colonial masters created a negative impression towards work. What is forgotten or not even talked about is the fact that in traditional Africa, communities depended for their livelihoods on communal participation. The unfortunate reality is that the wage or pay takes priority over work itself. People will accept doing certain things just for pay whether they want to or even qualify to do it. Instead of relegating *burungi bwansi* as a backward practice, efforts should be made to incorporate it into all management practices because of its potential to strengthen communities and organizations.

Management Theory Based on *Kirinju*

Kirinju is an honor and title given to the elders in the community; in its simple terms means "the one with grey hair" and in African culture, the more grey hair you get, the wiser you become. In fact, for the less respected elders in the community perhaps because of their contrary behaviors they are referred to as "*okurize enju zonka*" meaning "*the one with empty grey hair.*" Yefesi (2014) agrees with this finding when he highlights that management in Africa was based on age; *kirinju* were the custodians of wisdom. Highly respected individuals in every community, *kirinjus* in turn conducted themselves in a dependable manner. Respect for age and hierarchy means that superiors are expected to make decisions to be passed down to the subordinates; in fact, this is still expected. Young people are expected to choose elders who perform leadership roles in the community (Oghojafor and Chinyere, 2013). According to the *kirinju* theory, there are strong lines of authority, control, delegation, coaching, and mentorship. The study took time to reflect on the relationship between documentation, naming, and accepted models. We realized that for the most part, the African knowledge is in the hands of a few that can well tell the story. On the other hand, there was an argument as to whether knowledge transfer was/is equally effective through stories as it is through books. The transfer of management knowledge by *kirinju* was not through books and journals as with Western management but through other means such as stories told around fireplaces, dances, songs, rattles, and others. Stories were part and parcel of everyday life; stories told about the past shaped the future (Hanna, 1968; 1987).

The present study argues that integrating the *kirinju* philosophy into organizations in Africa today would achieve what is promoted by bureaucratic theory, but most important, people would recognize and own such processes. There is the notion of Western management theories that employees should be encouraged to participate in decision making, yet policies are formulated somewhere else, making it difficult for people to own them. Quite often, people tend to think that Western ideas or expertise are more accurate, advanced, and offer better solutions. This may be true in Western societies but may not be so in Africa. Some situations have failed Western interventions only to be solved by local African ones such as family and inheritance issues. When people talk in proverbs, they make meanings that are understood and respected by community members to which it is told. This study postulates that *kirunju* is a management practice that has a potential to contribute to addressing communication challenges within organizations.

Management Theory of *Ubuntu*

The expression of *ubuntu* generally means collective humanness (Mangaliso, 2001) and is a fundamental value in African cultures rooted in almost all socioeconomic processes. *Ubuntu* supports the ideal of togetherness among people, and the Africans put a lot of emphasis on the care for one another (Rich, 2012). *Ubuntu* underpins the basic values that manifest themselves in the ways African people think and behave towards one another and everyone else they encounter. When applied, *ubuntu* has the power to strengthen African values to build and reinforce strong teams. In traditional Africa, leadership and management was based on *ubuntu*, that is, according to accepted morals, values, and beliefs. Decisions therefore were made based on what was believed to be human and the ability to act in a way that is consistent with cultural values and consistent over time (Sergiovanni, 1984).

The idea of *ubuntu* focuses on shared values, individual contribution, encourages communal goals, and cuts across humanity. *Ubuntu* is therefore considered an important value of African culture that can form the foundation of an African management philosophy that is in line with the people's own culture (Mangaliso, 2001). African society is built on strong cultural beliefs in which answers and meaning are found. Considered as a management theory, *ubuntu* enhances organizations' effectiveness, filling organizations with humanness, a spirit of caring, community, harmony and hospitality, respect, and responsiveness. *Ubuntu* as a management theory emphasizes "teamwork, attention to relationships, mutual respect and empathy between leader and followers" Inyang (2008, p. 124). These are fundamental principles of management that hold promise for improving organization activities and functioning in Africa.

Discussion

Despite adopting management theories from the West, Africa is not only lagging behind the rest of the world but falling really further (Hofstede, 1991). To imagine that management theories developed in Western countries will serve globally is naïve, (Adegboye, 2013). The transplantation of Western management theories and models has not met the needs and aspirations of the people of Africa. It is unbelievable that, despite evidence towards the role of indigenous knowledge in development processes, management theories in Africa continue to ignore that position (Hofstede, 1991); after all, all management theories are built on specific cultural assumptions (Osarumwense, 2014). Theories advanced by scholars such as Fayol, Taylor, Maslow, Herzberg, and Likert confirm this assertion (McNamara, n.d). In the various theories, one is able to identify the sociocultural norms of the people with whom the theories originate. It is not surprising therefore that some of these theories have not necessarily transformed Africa as expected.

Theories developed in the West and exported into non-Western societies without considering the cultural assumptions that influenced their development (Hofstede, 1991) cannot serve African interests. Africa is culturally complex, and organizational leaders are faced with the challenge of dealing with this complexity. The different levels of cultural complexity lie between continents, nations, and ethnic groupings. Management theory is meant to enhance managerial efficiency by providing guidelines to help in problem solving. But the transfer of Western management theories and practices into African contexts does not only hinder the evolution of indigenous theories and cripple the few that are there, but also cause more harm than good (Adegboye, 2013).

The need to promote African management theories and practices is reinforced by the fact that management practice involves the translation of existing management knowledge and theories into action that will result in the achievement of efficiency and effectiveness. But in Africa, this does not happen; the traditional practices are all relegated and organization leaders are all striving to implement Western management theories. The study agrees with Osarumwense (2014), who argues that before the colonialists came, Africa had functioning political, economic, and administrative infrastructures. Adegboye (2013) posits that colonialism altered people's thinking processes and lived experiences, which already had forms of management. The old

African towns and villages had effective management practices under the guidance of village heads, chiefs, or kings. Villages, towns, and tribal groups had strong groups for their inter-tribal wars and protection. This kind of arrangement involved a great deal of organizational and managerial activity. Africans had ways of organizing their world of work. They had a way of exercising power and authority at the workplace to improve their lives and livelihoods. The ongoing discourse by management practitioners (Osarumwense, 2014) reviewing management theories does not consider indigenous African theories but instead concentrates on Western theories that in most cases are not applicable to African cultural dynamics. Management theories imported into Africa have failed to recognize the unique needs of the African worker who has a different background from their counterpart with a Western background. Management manuals and procedures used in the workplace ignore that an African worker comes from an extended family and has a responsibility to the community. Manuals and policies concentrate on output based on Western discourses. African workers are torn into two scenarios: either to respect their family and community as they work, or to work for a wage. The best way to merge these two positions would be through the identification and integration of African management practices into organizations.

The Untapped Strengths of Traditional Management Practices

Recognizing African practices in the management theory of organizations based on the continent is to appreciate the diverse nature of contexts and particular situation than think that what works in the West works in Africa. It is important to understand that unique organizational circumstances require different management styles. Yukl (2002) brings out a supportive argument that management is too difficult to depend on a set of standardized responses. Effective organizations will require adopting the appropriate response to the issue or situation (Morgan, 1997). Nwagbara (2012, p. 71) cites the work of Mbigi (2002), highlighting the many benefits of African management practices in today's organizations, including but not limited to "respect for the dignity of others, group solidarity, teamwork, service to others in the spirit of harmony and interdependence." Apart from Nwagbara (2012), other scholars such as Pietersen (2005); Bolden and Kirk (2009) and Bush (2007) have equally captured the strengths enshrined in African management practices, and the present study has highlighted some in the Table 11.1 below:

There are great strengths prescribed in Western management theories but there are equally more in the relegated traditional African management practices. However, from the above table, it is evident that African management theories were equally important in improving lives and livelihoods of communities. The evidence further shows that if African management theories are given a platform, they would improve community performance.

Table 11.1 The Strengths of *Burungi Bwansi, Kirinju* and *Ubuntu*

Western Management Theories	The Strengths of African Management Practices
Formal	Relationships
Subjective	Binding
Participative	Collective Responsibility
Transformational	Ownership
Individualistic	Equality
Transactional	Helping others
Modern	Respect for others
Instructional	Respect for human dignity
Domineering	Solidarity
Cooperative	Teamwork
Authoritarian	Service and harmony
Consultative	Interdependence
Democratic	Consensus
Foreign	Sharing
	Sanctity of commitment
	Compromise and consensus
	Accustomed
	Indigenous and cultural

They would even amplify the results since they are grounded in the local wisdom. Because organizations in Africa are strongly influenced by theories and concepts from the external environment, there is a struggle to relate these concepts to their situations rather than applying knowledge based on their circumstances (Adegboye, 2013). The challenge remains the ability to modify external theories to fit the prevailing values. The many management theories practiced in Africa replicate very different ways of understanding and interpreting events and behavior in organizations, largely representing the very different origins of the theory. They also represent what are often ideologically based, and certainly divergent, views about how organizations should be managed (Bush, 2007).

CONCLUSION

An effective management theory requires a firm foundation in the society it serves in order for it to be practical. Organizations in Africa have been made to copy everything from the West: ideas, concepts, and institutional designs, without considering that these are from highly developed countries. Although it is assumed that to succeed, you study success, the transfer of such theories from one cultural environment to another is full of pitfalls and barriers. Most of these ideas are very much intertwined in the social fabric of the country from which they originated. Challenges of transferring management knowledge across continental boundaries continue to fail to create

Figure 11.1 A Suggested Approach to Integrate African Management Practices

a working environment for all. Managers from the West keep on wondering what's wrong with their colleagues from Africa and vice versa. Issues of cultural conflict are paramount and are always at the center of an organization's struggles. The emphasis is on the need to develop local concepts and theories of management that are in line with Africa's inherent situations or circumstances and that will be most effective in achieving our development goals. There is a need to integrate African and Western management theories (Figure 11.1) in order to come up with a culturally feasible management theory for organizations based in Africa.

Whereas there has been little research on these African management practices, the principles of *burungi bwansi, kirinju* and *ubuntu* are well suited to the management of African organizations and support the development of indigenous African management theory. They bring out aspects of collective welfare—respect for the elders or authority and collective humane values—that when applied in management strengthen organizations. The general lack of management systems in Africa (Nzelibe, 1986; Inyang, 2008) is a result of overlooking some of the African management theories that had a moral responsibility that guided the operations of individuals. The Western management accountability tools can be manipulated, but the values of *ubuntu* cannot because it is an inner value that cannot just be compromised by models. African indigenous management practices offer concrete ways of how to effectively manage organizations based on and run by Africans. Management as a human responsibility supports all aspects of development. Studies have shown that the effective management is largely influenced by the traditions, values, and habits of a people and social contexts (Inyang, 2008). There is no better way to practice democracy and moral stability in any system than through *ubuntu* theory, no better way to act through hierarchy than through *kirinju*, and of course no better way to strengthen teams than through *burungi bwansi*. It is important to develop ethnically indigenous management theories to strengthen organizations based on the African continent. More in-depth research and documentation of African traditional management practices will bring about the reinvention of African management abilities and the recovery of the relegated strengths-based management practices.

REFERENCES

Adegboye, M. (2013). The applicability of management theories in Nigeria: Exploring the cultural challenge. *International Journal of Business and Social Science,* 4(10), Special Issue. pp. 205–215.

Ahiauzu, A. (1999). The African industrial man. Port Harcourt, Nigeria: Cimrat Publications.

Ajei, M. O. (2007). *Africa's development: The imperatives of indigenous knowledge and values* (Ph.D. thesis). University of South Africa.

Bartol, K. M., and Martin, D. C. (1991). *Management.* New York: McGraw-Hill.

Bolden, R., and Kirk, P. (2009). African leadership: Surfacing new understanding through leadership development. *International Journal of Cross Cultural Management,* 9(1): 69–86.

Bonnier, E., Poulsen, J., Rogall, T., and Stryjan, M. (2014). *Preparing for genocide: community work in Rwanda.* Retrieved August 10, 2014, from http://aswede.iies.su.se/papers/ASWEDE_C1_Stryjan.pdf

Bush, Tony. (2007). Educational leadership and management: Theory, policy, and practice. *South African Journal of Education (EASA),* 27(3), 391–406.

Hanna, J. L. (1968). Field research in African dance: Opportunities and utilities. *Ethnomusicology,* 12(1), 101–106.

Hanna, J. L. (1987). *To dance is human: A theory of nonverbal communication.* Chicago: The University of Chicago Press.

Hofstede, G. (1991). *Cultures and organizations: Software of the mind.* London: McGraw Hill.

Inyang, B. J. (2008). The challenges of evolving and developing management indigenous theories and practices in Africa. *International Journal of Business and Management,* 3(12), 122–132.

Itika, Josephat, Ridder, Ko de, and Tollenaar, Albertjan. (Eds.). (2011). *Theories and stories in African public administration.* University of Groningen / Mzumbe University, Ipskamp Drukkers, Enschede.

Jackson, T. (2012). Postcolonialism and organizational knowledge in the wake of China's presence in Africa: Interrogating South-South relations. *Organization,* 19(2), 181–204.

Kamugisha, D. (2011). Collective action. In J. Itika, Ko de Ridder, and A. Tollenaar (Eds.), *Theories and stories in African public administration.* Ipskamp Drukkers, Enschede.

Mangaliso, M. P. (2001). Building competitive advantage from Ubuntu: Management lessons from South Africa. *Academy of Management Executive,* 153(3), 23–23.

Mbigi, L. (2002). Spirit of African leadership: A comparative African perspective. *Journal for Convergence,* 3(4), 18–23.

McNamara, C. (n.d.). *Historical and contemporary theories of management.* Retrieved January 21, 2013, from http://managementhelp.org/management/theories.htm. Authenticity Consulting, LLC.

Mendelek, T. N., April, K., and Blass, E. (n.d.). *Context tension: Cultural influences on leadership and management practice.* Retrieved April 7, 2015, from http://www.ashridge.org.uk

Morgan, G. (1997). *Images of organization.* Newbury Park, CA: Sage.

Nwachukwu, C. C. (1992). *Management theory and practice.* Africana FEP Publishers Limited.

Nwagbara, U. (2012). Leading a post modern African organization: Towards a model of prospective commitment. *Journal of Pan African Studies*, 4(9), 75–92.

Nzelibe, C. O. (1986). The Evolution of African Management Thought. *International Studies Of Management & Organization, 16*(2), 6–16.

Oghojafor, A. B. E., and Chinyere, A. G. (2013). Indigenous management thoughts, concepts and practices: The case of the Igbos of Nigeria. *Australian Journal of Business and Management Research, 3*(1), 8–15.

Osarumwense, I. (2014). African values for the practice of human resource management. *Beykent University Journal of Social Sciences (BUJSS), 7*(1), 56–77.

Pietersen, H. J. (2005). Western humanism, African humanism and work organizations. *South African Journal of Industrial Psychology, 31*(3), 54–61.

Rich, J. (2012). *Embracing the spirit of Ubuntu: The essence of our humanity.* Retrieved April 15, 2015, from http://judithrich.com/embracing-the-spirit-of-ubuntu-the-essence-of-our-humanity/spirit-of-ubuntu-photo/

Said, E. W. (1978/1995). Orientalism, London: Penguin Books.

Sergiovanni, T. (1984). Leadership and excellence in schooling. *Educational Leadership, 41*, 4–13.

Yefesi. (2014). *A local person interviewed* in October 214 in S. Western Uganda.

Yukl, G. A. (2002). *Leadership in organizations* (5th ed.). Upper Saddle River, NJ: Prentice-Hall.

Xaba, T. (2008). Marginalized medical practice: The marginalization and transformation of indigenous medicines in South Africa. In B. De Sousa Santos (Ed.), *Another knowledge in possible: Beyond northern epistemologies (Reinventing social emancipation: Toward new manifestos).* New York: Verso. pp. 1–10.

Part IV

Organizational Practices and Management Challenges in Africa

12 Human Capital Development in Africa
Some Urgent Considerations

Bill Buenar Puplampu

INTRODUCTION

There is sufficient evidence that economic growth, societal transformation, organizational performance, and the general uplift of the standard of living within countries are more often than not a direct consequence of appropriately deployed human capacity and availability of productive skills through which natural resources are transformed to serve human needs (Kamoche, 1996; Kraak and Press, 2008; Walumbwa, Aviolo, and Aryee, 2011). It is, however, unclear the extent to which African governments and corporate leaders appreciate the need to adopt a strategic and far-sighted approach to the development of human capacity and productive skills (Puplampu, 2009).

If the evidence and logic is accepted—that human skills properly deployed facilitate social and economic development—then the consistently poor performance of many African countries on various development and economic indices may be attributed (directly and/or indirectly) to weak attention to the matter of human capital development (HC).

This chapter considers the matter of human capital development broadly and offers examples of what seems to have worked for some countries, then places the issue in the African context in terms of developing capacity for African organizations and concerns about innovation. It draws on examples from Ghana and offers a stakeholder view of the human capital development agenda and suggests that much needs to be done to proactively develop policy, synchronize the actions and initiatives of relevant agents, actors, and agencies—if Africa is to realize the full benefit of HC efforts.

HUMAN CAPITAL (HC) AND HUMAN RESOURCE DEVELOPMENT (HRD)

Human capital development is a well-worn concept. To varying degrees, nations, governments, organizations, and international agencies pontificate about it and engage in some actions meant to operationalize it. But what is it really? Why is it so important? Why is it a key consideration if appropriate skills and capacities are to be developed for African organizations?

In 1776, Adam Smith, in his *An Inquiry into the Nature and Causes of the Wealth of Nations* (Book II) identified four types of fixed capital that impact or afford the possibility of generating wealth:

- Machines and implements used for one's vocation;
- Buildings (profitable fixed assets from which one can procure an income or a return);
- Land and the associated enhancements; and
- Human capital (defined as the acquired and useful abilities *of all the inhabitants or members of the society*. These abilities are secured through "education, study, or apprenticeship," are domiciled in the person and constitute a fortune, asset, or stock for both the individual in whom they are domiciled as well as "of that of the society to which he belongs."

What is striking here is that over 235 years ago, Smith clearly postulated that the stock of skills and knowledge individuals possesses cumulatively constitute the human capacity and capital of the society to which the individual/s belongs. Since then, the concept of human capital has featured in human resource development, economics of labor, strategic human resource management, and related literatures (Becker, 1993; Bowles and Gintis, 1975; Keeley, 2007), and since then, the definitions and conceptualizations of HC have not changed much (Garavan, Morley, Gunnigie, and Collins (2001).

Human capital development and the related concept of human resource development are in essence a systematic and planned set of activities designed to provide the people of an organization or society with the necessary knowledge, skills, competencies, and mindset for present and future jobs, organizational and societal requirements. The core remit is to ensure that there are no competence and skill gaps now and into the future (Garavan et al, 2001).

From the organizational perspective, Cantrell, Benton, Laudal, and Thomas (2006) escribe a four-tier human capital development framework. This framework suggests that the organization's business results may be considered at Tier 1. This is composed of evidence such as revenue growth, return on investment, and future value. These are, however, derived from key performance drivers, which are Tier 2. Tier 2 is made up of factors such as productivity, quality, and customer sensitivity. These factors are in turn driven by Tier 3—human capital capabilities such as leadership capacity, workforce performance, talent management, and ability to change. To obtain appropriate sets of Tier 3 triggers and drivers, Cantrell, Benton, Laudal, and Thomas (2006) propose that there is a Tier 4: human capital processes. These processes include activities such as performance appraisal, succession planning, competency management, learning systems and knowledge management. Using an iceberg metaphor, one may say that this model suggests that the overt and easily seen edifice of business results actually sit on the not-so-evident foundation of clearly defined HC processes. This is an important point that policy makers in Africa should not miss. From the national perspective, research by Bontis, Keow, and Richardson (2000) indicate that human capital has been a critical influence on the performance of Malaysian industries and the Malaysian economy as a whole.

It seems that HC facilitates growth, performance, and development by unleashing directly applicable competences, knowledge, and capacities. Human behavior is often governed by level of knowledge, capacity for data and information, as well as intellectual and analytical insight. Behavior change is also often a question of attention to, consolidation, and annexation of the mental space, attitude frames, and sense of self-efficacy. Social psychologists have long concluded that there is a cognitive component to attitudes, attitude change, and behavior (Ajzen and Cote (2008).

To develop capacities for African organizations, therefore, it is necessary for focused attention on how in-country as well as regional organizations, agencies, and policy makers strategize towards building up both direct educational interventions as well as the more nuanced attitudes and competencies that facilitate productive engagement. To address this matter, brief attention will be given to Ghanaian policy lapses by way of example.

CHALLENGES IN NATIONAL POLICY—THE GHANAIAN EXAMPLE

In May 2006, the government of Ghana launched a Growth and Poverty Reduction Strategy II document (GRPS II 2006–2009; developed by Ghana's National Development Planning Commission). That document was to be applauded for its breadth of coverage on many of the critical matters that impinge on Ghana as a country and its socioeconomic future. However, the document operationalized government consideration of human capital development in a rather 'omnibus' way.

The omnibus character of the human capital stipulations in that policy document was evident in its range of intentions covered in Chapter 4 of the policy document. The areas set out as requiring attention with respect to developing human capital and human resources were the following 10 policy areas:

- Formal education
- Access to and participation in education
- Elimination of the gender gap
- Promoting science and technology
- Training and skills development

- Access to health care, malaria control and prevention of HIV/AIDS
- Population management
- Safe water and sanitation
- Urban development and regeneration
- Attention to the marginalized

These many areas are certainly worthy of attention. One can understand why the development economists who facilitated the crafting of the GPRS II incorporated so many areas. National policy often has to cover a broad enough range of areas to convince the populace that government is paying attention to as many of the issues that impinge on the welfare of citizens as possible. The trouble, however, is that this approach lumps many social factors and agendas together with the more specific HC issues under the umbrella term of 'human resource development'. This has potential to reduce the strategic focus, bite, and the monitoring and evaluation possibilities that would ensure that the nation can clearly track and follow the practical implementations and results of a focused attention on HC development.

This is even more critical, as today economists have returned to Adam Smith's propositions more forcefully and have concluded that a country's resources are largely made up of natural capital (natural resources), produced capital (manufactured goods), and intangible capital (knowledge and skills).

FOCUSED ATTENTION ON HUMAN CAPITAL— THE INTANGIBLE CAPITAL

Intangible capital is the country's stock of labor, human capital, the sum of a population's knowledge and skills, the level of trust in a society, the quality of its formal and informal institutions, as well as its levels of literacy. A World Bank study by Bailey (2007) places the following percentages on the various types of resources and their cumulative contribution to a nation's wealth: natural capital accounts for 5%; produced capital accounts for 18%; and intangible capital accounts for 77% of a nation's wealth.

This suggests that if African countries wish to tackle poverty, socioeconomic development, and general institutional/organizational capacity, a focused attention on developing intangible capital (skills, knowledge, attitudes and values, institutional capacities, processes and arrangements that facilitate synergization of national efforts) that by extension translates to human capital is *sine qua non*.

The Ghanaian example suggests that the country needs to decompose or un-bundle the human resource/human capital development conceptualizations in its growth strategy by removing those elements in relation to health care, population management, provision of water, urban development, and housing, etc. These must be carved out clearly as a social development growth agenda. It would then be possible to maintain the 'purity' of an HC agenda in terms of an articulated set of skills, literacy levels, organizational and human competencies, values and attitudes that are needed in significant proportions over the next 15–20 years (writers like Porter 1998, suggest that HC investments 'mature' in 10–15-year cycles). National economic policy would then need to set out a separate growth strategy focusing on, for example, human capital development for the next generation.

There are a number of advantages to this approach. Giving focused and strategic attention means the country can:

- Track skill development across sectors;
- Evaluate the impact of skill sets on commerce, industry, and wealth creation; and
- Set up particular institutions dedicated to building particular skills and monitoring these.

Skills and knowledge, properly deployed, almost always have a knock-on effect on other sectors of the economy.

OPERATIONALIZING HUMAN CAPITAL DEVELOPMENT

Operationalization of a focused attention on human capital development is a matter of policy, law, and institutional commitment. There are examples or precedents in history. We detail some of these below.

In 1862, the Congress of the United States of America passed the Morill Act, which was officially titled, "An Act Donating Public Lands . . . to provide Colleges for the benefit of Agriculture and the Mechanical Arts." The result was 69 higher education colleges and universities including what are today Cornell, Massachusetts Institute of Technology, and University of Wisconsin at Madison. These were the so-called 'land-grant' colleges. Backed by law and a clear understanding of what the US needed to do with regard to its skill base, these colleges had a dedicated focus on training in agriculture and industrial skills. The law indicated that:

> without excluding other scientific and classical studies and including military tactic, to teach such branches of learning as are related to agriculture and the mechanic arts, in such manner as the legislatures of the States may respectively prescribe, in order to promote the liberal and practical education of the industrial classes in the several pursuits and professions in life' (July 2, 1862, ch. 130, § 4, 12 Stat. 504; www.law.cornell.edu/uscode/text/7/304) Accessed August 26, 2015.

These policy directions led to skills, knowledge, and research paradigms that have facilitated food security and many other benefits for the US.

Another example is worth mentioning. In 1978–79, Singapore decided that in 10–15 years it would become a financial powerhouse of the Far East. Their resultant strategy had a number of foci. Firstly, the country identified the necessary skills for such financial capacity. They then researched the way the financial system works globally. This was followed by sending out young Singaporeans to understudy in the New York, London, and Zurich systems.

Finally, we refer to the example of Costa Rica. For many years culminating in the 1990s, Costa Rica decided to adopt a mix of developing skilled high-end technical expertise as well as a broad range of employee capacities with the appropriate work ethics so as to attract foreign direct investment. It went into close partnership with a group of experts known as CINDE (China Industrial Group, Inc.), who drew on significant research about their country, its skills, and competitiveness with particular reference to electronics and software. The country sought to position itself as the emerging electronics manufacturing center in the Americas. This led to close collaboration with the software giant, Intel. The results now include a string of forward and backward linkages and integrations that have established the country firmly on the road to a skill-based economy (Rodríguez-Clare, 2001).

Anecdotal evidence suggests that in some Scandinavian countries, the state mandates higher education institutions to produce a certain number of PhDs (for example) in certain skill areas due to the projections of what the country needs—and state funds are then appropriately channeled to those institutions that take up the challenge.

Clearly, countries in Africa need to articulate for themselves the intangible capital content needed, why such content is needed, within what time frame, and to what clearly identifiable ends. Ghana, for example, has struck oil in commercial quantities since 2007. What are the skill and competence implications of this discovery? Many advocates of the involvement of indigenes in the extractive industries in developing areas suggest that often the flashpoints of social unrest that result from mineral exploitation are the result of the inability of the indigenous people of an area to participate fully across all levels in the design, implementation, and benefits of mineral wealth extraction, often due to low levels of literacy, education, and absence of requisite skills.

AFRICA, INNOVATION, AND SOLVING SOCIETAL PROBLEMS

It seems, however, that in Africa, insufficient attention is given to developing human capital. While national budgets focus on education (primary, secondary, and university), the human capital concept and the development of human capital goes beyond the provision of education per se. Admittedly, political instability and difficult economic circumstances have contributed to the marginalization of human capacity development in Africa. However, it is perhaps precisely because of the economic marginalization of various countries that they must urgently turn attention to human capital issues. Tackling human capital and its development requires that nations have a clear sense of their future economic and social imperatives and carry out a full analysis of the potential contributions from their natural resource endowments. These must be placed in the context of their comparative advantages within their region, trade blocks, global trends, and the institutional and productivity challenges they face. These must then be used to determine the stock of knowledge, skills, and value orientations needed for the future in determined periodic cycles.

Economic growth that is innovation-driven means that talent pools made of highly skilled theorists, technologists, and technicians brought together through unique policy formulations, interlinked state-private structures, and programmatic arrangements collectively and through iterative efforts bend their capacities towards socioeconomic advances that transform the lives of people within and across national boundaries. This paper takes the view that African countries have not paid sufficient attention to systemic human capital development with innovation in mind. Such appropriately set-up human capital systems involve the creation of structures and schemes for developing human capacity towards two primary ends:

- Strategic attention to resolving the human capital needs of the nation and economy into the medium and longer term; and
- The availability of researchers, designers, incubators, and entrepreneurs who make economic capital out of scientific and social innovations.

The African problem is that their human capital development systems appear disjointed and lack coherent focus towards the achievement of the two aims noted above. This mitigates innovation and severely limits the ability of African countries to leverage the skill sets of their people towards socioeconomic growth.

Let us return to Ghana as an example for Africa. Ghana gained independence from the United Kingdom in 1957. Since 1992, it has been noted as a stable democracy in Africa with a vibrant economy (growth rate of approximately 5% per year over the last 10 years). The formal economy is distributed between agriculture (23%), services (50%), and manufacturing/extraction (27%). Experts suggest Ghana is an emerging economy with middle-income status. It is ranked 64th on the Ease of Doing Business Index (http://www.doingbusiness.org/data/exploreeconomies/ghana/). It has a GDP of about US $90 billion, is one of the fastest-growing economies in the world (www.worldfolio.co.uk), and has significant mineral and hydrocarbon reserves including oil, which was pumped in commercial quantities from 2010; it is the second-largest gold producer in Africa after South Africa, ninth in diamond production in the world, and the second-largest cocoa producer after the Ivory Coast. In the last 10 years, various developments have seen the country attain significant growth and progress in areas

212 Bill Buenar Puplampu

such as telecommunications (over 20 million cell-phone lines in operation, over 100 Internet service providers, over 100 VSAT (satellite) operators, five major telecom companies using the latest fiber-optic technologies); 27 commercial banks and over 120 rural and community banks; two major hydro dams with a third under construction; and the fourth-largest solar plant in the world under construction by Blue Energy (a UK firm). These and other indices show that Ghana is fast developing. Its educational sector has seen rapid growth from three public universities in 1980 to eight in 2013, and more than 40 private universities including international brands such as University of Lancaster (UK), Webster University (US), Sikkim Manipal University (Malaysia), and China Europe International Business School (EU/China). Government policy intention through Vision 2020 aims to position Ghana as a newly developed economy by 2030.

Despite the above indices and factors, development intentions may not be achieved without significant human talent, capacity growth in human resources, and innovation that facilitates indigenous solutions to the country's problems. Such innovation does have to translate into viable business propositions that offer entrepreneurs opportunity to both solve problems and make a decent profit. The question though, is does the country's system for human capital development facilitate preparation for industry? Does it facilitate innovation and entrepreneurial engagement with the country's resource base and economic opportunities?

Innovation

Broadly defined, innovation refers to events and processes that end in the development of new solutions to existing and/or anticipated needs of markets, governments, and society. Thus, while creativity is often a psychological phenomenon and inventions are the development of new, hitherto-unknown methods, items, or processes, innovation turns on the application and use of new ideas/processes/events towards the solution of extant problems in a dynamic and iteratively incremental manner. The key issue with innovation is its capacity to transform organizations, societies, regions, and lately, the global community. One has only to look at the impact of the World Wide Web: cell phones, credit cards, prosthetics, etc., which through human creativity and ingenuity moved from invention to problem solving and enhancement of human existence. Africa's current state may be attributable in part to its inability to innovate. Individuals are certainly creative and ingenious enough to navigate the uncertainties of life on the continent. However, these acts or instances of creativity have not led to significant shifts in the quality of life of African peoples because the innovative groundswell has been absent. But the continent is a prime candidate for innovation. Natural resources abound that may be converted to created/manufactured wealth. Many challenges exist, from malaria through malnutrition to desertification and fuel shortages—all calling for innovative solutions.

But who are the innovators and what systems support the emergence of creative talent? What frameworks and structures support the deployment of the outputs of such creative talent towards viable problem solution? How can progress be attained through innovation by combining solution development, human societal enhancement, and commercial viability? The answers can be found in systems of human capital development.

Many scholars (Bontis and Fitz-enz, 2002; Olaniya and Okemakinde, 2008; Son, 2010) suggest that the basic thrusts of human capital thinking include a number of points such as:

- Economic prosperity of countries (national development prospects, efficient functioning of institutions within countries, and ultimately positive social change and standard of living improvements, etc.) are attributable to the existence of a stock of relevant human skills and competencies within the country.
- The skills possessed within a society or an economy facilitate a greater ability to transform natural capital (raw materials, resource endowments, etc.) into consumable goods, services, and processes.
- The educational system within a country (number and types of schools; levels of schooling—primary, secondary, tertiary, etc.; years of schooling; gender representation in school; literacy rates, etc.) represents the single (albeit composite) most verifiable factor or metric that accounts for human capital efforts.

Education, Innovation, and Human Capital Frameworks

Given the numerous problems and challenges of African countries, it is rather disconcerting that going by one measure of human capital development (years of schooling) sub-Saharan Africa lags behind with an average of 5.43 years of schooling. The global average by 2010 was 8.12 years; the average for industrialized countries was 10.81 years (Son, 2010). A simple inference is that at this rate, Africa will be unable to solve its problems by itself. Africa will not innovate. The problem however is a little more complex than limited years of schooling. The problem appears to include disjointed and misaligned policy and institutional frameworks for human capital growth.

African countries like Ghana do not seem to have arrived at the point of recognizing that human capacity is the solution to social problems and that human capacity is built through education. They also do not seem to have realized that education requires investments and strategic linkages to result in resourceful innovators who would bend their efforts towards problem solution. They also do not seem to have realized that integrated country-level systems and frameworks are necessary to give operational voice and reality to the human capital-education-innovation linkage.

African countries should design educational and skill development systems that enable creative talent to be nurtured. Educational systems must

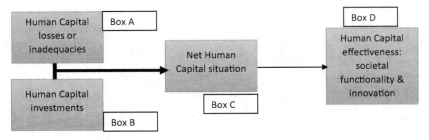

Figure 12.1   Human Capital and Societal Functionality

look to ensuring that skill gaps are properly understood and filled. This is captured by a model (Figure 12.1 below), which draws on Bontis and Fitzenz (2002).

THE DISJOINTS, MISALIGNMENTS, AND POLICY INADEQUACIES

Using a consideration of the stakeholders and actors within the Ghanaian human capital system, one may suggest that for much of sub-Saharan Africa, the ingredients for Box B (how the country makes HC investments) are ill considered, ill defined, and misaligned, and Boxes A (nature of HC attrition) and C (the prevailing HC situation) are poorly understood. While Box B represents the educational and human capital development process, Box C represents the prevailing situation along with the configuration of actors whose appropriate interlinkages would ensure that Box D actually happens. This notion of interlinkages is what drives the suggestion that a stakeholder analysis of the actors and players is necessary and important.

The Ghanaian situation is used here to discuss the matter. We need to look at the relevant stakeholders within the educational system to examine their policy direction and interlinkages with regard to human capital and innovation. In Ghana, the State Actors and Regulators for education include the National Council for Tertiary Education (which makes policy on higher education), the National Accreditation Board (which implements policy and accredits higher education institutions), and the Ministry of Education (which promotes the policy agenda of the ruling government).

Apart from the educational actors, there are research institutes such as the Council for Scientific and Industrial Research, Food Research Institute, Building and Road Research Institute, etc. They have the mandate to carry out research that may be directly applicable to solving human and social problems within their sphere. Then there are public and private universities, of which Ghana has over 50. These universities are the direct frontline actors in getting higher education delivered and appropriate skills built up within the country. Finally, there are industry players such as big firms and trade associations, for example, the Association of Ghana Industries, Ghana Employers Association, Association of Bankers, and National Board for Small Scale Industries, etc.

In a paper titled "Communities of Creation: managing distributed innovation in turbulent markets," Sawhney and Prandelli (2000) show that the economic system has various communities: communities of creation, production, and consumption. While the consumption community specializes in the use of finished products or services, the community of production "makes" the required services and products. The communities of creation include the organizations and groups that create knowledge, share ideas, develop thinkers and skills, and facilitate the turning of ideas towards problem solution. They suggest a number of important characteristics that are crucial to the viability of communities of creation. These include:

- Common interest;
- Explicit economic purpose and political/powerful sponsors who offer policy and material support;
- Shared means of communication and rules for participation; and
- Cooperation and mechanisms for protecting intellectual property rights and for facilitating development of appropriate intellectual capacities.

If policy, educational, research, and advocacy systems are fundamental to building national innovation talent and developing appropriate skill sets, then developing systems that link researchers, academia, and industry policy makers in a synergistic flow is critical. However, in looking at these players, it seems there are several disjoints and disconnects in the present policy, structural, and institutional arrangements. We argue that a fundamental issue at stake in Ghana (and Africa) is to interrogate why the present systems are mitigating skill development and innovation. Policy makers and higher education managers need to pause, reflect, and map out where skills are needed, where innovations are required, how structures may be realigned to deliver, and how the regional strengths may be leveraged to achieve regionally based skills that facilitate economic and social integration and growth.

In Ghana, the National Accreditation Board continues to accredit university-level institutions to offer business programs when the national need appears to be in the areas of science, technology, and medicine. Anecdotal evidence places graduate unemployment at about 15%–20%. A little over 60% of graduates are from the business and humanities specialities. Should not a policy review constrain the continued accreditation of institutions that seek to come on stream only to offer business and humanities programs?

Multiple government ministries and agencies have responsibilities for a variety issues all relating to education, skills, and skill deployment. These include the Ministry of Science and Environment, the National Council for Tertiary Education, the Research Councils, the Ministry of Education/ Ghana Education Service, etc.

It is unclear the extent to which these agencies "talk" with each other to arrive at the collaboration and cooperation referred to by Sawhney and Prandelli (2000) as key to communities of creation. The atmosphere that characterizes the relationship between regulatory bodies and the growing crop of private universities appears to be one of antagonism and policing rather than collaboration towards achieving a common goal of human capital development. In these regards, therefore, the policy direction with regard to human capital development is weak. In a country with a rather poor doctor-patient ratio (currently 1:16,000), it would be expected that policy supports would be evident towards facilitating more places for medical training. To date, professional training for lawyers is carried out only by the Ghana Law School, which has an annual intake of just about 200.

It is unclear whether the economic policy and natural resource potentialities have featured much in determination of skill development. It is unclear how developed skills may be nurtured and fostered to yield innovations that progressively remove socioeconomic disadvantages and address many problems such as sanitation, fuel, power, unemployment, poor health, institutional weaknesses, etc.

It is unclear whether the various actors have clear indications of what organizational capacities are required and at what level of competence—over the next decade or more—to foster organizational and institutional growth.

CONCLUSIONS: TOWARDS A STAKEHOLDER MODEL OF HUMAN CAPITAL DEVELOPMENT

Given the lapses noted above, a stakeholder model for developing human capital through education and achieving innovation for social and economic development is offered here in Figure 12.2. It builds on Figure 12.1.

Through Figure 12.2 above, we consider that Ghana (and other African countries) need to look very carefully at how to synergize the activities and efforts of all the parties to human capital development. Stakeholder inputs are critical and must be solicited on a regular basis. Relevant government departments must facilitate research and policy discourses on human capital needs and projections. Implementing agencies must be tasked with attention to the skill development imperatives of the country.

Ghana (and other countries in Africa) need to mainstream a human capital policy framework developed by a committee of experts who have the primary remit of engaging government and industry in discussion on what skills and knowledge the country truly needs over the next 15–30 years. The committee of experts should commission and use research findings on global high-end industry and commerce/corporate movements and innovations, regional realities, and comparative and competitive advantages.

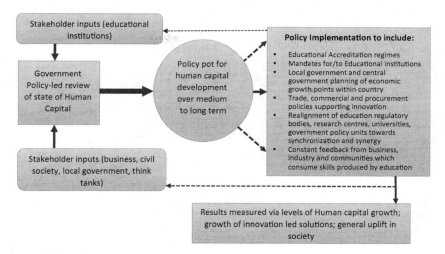

Figure 12.2 A Stakeholder Model of Human Capital Development

Universities and polytechnics need to engage in a focused interrogation of the range of program offerings and track the impact of the same on national wealth creation. This should then guide regulatory and implementing agencies and bodies such as the Ghana Education Service, National Accreditation Board, National Council for Tertiary Education, and so on in the formulation of the next line of action on skill consolidation. Ghana's National Accreditation Board, for example, should accredit programs and colleges not only because the programs or colleges have met critical pedagogical demands and measures set, but also because there is a clear sense of what accredited institutions and programs would contribute to the HC drive in the areas dynamically identified as critical for the nation. In this regard, it seems important to note that institutional capacity, organizational credibility and efficiency, national values, literacy, and work practices are key HC dimensions that need attention in the scheme of things.

South Africa has since 2003 published a Human Resource Development Review Report. This is a step in the right direction. Other countries on the continent need to adopt a model that starts with cogent analyses and research, leading to publication of national human capital, employment and productivity statistics that have integrity. These statistics should then be used by the committee of experts to map out human capital imperatives in 5–10-year cycles. These imperatives should become the basis for human capital public policy, educational policy, institutional policy, and regulatory convergence of bodies such as research councils, tertiary education institutions, accreditation agencies, university managements, and associations of public/private universities, polytechnics and colleges. At present it is unclear how/whether educational institutions are responding strategically to the economic future.

From the organizational to the national positions on HC, it is evident that HC growth does not occur as a matter of course. It requires specific interventions. If Hershberg (1996) argues that HC development is America's greatest challenge, it seems reasonable to suggest that African countries should take a cue and refocus attention on policy initiatives that address skills, values, literacy, competencies, and institutional capital that would insure to our good into the far future. In this chapter, we have suggested that what is required is a focused attention as well as synergistic interlinkage amongst all agencies and actors in the HC space in various African countries.

Future research needs to tackle a number of issues including exploring the apparent institutional/political resistance to crafting an encompassing and long-term educational and human capital policy regime, and the socio-economic implications of lapses in human capital planning using real-time data as well as baseline information on capacities and competencies in African countries—much like the work of Raven (1984) in the UK.

REFERENCES

Ajzen, I., and Cote, N. (2008). Attitudes and the prediction of behaviour. In W. Crano and R. Prislin (Eds.), *Attitudes and attitude change* (pp. 289–311). New York: Psychology Press.

Bailey, R. (2007). *Our intangible riches. World bank economist Kirk Hamilton on the planet's real wealth*. Retrieved May 10, 2008, from http://www.reason.com/news/show/120764.html

Becker, G. (1993). *Human Capital: A Theoretical and Empirical Analysis with Special Reference to Education*. University of Chicago Press.

Bontis, N., and Fitz-enz, J. (2002). Intellectual capital ROI: A causal map of human capital antecedents and consequences. *Journal of Intellectual Capital, 3*(3), 223–247.

Bontis, N., Keow, W., and Richardson, S. (2000). Intellectual capital and business performance in Malaysian industries. *Journal of Intellectual Capital, 1*(1), 85–100.

Bowles, S., and Gintis, H. (1975). The problem with human capital theory: A Marxian critique. *American Economic Review, 65*(2), 74–82.

Cantrell, S., Benton, J., Laudal, T., and Thomas, R. (2006). Measuring the value of human capital investments: the SAP case. *Strategy and Leadership, 34*(2), 43–52.

Garavan, T., Morley, M., Gunnigle, P., and Collins, E. (2001). Human capital accumulation: The role of human resource development. *Journal of European Industrial Training, 25*(2, 3, 4), 48–68.

Ghana Growth and Poverty Reduction Strategy (GPRS II 2006–2009). (2005). *Volume 1 Policy Framework*. National Development Planning Commission, Accra.

Hershberg, T. (1996). *Human capital development: America's greatest challenge*. Annals of the American Academy of Political and Social Science, 544, 43–51.

Kamoche, K. (1996). Strategic human resource management within a resource-capability view of the firm. *Journal of Management Studies, 33*(2), 213–233.

Keeley, B. (2007). *OECD insights: Human capital.* OECD Publishing.

Kraak, A., and Press, K. (2008). *Human resource development: Education, employment and skills in South Africa.* Cape Town: HSRC Press.

Olaniyan, D., and Okemakinde, T. (2008). Human capital theory: Implications for educational development. *Pakistan Journal of Social Sciences, 5*(5), 479–483.

Porter, M. (1998). *Competitive advantage of nations.* New York: The Free Press.

Puplampu, B. (2009). Developing Ghana's human capital editorial. *African Journal of Management Research, 18,* 1–8.

Raven, J. (1984). *Competence in Modern Society. Its Identification, Development and Release.* London: HK Lewis.

Rodríguez-Clare, A. (2001). Costa Rica's development strategy based on human capital and technology: How it got there, the impact of Intel, and lessons for other countries. *Human Development Report of 2001, UNDP.*

Sawhney, M., and Prandelli, E. (2000). Communities of creation: Managing distributed innovation in turbulent markets. *California Management Review, 42*(4), 24–54.

Smith, A. (1776). *An inquiry into the nature and causes of the wealth of nations. Book II.* Retrieved May 20, 2009, from http://www.adamsmith.org/smith/won-b2-c1.htm

Son, H. (2010). Human capital development. *Asian Development Review, 27*(2), 29–56.

Walumbwa, F., Aviolo, B., and Aryee, S. (2011). Leadership and management research in Africa: A synthesis and suggestions for future research. *Journal of Occupational and Organizational Psychology, 84*(3), 425–439.

13 Building the Next Generation of African Managers and Entrepreneurs

Henrietta Onwuegbuzie

INTRODUCTION

Management education in Africa at all levels has been characterized mainly by classroom teaching and learning (Safavi, 1981; Abdulai, 2014). The curriculum used has been based on colonial educational systems and models (Safavi, 1981). These models have been found to be inadequate for African culture and development (Hanson, 1971; Abdulai, 2014) as they do not accommodate the peculiarities of the African socio-cultural context and values (Kiggundu, 1991; Beugré, 2015). As Beugré (2015) explained,

> There is no doubt that management theories and techniques developed in the West or elsewhere cannot be applied to Africa, without considering the economic, technological, and, most importantly, social and cultural factors, specific to the continent (p. 1).

Further, the high failure rate of start-up businesses, ranging between 70% and 80% globally (Fatoki, 2014; Moya, 2015), suggests a fundamental weakness in preparation of individuals for entrepreneurship, and beckons the need for more adequate preparation. This preparation will facilitate a higher rate of successful entrepreneurial outcomes along with better management practices that enhance successful entrepreneurship. As SMEs (small- to medium-sized enterprises) tend to be the engine of economic growth and the greatest employers of labor in most countries (De Kok et al, 2013), strengthening management and entrepreneurial practices through appropriate training methods will greatly accelerate the attainment of the much desired inclusive growth and sustainable development.

This chapter explores an educational training framework aimed at improving management and entrepreneurial training, as well as prepare managers for African organizations. The proposed training format integrates a strong component of the traditional African indigenous entrepreneurial practice of apprenticeship with aspects of mainstream management learning practices to achieve a stronger preparation in terms of theory and practice of management and entrepreneurship.

As global unemployment rates continue to soar, with higher rates in Africa (International Labor Organization, 2014), there is an urgent need for an educational structure that emphasizes job creation over job seeking and adequately prepares students with entrepreneurial skills. This orientation is especially imperative for Africa, where the prevailing Western management systems are inappropriate and poorly applied and unemployment is higher. The proposed restructuring of the current educational system in this chapter allows more experiential management and entrepreneurial learning through the inclusion of a stronger apprenticeship component.

The traditional way of transmitting management and entrepreneurial learning was through apprenticeship, and this system trained individuals to learn by doing (Onwuegbuzie, 2014). These individuals successfully started and ran similar ventures to those in which they apprenticed. However, most of them faced a scaling challenge (Onwuegbuzie, 2014). On the other hand, current mainstream educational curriculum tends to emphasize preparation for paid employment. Considering the unemployment crisis resulting from having more job seekers than available jobs, there is an urgent need for the mainstream school curriculum to accommodate a stronger component of entrepreneurial and management training that adequately equips students to handle both management positions as well as successful entrepreneurship.

The proposed combination of the traditional apprenticeship system with current mainstream management training is therefore based on the realization that the traditional apprenticeship system effectively equipped individuals to successfully start and run a venture after the traditional six-year training period, though few tend to scale up (Srinivas and Sutz, 2008; Onwuegbuzie, 2014). On the other hand, the high failure rate among start-ups by those who have undergone mainstream training, even after many more years of schooling, reveals inadequate entrepreneurship preparation, even though those who succeed tend to scale up faster (Onwuegbuzie, 2014). Consequently, both the traditional and the formal systems of learning have advantages and shortcomings. Integrating both systems, as will be illustrated in the framework provided later on in the chapter, could help overcome the shortcomings in both systems. The combination is argued to provide a more effective training for management and entrepreneurship that could result in increased rates of successful and scalable forms of entrepreneurship.

The first part of the chapter provides a historical perspective of management education in Africa, discussing pre- and postcolonial management education in Africa and important aspects of the indigenous knowledge system that are relevant to contemporary management and entrepreneurship training. Apprenticeship as a specific example of indigenous African management practice is further discussed. Based on the case study provided, a framework is developed for management and entrepreneurship training that integrates traditional apprenticeship and mainstream learning, with the aim of deriving the advantages from both systems. This model, suggested for African scholars, could potentially inform global management training methods to increase the number and success rate of start-ups around the world.

HISTORICAL PERSPECTIVE OF MANAGEMENT EDUCATION IN AFRICA

This section highlights some of the historical features of management education in precolonial and postcolonial times. Kiggundu (1991) argues that management development specialists need to understand Africa's historical background to be able to contribute effectively to the continent's current management development needs. It is against this backdrop that we shall examine some aspects of Africa's historical background, especially as it relates to management development. It has been divided into these periods for clarity of understanding.

PRECOLONIAL MANAGEMENT EDUCATION

Education in precolonial times was an integral part of everyday life. It was linked to culture and tradition (Safavi, 1981; Ntuli, 2002; Fashoyin, 2005). It was more or less very practical and reflective of the needs and expectations of the community. One of the earliest universities in Africa and in the world was the University of Sankoré in Mali in West Africa. The university was founded in 989 by the Chief Judge of Timbuktu, Al-Qadi Aqib ibn Mahmud ibn Umar. It had its roots in the Sankoré Mosque and was financed by a wealthy Mandinka woman. It was a black intellectual institution renowned around the world between the 15th and 16th centuries, and also said to be the leading center of education at that time (Khair, 2015). The university was known for its high standards and attracted students from all over Africa and the Muslim world. For example, while the population of the whole city of Timbuktu was 100,000, the number of students who attended the university was 25,000. The subjects taught were Islamic studies, literature, medicine and surgery, astronomy, mathematics, physics, chemistry, philosophy, language and linguistics, geography, history, and art. Interestingly, however, the students at the University of Sankoré were also taught how to trade and matriculated with a specialization in a trade (Abdulai, 2014). The university's trade shops offered classes to train students in business, carpentry, fishing, farming, tailoring, shoe making, construction, and so on. The students were also taught business codes of conduct and ethics (Abdulai, 2014). Traditional African education was therefore linked to morality and respect for elders, as emphasized by Ntuli (2002).

Another phenomenon that displayed indigenous management knowledge in Africa was the pyramids of Egypt. The pyramids were a classic example of management and coordination. Built in 2900 BC, each pyramid required 100,000 men working for 20 years, covering 13 acres, and using 2.3 million blocks, each weighing an average of 2.5 tons. (Inyang, 2008). Management knowledge was clearly required to successfully coordinate workers to achieve results.

Traditional African communities were intrinsically entrepreneurial, as every family produced something they used as well as commercialized to earn a living (Vaz, 2006). They were known for producing and/or trading one solution or another, whether they were farmers, blacksmiths, fishermen, carpenters, herbal healers, or "baby-catchers" (those who specialize in delivering babies like midwives). Traditional communities especially in Nigeria could be described as a collection of entrepreneurs, with some more financially successful than others. The next subsection briefly describes the events after colonialism.

POSTCOLONIAL MANAGEMENT EDUCATION

The advent of colonialism in Africa in the 19th century disrupted cultural beliefs and traditions and thus triggered the beginning of what may be called "colonized African management" (Eze, 1995; Inyang, 2008). The African governments after independence almost invariably maintained the European approach to education. The objective of all systems was to provide a liberal arts education to all youths and to create labor power for public services. The design of educational programs did not fit the intrinsically entrepreneurial lifestyle of African communities. Neither did it train students in the kinds of skills, social education, and motivation they needed to contribute effectively to the socioeconomic enhancement of their communities (Small, 1978; Stabler, 1979; Safavi, 1981).

Yet another implication of colonial development and management transfer in Africa was the introduction of the concept of wage employment. Wage employment was uncommon in African countries as economic activities were centered around the family (Inyang and Akpama, 2002). There was hardly need for external recruitment of labor. The prevalent apprenticeship system provided additional hands. Apprentices were usually housed and fed, and after a period of about six years were rewarded for their labor by being provided the wherewithal to start a business venture in their field of learning. "The only thing akin to recruitment was communal exchange of labor, and of course, there was no cash nexus involved, that is, economic relations were not moderated by exchange of labor for payment of monetary rewards" (Eze, 1995; Inyang and Akpama, 2002, 15).

The closest in mainstream practice to traditional apprenticeship is the internship period required of students in some courses. Students are usually required to spend about 3–6 months in organizations getting hands-on experience. While this provides an opportunity to learn by doing, given the brevity of the period, the students are not as exposed to all ramifications of the business as apprentices who "intern" for as long as six years and even live with their masters. The traditional apprentices are therefore more embedded in every aspect of the business and imbibe greater learning regarding the business than modern-day interns who are usually restricted to a few departments in an organization, and even when they go round to all the departments, spend too little time to achieve in-depth learning, and so do not usually get a holistic understanding of the business. While the importance of classroom learning cannot be overlooked, the predominance of classroom learning over practical learning-by-doing in mainstream systems illustrates how Western forms of learning have overshadowed the predominantly practical learning system of apprenticeship in African tradition. A number of other traditional systems around the world also practiced apprenticeship as a means of transmitting management and entrepreneurial learning.

Throughout most of Africa, indigenous management theories and practices were inhibited by the advent of colonialism and Western management education (Inyang, 2008). The colonial administrations transferred their own educational systems with little adaptation to the colonies and trained teachers to provide the same curriculum of elementary and secondary schooling offered in the mother country (Clignet, 1974). As Gbadamosi (2003) further elaborates,

> Western management concepts and writings have dominated the thinking of academics and managers in Africa for a long time. Such writings have not shown how culture might be taken into account in managerial practice (p. 274).

Therefore, there was a clash between cultural norms and the formal Western systems in which most Africans have been schooled, resulting in the poor management practices evidenced in most African organizations. The struggle to reconcile cultural traditions with Western management styles has thus resulted in a situation of 'double jeopardy.' On one hand, African scholars were trained out of their intrinsic entrepreneurial orientation and reprogrammed to be wage seekers. On the other hand, they were made to subordinate, and to a large extent substitute traditional management practices that worked with Western-style management practices they frequently implemented poorly. Given that Western management practices are quite foreign to the prevalent culture in which they operate, it is not surprising that African professionals largely struggle with its practice.

The situation described above beckons a change that accommodates the positive traditional learning systems in each African country in achieving a more appropriate management and entrepreneurship training system for African scholars and practitioners.

APPRENTICESHIP AS AN AFRICAN
INDIGENOUS PRACTICE

The apprenticeship system in Africa serves a major purpose of learning trade and business practices that were culturally embedded (Kempner, Castro, and Bas, 1993). Every African community has its traditional code of conduct, which includes ways of showing respect to elders as well as practices considered taboos. Most modern-day Africans trained in the current formal learning systems are unaware of these norms, which would ordinarily have been communicated through the apprenticeship system.

The system successfully transmitted holistic knowledge of entrepreneurship through both tacit and explicit learning (Peil, 1970; Lave, 1977; Chuta, 1983; Gamble, 2002). The apprentice learned not just the skill he sought to acquire, but also virtues, values, and interpersonal skills from his more experienced master. The standard period of apprenticeship was six years (Onwuegbuzie, 2014). During this period, the apprentice served the master, usually without pay, while learning his trade or skill. At the end of the apprenticeship period, the master was expected to assist the apprentice in starting up his own venture by paying the rent for his first store and where applicable, providing his first stock of goods. This was a form of repayment to the apprentice, who, while learning by working for his master, also provided other domestic services.

The apprentice learned not just the skill or trade, but also learned how to manage people from watching his master deal with customers and staff. The cultural norms and values, which were known to all, made any aberrations or virtues in a master's behavior apparent to an apprentice, who then knew what to emulate or avoid. An apprentice therefore received comprehensive training to enable the successful management of a similar enterprise independently at the end of the established training period. Unemployment was therefore nonexistent in traditional African communities where this system was the norm, as there was no need to look for jobs.

Working and/or living with a master for the period left the apprentice with comprehensive knowledge about every aspect of managing the venture. The apprentices usually succeeded in running their own ventures, as they had experienced practically everything about the venture during apprenticeship. Consequently, business failure was unheard of as the level of preparation was extremely thorough. The only instances of failure, which were few and far between, were usually due to personal irresponsibility, such as drunkenness, where the individual chose to spend excessively on drinking rather than reinvesting into his venture.

The apprenticeship system therefore equipped individuals with the skills required to successfully start and manage a business venture. The fact that there were hardly any business failures in spite of operating in the least enabling environments attests to the thoroughness of the apprenticeship system, which also provided readily available cheap labor for the production of goods and services (Liedholm, McPherson, and Chuta, 1994). Nevertheless, these ventures usually did not scale up, though they provided a means for individuals to cater for their families.

The continued success of the apprenticeship system, which is currently practiced mainly in the informal system and rural areas, strongly suggests that the system may have evolved to develop more scaled businesses had its evolution not been truncated by colonization. This paper thus argues that the incorporation of the indigenous practice of apprenticeship in mainstream management education provides a more effective way to develop African scholars and entrepreneurs. The next section examines some aspects of indigenous knowledge systems that can be integrated in mainstream management curriculum.

INDIGENOUS KNOWLEDGE SYSTEMS

Indigenous knowledge systems (IKS) represent an accumulation of several years of experience based on observations, experiences, and the adaptive skills of several generations of people in a community that have been transmitted orally (Grenier, 1998; Warren and Rajasekaran, 1993). Indigenous knowledge, which played a major role as a means of survival in precolonial times, unearths a wisdom of old and continues to be relevant today, as evidenced by the increasing attention scholars are drawing to the importance of indigenous knowledge (Sen, 2005). They are applied to all aspects of life including the management of natural resources necessary for continued existence.

Some authors have emphasized the need to draw on local resources and indigenous knowledge systems for designing and implementing management programs (Thiong'o, 1987; Kiggundu, 1991; Ntuli, 2002) as a step towards decolonizing the African mind. Ntuli (2002) contends that "African history is a vast terrain of distortion, confusion and suppression." Ntuli (2002) further points out that in spite of the effort by the United Nation's Educational Scientific and Cultural Organization (UNESCO) to produce a nine-volume history of Africa by African scholars and other Africanists, ignorance still persists:

> The nine volumes are still unknown by African educators and where they are known, they are not prescribed, where they are prescribed, they are not taught, and where they are taught, they are taught from a western perspective thereby negating their very existence (p. 62).

Ntuli (2002) therefore, calls for a re-examination of indigenous knowledge systems with the aim of distilling valuable lessons that continue to be relevant to contemporary society and incorporated into management training taught in Africa.

Extant literature highlights some aspects of the indigenous management knowledge and practices in Africa that can be used in teaching formal education:

1. Learning through the *Amaghikiza system:* Education in the traditional African community was done through secret societies, initiation schools and through the *Amaghikiza system,* a type of mentorship program where older girls mentored younger girls to ensure sexual abstinence until the girls were ready to take full control of their affairs. Both male and female initiation programs sought to prepare youth to take control of their lives within the broader community. Group learning and group solutions to problems were employed, while emphasis was on horizontality rather than verticality in the learning process (Ntuli, 2002).

The above could be interpreted as modern-day mentoring, which some organizations practice. The mentoring in the above instance goes beyond the job, to the personal. Guiding the individual to grow in character, values, and discipline, which eventually impacts on how s/he works and relates with others on the job.

2. Strong emphasis on ethics, morality, and respect for elders: Underlying every effort toward learning and existing in the traditional African society was the culture of high ethical values, community, and respect. The ethos was "I exist because I belong: I belong because I exist" Ntuli (2002). Regarding African families, Safavi (1981) notes:

Families throughout Africa should be credited with instilling high ethical values in their children. Management educators acknowledged that their strong ethical foundation helped young managers resist the corruption prevalent in the government bureaucracies with which they must deal (p 321).

The above speaks to the value of integrating a strong component of cultural values in management learning to create the moral fiber necessary to resist corrupt or fraudulent practices. A well-known African proverb states, "a good name is better than a pot of gold," meaning that it is better to have a good reputation than to acquire wealth by corrupt means.

3. The Case of the Undugu Basic Education Program (UBEP) in Kenya (Ekundayo, 2001): The Undugu Basic Education Program (UBEP) was established by the Undugu Society of Kenya in 1978. The program's objective was to offer opportunities for the acquisition of functional literacy and practical skills to street and other disadvantaged children in the slums of Nairobi. The program was organized in three

phases, and each phase lasted a year. Subjects offered in Phases 1, 2 and 3 were similar to those offered in formal primary schools. After Phase 3, the learners received vocational training in carpentry, sheet metal works, and tailoring. The processes of learning were generally learner-centered. Learners with a preference for vocational training were apprenticed to artisans in the informal sector for the purpose of enhancing their practical skills and having insights into the world of work. At the end of the program, the apprenticeship system provided a link between learning and work and facilitated the transition from learning institutions to working life.

The above provides an example of indigenous management systems that are similar to aspects of current formal management education, from an indigenous cultural perspective. It contains a strong moral and practical component, which can work together with mainstream learning systems to produce better management and entrepreneurial learning. This combination will ensure that graduates are capable of becoming successful entrepreneurs and also honing their interpersonal skills and values to enable them handle scenarios that may not be contemplated during classroom learning, even when action learning tools such as case studies are used. The next section examines in detail the concept of apprenticeship and how it can be adopted as a strong component of management training in Africa.

THE CASE FOR APPRENTICESHIP

Underlying the discourse so far is the importance of apprenticeship in developing management scholars and entrepreneurs. Apprenticeship has also been seen to yield positive results not just in Africa, but in the world. Recent research conducted in United Kingdom (Clark, 2014) noted that only 5% of apprentices are unemployed 12 months after starting their job hunt compared with 16% of graduates and 13% of those with A-levels. This study, which was carried out by the Institute of Public Policy in the United Kingdom, further revealed that while unemployment rates had risen for all educational levels since the 2008–09 financial crash, the employment rate for apprentices remained unaffected.

Without downplaying the evident advantages of current formal management learning structures, the above suggests that the labor market tends to prefer those groomed through apprenticeship over school-leavers. Consequently, incorporating apprenticeship in the mainstream curriculum is likely to provide a stronger preparation that will make school-leavers more attractive in the job market. The following case study provides an example of how the combination of traditional apprenticeship and mainstream learning gives rise to effective management learning and successful apprenticeship that can be scaled.

Case Study

Madu was born in a rural community in Eastern Nigeria. The practice in the 1940s, when Madu was born, was for parents to send their children to primary school, and if they could afford it, also to secondary school, before putting them on apprenticeships to learn a trade or skill of their choice. Prior to this period, children just learned what their parents knew and there was no formal schooling.

Madu's parents could not afford to send him to secondary school, so after six years of primary schooling, Madu was asked what skill or trade he would like to learn so he could be sent on an apprenticeship. Madu had always looked on in admiration at older relatives who came to the village at Christmas in flashy cars. They sold spare vehicle parts in the city, and so Madu wanted to be like them, and told his parents, "I have always wanted to be a vehicle spare parts trader, just like my older cousins. I would like to apprentice with a motor car spare parts trader." Madu's parents initially could not find a spare parts trader they were friendly enough with, so Madu was sent to learn to trade in secondhand clothing with a relative.

Apprenticeship

Madu's first master sold secondhand clothing. Besides the fact that this was not what Madu really wanted, he treated Madu very badly. After a few months, Madu ran away from him and returned to his parents. Luckily for Madu, while home, he one day ran into an old family friend who was visiting. The family friend knew Madu was honest and hardworking and asked Madu if he was engaged in any way at the time. Madu explained his recent predicament, and so the friend asked Madu if he would like to come to apprentice with him in his motorcycle spare-parts business. Madu was elated and accepted. This was much closer to his dream of becoming a motorcar spare-parts dealer.

Madu worked hard while with his master and impressed him. Living with his master and watching the way he managed the shop and related with people was enlightening for Madu, who also learned to live a regular work schedule. He would wake early and go off to clean the store and arrange the stock before dawn broke to ensure early customers could be served. He would then have breakfast and spend the rest of the day helping to attend to customers and trying to get roaming customers into his shop. His master would usually come in soon after Madu had the shop cleaned and organized as he had been taught. There was a mechanic workshop next to the shop and Madu sometimes went over to help out. He loved this, as he enjoyed learning about cars and knew he wanted to be a car-parts dealer in the future.

In addition, Madu was learning from observing and doing; he read a lot. Having missed out on secondary schooling, Madu felt the need to make up by avidly reading. He read almost any book that came his way and bought quite a few from secondhand bookstores. Two books that influenced Madu for life were *The Power of Positive Thinking* by Norman Vincent Peale and *The Magic of Thinking Big* by David Schwartz. As Madu stated;

> I learnt the power of having a dream and thinking big. I learnt that once you have a dream, nothing on earth can stop it from happening. I also learnt that every problem around me is a business opportunity, so I am always thinking of solutions I can provide to the problems I see.

As the apprenticeship period drew to a close, Madu not only knew the business inside out but had started nurturing a vision to do the same thing on a larger scale. At the end of his apprenticeship, Madu's master wanted to make him the head of one of his branches in the East. But Madu, influenced by his readings, told his master he would prefer to go to Lagos, the commercial center of Nigeria, where he felt he would have more opportunities. His master was surprised that he rejected the offer. Apprentices were traditionally set up to start on a smaller scale and not usually presented with such an enviable opportunity as heading an established branch. He consequently felt Madu must have somehow made money for himself for him to be bold enough to decide to go to a large city like Lagos. He therefore gave Madu less money than he would ordinarily have been entitled to and bade him farewell.

In spite of the difficulties moving to the city entailed, Madu left for Lagos. While there, he had to squat with a friend, as he could not afford an accommodation of his own. As expected, life was tough for Madu in Lagos. He could only afford one meal a day, which he ate at night. He woke up early every morning and headed to the vehicle spare-parts market where his friend, who owned a shop, allowed him to hang around and help out. Madu creatively found a way to earn money by making commissions on the goods sourced for customers who came into the market. The sellers would give the needed product to Madu at a discounted rate so that he could earn a margin when the customer paid the going rate. In spite of how little money he made, Madu kept saving and hardly eating until he could rent a small store to start his own spare-parts business.

According to Madu, "My parents taught me to be hardworking, honest, and respectful. They told me that if I did all these, I would succeed in life." Madu took this advice to heart and displayed great interpersonal skills. When he eventually rented a store, he was able to get supplies on credit until his business was stable enough to pay as he purchased stock. Madu's personality endeared him to those he interacted with. Soon, people were willing to share trade secrets with him. One of Madu's friends eventually offered to take him along on one of his trips to import stock from China so that Madu could do the same, as his business was growing. Madu quickly learned the ropes, and after a few trips to China started getting curious about how the Chinese manufactured the parts he bought. He mentioned his curiosity to a Chinese supplier, who willingly invited him to visit his factory. Madu discovered that the production process involved making a mold, which was passed through a simple production line. The process was similar to that used by companies that manufactured plastic products. It then occurred to Madu that if he had the molds, he could actually manufacture the products in Nigeria through local plastic product manufacturers. He realized that local manufacturing would drastically bring down his costs and consequently the price to his customers.

Madu therefore ordered and purchased molds, which he brought back to Nigeria. He approached local manufacturers of plastic products such as buckets and convinced them that producing a motor vehicle spare part was more lucrative as they would make more gain per unit produced, even when the same quantity of input was used. The manufacturers were quick to embrace Madu's suggestion, and soon enough, Madu was stocking parts manufactured locally and supplying his customers at much lower prices. He soon became a game-changer in the industry, as he crashed historically higher prices to customers.

Other importers soon realized they couldn't compete with Madu as their costs were significantly higher than Madu's. Also, customers were already flocking to Madu to benefit from the cost savings. In order to survive, other importers of the same product soon became Madu's customers. Madu had therefore successfully changed the industry dynamics and rose to become a very profitable large-scale supplier of motorcar spare parts. On witnessing the success of this model, Madu continued to buy different molds of car parts that were both needed and difficult to find locally. The knowledge he acquired about cars during his apprenticeship period was a huge advantage for him, as it helped him easily identify what he should choose to provide.

> During my apprenticeship, there was a mechanic workshop beside my Master's shop. I used to spend some time helping out and I learnt a lot about cars . . . I can also repair cars. I know the parts that easily get worn out and so know, which parts will be in high demand. Those are the parts I stock.

Human Resources

Madu's staff were mainly apprentices who also lived with him. Apart from his computer-literate secretary and his driver, who were paid employees, his six staff were apprentices, who were provided with accommodation and feeding, along with some pocket money. They spent the first few weeks watching and learning before Madu was eventually able to entrust them with tasks. They kept the stock count, attended to customers, received deliveries from manufacturers, and cleaned the premises. The more they learned about the business and took charge, the more time Madu could dedicate to developing new product ideas. Madu's ability to keep identifying problems around him and developing solutions for them kept his business thriving. He had a notebook where he recorded ideas of solutions that were waiting to be developed. For instance, he designed racks to hold shoes, bags and belts, based on his observation that most people found it difficult to keep such items in order. The racks were an immediate hit when they reached the market, and he soon sold out.

Belief System

Madu treated all those who worked for him well. His apprentices looked up to him and it was obvious to them that he was developing them for the future. Madu's behavior was influenced by his Christian faith:

> I've always believed in God and the importance of keeping his teachings. I try my best not to do anything wrong to anyone. I believe that what one does to others comes right back, so I try to treat others as I will like to be treated. I also try to forgive those who have offended me. When it is difficult, I repeat out loud, three times, 'I forgive you', even when the person is not present. I feel better and can work better after that. I also make sure I repay all my debts. If I know I can't meet up with a repayment, I inform the lender in advance and crave more time. I don't wait for the due date before explaining.

Madu's actions were informed by his strong belief system. The sincerity of his actions inspired trust among his employees and apprentices who were very committed to the job. As his apprentices got to the end of their apprenticeship period, Madu unfailingly followed the traditional requirement of setting them up. He helped them financially with renting their first store and provided their first stock on credit. As they continue to replace their supplies by buying from Madu, their success also increased Madu's success.

CASE ANALYSIS

The case study showed how the knowledge Madu acquired during his apprenticeship period and through his wide reading both contributed to providing the strong foundation that led to his entrepreneurial success. Madu's knowledge of vehicle spare parts informed the choice of parts he imported, and that gave him a competitive advantage. The case consequently highlights the effectiveness of the traditional apprenticeship system, through which apprentices learn by doing, such that at the end of the stipulated period, they are prepared to successfully run and manage a similar venture of their own.

Madu's avid reading, which represents mainstream knowledge, provided him with a vision that went beyond the present size of his business and this encouraged him to work towards scaling his business. Madu was thus able to overcome the scaling challenge faced by most indigenous African entrepreneurs. The case therefore shows how the traditional and mainstream knowledge systems combine to provide complementary knowledge that allows for a successful entrepreneurial outcome. The case can be further analyzed under different themes that help to illustrate how the integration of indigenous and mainstream knowledge systems can work together to provide a more effective management and entrepreneurial preparation.

Learning by Doing

Madu learned how to manage a business by watching the actions of his master, and by working along with him. The way Madu's master managed resources and people provided a school of learning for Madu. While it could be argued that this system could foster both the virtues and vices of a master in an apprentice, the cultural norms that uphold values such as integrity, fair play, and industriousness actually allow the apprentice to discern when a master's actions are right and therefore worthy of emulation.

Learning Duration

The stipulated six-year apprenticeship period could also been considered one of the major success factors in the traditional apprenticeship model because it allowed sufficient time for the apprentice to get a thorough understanding of different facets of the business before launching into owning and running a business.

Madu was successful in managing his business as he had learned the fundamentals during his apprenticeship training. Consequently, the apprenticeship method if adopted in mainstream is likely to reduce the high failure rate recorded globally by mainstream start-ups.

Learning From Mainstream Systems

Madu had only six years of primary schooling in the formal system. However, his avid reading helped him develop a vision and the ability to think big. This led him to work towards scaling beyond counterparts in the industry he played in. The combination of Madu's apprenticeship and mainstream knowledge acquired through reading contributed to preparing Madu for a successful entrepreneurial outcome. While apprenticeship formed his knowledge of the trade, Madu's readings shaped his mind and stimulated his entrepreneurial alertness. Consequently, he was frequently thinking of solutions to problems around him. Unlike most indigenous entrepreneurs who fail to scale up, Madu was able to scale because he combined the mainstream knowledge he acquired through reading with his indigenous knowledge of the business, gained during his apprenticeship. The combination of both knowledge systems appears to provide a stronger preparation for learning. Madu's success was therefore as a result of both apprenticeship as well as mainstream learnings from reading widely.

Financial Support

The financial support traditionally provided to apprentices by the master is intended to support apprentices as they launch into their first venture. It can be likened to the SBA (Small Business Administration) loans given to start-ups in the US. In Madu's case, he did not get the usual financial assistance apprentices customarily receive at the end of the apprenticeship period because he turned down the offer to head a branch of his master's business. Madu nevertheless survived by dint of hard work and personal sacrifice. This suggests that while some financial support can facilitate business start-ups, it is not indispensable for a start-up to survive. Further, the hands-on learning during the apprenticeship period equips the apprentice with experience on how to manage during periods of scarce financial resources, which all businesses face in the course of their existence.

Belief System and Values

Madu's upbringing in the socio-cultural values of his community, as well as his faith, influenced his belief system and his behavior. This contributed to his entrepreneurial success as his pleasant character, interpersonal skills, and honesty endeared him to people, who facilitated his success by willingly sharing trade secrets with him. His personality facilitated the benefits he received from his network contacts and this accelerated the growth of his business.

Side Benefits of the Apprenticeship System

Finally, besides being a means of transmitting management and entrepreneurial skills, the apprenticeship system appears to provide cheap and committed labor, because as learners, apprentices, while working for the master are usually not paid a salary, especially when they are housed and fed by the master, which is not unusual. In some instances they receive a stipend.

Their level of commitment to the job tends to be high because of the relationship that usually exists between the family of the apprentice and the master, especially if the master treats the apprentice well. The master therefore enjoys committed and low-cost labor in exchange for sharing his knowledge. Depending on the nature of the business, a master can also grow through his apprentices, especially if the business entails buying and selling as the apprentices are likely to purchase supplies from their master rather than go elsewhere, especially if the master gives them a special discount for being his trainees. On the whole, the case illustrates the learning-by-doing that occurs during traditional apprenticeship and the potential benefits derivable from combining the traditional apprenticeship system with mainstream learning. The proposed new learning format is likely to provide a stronger preparation for African management scholars and entrepreneurs. A proposed framework for combining both traditional and mainstream knowledge systems is discussed in the following section.

THE NEW PARADIGM

A number of authors have argued that the best way to enhance economic, social, and political development in Africa is by institutionalizing indigenous African management systems (Blunt and Jones, 1997; Mbigi, 1997; 2005; Kamoche, 2000; Anyansi-Archibong, 2001; Mangaliso, 2001; Ngambi, 2004). This argument, as explained by Thairu (1999), is based on the fact that our African indigenous knowledge contains valuable information that is relevant to contemporary society:

> African societies have built up a wealth of indigenous knowledge in response to dynamic changes experienced in their environments. This knowledge must be taken into account when one is trying to improve the way an African organization is managed, how it is structured, and how decisions are made (p. 267).

Apprenticeship, as illustrated above, has traditionally been an effective means of transmitting both management and entrepreneurial learning. Even though the internship practice in mainstream learning systems provide a similar opportunity, the shortness of its duration does not permit the same depth of learning that is achieved through the apprenticeship system, which lasts for a longer period and during which the apprentice is fully embedded into the business. While acknowledging the importance of classroom learning, the proposed learning system combines the best of mainstream and traditional learning systems, as also advocated by Beugré and Offodile (2001), in their 'culture-fit model'.

The proposed format for teaching the next generation of management scholars and practitioners is hinged on the belief that management is culture-dependent (Drucker, 1969; Hofstede, 1980a; 1980b; 1991; Beugré and Offodile, 2001). The training model is premised on a six-year tenure and directed at individuals who are 18 years and above, with the aim of attaining a master's degree in management.

The proposed structure starts with the first phase, which involves a preliminary preparation of one year of classroom training, in which students are provided with historical perspectives and reasons behind the cultural values and norms of their country and most of the African continent. This will provide a foundation to guide students' behavior and decision making during the rest of their studies. Subsequently, in the second phase, which may be referred to as the immersion phase, students are sent to companies in industries of their choice for another four years. During this period, students will pass through departments representing different functional areas of management. The students in each cohort will all go through similar departments (in different companies) during the same period and return to the classroom for 2–3 weeks after each six-month period of apprenticing in a particular department of the company. For instance, in each set, all students will be in the HR department of different companies at the same time for a stipulated period of six months, so that when they return to the classroom, the sessions will be on HR. When they leave for another six months to say, the finance department of different organizations, when they return to the classroom, they take sessions on finance. The classroom sessions will facilitate a deeper understanding of their practical experiences during the six-month apprenticeship period and provide a forum for them to exchange ideas and lead to the discovery of theories. Following this pattern, they can apprentice in at least eight different departments and take the corresponding courses.

The sixth and final year can be dedicated to classroom work where a project or "thesis" on their learning experience will distil key learning points they can reflect on as they either start businesses of their own or take up paid employment. Figure 13.1 below provides an illustration of the 1–4–1 model, where the students begin with one year of classroom preparation and four years of in-company apprenticeship training, interspersed with relevant classroom learning and one year of guided research written up in a thesis that illustrates theories from knowledge acquired from the African context and key learning points.

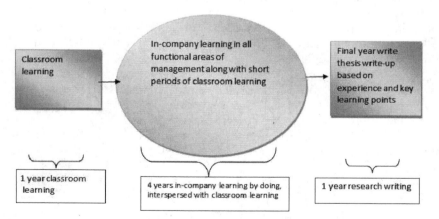

Figure 13.1 The 1–4–1 Model for Preparing the Next Generation of Management Scholars and Practitioners

The proposed model implies an increased interface between scholars and organizations/entrepreneurs. Abdulai (2014) notes that putting students to apprentice in corporate organizations will enable them acquire management skills before they graduate.

CONCLUSION

The discourse above presents apprenticeship as a method of learning and transferring knowledge that worked in the past and still works, and argues that it should be incorporated into mainstream learning systems to strengthen the preparation of African management scholars and entrepreneurs. The proposed learning framework implies that tertiary institutions would ordinarily be attached to companies in different industries. The 1–4–1 model, which entails one year of cultural learning and four years of immersion in different departments of an organization, during which they receive some interspersed classroom training for 2–3 weeks after every six months of working, and then a final year when the students would be required to distil their learning in the form of a research project or "thesis." During this final year, they will develop theories around their learning as well as articulate key learning points that will be useful to them as well as form a learning tool for others. The system is expected to deliver a stronger preparation for African management scholars and entrepreneurs.

This proposed framework for teaching management and entrepreneurship in African business schools can indeed be applied in other parts of the world, and could provide a potential solution to the global challenge of unemployment, as it has a strong entrepreneurial orientation that allows students become more confident about starting and running entrepreneurial ventures.

The proposed system would be greatly facilitated by government policies that create incentives for organizations to collaborate more closely with schools in order to achieve stronger management and entrepreneurial learning.

REFERENCES

Abdulai, David. (2014). *African-centered management education: A new paradigm for an emerging continent*. Ghana: Gower.

Agulanna, C. (2006). Democracy and the Crisis of Leadership in Africa. *The Journal of Social, Political, and Economic Studies, 31*(3), 255.

Anyansi-Archibong, Chiekwe. (2001). Towards an African-oriented management theory. In Felix Moses Edoho (ed.), *Management challenges for Africa in the twenty-first century: Theoretical and applied perspectives*, 1st ed., 63–72. Westport, CT: Praeger.

Beugré, Constant. (2015). The challenge of management scholarship in Africa. *Africa Journal of Management, 1*(1), 94–98. doi:10.1080/23322373.2015.994429

Beugré, Constant, and Offodile, Felix. (2001). Managing for organizational effectiveness in sub-Saharan Africa: A culture-fit model. *International Journal of Human Resource Management, 12*(4), 535–550. doi:10.1080/09586190110037083

Blunt, P., and Jones, Merrick. (1997). Exploring the limits of Western leadership theory in East Asia and Africa. *Personnel Review, 26*, 6–23.

Chuta, Eyinna. (1983). Upgrading the managerial process of small entrepreneurs in West Africa. *Public Administration and Development, 3*(3), 275–283.

Clark, Laura. (2014). Apprentices beat graduates in job race. *Daily Mail Newspaper.* http://www.dailymail.co.uk/news/article-2848218.

Clignet, Remi. (1974). *Liberty and equality in the educational process.* New York: Wiley.

De Kok, J., Vroonhof, P., Verhoeven, W., Timmermans, N., Kwaak, T., Snijders, J., & Westhof, F. (2013). Do SME s create more and better jobs? EIM Business & Policy Research Report.

de Noronha Vaz, T. (2006). Entrepreneurship in small enterprises and local development. *The new European rurality: Strategies for small firms,* 13–28.

Drucker, Peter. (1969, November–December). Management's new role. *Harvard Business Review,* 49–54.

Ekundayo, Thompson. (2001). *Successful experiences in non-formal education and alternative approaches to basic education in Africa.* Presentation, Tanzania.

Eze, N. (1995). *Human resource management in Africa: Problems and solutions.* Lagos: Zomex Press.

Fashoyin, T. (2005). Management in Africa. *Lagos Organization Review, 1*(1), 43–45. First published in the *Regional Encyclopedia of Business and Management: Management in Emerging Countries* (pp. 169–175) edited by Malcolm Warner, 2000, Thomson Learning.

Fatoki, O. (2014). The causes of the failure of new small and medium enterprises in South Africa. *Mediterranean Journal of Social Sciences, 5*(20), 922–927.

Gamble, Jeanne. (2002). Teaching without words: Tacit knowledge in apprenticeship. *Journal of Education, 28*, 63–82.

Gbadamosi, Gbolahan. (2003). HRM and the commitment rhetoric: Challenges for Africa. *Management Decision, 41*(3), 274–280.

Greiner L (1998). Working with Indigenous Knowledge, A guide for researchers. International Development Research Center. Ottawa, Canada.

Hanson, John. (1971). *Enhancing the contribution of formal education in Africa: Primary schools, secondary schools, and teacher training.* Washington, DC: Overseas Liaison Committee, American Council on Education.

Hofstede, G. R. (1980a). *Culture's consequences: International differences in work relations.* Newbury Park, CA: Sage.

Hofstede, G. R. (1980b, Summer). Motivation, leadership, and organization: Do American theories apply abroad?' *Organizational Dynamics,* 42–63.

Hofstede, G. (1991). *Cultures and organizations: Software of the mind.* London: McGraw Hill.

International Labour Organization. (2014). *Global employment trends 2014.* http://www.ilo.org/global/research/global-reports/global-employment-trends/2014/WCMS_233936/lang—en/index.htm

Inyang, Benjamin J. (2008). The challenges of evolving and developing management indigenous theories and practices in Africa. *International Journal of Business and Management, 3*(12), 122–132.

Inyang, Benjamin J., and Akpama, A. M. (2002). *Personnel management practice in Nigeria*. Calabar, Nigeria: Merb Business Center.

Kamoche, K. (2000). *Sociological paradigms and human resources: An African context*. Aldershot: Ashgate.

Kempner, Ken, de Moura Castro, Claudio, and Bas, Daniel. (1993). Apprenticeship: The perilous journey from Germany to Togo. *International Review of Education, 39*(5), 373.

Khair, Zulkifli. (2015). The University of Sankore, Timbuktu. *Muslimheritage. Com*. Retrieved February 16 from http://www.muslimheritage.com/article/university-sankore-timbuktu

Kiggundu, M. N. (1991). The challenges of management development in sub-Saharan Africa. *Journal of Management Development, 10*(6), 32–46.

Lave, Jean. (1977). Cognitive consequences of traditional apprenticeship training in West Africa. *Anthropology and Education Quarterly, 8*(3), 177–180.

Liedholm, C., McPherson, M., and Chuta, E. (1994). Small enterprise employment growth in rural *Africa. American Journal of Agricultural Economics, 76*(5), 1177–1182.

Mangaliso, M. P. (2001). Building competitive advantage from Ubuntu: Management lessons from South Africa. *Academy of Management Executive, 153*(3), 23–23.

Margaret, Peil. (1970). The apprenticeship system in Accra. *Journal of the International African Institute, 40*(2), 137–150.

Mbigi, L. (1997). *Ubuntu: The African dream in management*. Pretoria: Knowledge Resources.

Mbigi, L. (2005). *The spirit of African leadership*. Johannesburg: Knowledge Resources.

Moya, Mason. (2015). Research on small businesses. *MKM Research*. Retrieved February 16, from http://www.moyak.com/papers/small-business-statistics.html

Ngambi, H. (2004). African leadership: Lessons from the Chiefs. In Terry Meyer and Italia Bonineli (eds.), *Conversations in leadership: South African perspective*, 1st ed., 107–132. Johannesburg: Knowledge Resources.

Ntuli, P. (2002). Indigenous knowledge systems and the African renaissance: Laying a foundation for the creation of counter-hegemonic discourses. In Catherine Alum Odora Hoppers (ed.), *Indigenous knowledge and the integration of knowledge systems: Towards a philosophy of articulation. New Africa Book*, 1st ed., 53–66. Claremont: South Africa.

Onwuegbuzie, Henrietta. (2014). *The entrepreneurial learning process of indigenous knowledge entrepreneurs*. Ph.D. Lancaster University Management School, Lancaster.

Safavi, F. (1981). A model of management education in Africa. *The Academy of Management Review, 6*(2), 319–331.

Sen, B. (2005). Indigenous knowledge for development: Bringing research and practice together. *International Information and Library Review, 37*(4), 375–382.

Sillitoe, P. (1998). The development of indigenous knowledge. *Current Anthropology, 39*(2), 223–252.

Small, N. J. (1978). Getting ideas across: Limitations to success engineering in a new state. *African Affairs, 77*, 531–533.

Srinivas, S., and Sutz, J. (2008). Developing countries and innovation: Searching for a new analytical approach. *Technology in Society, 30*(2), 129–140.

Stabler, E. (1979). Kenya and Tanzania: Strategies and realities in education and development. *African Affairs, 78,* 33–56.

Thairu, W. (1999). Team building and total quality management (TQM) in Africa. In Julis Muruku Waiguchu, Edward Tiagha, and Muroki Francis Mwaura (eds.), *Management of organizations in Africa: A handbook of reference,* 1st ed., 267–279. Westport, CT: Quorum Books.

Thiong'O. W. (1987). Decolonizing the mind; the politics of language in African Heinemann, Nairobi: Portsmouth.

Warren, D. M., & Rajasekaran, B. (1993). Putting local knowledge to good use. *International Agricultural Development, 13*(4), 8–10.

14 Public-Private Partnerships for Enhancing Organizational Capabilities in Nigeria

Osikhuemhe O. Okwilagwe and Christos Apostolakis

INTRODUCTION

Public-Private Partnerships (PPPs) have become increasingly predominant as an effective way of delivering policy interventions rather than government-led approaches. As governments growingly experience huge infrastructure investment requirements, budgetary constraints, economic and technological changes, partnerships are looked upon as alternative ways to finance and deliver certain government services (de Bettignies and Ross, 2009; Drumwright, Cunningham, and Berger, 2004). It has been argued that the changing governmental role of coordinating and offering public services has created a systematic shift from bureaucratic hierarchy to the market and furthermore to networks. In this respect, partnerships are regarded as a new form of governance (Clarke and Glendinning, 2002).

Forrer, Kee, Newcomer, and Boyer (2010, p. 476) define partnerships as "long-term agreements between the government and private sector organizations in which the private organization participates in the decision-making and delivery of a public good or service that has traditionally been provided by the public sector and in which the private sector shares in the risk of that agreement." Local regeneration partnerships are thus argued to be an expression of the desire for and utility of such collaborations for the physical, economic, and social renewal of areas that have been subject to decline (de Bettignies and Ross, 2009; Davis, 2002).

The UK government in 1992 announced its Private Finance Initiative in the use of regeneration programs in cities like Manchester and Leeds and parts of London (Tsenkova, 2002; Broadbent and Laughlin, 1999). From this period onwards, the interest in partnerships grew rapidly to other developed countries, including Australia, United States, Canada, Germany, Japan, and the Netherlands. Emerging economies, like the BRIC countries Brazil, Russian Federation, India, and China have also adopted partnerships as a better approach for keeping up with the growing need for sufficient and effective public services and have been used extensively in road infrastructure and urban transport. An example of this is the São Paulo Metro Line 4 in Brazil (Willoughby, 2013; Kateja, 2012). In the face of a slow world economy, the economic conditions in Sub-Saharan Africa have remained relatively strong and growth in the region was projected at about 5.25% a year in 2012 to 2013 (IMF, 2012). According to Sanni and Hashim (2014, p. 134), "in order to address these developmental challenges, the governments in sub-Saharan Africa are now recognizing that public private partnership work is probably the most effective way for them to go forward." In these countries, PPPs have been used across various programs such as water, housing, transport, and road infrastructure.

In 2013, the World Economic Forum estimated that greater investment of about US$1 trillion per annum was needed globally for regeneration programs such as infrastructure development (WEF, 2013a). Of this amount, it is estimated that Africa needs to invest about US$93 billion annually to close its infrastructure funding gap (WEF, 2013b). A funding gap that is advocated can be filled up by bringing together capital investments, as well as expertise from both the public and private sectors (WEF, 2013a). Furthermore, whereas the huge capital investment may be a reason for such partnerships (Andrews and Entwistle, 2010; de Bettignies and Ross, 2009), on the other hand, partnerships also enable different organizations to support each other by ensuring more efficient mobilization of resources, leveraging and capitalizing on their complementary strengths and capabilities and addressing the nexus of local regeneration problems using more comprehensive approaches (Tsenkova, 2002).

In Nigeria, PPPs are beginning to play a key role in keeping up with the growing need for sufficient and effective public services. PPPs are envisaged to play a significant role in fulfilling the objectives of the National Integrated Infrastructure Master Plan (NIIMP) approved by the Federal Executive Council in 2014. The Master Plan is a 30-year plan and is to be implemented using 10-year operational plans and 5-year medium-term plans (Leke, Fiorini, Dobbs, Thompson, Suleiman and Wright, 2014; World Bank, 2014). It has thus been suggested that the desire and need for local regeneration is one of reasons the government of Nigeria looked at the practices of PPPs, because an estimated US$350 billion is needed by the country to meet its infrastructure needs (World Bank, 2014; AfDB, 2013a). In other words, local regeneration partnerships have come to be symbolized by a number of projects that enhance the capacity of economic activities in Nigeria.

The collaborative endeavors of partners can help to shape and steer local regeneration issues and also improve the chances of addressing them successfully (Lasker, Weiss, and Miller, 2001). Additionally, Huxham (1996) and Huxham and Vangen (2005) confirm that the aspiration of partnerships is to gain some form of collaborative advantage from their arrangements. This distinguishing feature and overarching goal of partnerships is the key mechanism through which these partnerships gain an advantage over individual organizations in addressing local regeneration issues. On the other hand, Macdonald and Chrisp (2005) and Lasker, Weiss, and Miller (2001) believe that the ability of a partnership to achieve some form of collaborative advantage is likely to be influenced by internal factors in the partnership such as the opportunistic behaviors exhibited by the partners and delays caused by renegotiations or cost overruns. They further argue that partnerships can also be influenced by factors in the external environment that are beyond the ability of any partnership to control, such as a change in the political climate where the partnership operates. Some have also argued that certain collaboration elements such as mutual interdependence, trust, and transparency between partners appear significant for collaborative arrangements to progress (Willems and Van Doreen, 2012; Bovens, 2010; Brunetto and Farr-Wharton, 2007; Vangen and Huxham, 2003).

Nevertheless, the difficulties in reporting the potential benefits of any form of collaboration in a developing country have been raised from various research (Ramiah and Reich, 2006; Selsky and Parker, 2005; Miraftab, 2004; Otiso, 2003). According to Selsky and Parker (2005) and Otiso (2003), this may be due to the form of partnerships that operate at subnational levels outside the attention of researchers and most of these activities are usually funded and published by donor agencies as promotional materials. Mitchell-Weaver and Manning (1991, p. 16) also argue that "partnerships need to be defined and categorized as to their role in development planning and decision making under different development strategies and at different scales of action." Further to the these arguments, Selsky and Parker (2005) in their research on cross-sector partnerships to address social issues suggested that it was imperative to investigate how partners overcome or exploit sector differences to learn about their social issue, learn from each other, and/or encourage partners learning to reach intended outcomes.

To contribute to this limited literature, this chapter will investigate the capability of partner organizations to benefit from the full potential of their collaboration and the effectiveness of their partnership arrangement to achieve their intended goals from the context of a developing African country, Nigeria. This is in contrast with most studies that have focused on these regeneration partnerships in developed countries and are consequently better reported than in developing ones (Couch, Olivier, and Borstinghaus, 2010; Ramiah and Reich, 2006; Selsky and Parker, 2005). This investigation was carried out using data collected from semi-structured interviews between March and April 2014 from key officials involved in a toll road partnership arrangement in Lagos, Nigeria.

The chapter provides the theoretical basis for the research; it begins by developing a theoretical framework that integrates the literature on collaborative advantage in partnership arrangements. The following section discusses the methodological approach, the context of the empirical research as well as the case study investigated. Following from this, the discussion of the findings are presented. The chapter concludes with a discussion of the contribution of the research, managerial implications, the research limitations, and suggestions for further research.

PUBLIC PRIVATE PARTNERSHIPS: NECESSITY OR OPPORTUNITY

The process of local regeneration through infrastructure development (both economic and social infrastructure) by the public sector could be slow and inefficient. This quandary of inefficient public infrastructure delivery is worsened in developing African countries by government coffers not being able to finance and deliver on infrastructure development so as to meet population growth and ease the pressure on existing infrastructure (Willoughby, 2013). In these African countries, PPPs can be a viable way forward to overcome the limitations of the traditional delivery models by accelerating major rehabilitation and renewal projects, particularly the ones with large capital expenditure involved, and are also best suited to greenfield infrastructure projects, with their greatest potential positioned in emerging and developing African countries (WEF, 2013a). Like any other delivery model, PPP arrangements can be stalled with difficulties preventing them from getting off the ground or be prone to opportunistic activities; hence, they need to be properly structured to ensure they run a successful life cycle (Farlam, 2005).

Collaborative Advantage: The Notion

It is evident from literature that the collaboration process from the formation stage through to the evaluation stage of a partnership life cycle can be a difficult journey for public and private sector partners. Although these forms of collaboration are usually taken to be a good thing, Asthana, Richardson, and Halliday (2002) argue that it is significant to determine the conditions or factors that increase the probability of successful collaborations emerging. Himmelman (1996, p. 28) defines collaboration as "exchanging information, altering activities, sharing resources and enhancing the capacity of another for mutual benefit and to achieve a common purpose."

In the context of PPPs, Gray (1996) offered a framework conceptualized along two dimensions in which she classified different interorganizational collaborations, the factors that motivate partners to collaborate, and the type of outcomes expected. According to this framework, collaborations involving collective strategies on how partners can implement a shared vision can be labeled as partnerships, whereby through their collaborative capacity, the partners gain appreciation of their interdependence.

Furthermore, the value of collaboration could be identified within the capacity of partners from different organizations to combine their resources and expertise in order to create and sustain successful partnership working; this notion has been termed 'collaborative advantage' (Huxham, 1996; Kanter, 1994). Giving the high investment in resources involved in partnerships, it will often be difficult to justify collaborating except when real advantage can be gained from it. According to Huxham (1996, p. 14), "collaborative advantage will be achieved when something unusually creative is produced—perhaps an objective is met—that no organization could have produced on its own and when each organization, through the collaboration, is able to achieve its own objectives better than it could alone." The emphasis of this definition is that it focuses on the need for each individual organization to achieve its own objectives better than it could alone and from the recognition that it is a necessary requirement for successful outcomes of the collaboration.

Apostolakis (2004) and Kanter (1994) further argued that collaborative advantage defines a high value and ambitious form of collaboration and is vital to the growing practice of partnerships. Consequently, when partners are encountering challenges in operationalizing their strategies, according to Huxham and Vangen (2004), the main values of the concept of collaborative advantage can raise the profile of collaboration and legitimize it as an activity worthy of resource investment. Partners therefore need to engage in a continuous process of encouraging the collaborative processes within the partnership working. Considering that collaborative advantage can maximize the value gained when collaborating, the theoretical framework that guides this chapter is the theory of collaborative advantage. The theory of collaborative advantage is to support partners who seek to understand and capture the complexity of collaborative advantage in practice and convey it in a way that will seem real to those who experience it in their partnership process (Huxham and Vangen, 2005). This helps reinforce the rationale for translating the methodologies of the theory into a different geographical context.

Collaboration Elements in a Public-Private Partnership Working Context

Looking inwards into region-based economic and social issues, many PPPs experience local context factors, such as changes in the political climate where the partnership operates or the way business is conducted in that area that are likely to make achievement of collaborative advantage challenging. These context-specific factors are influential for the applicability of new policy approaches in any geographical context; therefore it is useful to conceptualize the collaboration elements in a partnership working as close as possible to the geographical contexts the PPPs operate in (Faehnle and Tyrvainen, 2013; Slater, Frederickson, Thomas, Wield, and Potter, 2007). Furthermore, according to Hudson and Hardy (2002), partnership working can be laden by excessive bureaucracy and cumbersome working arrangements. In such instances, bureaucracy can reveal a partner organization's true intentions.

Defining the relevant collaboration elements in partnership working within its context can further assist in exploring the concepts of collaboration and collaborative advantage. Therefore, taking this into consideration, collaboration elements in partnership working in the context of this chapter are defined as (a) *mutual interdependence* of the partners in the collaboration process; (b) *trust* between partners in the partnership working; and (c) *transparency* in the decision-making processes.

Lachapelle and McCool (2012); Lookwood (2010) and Slater et al (2007) argue that trust and transparency of partners are increasingly considered to be significant components of a successful partnership working. In other words, any activity that is seen to be nonopportunistic and to increase the partnership working experience, alongside the expectation to achieve the partnership goals, increases collaborative advantage between the partners. These collaboration elements will now be defined and discussed in relation to the collaborative advantage theory.

Mutual Interdependence, Trust, and Transparency: Enablers of Collaborative Partnership

Furthermore, within the context of the debates above, researchers have also argued that collaborative advantage is the proximal outcome of partnership working that gives them their unique advantage (Huxham, 1996; Kanter, 1994). This debate has benefited from the support of various researches conducted in developed countries; Wilson (2014) explored key factors in the dynamics of the collaborative process and identified both congruence and discord in the perspectives of academics and employers in Northern Ireland. Yet, it is a testable theory that can be investigated based on the underlying assumptions of collaborative advantage and in a reasonably clear way of asking the members of these partnerships in another empirical context if their experiences conform to these underlying assumptions of the theory of collaborative advantage.

It is imperative to note that there is the danger that PPPs are treated as models that could be implemented without restriction in every geographical context. Within the context of developing countries, such as Sub-Saharan African countries, Miraftab (2004) suggested that political, social, economic, and cultural environments greatly influenced partnerships in ways that led them to deliver outcomes opposite to those they claim. According to Rein and Stott (2009), it is often difficult to assess whether the good intentions behind partnerships are translated into real benefits for partners and the intended beneficiaries. In their study on six cross-sector partnerships in Southern Africa, they found that proper monitoring and evaluation processes were usually absent in these partnerships. The study concluded that the potential value of partnerships lies in their ability to deliver tangible developments in social and economic infrastructure and the opportunities they can give to relatively declining areas of a community.

This chapter contributes to this debate by reporting research that investigated mutual interdependence, trust, and transparency from a collaborative advantage theory perspective against the experiences of key officials involved in local regeneration PPPs in Nigeria, as it has been established in the literature theoretically and empirically as a paramount theory tool under which PPP arrangements can be examined, based on the value they add to the partnership working (Vangen and Huxham, 2003; Huxham, 1996). Rein and Stott (2009, p. 86) emphasize that "there is a real danger when replicating partnership models and projects as certain factors may not be taken into account, for what has being proven successful in one context can be valuable both as a learning resource and as an inspiration, but cannot necessarily be transferred directly, in the same form, to a new context, without a thorough and locally informed analysis of the new environment." Considering the political, cultural, social, and economic diversity of African countries, collaborative advantage theory provides the tool to investigate how partners benefit from the full potential of their collaboration and influence the capacity of their partnership to achieve their intended goals.

Mutual Interdependence of the Partners in the Collaboration Process

From the discussion in the previous sections, the chapter conceptualizes mutual interdependence in arrangements as involving the collaborative processes that contribute to and strengthen the partnership working, for instance, commitment and ownership, resource and information sharing, collaborative decision making, community involvement, and collaborative communication and governing of partner organizations (Huxham and Vangen, 2005; Apostolakis, 2004; Hudson and Hardy, 2002). Mutual interdependence thus acts as an incentive to enter into partnership arrangements and motivates partners to pursue collective goals. The application of partnership work in Sub-Saharan Africa has been based upon the argument by all sector participants that it can flourish only if stable communication channels are established. Partnerships have been implemented, although lack of capacity and policy direction, mistrust among government and other implementing agencies, policy bias against PPP, high participation costs, low technology, socio-cultural and macroeconomic issues, delay in negotiation, and poor performance are among the challenges that one can identify affecting the smooth management and implementation of the PPP projects in Sub-Saharan Africa (Sanni and Hashim, 2014).

According to Lasker, Weiss, and Miller (2001), the collaborative advantage that partnerships achieve is reflected in the way partners think about the partnership's goals, strategies, the type of activities the partnership carries out, the partnership delivery and the relationship the partnership develops with the local community. The innovative interventions and holistic functioning of partnerships are likely to be revealed in the development of strategic plans and partnership delivery that have a considerable potential for success; the achievement of the partnership goals is likely to be reflected in the scope of the partnership efficiency and management effectiveness as part of their collaborative advantage.

Furthermore, the capacity of PPP arrangements to identify and concentrate on the issues that matter to the community, to communicate how its activities will deal with these issues, to evaluate its activities and to obtain widespread community participation can strengthen the sustainability of the partnership, thus allowing it adequate time for its activities to have a meaningful influence on the delivery of local regeneration initiatives and consequently have a long-term effect on outcomes (Cropper, 1996).

Trust Between Partners in the Partnership Working

Partnerships are characterized by mutually beneficial interactions of partners and the expectation that these partners will act in favor of the partnership arrangement (Forrer et al, 2010). In other words, positive actions of the partners to decrease opportunistic activities will increase their trust in the partnership. According to Hudson and Hardy (2002, p. 57), "development and maintenance of trust is the basis for the closest, most enduring and most successful partnerships."

According to Krishnan, Martin, and Noorderhaven (2006), trust is suggested to bring about good faith in the intent, reliability, and fairness of partner behavior. In this chapter, trust is defined as the expectation that a partner organization can be relied upon to fulfill its obligation and will behave in a predictable manner and will act fairly when the possibility for opportunism is present (Zaheer, McEvily, and Perrone, 1998). It plays a key role in the development and sustainability of long-term collaborations, which allows for practical interpretation of partner intentions, facilitates more open communication, and reduces the potential for conflict, resource sharing, strategic flexibility, and predictability (Seppänen, Blomqvist, and Sundqvist, 2007).

Trust is also suggested to have different effects on partnership arrangements depending on the environmental and internal factors within which partners interact (Lachapelle and McCool, 2012). Therefore, it is useful to conceptualize trust as close as possible to the geographical contexts the partnerships operate in (Faehnle and Tyrvainen, 2013; Slater et al, 2007). As argued by Ng, Lau, and Nyaw (2007); Zaheer and Zaheer (2006); and Dyer and Chu (2000), depending on how trust is perceived, the institutional and cultural support for trust can vary considerably across national contexts and may also have an effect on the partners' opinions and awareness of trust. Moreover, as trust is a context-specific concept, partnerships are likely to experience local context factors that make it more difficult for them to achieve collaborative advantage (Appuhami, Perera, and Perera, 2011). To establish and sustain trust throughout a partnership is not an easy process; this has been attributed to the complexity that is attached to the formation of the partnership arrangements and to uncertainty within its environment (Lachapelle and McCool, 2012). From the partnership work produced in these Sub-Saharan countries, it seems that building trust is a complex endeavor, heavily loaded with ethical, social, and cultural issues.

These challenges significantly affect the policy with skepticism and concerns regarding private-sector involvement and can affect partnership operation (Ezezika et al, 2013).

Transparency in the Decision-Making Processes

Transparency is defined as the visibility of a decision-making process, and it is a requirement that is grounded in governance ethics, of each partner organization's right to know about matters and decisions that affect the partnership arrangement (Lookwood, 2010). Decision support systems such as detailed information indicating the reason and procedures behind each decision reached and the clarity and justification of every particular course of action is vital (Willems and Van Doreen, 2012).

Akkermans, Bogerd, and van Doremalen (2004) argue that transparency in partnerships is as a result of reinforcing dynamic interactions between partners. They also argue that the more partners work closely together, the more they will trust each other and the more mutual their collaborative working. This will improve their performance level when working together, while further improving trust in the collaborative process. Performance reporting is also an important aspect of transparency; it is essential that these partnerships regularly disclose their progress through various mechanisms such as annual reports, reports of achievements as against intended goals and management effectiveness evaluations (Forrer et al, 2010; Lookwood, 2010).

NIGERIA'S INFRASTRUCTURE FUNDING GAP THROUGH LOCAL REGENERATION PARTNERSHIPS

Nigeria is viewed as an emerging market, a middle-income economy with fast-developing financial, service, telecommunication, and entertainment sectors. To better measure the size of its economy, the country re-based its GDP in April 2014 from $454 billion in 2012 and $510 to 2013 by changing its base year from 1990 to 2010; this brought the country's GDP ahead of South Africa's GDP of $354 billion, making Nigeria the 26th-largest economy in the world from the previous 30th position (Leke et al, 2014). These new figures can be attributed to the attraction of international investors since 2009 to the country's strong growth indices, enhanced macroeconomic stability, increase in population, and unsaturated markets (Masetti, 2014; AfDB, 2013a). Furthermore, the ongoing economic reforms in Nigeria have also aided the country as the largest economy in Africa. These economic reforms have influenced the country's institutional environment through the process of decentralization, leading to a rise in privatization and commercialization (Olaseni and Alade, 2012).

Another feature of the economic reform process has been the introduction of PPPs targeted at the local regeneration of communities through infrastructure development. With the rapid growth of the country's population, which currently stands at about 174 million, and the increase in rural to urban migration, there is the need to mitigate the pressure this growth puts on housing and energy as well as to consider other social concerns such as poverty and the deterioration of the local environment (AfDB, 2013a). However, with the responsibilities for addressing local regeneration issues passed on from federal to state levels, state governments are expected to do more with the available financial funding in maintaining local infrastructure and service provisions (Babatunde, Opawole, and Akinsiku, 2012).

The desire and need for infrastructure development could indicate why PPPs as a policy approach have extended to various states in the country (Olaseni and Alade, 2012). According to Couch et al (2010), when policy makers in a country are faced with a new crisis, there is usually the trend to use or adopt solutions that have been implemented in the past or implemented in another country. Though Nigeria has become Africa's largest economy, it still lags behind South Africa in terms of economic development. The country is still a long way off in bridging the gap in infrastructure development (Babatunde, Opawole, and Akinsiku, 2012). Ongoing reforms in the public sector can only affirm the need for the adoption of PPPs in the country. Oluwasanmi and Ogidi (2013) believe that the government is moving progressively towards a private sector–driven economy, and one of the major objectives is to facilitate the effective implementation of necessary policies such as enabling laws to regulate the PPP arrangements.

Furthermore, in order to promote the implementation of PPPs in the country, the Infrastructure Concession Regulatory Commission (ICRC) Act was enacted into law in 2005 by the government to ensure adherence to best practices (ICRC, 2009). The Infrastructure Concession Regulatory Commission was also established as a federal government agency tasked with the responsibility of monitoring PPPs by an act of parliament the same year. The ICRC has the mandate to regulate the PPP environment; develop the relevant legislation, guidelines, and specific procedures for PPPs as well as to monitor compliance of PPP contracts (ICRC, 2009).

There has been some degree of success in the implementation of PPPs since 2001; an example of this is in the revitalizing of the power sector in 2014, leading to an improved power supply per day. Also in the transportation sector, the modernization of the Abuja-Kaduna railway line is at 46% completion and the Lagos-Kano and Lagos-Ibadan lines have been rehabilitated, where access to local communities has been increased as well as a reduction in travel time to these communities (AfDB, 2013b). This is amid a few past failures in the quest to fully implement PPP arrangements; the rehabilitation of the Lagos-Ibadan Expressway into five lanes, which was a concession agreement with Bicourtney Nigeria Ltd., failed because a financier could not be gotten for the concession. This was inevitably reverted to the traditional procurement method of contracting (Oluwasanmi and Ogidi, 2013). Another failure was recorded in the PPP arrangement between the federal government and the state governments of Kogi and Nasarawa for the construction of the Guto-Bagana bridge over the River Benue. According to Oluwasanmi and Ogidi (2013), the failure of this arrangement was due to one or more of the partners not being able to meet up with the terms of the contractual agreement.

From the discussion above, it can be argued that although considerable changes in reforms across various sectors are taking place in Nigeria, this is evident with the establishment of institutions with the relevant authority to promote PPPs, it might be too soon to praise the commitment of the federal and state governments towards considering the adoption and implementation of PPPs, the willingness of interest groups to adopt the policy or to depict that there is a favorable PPP policy climate in the country.

RESEARCH STRATEGY

To understand collaborative advantage between public and private sector partners, a qualitative case study approach was used. A case study research was extensively used to explore the opinions and behavior of individuals and groups within organizations (Gibbert, Ruigrok, and Wicki, 2008). Case studies rely on multiple sources of evidence, with the data converging through triangulation, and as a result, they benefit from the development of the theoretical propositions to guide data collection and analysis. This helps to generate rich and contextual interpretations of the data collected (Yin, 2009). Case study research is a beneficial approach where there is little previous empirical research and also in situations where there are complex and multiple processes, thus necessitating the use of a qualitative, explorative approach (Yin, 2009).

Eisenhardt (1989, p. 534) defines a case study as "a research strategy which focuses on understanding the dynamic present within its natural settings." Case studies are advocated as methodological tools for providing descriptions and to test theories. They are the preferred strategy for asking "how and why" questions and the researcher has very little influence over the events and the entire emphasis lies on an existing phenomenon within a real-life context (Yin, 2009). The developing African country context provides an opportunity to study PPPs outside of the developed world and to test whether the theories developed in the developed world make sense in this context. Though a single case is used in this research, the participants were from the public and the private sectors to provide a rich research context. More specifically, interviews were carried out with participants from government organizations, regulatory and advisory bodies, funding organizations, financial and investment organizations, consulting and infrastructure development firms.

Research Design, Case Selection, and Description

The poor condition of roads throughout the country is quite evident due to the low quality of construction and maintenance (ADF, 2010). Road networks are vital to the country's economic growth because about 80% of Nigerian traffic (including people and goods) are conducted by road. However, it is estimated that about 42% of federal roads, 70% of state-owned roads, and 90% of local government roads are in poor and unmaintained condition (AfDB, 2013b). The case selected involved the building and designing of a toll road to link various communities within Lagos, a western state in Nigeria. According to (OPPP, 2011), one million motor vehicles are estimated to be stationed within Lagos State with a daily traffic flow of about 500,000 motor vehicles to and from the commercial business center of the state to other environs (LCC, 2015).

The toll road partnership was signed in 2006 and was a partnership among a Special Purpose Vehicle (SPV) and the state government. The partnership was formed based on the Design, Finance, Build, Operate and Transfer (DFBOT) partnership model to construct and maintain a toll road for a 30-year concession agreement (Ekanem, 2010). The financial close was achieved in 2008. The agreement was scheduled for two phases: the first phase was the expansion and upgrade of 49.4 km of road and the construction of a ramp. The 50 billion naira (US$333 million) estimated project cost financed by the SPV was to be recovered through charging tolls, advert fees, duct leases, and so on (Ekanem, 2010). The second phase was the construction of 20 km of coastal road. The state government was able to provide 5 billion naira of mezzanine finance and the federal government provided a sovereign support for the financing. Lagos State established the "Roads Law" in 2004 as an enabling framework for such PPP arrangements (LCC, 2015).

The partnership was selected because it was the pioneering local regeneration partnership arrangement at a state level using the PPP model. The Lagos state government in 2014 re-acquired the concession rights from the private partners six years into the concession agreement. The decision to buy back the concession rights has been linked to the request of the SPV company to raise the rates of tolls on the first toll plaza by 20% and also to commence toll collection at the second toll plaza. which is about 10 km from the first at the new rate. This was to enable the SPV to raise the needed funds for further construction and to cover the costs of construction resulting from the increase in interest rates (Vanguard News, 2013).

Data Collection and Analysis

The primary method for data collection was through semi-structured interviews. Fourteen interviews were conducted with participants drawn from seven organizations; the participants were from the public and private sectors, from different business units, and from different managerial levels to ensure that diverse perspectives on the partnership had been captured. It was an opportunity to investigate the activities and interactions that existed between the partners in the partnership arrangement. The selected participants were either currently or recently involved in the decision-making process of the contract negotiation and in the operations and coordination of the activities of the partnership arrangement (summarized in Table 14.1). The interviews followed a flexible thematic guide. This was to allow the participants the opportunity to freely express their views and bring up new issues they felt were important (Yin, 2009). The interviews were conducted on the premises of each organization and they varied between 42 and 125 minutes.

The participants were asked to discuss their reasons for participating in the local regeneration partnership and their experiences with regards to the partnership collaborative processes and partnership working. Additional data was collected from some of the participants by way of documents such as policy frameworks and reports on the partnership activities. This was to enable triangulation of findings in order to elicit a better understanding of

Table 14.1 Overview of the Demographics of the Participating Organizations and Participants as It Came Up From the Research Findings

Sector	Organization	Number of Interviews	Position of Participants
Public Sector	Government Institution	n = 4	Team leaders for core and social infrastructure, contract administration and contract management and an infrastructure engineer
Public Sector	Economic Reform Agency	n = 1	Director
Public Sector	Regulatory Agency	n = 1	Director
Private Sector	Infrastructure Development Institution	n = 1	Director
Private Sector	External Consultant	n = 1	PPP expert and consultant
Private Sector	Financial and Investment Adviser	n = 1	Director
Private Sector	International Funding Body	n = 5	Private sector and transport specialists, economist, disbursement and procurement officers

the phenomenon being investigated and to improve the validity of the findings (Gibbert, Ruigrok, and Wicki, 2008).

Data analysis was carried out in line with the process of engaging inductive theory with the use of case studies. The data analysis began by initially transcribing the interviews and thereafter the transcripts and documents collected were reviewed to identify important issues and highlight patterns in the data. A thematic analysis approach was used to analyze the primary data collected with the assistance of the NVivo software. Analyzing with NVivo consisted of logging data movements, coding patterns, and mapping conceptual categories. This made all stages of the analytical process traceable and transparent, thus facilitating the production of a better detailed and comprehensive audit trail than a manual mapping of the process can allow.

According to Braun and Clarke (2006), thematic analysis strategy offers the means by which to access and analyze the articulated perspectives of the participants so that they may be integrated into a model that looks to explain the social processes under investigation. This analytical strategy involved categorizing the data as an indication of themes that related to the partners, the resources as well as their operations, which are the building blocks of collaborative-advantage partnership arrangements.

Findings and Interpretations

The analysis of the empirical data depicted how three key collaboration elements identified in the context of Nigeria—*mutual interdependence* of the partners in the collaboration process, *trust* between partners in the partnership working, and *transparency* in the decision-making processes—are pertinent in facilitating the collaborative processes in partnerships and how the collaborative processes in turn influence the local regeneration partnership performance and outcomes of the partnership working.

Analysis of the empirical data involved carefully reviewing and coding the 14 interview transcripts. This also involved re-reading the transcripts while making constant comparisons and coding important themes into categories as guided by the research question. As this process progressed, categories were expanded and refined, and data were re-coded to fit the latest theme identified. Compilations of transcript-quotes representing the different themes were then reviewed for coherence, and these themes are used in selecting quotations for discussing the findings.

In the discussion of the findings, the themes identified from the data analysis are put in italics and are used in organizing the results below (summarized in Table 14.2). The participants from the different organizations are denoted by both alphabetical and numerical codes: the four participants from the public-sector government institution are denoted by PG1, PG2, PG3, and PG4; the two participants from the public-sector regulatory institution are denoted by PR1 and PR2; the participant from the private-sector infrastructure development institution is denoted by PD1; the participant

Table 14.2 Summary of the Findings That Indicate the Implication of Collaboration Elements for the Collaboration Processes in the Public-Private Partnership Working in Nigeria

PPP policy implementation and collaboration elements in a partnership working in the context of Nigerian local regeneration	The influence of the collaboration elements on the collaborative processes
Antecedents to partnership arrangements	• budgetary restraints experienced by the government • seeking alternative sources of capital investment • the need for rapid infrastructure expansion through huge investments • advocated as a well-established global model to improve the delivery of services • the need to revisit and redefine the institutional structures for PPP projects • a need for the stability of legal frameworks and regulatory guidelines • the willingness of interest groups to participate in the implementation of PPP initiatives • a greater potential for economic growth through increased infrastructure development in Nigeria
Mutual interdependence of the partners in the collaboration process	• respect for the commitment made at the formation stage • understanding the skill gaps needed for the partnership working • the need to focus on the right capabilities needed for partnership progress • the need for clearer and transparent competitive tendering procedures and guidelines • monitoring of the operations of the partnership
Building trust among stakeholders in the partnership	• making a long-term commitment to the PPP life cycle and contractual arrangement • the inclusion of guarantees into the contracts as a risk-sharing mechanism • the negotiation of a robust contractual agreement and clearly defined framework • enlisting partners with the needed capabilities, the need for the partners to act with integrity and commitment • focus on the priorities and intended outcomes • the availability of relevant information about the partnership performance • clarity of the decision-making process

(Continued)

Table 14.2   (Continued)

PPP policy implementation and collaboration elements in a partnership working in the context of Nigerian local regeneration	The influence of the collaboration elements on the collaborative processes
Ensuring transparency in the decision-making processes	• clarity in terms of negotiation at the formation stage • visibility of the decision-making processes • ensuring greater credibility among partners going forward into the partnership arrangement • the building of credible pipelines of investable opportunities and enabling institutional investors • transparency was an important collaborative element in facilitating the partnership working • effective management of the various interest groups is deemed equally important throughout the life cycle of the partnership
Evaluating the partnership's overall performance	• allocation and acceptance of the responsibility for decisions and actions of the partnership members • introduction of delivery units that anticipate and manage threats, opportunities, and associated risks of a project • the ability of the partners to fulfill the terms of the contract negotiated

from the private-sector consulting organization is denoted by PC1; the participant from the private-sector financial and investment advisory organization is denoted by PA1 and five participants from the private-sector international funding body are denoted by PF1, PF2, PF3, PF4, and PF5.

REGENERATION PARTNERSHIPS: NIGERIA'S INFRASTRUCTURE DEVELOPMENT

Findings indicate that economic and social infrastructure development in Nigeria have in the past received little attention from the government and this could be attributed to the budgetary restraints experienced at both the federal and state levels of government, coupled with the growing population in the country, which currently stands at about 174 million. The resultant effect of this has been the decline of existing infrastructure and services in certain communities within different states of the country. Participants within the research voiced the need for rapid infrastructure expansion through huge investments. In an effort to meet the demands of the infrastructure and service provision, the federal government has had to implement policy initiatives aimed at improving the quality of life of the local residents living in these communities, local regeneration partnerships being one of such initiatives serve as alternative sources of capital investment.

In the words of participant PG2:

> Public funds are drying out, the treasury is inundated, government is also coming down with very huge overheads, so what is left for development keeps diminishing. I guess that is why the PPP option is very useful.

Similarly, participant PO1 was of the opinion that

> Most importantly, finances are limited and many governments in Nigeria have all come to realize that services cannot wait, the users of government services cannot wait, road project development cannot wait. Meanwhile, their resources are finite and they need these things, so they have come to realize that PPPs are a way out for them to achieve them, hence they can eat their cake and have it.

Findings also indicate that the Nigerian government consideration for implementing PPPs not only stems from the financial benefits as an alternative source of funds, but also in the belief that they are advocated as an established global model that serves to improve the delivery of economic and social infrastructure across the country.

This was reflected by some of the participants interviewed:

> Ultimately, we believe it is a model that would help to serve our purposes, as well as the nation's purposes of course there is another very important thing as well, it is not just about doing projects to optimize share-holders' value. (PD1)
>
> With the deficit in infrastructure, any government knows the reality that there is no way your development, renewal, regeneration of infrastructure can happen without external funds, PPP is becoming a fashionable, tested model. (PG1)

REGENERATION PARTNERSHIPS: OPPORTUNITY TO ATTRACT THE CAPABILITY

It was a common consensus among the public sector participants that projects that involve the private sector have a greater potential to succeed. They believe that the private sector partners tend to be more efficient in fulfilling the term of a contract and in managing such projects over their life cycle than when the public sector partners are in charge of managing similar projects.

> So you have people managing the partnership who do not have a full understanding of the arrangements and when it comes to making informed decisions, they cannot make informed decisions and they cannot even advice their management to make appropriate decisions, so some these process have taken up by the private sector. (PR2)

Having the right skills and capabilities, though, might enable a partnership to take advantage of the strengths of both the private and public sectors and thus reap the collaborative rewards of the partnership. It also entails that the partners be more efficient in the mobilization of resources and in leveraging and capitalizing on their complementary strengths and capabilities (Huxham and Vangen, 2004).

In the toll road partnership, it was important that needed capacity to deliver the intended goals was available, although certain issues were not fully addressed at the contract negotiation stage. These issues pertained to questions about the risks each of the partners were ready to take on, how the risks were going to be mitigated to ensure that the partners delivered on the terms of the contract, and if the partners had relevant knowledge of partnership arrangements. It therefore became imperative to ensure the negotiation of a robust contractual agreement and a clearly defined project framework before the commencement of the partnership. Participants reported that the expertise and past work records of potential partners need to be taken into consideration during the bidding and tendering stage.

> The thing is who is going to deliver it; we have to look at who the counterparties are. What the government would deliver on its own end, can the private investor deliver on its own end? Do we have the right contractors for example, not everything is done by the private investor, also some of these things are outsourced as well, and do we have the right input? (PR1)
>
> I think the critical thing is that the partners have a track record, see what they've done and importantly see what they've done in similar environments. Doing business in Nigeria is not the same as doing business in London or doing business in some states of the United States. It is not the same thing, there are some issues that are unique to Nigeria and there are some difficulties too. (PF1)

The interest and commitment of stakeholder groups to participate in the partnership led to a greater potential to fulfill the terms of the contract and the success of the partnership in achieving its intended goals. As argued by Coote, Forrest, and Tam (2003), the long-term orientation of these partnerships, where the partners focus on long-term goals and believe the collaboration will achieve the desired outcomes, creates commitment among the partners.

One participant warns that interest and commitment does not come only from the internal stakeholders but other external stakeholders:

> The way you can ensure that it works is to manage the entire chain. The end user must be happy to pay for it, have the ability to pay for it, pay for it consistently and of course you have to provide the level of support and service that goes with that, otherwise people won't want to pay and that is what flows up the chain and to the very end of the delivery chain. (PF3)

Furthermore, Doz (1996) suggests that commitment is an important goal for the partnership working, as it counters opportunism and determines trustworthiness, as well as the willingness to collaborate because the partners can then put their efforts towards desired outcomes. Participants in the research reported that although there were challenges associated with fulfilling the terms of the partnership agreement, there was a commitment to achieve the set goals of the partnership.

> By and large it delivered a road, a good world class road, I think it initially underrated the problem, the community issues, the stakeholder issues, but in the end its being a success. (PC1)
>
> As seen with the construction of the toll road, the massive development it has catalyzed that therefore as a multiplying effect on industries and they create new jobs, and other industries are built further down the axis. What we find in all of this, is that a critical infrastructure was put in place. (PD1)

CONTEXTUAL ELEMENTS ASSOCIATED WITH PARTNERSHIPS WORKING IN NIGERIA

This section aims to identify the contextual elements that are likely to affect the building of credible pipelines of investable opportunities and to enable institutional investors who can manage and adequately implement PPP projects in Nigeria. The findings of the research indicate some of these contextual elements and these are presented below.

Mutual Interdependence of the Partners in the Collaboration Process

Goodman and Dion (2001) pointed out that confidence in a partner is the perceived level of certainty that the partner organization will pursue

mutually compatible interests in the collaboration, rather than act opportu-
nistically. Some of the participants indicated that perhaps the project risks
were not assigned to the best partner to mitigate them.

> The bottom line in the partnership, there is risk on both sides, either that
> the private sector would overwhelm the government, structure a trans-
> action that would unduly favors the private side, there are some who
> believed that the transaction was unduly favorable to the private investor
> and there are others who would argue to the contrary. (PC1)

Following from the collaborative advantage theory, the extent of the collaboration between partners has been identified as important to its ultimate
success and the quality of collaboration between partner organizations, and
has obvious implications for outcomes (Wilson, 2014). The participant further suggested that "There has to be openness, fairness in negotiation, confidence, trust on both sides to negotiate and to put appropriate structures in
place for both interests." (PC1)

Collaborative decision making is considered to be a mechanism for ensuring mutual interdependence and trust in the partnership. The key to success,
however, as suggested by Thompson and Perry (2006) lies in the willingness of partners to monitor the partnership and each other's adherence to
the agreed-upon rules and to impose credible sanctions on non-compliant
partners. Within the partnership, the fulfillment of the terms of contract was
depicted in the visibility of the decision-making processes.

> The other one thing that must be offered to the investor is the certainty
> that the government must keep its side of the bargain. The political risk
> involved, especially if government changes. (PF5)

In spite of the ongoing regulatory reforms in the state, which has set an
enabling environment for PPPs, some of the participants from the private
sector are of the view that the government still needs to revisit and redefine
the institutional structures in place to enhance the rapid implementation
of the PPP within the state. This was reflected by some of the participants
in the research:

> One of the reasons investors ask for guarantee is not because of the fear
> of defaulting, but the fear of exploitation (forcefully taking an organiza-
> tion's possession for the enjoyment of the government). Foreigners are
> always weary of exploitation. (PF2)
>
> The regulations need to be able to protect the public interest, because
> many of the facilities they have monopoly characteristics where you
> have, a single provider and you don't want a situation where they are
> going to extort money from the consumer, so things like tariff have to
> be regulated, you have technical standards, the roads have to be of cer-
> tain quality, so that kind of regulation needs to be in place. (PF1)

Ensuring Transparency in the Decision-Making Processes

The need for clearer and transparent competitive tendering procedures and guidelines was inferred from the concerns of the participants in the research, that transparency in the tendering process has a direct implication for obtaining adequate funding for the partnership's project. One of the participants raised a concern stating that

> If there isn't competitive tendering banks get nervous because they think there isn't proper competitive tendering, because they think if a new government comes in they would come and revoke it. (PD1)

As further explained that by participant PF5, it is important to ensure that the project is bankable and to ensure that the way the project is conceived is likely to attract bidders and be able to raise the needed funds. So also the confidence that partners would ensure efficient project delivery is attributed to the clarity in terms of negotiations at the formation stage, ensuring greater credibility among partners going forward into the partnership arrangement.

Partners from different sectors may bring distinctive advantages to the partnership arrangement. Lasker, Weiss, and Miller (2001) reinforce that the private sector partners most possess the ability to maximize value for money and thus deliver outcomes at lower costs, and that the public sector has to be accountable and ensure the protection of public good as well as ensure the more justifiable interests of the local communities where the partnership would operate. Participant PD1 was of the opinion that a sense of satisfaction could be felt from collaborating with the government in achieving its objectives by opening up the area for people and to catalyze growth. Another participant shared a similar view:

> I think that one thing we can say this project illustrates is the need for transparency around the terms of concession. (PA1)

Building Trust Among Stakeholders in the Partnership Working

Participants in the research expressed their concerns and views about the inability of the partnership to actively engage with the local community where the toll road was constructed. They were of the opinion that more could have been done to encourage public opinion and to avoid challenges and public disruption by way of demonstrations that came about as a result of the partnership's oversight in doing so. Some participants expressed the need for greater engagement by both sectors with all stakeholders.

> There are many ways of doing this and you need to encourage the community and this can take many forms. You can have meetings where you can speak with people, you can have small focus groups where you can get into people's minds and you can pass messages. (PF4)

> It is considered from the very beginning of the project, from the beginning we get their consent, we tell them this is what we want to do. We speak with their leaders, and the community. Otherwise they can sabotage your operations. (PG1)

Furthermore, by genuinely engaging the local community, an atmosphere of trust and transparency in the decision-making process is created and may have positive implications for local residents. Some interviews indicated that engaging with leaders who are the influencers in the communities could encourage them to have a positive attitude towards the project.

> It pays the government to do so, because when we get the buy in of the people they can advise us of some peculiarities in that area, they can help facilitate the operations. (PG2)

Another participant was of the opinion that people fear change because they think they would be disenfranchised and sometimes it might be in the interest of all involved to reach a compromise.

> The process starts early, you get them involved early, sometimes they would tell you what they want before the operations can go forward, compromise and understanding and it is a continuous one. (PG3)

Findings also indicated the need for effective management of the various stakeholder groups throughout the life cycle of the partnership. Participants indicated that being proactive in getting across relevant information involves multiple communication channels and plays a key role in avoiding conflicts. The importance attached to opening up and ensuring wider channels of communication can affect how decisions are made and how the partnership's working is taken forward (Andrews and Entwistle, 2010). This is because conflict resolutions are deemed as tedious processes and if taken through Nigerian courts tended to be time consuming with an adverse effect on the delivery timeline of the project. Although this was not the case in the partnership, participants however made mention of it based on their experiences from past PPP projects.

> The contract has dispute resolution clauses, we usually start with meetings, depending on the contract and the partners involved, there could be 30 days in which to remedy the dispute, then 7 extra days which is the final notice, or we go to mediation or arbitration, or even a dispute process court. (PG4)

Evaluating the Partnership's Overall Performance

In evaluating the effectiveness of the partnership, the allocation and acceptance of the responsibility for decisions and actions of the partnership members can be linked to the partnership's performance management and problem solving. The availability of relevant information about the partnership performance and clarity of the decision making process are also deemed important. Participants suggest that it is also imperative that some form of joint monitoring and management mechanisms involving stakeholder groups are negotiated into the contract. According to Kelly (2012), evaluation of PPP arrangements can serve many different purposes and the approach taken will depend on the environment, participatory mechanisms, and in addition, the objectives that lie behind the drive to evaluate. In other words, evaluation assists in determining the merit or the worth of the PPP arrangements and partnership working.

> They signed an agreement and there is reprimand for any breach of those clauses; they do the monitoring through the supervision missions, which is done 2 to 3 times a year. (PF2)
>   At the end of the day, if you deal with somebody who cannot deliver, it is a waste of time. You need to be satisfied, especially when you sign the bottom lines that it is a good prospect that you would be able to see your budget through to the end in its entirety, the delivery mechanisms in terms of the physical deliverables, the service levels people would be willing to pay for. (PR1)

It is the opinion of some participants that although the entire toll road has not been completed and the concession rights of the SPV had to be bought back by the Lagos state government, the idea of the toll road infrastructure would not have been conceived if the private sector had not stepped in.

> Infrastructure helps to promote economic development and growth, infrastructure especially social infrastructure, roads, water and others, help to improve the quality of life. We have seen with the construction of the toll road, the massive development it has catalyzed that therefore as a multiplying effect on industries and they create new jobs, and other industries are built. (PF1)

MANAGERIAL IMPLICATIONS

The purpose of this chapter was to investigate the capability of partner organizations to benefit from the full potential of their collaboration and the effectiveness of their partnership arrangement to achieve their intended goals from the context of a developing African country, Nigeria. The country's sizable and growing population continues to put pressure on the already evident infrastructure deficit. Local regeneration partnerships from the findings thus represent both a necessity and an opportunity for diversifying income and economic growth as a result of a certain degree of political willingness of the government to advocate for improvements in the infrastructure sector. Although PPP implementation in Nigeria is in its early years, the country is however keen to adapt PPP models to suit the country's own business and cultural contexts.

Discussion

Despite the difficulties encountered from setbacks and delays in the construction of the toll road in Lagos State, PPPs are considered models with great potentials. This is the case in most developing African countries as the policy portrays a positive contribution to infrastructure development. An essential element in the success of the investigated partnership arrangement was seen in the collaborative efforts of the partners through coordinated activities right from the formation stage. It was evident from the case study that the government and decision makers alike took into consideration the long-term nature of the partner arrangement by ensuring that the right partners with the appropriate expertise and knowledge were selected, as well as ensuring that right from the formation of the partnership a well-structured contract was negotiated. Although the contract had to be renegotiated at a later stage of the life cycle of the partnership, the overall results were nonetheless positive as the intended goals of linking various communities together and reducing the traffic congestion in the area was achieved.

Mutual interdependence, trust, and transparency in this chapter have been investigated from the collaborative advantage theory perspective. This theory also perceives organizations as social systems that constantly need collaborative working through mutual agreements and interdependence of partners in order to achieve intended goals (Vangen and Huxham, 2005). From the findings, these three collaboration elements are seen to be influenced by the contextual factors in the case investigated. The findings indicated that these collaboration elements acted as enablers of the collaborative processes without which the partnership would have been plunged into very troubled waters.

Findings indicate that the funding institutions, both indigenous and foreign, were wary about the existing regulatory framework, as there was a limit to which it could be enforceable in partnership arrangements. It is inferred from the opinions of the participants that transparency of the tendering process had a direct implication for obtaining adequate funding, as the visibility of the process boosted financiers' confidence in financing the toll road project. Trust among the partners was subject to the negotiated contract that bound the working partnership and ensured that the partners adhered to their obligations and carried out the actions needed to achieve the mutually set goals. The resultant effect of this was that it enabled mutual rules for the collaboration to be established and this assisted the partners in the renegotiation of part of the contract when issues such as the 'right of way' arose during the construction of the toll road. Evidently, trust was necessary for initiating and building confidence in the partnership.

Mutual interdependence and trust from the case study was also seen to be evident in the selection of partners with the right skills and capabilities. Getting this process right enabled the partnership to take advantage of the strengths of both the private and public sectors partners and to reap the collaborative rewards of the partnership. The collaborative rewards of the partnership can only be fully reaped when such collaborative efforts not only help promote economic growth and infrastructure development and improve the quality of life of the local residents in the communities where the partnerships are implemented, but also lie with the ability of the partners to fulfill the terms of the contract negotiated. The decision of the Lagos state government to buy back the concession rights of the private sector indicates that the completion of the other phases of the toll road would be through the traditional procurement method of contracting. This action can be interpreted as defeating the objective of implementing PPPs in the first place.

It is inferred that certain risks that arose from the increase in interest rates had not been factored into the contract at the time of negotiation and that community residents' unwillingness to pay the tolls could have been resolved by better, proactive communication strategies. Consequently, there was the need for appropriate risk identification and allocation to partners, the acceptance of the responsibility for decisions and actions in the partnership process, as well as an effective management procedure to be put in place. Furthermore, there were opportunities missed in the management of the partnership to introduce dedicated project delivery units to help anticipate opportunities and manage threats and other associated risks during the partnership process.

Managerial Implications

This chapter demonstrates that a partnership's collaborative advantage is influenced by certain contextual collaboration elements that may hinder the implementation of PPP arrangements in local regeneration in Nigeria. Diffusion of the findings from local regeneration partnerships such as the one investigated in this chapter could contribute to the quality of decisions that need to be made in deciding on the appropriate PPP models to be implemented in funding local regeneration projects in other similar developing countries in, for instance, Sub-Saharan Africa. Such decisions can be influenced by having relevant knowledge about the selection of the most appropriate partners at the formation stage with the needed expertise, core capabilities, and competencies. Careful partnership formation and functioning can facilitate collaborative advantage. The institutionalization of partnerships can also be a great asset to strengthen the partnership interrelationships such that the partners are able to share the same vision and enthusiasm that can lead to the delivery of innovative solutions and services. Finally, better risk management can contribute to the collaborative advantage potential of the partnership such that proper identification of risk and optimal allocation of risk can lead to overall cost efficiencies, be a determinant of value for money, and ensure greater certainty of partnership success.

Limitations

This chapter is based on the analysis of a single case; hence, contextual factors that could limit generalizing it should be carefully considered. Despite it being a single case, there is the possibility for analytic generalization whereby the purpose is to reach an interpretation of the studied phenomenon that could be transferable to other similar empirical contexts (Yin, 2009). A varied range of participants were considered from both the public and private sector to increase the relevance of the findings to other contexts and to enhance the validity of the conclusions. The selection of the local regeneration partnership also gave a picture of the varied nature of key officials, resources, and activities needed to reveal a much broader picture of the phenomenon researched. Furthermore, the findings of this research could be further checked by conducting comparative case studies across a number of PPPs.

A longitudinal study of the empirical case could be conducted so as to improve the quality of findings. Another limitation concerns the empirical perspective and scope of the research as it was based on the perception of the key officials who were asked to discuss their reasons for participating in the local regeneration partnership; hence, their opinions related to their own experiences of the partnership activities and collaboration processes. There is the opportunity to include the local community in the framework as they are the end users of the partnership activity and the ones that can ultimately benefit from the partnership's activities and resources.

REFERENCES

African Development Bank (AfDB). (2013a, August). *An infrastructure action plan for Nigeria—closing the infrastructure gap and accelerating economic transformation.* African Development Bank. http://www.afdb.org/en/documents/document/an-infrastructure-action-plan-for-nigeria-closing-the-infrastructure-gap-and-accelerating-economic-transformation-33031/

African Development Bank (AfDB). (2013b, January). *Federal Republic of Nigeria country strategy paper (2013–2017).* African Development Bank and African Development Fund: Regional Department West. http://www.afdb.org/fileadmin/uploads/afdb/Documents/Project-and-Operations/Nigeria%20-%202013–2017%20-%20Country%20Strategy%20Paper.pdf

African Development Fund (ADF). (2010, August). *Capacity building for PPP infrastructure (C84PPPi) in Nigeria.* African Development Fund Project Appraisal Report. http://www.afdb.org/fileadmin/uploads/afdb/Documents/Project-and-Operations/NIGERIA_-_PAR__-_CB4PPPi_.pdf

Akkermans, H., Bogerd, P., and Van Doremalen, J. (2004). Travail, transparency and trust: A case study of computer-supported collaborative supply chain planning in high-tech electronics. *European Journal of Operational Research, 153*(2), 445–456.

Andrews, R., and Entwistle, T. (2010). Does cross-sectoral partnership deliver? An empirical exploration of public service effectiveness, efficiency, and equity. *Journal of Public Administration Research and Theory, 20*(3), 679–701.

Apostolakis, C. (2004). Citywide and local strategic partnership in urban regeneration: Can collaboration take things forward? *Politic, 24*(12), 103–112.

Appuhami, R., Perera, S., and Perera, H. (2011). Coercive policy diffusion in a developing country: The case of public-private partnerships. *Sri Lanka Journal of Contemporary Asia, 41*(3), 431–451.

Asthana, S., Richardson, S., and Halliday, J. (2002). Partnership working in public policy provision: A framework for evaluation. *Social Policy and Administrative, 36*(7), 780–795.

Babatunde, S. O., Opawole, A., and Akinsiku, O. E. (2012). Critical success factors in public-private partnership (PPP) on infrastructure delivery in Nigeria. *Journal of Facilities Management, 10*(3), 212–225.

Bovens, M. (2010). Two concepts of accountability: Accountability as a virtue and as a mechanism. *West European Politic, 33*(5), 946–967.

Braun, V., and Clarke, V. (2006). Using thematic analysis in psychology. *Qualitative Research in Psychology, 3*(2), 77–101.

Broadbent, J., and Laughlin, R. (1999). The Private Finance Initiative: Clarification of a future research agenda. *Financial Accountability and Management, 15*(2), 95–114.

Brunetto, Y., and Farr-Wharton, R. (2007). The moderating role of trust in SME owner/managers' decision-making about collaboration. *Journal of Small Business Management, 45*(3), 362–387.

Clarke, J., and Glendinning, C. (2002). Partnership and the remaking of welfare governance. In C. Glendinning, M. Powell, and K. Rummery (Eds.), *Partnerships, new labour and the governance of welfare*. Bristol: the Policy Press, 393–414.

Coote, L. V., Forrest, E. J., and Tam, T. W. (2003). An investigation into commitment in non-Western industrial marketing relationships. *Industrial Marketing Management, 32*(7), 595–604.

Couch, C., Olivier, S., and Borstinghaus, W. (2010). Thirty years of urban regeneration in Britain, Germany and France: The importance of context and path dependency. *Progress in Planning, 75*, 1–52.

Cropper, S. (1996). Collaborative working and the issue of sustainability. In C. Huxham (Ed.), *Creating collaborative advantage* (pp. 80–100). London: Sage.

Davis, J. S. (2002). The governance of urban regeneration: A critique of the governing without government thesis. *Public Administration, 80*(2), 301–322.

De Bettignies, J. E., and Ross, T. W. (2009). Public- private partnerships and the privatization of financing: An incomplete contracts approach. *International Journal of industrial Organisation, 27*(3), 358–368.

Doz, Y. L. (1996). The evolution of cooperation in strategic alliances: Initial conditions or learning processes? *Strategic Management Journal, 17*(Summer Special Issue), 55–83.

Drumwright, M. E., Cunningham, P. H., and Berger, I. E. (2004). Social alliances: Company/nonprofit collaboration. *California Management Review, 47*(1), 58–90.

Dyer, J. H., and Chu, W. (2000). The determinants of trust in supplier-automaker relationships in the US, Japan, and Korea. *Journal of International Business Studies, 31*(2), 259–285.

Eisenhardt, K. M. (1989). Building theories from case study research. *Academy of Management Review, 14*(4), 532–550.

Ekanem, N. G. (2010). *Nigeria: The most dynamic market in Africa?* SADC PPP Forum and Network Launch Midrand. South Africa, February 2010.

Ezezika, O. C., Deadman, J., Murray, J., Mabeya, J., and Daar, A. S. (2013). To trust or not to trust: A model for effectively governing Public- Private Partnerships. *AgBioForum, 16*(1), 27–36.

Faehnle, M., and Tyrväinen, L. (2013). A framework for evaluating and designing collaborative planning. *Land Use Policy, 34,* 332–341.

Farlam, P. (2005). *Working together: Assessing public-private partnerships in Africa.* The South African Institute of International Affairs. NEPAD Policy Focus Report No. 2.

Forrer, J., Kee, J. E., Newcomer, K. E., and Boyer, E. (2010). Public–private partnerships and the public accountability question. *Public Administration Review, 70*(3), 475–484.

Gibbert, M., Ruigrok, W., and Wicki, B. (2008). What passes as a rigorous case study? *Strategic Management Journal, 29*(13), 1465–1474.

Goodman, L. E., and Dion, P. A. (2001). The determinants of commitment in the distributor–manufacturer relationship. *Industrial Marketing Management, 30*(3), 287–300.

Gray, B. (1996). Cross-sectoral partners: Collaborative alliances among business, government and communities. In C. Huxham (Ed.), *Creating collaborative advantage* (pp. 57–79). London: Sage Publications.

Himmelman, A. T. (1996). On the theory and practice of transformational collaboration: From social service to social justice. In C. Huxham (Ed.), *Creating collaborative advantage* (pp. 19–43). London: Sage Publications.

Hudson, B., and Hardy, B. (2002). *What is 'successful' partnership and how can it be measured?* In C. Glendinning, M. Powell, and K. Rummery (Eds.), *Partnerships, new labour and the governance of welfare.* Bristol: The Policy Press.

Huxham, C. (1996). Collaboration and collaborative advantage. In C. Huxham (Ed.), *Creating collaborative advantage* (pp. 1–18). London: Sage Publications.

Huxham, C., and Vangen, S. (2004). Doing things collaboratively: Realizing the advantage or succumbing to inertia? *Organizational Dynamics, 33*(2), 190–201.

Huxham, C., and Vangen, S. (2005). *Managing to collaborate: The theory and practice of collaborative advantage.* London and New York: Routledge.

Infrastructure Concession Regulatory Commission. (ICRC). (2009). *The National Policy on Public Private Partnership.* Abuja, Nigeria.

International Monetary Fund. (IMF). (2012). *Sub-Saharan Africa: Maintaining growth in uncertain world.* Regional Economic Outlook, Washington, DC. https://www.imf.org/external/pubs/ft/reo/2012/afr/eng/sreo1012.pdf

Kanter, R. M. (1994, July–August). Collaborative advantage: The art of alliances. *Harvard Business Review, 72*(4), 96–108.

Kateja, A. (2012). Building infrastructure: Private participation in emerging economies. *Procedia-Social and Behavioral Sciences, 37,* 368–378.

Kelly, C. (2012). Measuring the performance of partnerships: Why, what, how, when? *Geography Compass, 6*(3), 149–162.

Krishnan, R., Martin, X., and Noorderhaven, N. (2006). When does trust matter to alliance performance? *Academy of Management Journal, 49*(5), 894–917.

Lachapelle, P. R., and McCool, S. F. (2012). The role of trust in community wildland fire protection planning. *Society and Natural Resources, 25*(4), 321–335.

Lasker, R. D., Weiss, E. S., and Miller, R. (2001). Partnership synergy: A practical framework for studying and strengthening the collaborative advantage. *The Milbank Quarterly, 79*(2), 179–205.

Leke, A., Fiorini, R., Dobbs, R., Thompson, F., Suleiman, A., and Wright, D. (2014, July). *Nigeria's renewal: Delivering inclusive growth in Africa's largest economy.* McKinsey Global Institute.

Lekki Concession Company (LCC). (2015). *Project information.* http://www.lcc.com.ng/tolls.asp

Lookwood, M. (2010). Good governance for terrestrial protected area: A framework, principles and performance outcomes. *Journal of Environment Management, 9*(3), 754–766.

Macdonald, S., and Chrisp, T. (2005). Acknowledging the purpose of partnership. *Journal of Business Ethics, 59*(4), 307–317.

Masetti, O. (2014). *Nigeria- the number one African economy.* Briefing on emerging markets. Deutsche Bank Research.

Miraftab, F. (2004). Public-private partnerships: The Trojan Horse of neoliberal development? *Journal of Planning Education and Research, 24*(1), 89–101.

Mitchell-Weaver, C., and Manning, B. (1991). Public-private partnerships in third world development: A conceptual overview. *Studies in Comparative International Development, 26*(4), 45–67.

Ng, P. W. K., Lau, C. M., and Nyaw, M. K. (2007). The effect of trust on international joint venture performance in China. *Journal of International Management, 13*(4), 430–448.

Office of Public-Private Partnership. (2011). *Building the Lagos of our dream.* Office of Public-Private Partnerships, Lagos State.

Olaseni, M., and Alade, W. (2012). Vision 20:2020 and the challenges of infrastructural development in Nigeria. *Journal of Sustainable Development, 5*(2), 63–76.

Oluwasanmi, O., and Ogidi, O. (2013). Public private partnership and Nigerian economic growth: Problems and prospects. *International Journal of Business and Social Science, 5*(11), 132–139.

Otiso, K. M. (2003). State, voluntary and private sector partnerships for slum upgrading and basic service delivery in Nairobi City, Kenya. *Cities, 20*(4), 221–229.

Ramiah, I., and Reich, M. R. (2006). Building effective public–private partnerships: Experiences and lessons from the African Comprehensive HIV/AIDS Partnerships (ACHAP). *Social Science and Medicine, 63*(2), 397–408.

Rein, M., and Stott, L. (2009). Working together: Critical perspectives on six cross-sector partnerships in Southern Africa. *Journal of Business Ethics, 90*, 79–89.

Sanni, A. O., and Hashim, M. (2014). Building infrastructure through public private partnerships in Sub-Saharan Africa: Lessons from South Africa. *Procedia-Social and Behavioral Sciences, 143*, 133–138.

Selsky, J. W., and Parker, B. (2005). Cross-sector partnerships to address social issues: Challenges to theory and practice. *Journal of Management, 31*, 849–873.

Seppänen, R., Blomqvist, K., and Sundqvist, S. (2007). Measuring inter-organizational trust—a critical review of the empirical research in 1990–2003. *Industrial Marketing Management, 36*(2), 249–265.

Slater, R., Frederickson, J., Thomas, C., Wield, D., and Potter, S. (2007). A critical evaluation of partnerships in municipal waste management in England. *Resources, Conservation and Recycling, 51*(3), 643–664.

Thompson, A. M., and Perry, J. L. (2006, December). Collaboration processes: Inside the black box. *Public Administration Review, 66*(Issue Supplement s1), 20–32.

Tsenkova, S. (2002). *Partnership in urban regeneration: From 'top down' to 'bottom up' approach.* In S. Tsenkova (Ed.), *Urban regeneration: Learning from the British experience* (pp. 73–84). Calgary, University of Calgary: Faculty of Environmental Design.

Vangen, S., and Huxham, V. (2003). Nurturing collaborative relations: Building trust in inter-organizational collaboration. *The Journal of Applied Behavioural Science, 39*(1), 5–31.

Vanguard Newspaper. (2013). *Lekki-Epe expressway concession buy-back: Begging posers.* http://www.vanguardngr.com/2013/11/lekki-epe-expressway-concession-buy-back-begging-posers/.

Willems, T., and Van Doreen, W. (2012). Coming to terms with accountability: Combining multiple forums and function. *Public Management Review, 14*(7), 1011–1036.

Willoughby, C. (2013). How much can public private partnership really do for urban transport in developing countries? *Research in Transportation Economics, 40*(1), 34–55.

Wilson, G. (2014). Building partnerships in social work education: Towards achieving collaborative advantage for employers and universities. *Journal of Social Work, 14*(1), 3–22.

World Bank. (2014). *Nigeria—Country partnership strategy for the period FY2014-FY2017.* Washington, DC; World Bank Group. http://documents.worldbank.org/curated/en/2014/03/19341853/nigeria-country-partnership-strategy-period-fy2014-fy2017

World Economic Forum (WEF). (2013a). *Strategic infrastructure: Steps to prepare and accelerate public-private partnerships.* Prepared in collaboration with The Boston Consulting Group. May 2013. Switzerland: World Economic Forum. http://www3.weforum.org/docs/AF13/WEF_AF13_Strategic_Infrastructure_Initiative.pdf

World Economic Forum (WEF). (2013b). *Strategic infrastructure in Africa: A business approach to project acceleration.* Prepared in collaboration with The Boston Consulting Group. May 2013. Switzerland: World Economic Forum. http://www3.weforum.org/docs/AF13/WEF_AF13_African_Strategic_Infrastructure.pdf

Yin, R. K. (2009). *Case study research: Design and methods* (4th ed.). Newbury Park, CA: Sage Publications.

Zaheer, A., McEvily, B., and Perrone, V. (1998). Does trust matter? Exploring the effects of interorganisational and interpersonal trust on performance. *Organisation Science, 9*(2), 141–159.

Zaheer, S., and Zaheer, A. (2006). Trust across borders. *Journal of International Business Studies, 37*(1), 21–29.

15 The Role of the Legal Profession in Facilitating a Regulatory Framework for Public-Private Partnerships in Ghana

Bill Buenar Puplampu

INTRODUCTION

Public-Private Partnerships (PPPs) are a growing policy option through which governments in Africa seek to bridge the gap between infrastructure, social service provisions, limited state resources, and competing socioeconomic planning needs. In Africa, however, the regulatory regimes around PPP are rudimentary at best and nonexistent in places. This paper examines the role that the legal profession could have in developing regulatory frameworks, but positions this contribution within the context of trust, business relations, and the very visceral concerns and anticipated outcomes that the interested parties to any PPP arrangement have. The paper is based on the Ghanaian situation and offers some policy pointers that may be of use elsewhere.

The Background for Understanding Public-Private Partnerships

Good governments everywhere that have the interests of their people at heart and recognize that citizens have the right to demand their due are motivated to deliver social, educational, health, business, and infrastructural facilities and opportunities. The reality, however, is that hardly any nation on earth has been able to deliver these services purely from state revenues. There are ideological differences as to how to bridge the gap between what the state can provide and what it cannot and the nature of power allocations, resource use, and how open the discussions around these issues could be (Chomsky, 2013). These ideological differences undergird the variances between 'left'- and 'right'-leaning political parties and policy formulations. These differences notwithstanding, neither ideological traditions when in government have achieved sufficient income generation to enable them deliver services and economic well being to their countries. In Africa, various scholars and commentators have noted that these deficits have led to a resort to loans, grants, aid, technical assistance, budget support, unfavorable trade deals, and severe natural resource depletion through over exploitation (Arnold, 2006). These have been aimed at generating or securing sufficient revenues to finance infrastructure projects, economic transformation, as well as recurrent expenditures. The reality is that these financing efforts have not been sufficient.

In the immediate post-independence years, African governments such as those in Ghana led by Kwame Nkrumah, Zambia led by Kenneth Kaunda, and in Tanzania led by Julius Nyerere adopted government-to-government direct infrastructure financing (Tanzam Railway, Accra-Tema Motorway, Tema Harbor, etc.). Often, however, such projects have tended to be heavily skewed in favor of the northern donors where conditionalities demand that materials are procured from donor countries, expertise should be imported, and even designs have to fit not local conditions but rather the preferences and political propaganda intents of the donor countries. A similar situation is recurring with the significant entry of Chinese support into Africa: Many Chinese projects in Africa are executed completely with Chinese labor and Chinese-manufactured materials. The disadvantages of the government-to-government approaches, the continuing deficits and gaps between revenue mobilization and necessary ideals in economic planning, constricting aid budgets of northern metropolitan powers as well as the propensity of private, public sector, and institutionalized corruption to enter the government-to-government arrangements have led to efforts towards identifying alternative financing, project management and economic management models. PPP has come in as a viable option.

Another driver for PPP has been the growth in state debt. Debt-to-GDP ratios for many countries have been deteriorating, placing pressure on currencies, dislocating fundamental fiscal discipline and controls within the economy, crowding out space for bank lending to the private sector, forcing government budgets to focus on debt servicing, and forcing governments to engage in raising bonds, bills, and other government instruments. These instruments create an artificial vehicle for profits by the treasury units of banks and other major corporates who buy government instruments and make their money therefrom instead of thinking up innovative services and products to address continued growth in the economy.

In the face of such dislocations and resource provision gaps, many countries including the UK, Australia, Canada, India, Japan, and Russia have since the late 1980s adopted the PPP model to support various infrastructural and service provisions. Estimates have it that in the EU the PPP sector has been valued at over 200 billion euros in the last decade; in India, it has been valued at over US$300 billion. In Africa, PPPs have been noted in Gabon, South Africa, Lesotho, Zambia, and elsewhere, with total estimated values of over US$10 billion in the last decade. In Ghana, the World Bank has an ongoing PPP project with a value of US$30 million, project ID Code P125595 and a proposed closing date on August 2016. This project aims to improve the legislative, institutional, financial, fiduciary, and technical framework to ensure that in time Ghana has a 'pipeline' of 'bankable' PPP projects.

THE INFRASTRUCTURE AND RELATED
DEFICITS IN AFRICA

According to the South African Institute for International Affairs (Farlam, 2005), nearly 600 million people in Sub-Saharan Africa lack access to electricity, 300 million have no access to safe drinking water and even with mobile telephony, phone line penetration still hovers at less than 20% of the over 1.1 billion people in Africa. In the freshly minted Republic of South Sudan, estimates suggest there are less than 200 kilometers of tarred roads across the whole country, which is about the size of France and three times the size of Ghana. Despite considerable improvements, it is still more difficult, takes longer, and involves more hassle to fly from Accra to Entebbe Kampala than to fly from Accra to London, New York, or Rome. Flying into any major international airport in Africa during the day, one is confronted with the aerial view of rusted tin roofs, footpaths instead of tarred roads, gullies where drains should be, and so on. Every year, many African countries experience severe floods often due to poor storm drains. Countries like Nigeria that are net exporters of crude oil and natural gas still have major issues with power generation and distribution, resulting in regular power outages and brownouts. The painful reality is that women die in pregnancy simply because they live in parts of their country where there are no health facilities, or access to such facilities is encumbered by poor roads or absent bridges. These all point to the service and infrastructure deficit that is the reality of our African existence. While Agulanna (2006) suggests that the leadership challenges that underscore much of Africa's underdevelopment and the matter of political corruption are well known (Arnold, 2006), and the reality is that much of Africa suffers a severe infrastructure deficit.

The hope of responsible governments is that this deficit may be bridged in part through innovative partnerships and involvement of private sector businesses; hence, recourse to PPP. However, it is important to set this within the context and never expect that PPPs will replace what duly elected governments are supposed to do. Any government that defaults to PPPs in order to allow it space to use monies for other nonpriority expenditures is being disingenuous and must be roundly condemned.

WHAT IS PUBLIC-PRIVATE PARTNERSHIP?
THEORY AND PRACTICE

PPP is in principle and in the narrowest sense a contractual arrangement between a government agency and a private business entity for the provision of a specific service or product that has not been captured under the regular process of procurement of service or open bid for infrastructure construction or other such initiative. The UN Economic Commission for Europe Guidebook on Promoting Good Governance in the Public-Private

Partnership Handbook (2008) describes PPPs as "innovative methods used by the public sector to contract with the private sector . . . towards financing, designing, implementing . . . and operating public sector facilities and utilities . . ." (p. 1). The Asian Development Bank describes PPP as "a range of possible relationships among public and private entities in the context of infrastructure and other services" (p. 1). PPP is not privatization. A PPP is not a standard public procurement of goods, services, or engineering development. PPP is not grant or aid. PPP is also not PSP (private sector participation). However, PPP may occur within the context of any of these options that are available to the state. PPPs have several characteristics that distinguish them from other forms of ventures. These characteristics may not all appear in the case of each PPP, but rather may exist in permutations. They include the following:

- Private performance of services often seen as the preserve of the state
- Governmental contract that allows a private entity to own a state asset for a period
- Build-Operate-Transfer projects and other such arrangements
- Significant shift of business risk burden to a private entity away from the state or community
- Significant injection of private funds, skills, expertise, and operating models into some state operations
- Private entity profits/payments derived from government payments or/ and service fees collected by the private entity
- Long-term contracts that share costs, risks, benefits/rewards between government, business, and community.

Theoretically, PPP emerges from the range of concerns articulated by public choice theorists (Grindle and Thomas, 1991), advocates of privatization (Vickers and Yarrow, 1995), and economists (Mansfield, 1997) who variously discuss mixed-economy models in which the atate facilitates regulation, supports private enterprise, and encourages private sector participation in economic sectors otherwise dominated by the public sector.

The aim or reason for entering into a public-private partnership is that the state or local government wishes to derive maximum benefit from private sector expertise, achieve prudent fiscal management, obtain efficiencies in the management and operation of key assets that if left in public hands could be subjected to poor maintenance, weak controls, and weak business operating models; the nation also seeks through PPP to develop local financial markets and increase private sector participation in the economy. The literature suggests that there is an increasing growth in the use of PPP as an intervention tool and as a means of addressing limitations in local economic development (LED) (Rogerson, 2010). On balance, various bodies such as the South African National Treasury, Provincial Government of British Columbia in Canada, the World Bank, the UN, the Asian Development

Bank and others suggest that global PPP projects have been in areas such as: power generation, water supply, sanitation and refuse management, housing, health and educational facilities, infrastructure development such as roads, airports, railways, and lately, eco-tourism and rural enterprise growth/value chain additions. Increasingly, ICT systems for telecoms, traffic management and so on have also come on stream within the PPP space.

Literature

South Africa and Ghana have emerged as two African countries keen on PPP. Sinanovic and Kumaranayake (2010) note that PPPs are being used in the battle against tuberculosis in South Africa. They found that the motives for private sector involvement include financial as well as concern for community well being. They conclude that competition between private providers, social and political awareness, as well as a regulatory framework are all crucial elements in PPP success. Brunne (2009) also discusses PPP within the South African health sector with regard to HIV/AIDS interventions. She argues that historical realities and the social fabric including the nature of collaborations between business, government, and society inform the viability of PPP in the health sector. Fombad (2012) discusses the matter of accountability within the PPP space in South Africa, noting that accountability may be conceived as a mechanism (process by which an agent or official renders due account of responsibilities entrusted), as management of expectations (amongst interested groups), and as a virtue that moderates and motivates particular behaviors. Fombad notes seven strategies through which accountability may be achieved in PPP. These are: public accountability (processes of government answering to the character of each PPP); communal accountability (civil society involvement); monitoring structures within each PPP (within-PPP governance mechanisms); transparency (open communication, answerability, and access to both documentation and officialdom); rule of law (regulations that have legal backing); ethical accountability (moral obligations); and institutional reforms (building relevant structures, internal capacity, skills, and processes).

Williams (2012) suggests PPP can be a tool that brings telecom service into rural areas in Africa—by offering both profit, innovation, and community development. In a similar vein, Oluwole and Kraemer (2013) describe how the Pink Ribbon Red Ribbon PPP aims to address women's cancers in Africa.

Asare and Frimpong (2013), writing on PPP used in addressing sanitation issues in Ghana, suggest that the picture is mixed. Their study arrived at some rather interesting conclusions, which must inform policy and further research. For example, they find that public fear that private participation leads to higher tariffs for certain services is not always so. They also suggest that the absence of a culture of civic responsibility amongst citizens can be a negative factor in PPP in the area of sanitation. An important finding has to do with the need for strong political will balanced by respect for contractual arrangements, which ensures that successive governments respect contracts, do not interfere in the running of PPPs, and offer sufficient open discourse with stakeholders. Open communication, careful planning, and open competition amongst private service providers as they bid for PPP involvement are key issues that undergird the success of PPPs. Ameyaw and Chan (2013), discussing water supply PPP arrangements in Ghana, identify a useful set of risks that need to be considered. These include: political and regulatory risks, operational risks, market/revenue risks, financial risks, relationship, social and third-party risks, as well as risks around the selection of projects and consortia to engage the PPP. In a related study, Abubakari et al (2013) examine urban water supply in Ghana. They study the case of the Ghana Water Company Ltd. and Aqua Vitens Rand Ltd. (AVRL), the consortium that had a management contract to manage urban water supply for Ghana Water. It is questionable whether their case study qualifies as PPP strictly since the AVRL involvement was a management contract in which risks were hardly passed on to the consortium. Nevertheless, they arrive at some relevant conclusions, chief of which is that the problems of Ghana Water that led to the involvement of AVRL go deeper than simply changing or augmenting management. This finding is consistent with Ameyaw and Chan, who suggest that project and consortium selection constitutes an important risk element in PPP. The point here is that governments and others who may wish to enter a PPP should consider very carefully whether the issue or project in question qualifies for or merits a PPP. It also means the idea of PPP should not be applied to any public-private involvement simply because it is thought of as such. This is why earlier on the point was made that PSP is not PPP.

A number of points are worth noting from the above limited review of some of the more recent literatures on PPP in Africa. Firstly, careful planning and thought needs to go into the choice of PPP; secondly, given that there are risks to be shared between partners, contractual arrangements are necessary and must be respected. Importantly, regulation and legal supports seem to emerge as critical. This leads us to the principal object of this paper, which is to consider the role of the legal profession in fostering a regulatory framework for PPP in Ghana.

Regulation and Its Place in Economic and Social Development

In a PPP, the state effectively cedes responsibility for providing certain services to actors in the private sector. It may in the process also offer state assets for use. It may also mean citizens are "exposed" to the profit motives of entities who are in partnership with the state. How are the partners to behave? What are the redress and adjudicatory mechanisms? What limits, rights, and responsibilities are conferred on the proximate parties to the PPP? And what legitimate expectations and duties extend to distal and peripheral stakeholders such as community dwellers? It is these many questions that call for regulation.

Regulation comes in various forms (Vickers and Yarrow, 1995) and exists along a continuum of enforcement regimes and a matrix of internal versus externally generated rules. By enforcement regimes, we mean whether the regulation is voluntarily complied with or enforced by law; by internal versus external, we mean whether the regulatory frame arises from within the business/organization/contract as opposed to arising from a regulatory body or association. Regulation is a societal prerequisite. A fundamental difference between modern and traditional society is the character of the regulatory framework. Whereas in traditional society, regulation is created through a complex system of social hierarchy, recourse to spiritual and cosmic interventions, rules of social intercourse that are domiciled in the chief, elders and clans, in modern society regulation is achieved through the formalization and documentation of enacted rules and operative guidelines.

Regulation supports societal growth by suppressing mob and/or unilateral action and fostering a process of structured interlocution. Regulation supports fair and even-handed social and economic interactions. Regulation provides safety and security and peace for citizens to go about their normal pursuits confident in the adjudicatory and boundary-defining systems that repose in regulatory frameworks. It is therefore reprehensible when the principal architect of regulation, the state, becomes the principal attenuator of regulation through complicity, duplicity, inaction, political interference, impunity, violation of constitutional provisions and more.

Regulation may be derived from internal sources such as ethical guidelines, standards of moral behavior, organizational norms, and the capacity of corporate and institutional leaders to instill levels of behavioral discipline within their people. Regulation may also be derived from external codes, laws, professional standards, business association requirements, international compacts and conventions. Whichever one of these or combinations of these we use depends on how we define the space within which PPP and other business transactions take place.

Defining the Space

Paul Boateng, former British Ambassador to South Africa, in a lecture at the University of Ghana ("Aggrey Fraser Guggisberg Memorial," 2012), defined the civil society space as the place from outside one's front door or gate all the way to the doorstep of the presidential palace. In the same way, the space within which a PPP operates is defined by the name: public-private partnership. The "public" in PPP is that space occupied by public services, public servants, state ownership, and public agencies. It is public because it is held in trust by the state for all citizens past, present, and future. It therefore demands within the regulatory regime a recognition of duty of care and trusteeship. By 1655, this notion of trustee had come to imply "one who is held responsible for the preservation and administration of anything" (The Oxford Universal Dictionary, 3rd Edition 1964).

The "private" in PPP is that space occupied by individuals, groups, and corporates who by dint of hard work, ingenuity, and foresight have created for themselves sufficient capacity to do business and make profit therefrom. It also represents that space occupied by citizens for whom public servants have a duty to create an amiable environment. The "partnership" space is inhabited by all who are brought into collaborative endeavor by any PPP project. A partner is one who is associated with, takes part in, or is joined in common cause with another. In partnership, therefore, we are talking about mutual association to carry out the endeavor with a mind to share in expenses, profits, and losses.

From this consideration of the space, we can identify that there are significant rights, expectations, and responsibilities across it. In addition, there is no room for any party to assume that they have a greater right than another within the PPP space. The public space requires that public accountabilities are met and public accounts are safeguarded. The private space requires that businesses make their due profit, citizens obtain the services or facilities to which their tax and citizenship entitles them, and that ordinary people can enter into business relationships without fear of state unilateral abrogation and arrogations. The partnership space presumes and assumes good faith, mutuality, and common purpose.

Legal Profession in Ghana: Life Is Larger Than the Courts

If lawyers and their colleagues in various arms of the legal and judiciary profession are going to "do good by PPP," they must remember these three spaces set out above and endeavor to ensure that regulation both in spirit and the letter preserves the rights and responsibilities of all. This point is important because the Ghanaian historical situation included a certain suggestion during periods of upheaval that the private business person has no right to the profits they derive from prudent and skillful enterprise. It is also worth mentioning the tendency in Ghana for citizens to overlook the cost of providing facilities and instead expect services to be provided for free. Anecdotal evidence on this may be drawn from the furor in February–March 2014 regarding the tolling of access roads into and out of the University of Ghana, in which public sentiment raged against the fact of tolls imposed, completely ignoring the US$3.5 million commercial bank facility that was used to finance the first full road rehabilitation within the university in 50 years. These points underscore the concern raised by Brunne (2009) that histories and social sensibilities are important factors in PPP success. At this point in Ghana, when there is consideration towards a PPP law, the Ghana Bar Association is expected to provide input. Drafters will be expected to draft a cogent draft bill. The cabinet will likely sit and discuss before sending to parliament for debate. So, we turn our attention to the Ghanaian situation and the Ghanaian legal professionals.

The Legal Profession and Its Litigation Stance

Puplampu (2013) in a survey of the business culture in Ghana found as follows:

- Businesses in Ghana are averse to contractual arrangements as a basis for managing their business relationships.
- Lawyers are seen as driven by litigation rather than holistic business advice.
- Rather than resort to the courts, many business people would rather cut losses and suffer in silence because the legal system is seen in part as not so upright and in part as preferring overly lengthy adjudication periods.

The relevant finding here is the characterization that the legal profession is stuck in a litigation mode. The public is very much aware of a certain predilection of the profession towards a narrow definition of legality and legal service, the law and the courts. From a psychological standpoint, life is larger, more complex, nuanced, and irreducible to litigation. Indeed, the Christian bible suggests that Moses gave the law because of the stubbornness of Israelite attitudes and recognized that the law did not solve the fundamental problem of human capacity for deviation from good. The consideration here is that in considering how the members of the legal profession may impact and contribute to the regulatory frame of PPP, the profession needs to redefine for itself a wide range of potential behavioral issues inherent in the coming together of the state and private business (both national and international) as corresponding actors. It is life and death for some. It is potential for economic uplift for others. It offers immense opportunity for ill-gotten wealth for others. It is an opportunity to re-create the existence of some communities. In other words, in regulating PPP one must see into the totality of the human and institutional concerns that arise from the partnership. Regulation must focus on ensuring that if the PPP comes to litigation, the parameters are sufficiently clear to enable the courts to deliver justice. In this respect, this chapter now considers what it means to bring the state and its actors together in collaborative business ventures.

A Consideration of Interests

To advance the notion of an appropriate regulatory framework, we need to consider the dynamics that emerge when a PPP is created. The state, by coming together in a PPP, accepts and recognizes its inability to execute and deliver on its promised mandate. This calls for a certain level of humility from state actors and their agents. But humility is often in short supply. What are the concerns of the state? These may be set out under three headings: political, social, and economic. Politically, often governments in Africa—which represent the State—wish to use whatever collaborative ventures they engage in to achieve political capital. They use the results to show how 'good' they are, seek perpetuation of rule, and accumulate a cadre of beholden and obligated individuals as well as a horde of financiers for whom government business and state patronage are key. Socially, the state is often concerned to use collaborations to achieve certain social agendas that it should (strictly speaking) achieve through its own direct initiatives, for example, hospitals, schools, and social mitigation programs. Economically, collaborative endeavors allow the inflow of monies that support government business, help sanitize public finances, and ideally facilitate local content, stimulate local economic growth and create private sector businesses. Importantly, however, political concerns often outweigh all others.

Private Business

What are the concerns of the private sector? Private businesses have a number of concerns. These are: to turn a profit, have access to necessary skill sets within the locality or country, leverage each business transaction as an aid to consolidate the footprint in the market, and be able to enjoy ease of doing business, regulatory support and absence of arbitrary government behavior. This need to enjoy hassle-free business must be seen in the light of a history in which political processes have demonized, castigated, scolded, and rebuked private business to the point of physical hostility and verbal conflagrations. Importantly, however, these laudable concerns do not always characterize private business, for there are instances of unethical business perpetrated by persons who seek any opportunity to swindle the state, local authorities, gullible persons, and traditional areas and use the existence of equally dubious public officials to collect rent on properties they do not own and receivables on assignments and contracts against which they have no claim.

The Citizen

What are the concerns of the ordinary citizen? To have the services, infrastructure, and environment that allows us all to be able to say in truth that we live in a civilized, prosperous, and caring society. When all these are put together, one begins to see that the matter of regulatory framework for PPP goes beyond contracts and obligations to the active consideration of the aspirations of a whole range of people, interest groups, and stakeholders.

Sensitivity of the Legal Profession

How sensitive is the legal profession to the concerns, needs, and issues arising from the nuanced realities raised above? When we talk about being 'sensitive,' we are referring to having the power to sense something—this implies that the profession should possess the soft and hard structures with which to receive appropriate stimulation. The question is, does it? When was the last time the Ghana Bar Association (GBA) commissioned a survey of Ghanaian business community views about lawyers? When was the last time the GBA surveyed the skills and capacities of those serving in company secretarial and related roles as to their advice-giving and relationship management with board chairs? Does the GBA or any other related bodies have the committees and systems by which to collect and collate ongoing information with particular reference to business and the emerging PPP domain and any other such relevant issues? By sensitivity, we also mean that the legal profession is sufficiently affected by external conditions and stimulations and thereby engages in a constant process of self-renewal. Does it? By sensitivity, we also mean that the profession is sufficiently responsive to issues.

How knowledgeable is the legal profession about the structure of the Ghanaian economy, which is approximately 33% agriculture, 33% service, and 33% manufacturing, and which draws nearly 70% of GDP from SMEs (small and medium-sized enterprises), rural areas, and remittances (Aryeetey and Kanbur, 2008)? If we consider some of the areas where PPP may be most useful—agribusiness and eco-tourism, roads and related infrastructures, exploitation of below-surface resources—we note that each of these areas have something to do with rural communities. How sensitive is the profession to the nature of regulatory arrangements that would best protect the interests and involvement of rural communities while also advancing business?

Ghana's Current PPP Arrangements

Ghana's PPP history is rather short and poorly developed. AVRL and Telenor Management Partners (Ghana Telecom) came as management contractors. In 2004, a policy guideline was developed but never really operationalized. This has now been revamped as of 2011. In 2009, a PPP Unit was set up at the Ministry of Finance. The closest Ghana came to a true PPP was in the immediate post-independence years under Dr. Kwame Nkrumah when Kaiser Aluminum of the US provided the financing that built the Akosombo Dam. Here, private capital built the dam. Government guaranteed tolling rates and purchase of excess power into the national grid for domestic and business consumption. Private capital was to make its money via the smelting of imported bauxite at the port city of Tema (through the company known as VALCO). In more recent times, another example has been the GCNet system where private capital and expertise came in to design and deploy an online and ICT-based import duty and port clearance regime to facilitate trade flow at the country's ports of entry. GCNet, a consortium of private entrepreneurs, banks and a pension fund, makes its money from fees charged for ICT online services at the ports; Ghana obtains more efficient port clearance processes as well as more efficient and traceable import duty (tax) inflows into state coffers.

There is an 18-page national policy document on public-private partnerships (June 2011) that purports to offer guidance in the interim until a law is passed. This is a most unfortunate situation. PPP assumes a framework of sharing risk, assets, and returns among partnering actors. The policy document is very nebulous in many of its cryptic statements and definitions about all these issues, including a weak statement of the potential range of partners and stakeholders. Risk sharing is key aspect of PPP. The policy document is rather banal in its six sentences on risk. The suggestion that value for money is a key driver for PPP in Ghana is a very narrow approach to considering what are truly huge, far-reaching, and potentially seismic economic end products from PPP collaborations. There is no evidence of assessment of PPP projects so far executed under the limited PPP arrangements so far to see where the problems, loopholes, potentialities, and challenges are. Compared with the volume and scope of PPP policy documents such as those of the Asian Development Bank (2008), UNECE (2008) and others, clearly Ghana's policy document is rather weak.

HOW WILL GHANA MAKE PPP WORK?

In considering an appropriate regulatory regime, drafters need to consider the following points. State actors need to ask the question: Which areas of the economic and social existence as a nation require the most in terms of PPP projects? The value-for-money proposition on its own is inadequate. In its place, policy makers must have a far-reaching holistic and strategic consideration of how any particular project will meet proximate as well as distal needs, and consider inter alia, potential to spur economic activity, support social and physical infrastructure, and create synergistic knock-on effects within the socioeconomic context of any particular community. Take mining as an example. Anyone who has visited mining towns such as Tarkwa or Obuasi in Ghana can see that that resource extraction has not been synergistically executed.

Second, what are the legal instruments currently available to regulate business and government relations, and how compliant is government? There is the constitution. There is the law on investment promotion, the Financial Administration and Procurement laws, the Bodies Corporate (Official Liquidation Act, which is relevant because often PPPs require creation of special purpose vehicles that may assume a legal status of their own), the Companies Code, and many others. What is the history of reprieve, redress, and justice served through the current regimes? What are the difficulties of the justice delivery system, which PPP can ill afford to experience? For example, anecdotal evidence has it that some commercial cases have taken up to 16 years to receive a ruling. PPP regulations perhaps have to incorporate alternative dispute resolution mechanisms right from the start.

Third, how trustworthy are the underlying transactions within government and business? The law is a collection of philosophical abstractions reified and given life by the artifact of human social intercourse. It therefore needs underlying transactions to give it life. What is the nature of those underlying transactions where the government is concerned? When parties enter a PPP, what are the underlying hopes, aspirations, and expectations that emerge as overt transactions? Related to the issue of underlying transactions are some critical human issues: trust, confidence, integrity, and the rule of principles. Lawyers and drafters need to mainstream into the regulatory regime matters and mechanisms of trust and confidence. The psychological failure of regulation is directly related to the impunity with which key actors flout various rules and regulations. The psychological failure of regulation means there is an internal disposition to flout regulation without thought for the consequences.

Fourth, the matter of corporate governance is another area requiring attention. Although distinctions are being made between good governance (relating to the state and how it is run), project governance (relating to how specific short-term projects are executed and handed over), PPP governance (relating to governance arrangements under public-private partnerships), and corporate governance (mechanisms for protecting the rights and interests of stakeholders in and around business and institutional entities), the essential principles are the same:

- Defined relationships between principal and agent;
- Protection of multiple stakeholder interests, rights, expectations, and fair mechanisms for redress;
- Responsibility mechanisms for holding officials and executives accountable through openness, transparency, and answerability; and
- Execution mechanisms for ensuring that agreed-upon objects and strategic aims are delivered through systems of operation that are consistent with policy, regulation, and sustainability.

These principles are fundamental to all and any governance arrangements, although the salience of any one may be different under particular governance circumstances. In this regard, therefore, while it may be expected that in a paper such as this one, greater focus may be given to discussing PPP governance, it seems a more beneficial approach to consider corporate governance because the success of a PPP often hinges on the arrangements within the PPP as well as (and perhaps more so) governance mechanisms within stakeholder institutions, regulatory bodies, supplier businesses, banks, and so forth. This is because the supply and value chain permutations for any PPP often spread far and deep within the national, regional, and sometimes international economy. Corporate governance underpins the confidence that all citizens and businesses and institutions may place in the capacity and disposition of any business partnership to be executed with due regard for law, principle, and contract. Governments have been known to violate corporate governance principles through interference and appointment and dissolution of boards and so on—regardless of the provisions that may be available in the constitution or other governing laws. How confident can private businesses be that special purpose vehicles created to handle a PPP would be free of violations of good corporate governance? The impunity, bravado, ignorance, and culpability that surrounds governance of corporates, especially in terms of behavior of public officials, is sometimes a cause for concern. In Ghana, some recent anecdotal events are worth mentioning: the President dissolves a board without recognition of limitations in the appointing powers of the state, National Security unilaterally demolishes the toll gate of a public institution without subjection to legal process, a regulator apparently varies due diligence processes in order to facilitate the sale of a financial institution due to the political interests at play, the state takes unduly long periods of time to pay contractors who have duly completed properly sanctioned contracts, private businesses involved in government contracts are known to never have filed an annual return to the registrar of companies, executives of financial institutions circumvent laid-down procedures for advancing credit facilities, poor building inspection processes and corruption of municipal building planning/permit issuance leads to significantly bloated costs of infrastructure projects and/ or poor quality work. Without prejudice to specific circumstances, one may argue that such lapses in governance would most invariably impact the success of PPP. In regard to PPP, therefore, members of the legal profession need to build into regulatory regimes issues and tools to foster reciprocity, fairness, just and right procedures. Through their roles as company secretaries, drafters, corporate advisors, solicitors, chairs/members of public commissions and boards of inquiry, legal professionals can facilitate deep commitment to both the spirit and the letter of the rule of law, due process, and sound adjudication.

Fifth, the matter of traditional rulers and traditional areas is of great importance. Based on South African evidence, PPP could be a tool with which to address a wide variety of socioeconomic transformation agendas. Therefore, its use in fostering LED in rural and traditional areas is worth considering. The issue, however, is: How able are those communities to navigate what it will take to derive the most from PPPs? At the present time, there is more than anecdotal evidence about the pressure being brought to bear on traditional communities in the western region of Ghana as a result of offshore oil and the attendant business possibilities arising therefrom. Rural dwellers, traditional chiefs, and others are under pressure to sell land, enter into tenancy agreements, etc. Illegal Chinese miners have invaded many areas in the gold-producing parts of Ghana, often under the pretext of having been invited in by Ghanaian entrepreneurs under some form of partnership. While these are not PPP, the issue here is the capacity of the traditional and rural communities to navigate arrangements that are placed before them. Where is the state? Where is the voice of legal advocacy? How can civil society challenge impunity of the state in its dealings with rural people?

The above points should inform the drafting of regulatory instruments and the general operating regime around PPP. In addition, consideration should be given to a number of challenges that may mitigate PPPs in developing countries. These include:

- Conflicts and nebulous positions around what each PPP project is supposed to achieve. This means that the regulatory regime must demand sufficient and inclusive discourse on PPP benefits.
- Weak award procedures. This means consideration must be given to how sound the current public procurement rules are. Despite the provisions of public procurement legislation, political cronyism affords many instances of direct and sole sourcing.
- Lack of clarity in the competing roles of various public bodies that seek to have a say or enforce various rules in the conduct of any PPP. In other words, regulation must ensure a simplified situation of interactions between existent state regulators and the contractual arrangements made for any particular PPP.
- Failure to disengage existing service providers in situations where a PPP requires new entities within the supply chain. The point here is that should a new PPP imply that existing suppliers to the state, municipality, or institution are no longer needed, appropriate mechanisms of disengagement should be provided for by the regulation.
- Political expediency and immaturity is known to create a situation where new governments simply repudiate or renege on previously executed contractual arrangements. This would be most inimical to PPP, and regulation must tackle this prospect.

Given all of the above, some specific recommendations to the legal profession in Ghana in its quest to contribute to the regulatory framework are in order. These are articulated below.

Business Education—Members of the legal profession must educate themselves in the issues raised here and in other business matters.

Build trust and confidence—Build trust in your role and capacity to help Ghanaian businesses receive justice; become advocates of sound state-sector business practices.

Promote the use of alternative dipute resolution (ADRs)—From the evidence available in the literature, PPP may come in various forms and may be used to address a variety of issues from the operation of libraries to HIV/AIDS interventions. In resolving disputes that may arise, the business community must be helped to recognize that not all disputes must necessarily end up in a court or remain unresolved due to aversion for court processes.

Locate contract terms under Ghanaian law—Reverse the trend in which foreign entities demand that operating laws should be laws based in their home countries. It is unfortunate when contracts are being drawn up for projects in Ghana, Nigeria, Sierra Leone, etc. and local partners are forced to accept the jurisdiction of foreign courts.

The spirit of business—In considering the regulation framework, lawyers and drafters must bear in mind that in business, time is valuable. In business, capital tied up is shareholder value wasted. In business, expeditious action facilitates value. In business, four key justice propositions are always sought: procedural justice, distributive justice, relational justice, and informational justice. While business has moral obligations, businesses do not exist to do charity work. They must make money—legitimate money. Regulation of PPP must therefore recognize the business imperative, and the legal profession must come to appreciate the way business works and the concerns of business. Business confidence often revolves around participation, decency, transparency, accountability, fairness, and efficiency. These must be stressed in any PPP regulatory regime.

CONCLUDING SUGGESTIONS

This chapter explored the role and input that the legal profession may provide towards a PPP regulatory framework in Ghana because a PPP law has been mooted, and drafters, consultants, and others from the legal profession are being called upon to work on draft laws and make necessary input. As part of the build-up towards a formal legal regime, the Ghana Bar Association must spearhead the formation of a committee to draft and launch a code to guide PPP in Ghana. This committee must be made up of members from the Bar Association, Association of Ghana Industries, the Chamber of Commerce, and business advocacy groups. The committee's work and resultant code must address the points made above as well as the following:

- The issue of state and government behavior;
- Anxieties and behavior of the private sector;
- Preservation of corporate governance and the status of special purpose vehicles and mechanisms for inspection, internal control, and audit of PPP processes;
- Interests of traditional areas and rural communities;
- Financing arrangements and risk assessment tools;
- The place of trade associations;
- The adjudication processes; and
- An advocacy platform.

Clearly, PPPs are a growth area that holds promise towards assisting economic growth as well as inclusive attention to many of society's problems. The state should revisit the matter of public sector reforms and establish an agency or department dedicated to corporate and institutional governance, public sector reforms and policy, and monitoring and evaluation of PPP in Ghana. These three (governance, reforms, and PPP monitoring) when taken together should ensure that the most benefits are derived from PPP and other vehicles for economic growth and societal transformation.

REFERENCES

Abubakari, M., Buabeng, T., and Ahenkan, A. (2013). Implementing public private partnerships in Africa: The case of urban water service delivery in Ghana. *Journal of Public Administration and Governance, 2*(1), 41–56.

Aggrey Fraser Guggisberg Memorial Lecture Ends. (2012, March 12). Retrieved February 12, 2016, from Ghana News Agency website: http://www.ghananews agency.org/print/40430

Ameyaw, E., and Chan, A. (2013). Identifying public-private partnership (PPP) risks in managing water supply projects in Ghana. *Journal of Facilities Management, 11*(2), 152–182.

Arnold, G. (2006). *Africa: A modern history.* London: Atlantic Books.

Aryeetey, E., and Kanbur, R. (2008). *The economy of Ghana: Analytical perspectives on stability, growth and poverty.* New York: James Curry.

Asare, B., and Frimpong, M. (2013). Public-private partnerships and urban sanitation: Do expectations meet realities in Madina-Ghana? *Journal of African Studies and Development, 5*(5), 113–124.

Brunne, V. (2009). Public-private partnerships as a strategy against HIV/AIDS in South Africa: The influence of historical legacies. *African Journal of AIDS Research, 8*(3), 339–348.

Chomsky, N. (2013). *Necessary illusions: Thought control in democratic societies.* Cambridge, MA: House of Anansi.

Farlam, P. (2005). Working together: Assessing Public-private partnerships in Africa. The South African Institute of International Affairs (NEPAD Policy Focus Series Report no. 2).

Fombad, M. (2012). Strategies for accountability in public-private partnerships in South Africa. *African Journal of Business Management, 6*(38), 10260–10272.

Grindle, M., and Thomas, J. (1991). *Public choices and Policy change: The political reform in Developing Countries.* London: Johns Hopkins University Press.

Mansfield, E. (1997). *Microeconomics.* New York: W. W. Norton and Company.

Oluwole, D., and Kraemer, J. (2013). Innovative public-private partnership: A diagonal approach to combating women's cancers in Africa. *Bull World Health Organ, 91,* 691–696.

Puplampu, B. B. (2013). Business culture in Ghana—An exploratory study. *Global Management Journal, 5*(1/2), 35–45.

Rogerson, C. (2010). In search of public sector-private sector partnerships for local economic development in South Africa. *Urban Forum, 21,* 441–456.

Sinanovic, E., and Kumaranayake, L. (2010). The motivations for participation in public-private partnerships for the provision of tuberculosis treatment in South Africa. *Global Public Health, 5*(5), 479–492.

Vickers, J., and Yarrow, G. (1995). *Privatization: An economic analysis.* Cambridge, MA: The MIT Press.

Williams, I. (2012). Infrastructure development: Public private partnership path for developing rural telecommunications in Africa. *Journal of Technology Management and Innovation, 7*(2), 63–71.

Resources

Farlam, P. (2005). *Working together: Assessing public-private partnerships in Africa.* The South African Institute of International Affairs (NEPAD Policy Focus Series Report no. 2).

Guidebook on promoting good governance in public-private partnerships. (2008). UNECE, NY. Retrieved from http://www.unece.org/fileadmin/DAM/ceci/publications/ppp.pdf

An introduction to public private partnerships (2003). Partnerships British Columbia.

National Policy on Public-Private Partnerships. (PPP). (2011). Government of Ghana, Ministry of Finance and Economic Planning. Retrieved from

Public-Private partnership Handbook. (2008). Asian Development Bank. Manila. Retrieved March 2014, from http://www.adb.org/documents/public-provate-partnerships-ppp-handbook

16 A Framework for Building Organizational Capabilities in Africa

Hamid H. Kazeroony

INTRODUCTION

Creating sustainable management and organization development in Africa requires a holistic approach. The continent's sociopolitical and economic infrastructure requires a systematic review and planning. This chapter will explain what Africa has achieved through African efforts and international institutions in moving forward. Simultaneously, the chapter will explain the challenges in and a framework for building organizational capabilities to serve Africa.

A FRAMEWORK FOR HIGHER EDUCATION TO DEVELOP HUMAN CAPITAL

In addressing the continental need, Africa has been undergoing reshaping by a new ethnocentric continental branding, leading to a positive image in its individual countries (Papadopoulos and Hamzaoui-Essoussi, 2015). Help has been provided to reshape Africa's image by various global institutions despite the existing challenges. The IMF's 2015 report provided a favorable cross-border cooperation among African countries attempting to regulate their financial services despite the existing challenges (Enoch, Mathieu, and Mecagni, 2015). The World Bank reported an extensive undertaking in 2015 to address infrastructural, social inequity, and gender gap challenges to shore up the North African region (IMPACT: IFC in the Middle-East, 2015). The World Bank has undertaken addressing many basic structural issues, ranging from the creation of a more inclusive business environment to engagement of the private sector in the expansion of educational sector, despite the unique challenges to many parts of Africa ranging from gender equity to the banking system, which must follow Islamic rules in some countries (*Africa*, 2015). The African Union has provided a collective approach with the framework to create an integrated and inclusive Africa (African Union, n.d.). However, in many African countries such as South Africa and Egypt, although comparable to China in terms of per capita income, their governments lack enthusiasm and clear policy for creating adequate structural support to shore up economic activities (Kynge and Weatley, 2015). A major part of the framework is creating sustainable higher education to provide the required human capital for building capabilities in African organizations. As Nelson Mandela stated, "Education is the most powerful weapon you can use to change the world" (Education for Sustainable Development, n.d.).

The African Development Bank began developing its education policy starting in 1986 in response to a host of concerns ranging from educational access, equity, quality, and relevance to internal and external efficiency, educational management, organization and planning, and cost and effectiveness. In 1999, the bank revised its approach to be more focused on addressing educational issues (African Development Bank, 2009). UNESCO, through a series of conferences in 2009, adopted some general principles in addressing education in general, which can be suitably applied to the management and organizational field of studies in Africa. Applying UNESCO's principles to the management and organizational field of studies can help address the environmental, social, cultural, and economic orientation of graduates, using a variety of pedagogical techniques promoting participatory learning and higher-order thinking skills, which can lead to lifelong learning, locally relevant and culturally appropriate stewardship, and an adaptable workforce (Education for Sustainable Development, n.d.). However, international institutions should recognize that when creating information literacy to serve African management and organizational studies in higher education, one should be cognizant that Western models do not apply to the sociopolitical and economic background of those who require it (Raju, 2013). Additionally, Africa continues to face other major challenges in its higher education. Challenges range from lack of space to a continuation of colonial teaching imposing its will on the postcolonial learners (Visser, 2008).

Challenges also provide opportunities in creating a framework for improvement. First, accreditation by various international bodies can help improve the programmatic and pedagogical quality of higher education institutions and the programs as discussed Chapter 4 (see Okonedo and Aluko, this volume). Second, the effectiveness of investment and improvement in higher education should be subjected to continual monitoring and evaluation for making improvements and adjustments to meet the shifting demands for new skills, knowledge, and addressing the changing nature of economies with each African country as discussed Chapter 2 (see Mpabanga, this volume). Third, as addressed Chapter 3 (see Mukwevho and du Plessis, this volume), African governments must develop policies to better support indigenous population's effort for access to the academic channels in building a cadre of local scholars and reducing dependency on foreign knowledge workers (see Mukwevho and du Plessis, this volume).

CULTURE'S INFLUENCE IN BUILDING MANAGERIAL
AND ORGANIZATIONAL CAPABILITIES

In an ever-evolving globalization where economies become more interdependent and organizations must operate in multiple geographic areas with diverse demographics, culture plays a central role in equipping managers with the right tools to navigate through human interactions, supporting internal stakeholders, responding to the external constituents' concerns, and creating effective an organizational environment for optimal performance. Culture influences ethical practices, individuals' value systems, production of knowledge, nature of relationships at work, and behavioral conformity, which in turn impact organizational effectiveness for implementation and processes (Abimbola, 2013; Arowolo, 2011; Beugré and Offodile, 2001; Ika, 2012; Mufune, 2003; Nussbaum, 2003; Prinsloo, 2000; Sims and Gegez, 2004; van Tonder and Ramdass, 2009; West, 2014).

Ethics and principle-based decisions provide a window to one dimension of management behavior and its impact on organizational processes (Abimbola, 2013). Here, the focus is not on what are acceptable or unacceptable ethical or principle-based decisions but rather the differences in each player's cultural perspective of ethics and principles that can lead to differences in interpretation of interactions, situations, needs, and the resulting actions. A clear example of contrast between African and Western value systems can be derived from the African concept of Ubuntu—interconnection between the self and community (Nussbaum, 2003). The concept of Ubuntu has also influenced knowledge creation and the way managers interact and respond to situations (Arowolo, 2011; Mufune, 2003; West, 2014). In contrast to Ubuntu, Western mangers operate based on organizational contractual relationships and processes rather than the human relationships. More precisely, Ubuntu reflects workplace spirituality, a sense of connectedness, belonging, compassion, and appreciation (van Tonder and Ramdass, 2009).

When implementing a decision within a multinational African organization, managers must be mindful of cultural traps, particularly if an organization is based on any Western model (Ika, 2012). Too often Western-style organizations or projects operate based on a top-down hierarchy that does not follow many African participatory traditions, and hence, result in failure (Ika, 2012). Unlike the Western concept of dualism (mind and matter), Ubuntu juxtaposes one individual entity (ethical values, consciousness, behavior, etc.) through others; and hence, an entire organization can be seen through the eyes of one employee who is seen through all others in the organization (Prinsloo, 2000). Therefore, culture requires methodical and continuing training within African higher education to prepare managers for the future workforce as well as continuing training inside African organizations to mitigate rising issues and minimize their impact by striving to create the same perception of issues, processes, and their consequences within an organization for effective decision-making. Cultural fit should be considered in organizations operating in African to make sure neither the Western approach nor the African cultures are given supremacy but rather unique situations are examined to assess the fit (Beugré and Offodile, 2001). Currently, there are two divergent views on African management behavior. One view holds that due to enculturation African managers behave completely differently than managers elsewhere, whereas the second view holds that African managers' behavior converges with managers' behavior in other places (Mufune, 2003).

To effectively address cultural challenges in improving organizational capabilities in Africa, there are different tools that can be used. As discussed Chapter 6 (see Bobina and Grachev, this volume), African organizations can build on cumulative information in cross-cultural studies and awareness of differences and similarities, which can strengthen African managers' skills, especially for those lacking experience and exposure to international business transactions (see Bobina and Grachev, this volume). The nature of communication also plays a pivotal role in establishing effective cross-cultural understanding within African organizations. Competency-based training can help expat and local managers arrive at shared meanings for effective communications within organizational channels as addressed Chapter 7 (see Abugre, this volume). An important part of cross-cultural communication in the context of African organizations is understanding the nature and rationale for corruption and resolving the legal and social differences in understanding what constitutes corruption to effectively deal with the issues, as discussed Chapter 8 (see Adewale and Khalid, this volume).

THE NEED FOR AFRICAN MANAGEMENT AND ORGANIZATIONAL THEORIES

Inadequate attention to theory has contributed to the lack of sustainable development in African managerial and organizational practices (Bagire and Namada, 2015). In addition, lack of attention to language as the mediating factor and discourse that intermingles meaning and contextualizes the differences in meanings (Boje, Oswick, and Ford, 2004) has further exasperated meaningful construction of theoretical work to help develop African management and organizational theories. The language communicating foundational ideas currently undermines the African context of management and organization as Western ideas are taught in creating new managers leading organizations and theoreticians creating new paradigms of thinking in Africa (Harries, 2013). Therefore, constructing theories from African perspectives to serve management and building capabilities for African organizations can help as long as one is mindful that attempts in constructing theories are subject to historical interpretation of language and discourse; it should be contextualized within a particular historical period that may limit the reach of a theory (Boon, 1982). Yet, other foundational challenges in management and organization theory construction continue to exist.

One structural challenge is the ambiguous and politically based subject of what lies beyond postmodernism and deconstructionism (Calas and Smricich, 2009; Derrida, 1978; Foucault and Lotringer, 1996; Tsoukas, 1992) that can adequately and objectively lead to workable management and organizational theories in general, and in Africa, in particular. The other challenge in creating theories is that although the continent has been passed to Africans from the colonialists, the literature and writing is besieged by dictatorial rule in the postcolonial era, making meaningful learning theories impossible (Kubayanda, 1997). Finally, moving to a technological age, beyond industrialization where metaphors, discourse, and textual presentation has changed, new methods are required (Rodgers, 2012). However, recent efforts indicate a gradual rise in concentrated efforts for advancing African management and organizational theories.

Increasing data by various international organizations makes empirical research in Africa more tenable, particularly when research uses a randomized controlled trial (Klingebiel and Stadler, 2015). Perhaps, one way to Africanize management and organizational theories is to refocus their construction on Ubuntu (community-centered spirit) and Kgotla (participatory democracy) to appropriately channel the management and organizational research (Beugre, 2015). In pursuing unique African approaches to theory building, as discussed Chapter 9, this vol., the influences of mediating factors such as language, culture, epochal context, relevance, and applicability should be examined and meaning shared through the research process by the researcher and the researched, irrespective of the research method (see Kazeroony, this volume). Some approaches that can help advance African management and organizational theory construction can be interventionist research, graphic scaling, and hermeneutics as detailed Chapter 10 (see Puplampu, this volume). Therefore, when constructing new African management and organizational theories, Western theories can be used to build foundational structures that are universal in nature with the recognition that the attempts should become culturally relevant, as addressed in Chapter 10 (see Mutungi, Mutungi, and Fuentes, this volume). For example, cultural-historical activity theory, drawing on a particular culture within a given historical context, based on a given community engaged in relational and interactional processes, can help the researcher examine and analyze complex African management issues and organizational processes (Foot, 2014).

FUTURE PATHWAY FOR AFRICAN MANAGEMENT AND ORGANIZATION

Sustainable management development in Africa for building capabilities to serve African organizations requires proper positioning and development of human capital, assessing the experiential learnings needs of the next generation of African entrepreneurs, building partnerships between public and private sector, and creating a legal framework to facilitate the working of organizations and the regulatory environment in which they can operate. Building capabilities to serve African organizations requires a comprehensive framework.

Whereas in the global context, a contingent workforce has become the new reality, its psychological contract in building a relational-transactional bond between the worker and employer in African organizational context presents a challenge in defining the obligation of each and has become a distracting factor for managers and an impediment in organizational processes (Lee and Faller, 2005). As detailed in Chapter 12 (see Puplampu, this volume), from a broad perspective, human development requires a comprehensive social policy in any country to narrow the gaps between genders and income to enable and empower its labor force to develop the necessary skills and knowledge to help build the capacity needed for growing organizations (see Puplampu, this volume). From a narrower perspective, addressing contingent workforce issues requires the creation of a cadre of entrepreneurs through mentorships and providing experiential learning in addition or away from the educational setting as proposed Chapter 13 (see Onwuegbuzie, this volume). This approach combines indigenous apprenticeship models with management training practices to create successful entrepreneurs (see Onwuegbuzie, this volume). Once human capital challenges are overcome, one should turn his/her attention to creating strong collaborations between public and private entities to smoothly advance the interest of the public while enabling private organizations to grow and serve consumers, as suggested Chapter 14 (see Okwilagwe, Apostolaki, and Erdelyi, this volume).

The final building block in creating viable organizations in Africa is to address the harmonization of their legal practices congruent with international practices (Fombad, 2013). As suggested Chapter 15 (see Puplampu, this volume), legal frameworks should be reexamined to improve the clarity of each party's expectations in the legal process (including public and private institutions, regulatory agencies, and all stakeholders) to create transparent mechanisms by which managers and organizations can operate (see Puplampu, this volume).

As change agents, we should consider that temporal, spatial, philosophical, and structural shifts deserve monumental attention to details (Quy Nguyen, 2001) when implementing change on a continental basis. The future pathway for building capabilities to serve African management and organizations is vibrant, yet there are research areas and practical issues that deserve considerable reflection and analysis.

REFERENCES

Abimbola, K. (2013). Culture and the principles of biomedical ethics. *Journal of Commercial Biotechnology, 19*(3), 31–39. doi:10.5912/jcb.598

Africa [Fact sheet]. (2015, October 22). Retrieved December 7, 2015, from http://www.worldbank.org/en/region/afr/overview#1

African Development Bank. (2009). *African development strategy for higher education, science, and technology.* Retrieved June 15, 2014, from African Development Bank Group website: http://www.afdb.org/fileadmin/uploads/afdb/Documents/Policy-Documents/yol%20%C3%A9duc%20eng.pdf

African union [Fact sheet]. (n.d.). Retrieved September 19, 2015, from http://www.au.int/en/about/vision

Arowolo, A. (2011). African traditional knowledge systems management: The struggle between science and tradition. *IUP Journal of Knowledge Management, 9*(4), 7–26. Retrieved from http://search.proquest.com/docview/922985640?accountid=35812

Bagire, V., and Namada, J. (2015). Management theory, research, and practice for sustainable development in Africa: A commentary from a practitioner's perspective. *Africa Journal of Management, 1*(1), 99–108.

Beugre, C. D. (2015). The challenge of management scholarship in Africa. *Africa Journal of Management, 1*(1), 94–98. http://dx.doi.org/10.1080/23322373.2015.994429

Beugré, C. D., and Offodile, O. F. (2001). Managing for organizational effectiveness in sub-Saharan Africa: A culture-fit model. *International Journal of Human Resource Management, 12*(4), 535–550. doi:10.1080/09586190110037083

Boje, D., Oswick, C., and Ford, J. (2004). Language and organization: The doing of discourse. *Academy of Management Review, 29*(4), 571–577.

Boon, J. A. (1982). *Other tribes, other scribes: Symbolic anthropology in the comparative study of cultures, histories, religions, and texts.* Cambridge [Cambridgeshire]: Cambridge University Press.

Calas, M., and Smricich, L. (2009). Past modernism? Reflections and tentative directions. *Academy of Management Review, 24*(4), 649–671.

Derrida, J. (1978). *Writing and difference.* Chicago: University of Chicago Press.

Education for sustainable development [Fact sheet]. (n.d.). Retrieved December 8, 2015, from UNESCO website: http://www.unesco.org/new/en/education/themes/leading-the-international-agenda/education-for-sustainable-development/education-for-sustainable-development/

Enoch, C., Mathieu, P., and Mecagni, M. (Eds.). (2015, April). *Pan African banks: Opportunities and challenges for cross-border oversight [White paper].* Retrieved December 7, 2015, from http://www.imf.org/external/pubs/ft/dp/2015/afr1503.pdf

Fombad, C. (2013). Some reflections on the prospects for the harmonization of international business laws in Africa: OHADA and beyond. *Africa Today, 59*(3), 51–80.

Foot, K. A. (2014). Cultural-historical activity theory: Exploring a theory to inform practice and research. *Journal of Human Behavior in the Social Environment, 24,* 329–347. http://dx.doi.org/10.1080/10911359.2013.831011

Foucault, M., and Lotringer, S. (1996). *Foucault live: (interviews, 1961–1984).* New York, NY: Semiotext(e).

Harries, J. (2013). The glaring gap, anthropology, religion, and Christianity in African development. *Exchange, 42*(3), 232–251. doi:10.1163/1572543X-12341273

Ika, L. A. (2012). Project management for development in Africa: Why projects are failing and what can be done about it. *Project Management Journal, 43*(4), 27–41. doi:10.1002/pmj.21281

IMPACT: IFC in the Middle-East and North Africa Fiscal Year 2015 [White paper]. (2015). Retrieved December 7, 2015, from http://www.ifc.org/wps/wcm/connect/001b83804a5cce1e91d6dd9c54e94b00/FY15+MENA.pdf?MOD=AJPERES

Klingebiel, R., and Stadler, C. (2015). Opportunities and challenges for empirical strategy research in Africa. *Africa Journal of Management, 1*(2), 194–200. http://dx.doi.org/10.1080/23322373.2015.1026758

Kubayanda, J. (1997). Unfinished business: Dictatorial literature of post-indepen dence Latin America and Africa. *Research in African Literatures, 28*(4), 38.

Kynge, J., and Weatley, J. (2015, August 4). Redrawing the World map. *Financial Times*, 5.

Lee, G. J., and Faller, N. (2005). Transactional and relational aspects of the psychological contracts of temporary workers. *South African Journal of Psychology, 35*(4), 831–847.

Mufune, P. (2003). African culture and managerial behaviour: Clarifying the connections. *South African Journal of Business Management, 34*(3), 17–28.

Nussbaum, B. (2003). Ubuntu: Reflections of a South African on our common humanity. *Reflections, 4*(4), 21–26. doi:10.1162/152417303322004175

Papadopoulos, N., and Hamzaoui-Essoussi, L. (2015). Place images and nation branding in the African context: Challenges, opportunities, and questions for policy and research. *Africa Journal of Management, 1*(1), 54–77.

Prinsloo, E. D. (2000). The African view of participatory business management. *Journal of Business Ethics, 25*(4), 275–286.

Quy Nguyen, H. (2001). Time, temporal capability, and planned change. *Academy of Management Review, 26*(4), 601–623. doi:10.5465/AMR.2001.5393897

Raju, J. (2013). Viewing higher education information literacy through the African context lens. *African Journal of Library, Archives and Information Science, 23*(2), 105–111.

Rodgers, D. (2012). Busy as a bee or unemployed? Shifting scientific discourse on work. *Minerva: A Review of Science, Learning and Policy, 50*(1), 45–64. doi:10.1007/s11024–012–9187–5

Sims, R. L., and Gegez, A. E. (2004). Attitudes towards business ethics: A five nation comparative study. *Journal of Business Ethics, 50*(3), 253–265.

Tsoukas, H. (1992). Postmodernism, reflexive, rationalism and organizational studies: A reply to Martin Parker. *Organizational Studies, 13*(4), 643.

van Tonder, C. L., and Ramdass, P. (2009). A spirited workplace: Employee perspectives on the meaning of workplace spirituality. *South African Journal of Human Resource Management, 7*(1), 230–241. doi:10.4102/sajhrm.v7i1.207

Visser, H. (2008). *Listen to the urgent sound of drums: Major challenges in African higher education.* New Directions for Institutional Research, 200865–77

West, A. (2014). Ubuntu and business ethics: Problems, perspectives and prospects. *Journal of Business Ethics, 121*(1), 47–61. doi:10.1007/s10551–013–1669–3

Contributors

Hamid H. Kazeroony is Professor of Business at Minnesota State Colleges and Universities, Inver Hills, USA, Academy of Management Membership Committee Chair, the *Transnational Journal of Business* Managing Editor for Accreditation Council for Business Programs and Schools, and co-chair of the European Academy of Management's Gender, Race, and Diversity track. His research reflects his interest in the way methods of production impact organizational leaders, institutions, values, and ethics, which has been manifested through his recent contributions to a wide range of academic books and journals.

Yvonne du Plessis is a Full Professor at the Graduate School of Business and Government Leadership at the North-West University in South Africa. She manages the Organizational Behavior and Human Resource Management programs. Her research focuses on contemporary management challenges in cross-cultural work settings, and she specializes in the behavioral aspects of project management. She has published in various national and international journals and has contributed in a wide range of academic books.

Bill Buenar Puplampu is an Associate Professor of Organizational Behavior and Chartered Psychologist (BPS), and Dean of the Central Business School of Central University College, Ghana. His work has appeared in *Business and Society Review, Acta Commercii, Ife PsycholoGIA, European Business Review, Canadian Journal of Development Studies*, and *Consulting Psychology Journal*.

James B. Abugre is a Senior Lecturer in the department of Human Resource Management of the University of Ghana Business School, Legon in Ghana. He is a member of the International Academy of African Business and Development, a member of the Academy of Management, and ambassador representing Ghana. His research is in cross-cultural management and communication, international human resource management including training and development of actors in organizations.

Adeyinka Adewale is a doctoral researcher and teaching assistant at the Centre for Social and Organizational Studies, School of Leadership Organizations and Behavior, Henley Business School, United Kingdom. He is a member of the Africa Academy of Management and a reviewer with the *Journal of Managerial Psychology*. His research interests are in ethics and the influence of organizational factors on the morality of individuals working in them. His most recent works have focused on the ethics of bureaucracy, aimed at contributing to the literature of organizational ethics and ethical misconduct in the workplace.

Christos Apostolakis holds an MA in Business Administration from Bournemouth University, an MA in Public Administration and Public Policy from the University of York, and PhD from De Montfort University—Leicester, all in the UK. He is currently a senior lecturer in Strategy at Bournemouth University Business School. His research interests revolve around strategy, collaboration, and public-private partnerships as well as social entrepreneurship.

Mariya Bobina is a Fulbright Scholar conducting research on economic effects of culture in emerging markets. She published a book on international strategic alliances and articles in *Thunderbird International Business Review*, *Journal of International Business Studies*, *Venture Capital*, and *International Journal of Leadership Studies*. Mariya Bobina served as Country Co-investigator in 62 societies' Global Leadership and Organizational Behavior Effectiveness (GLOBE) research project and as Associate Member at the University of Chicago's Center for East European and Russian/Eurasian Studies, and conducted research at the Woodrow Wilson International Center for Scholars in Washington, D.C.

Rosalina O. Fuentes is the President of SAIDI (Southeast Asia Interdisciplinary Development Institute) Foundation, and Dean of the SAIDI School of Organizational Development (OD). She has been immersed in educating, training, engaging in education, and OD consulting and research activities, most recent of which includes her advocacy of Positive Organization Development and Appreciative Inquiry. She is recognized in the Philippines as a 'guru of AI' for spreading knowledge and use of Appreciative Inquiry in different organizational processes. Other areas she has extensive experience in include culture building, strategic and tactical planning, re-engineering, and the whole gamut of Organization Development interventions for clients and partners in corporate, nongovernment, church, and local government sectors in both local and international settings. Her coaching and mentoring expertise has allowed her to journey with owners and heads of entities and more than 100 candidates in the course of their MA and PhD study and research in OD.

Mikhail Grachev is Professor of Management at Western Illinois University and University of Iowa with interests in cross-cultural management and emerging markets. He is the author of four books, case studies, and articles in *Advances in International Management, Advances in Global Leadership, Journal of International Business Studies, Journal of Management History, Small Business Economics*, and *Problems of Post-Communism*. Mikhail Grachev served as Country Co-investigator in the GLOBE research and as an International Leadership Association board member. He was named Stanford and Wharton Research Scholar, and his "Making the Most of Cultural Differences" was featured in *Harvard Business Review*'s Breakthrough Ideas.

Sharif M. Khalid is a researcher and teaching assistant at the Henley Business School, University of Reading, United Kingdom. He is currently at the twilight of his doctoral research and has just recently joined the University of Sheffield Management School, University of Sheffield as Lecturer in Accounting. He is a member of the British Accounting and Finance Association, the Centre for Social and Environmental Accounting Research and the Governance and Responsible Investment Research Centre. His research interest lies within Critical and Emancipatory Accounting encapsulating: corporate social responsibility, corporate governance, responsible and ethical investment, integrated reporting as well as public sector management, accountability and transparency.

Olusegun Matanmi is a professor of human resources and industrial relations in the Department of Industrial Relations and Personnel Management, Faculty of Management Sciences as well as Dean of the Postgraduate School (the latter administrative function spanning August 2012–July 2015) at Lagos State University, Ojo Main Campus, Lagos, Nigeria. His core areas of academic and professional competencies include: strategic human resource management, labor and employment relations, entrepreneurship, diversity management, and research and evaluation methodology. He is a Fellow of the Institute of Strategic Human Capital Managers (Nigeria).

Dorothy Mpabanga is a Director in the Center of Specialization in Public Administration and Management (CESPAM) and Senior Lecturer of Human Resource Management in the Department of Political and Administrative Studies (PAS), University of Botswana. Dorothy obtained her undergraduate degree in Public Administration and Sociology from the University of Botswana, and an MSC in Development Economics and Project Planning and Appraisal from the University of Bradford in the UK. Mpabanga holds a PhD in Human Resource Management from the University of Strathclyde in Glasgow, Scotland in the UK. In joining the University of Botswana, Mpabanga brought with her vast industry experience from public sector and the Central Bank of Botswana. Her research interests and publications are in human resource management, constraints to industrial development in Botswana, NGO management, higher education management, performance management systems, ICT in Botswana, governance, elections and electoral processes in Botswana.

Emmanuel Mukwevho is an Associate Professor of Biochemistry at the department of Biochemistry, North-West University (NWU), South Africa. He holds an MSc degree in Molecular and Cellular Biology and a PhD degree in Anatomy and Cell Biology both from University of Cape Town (UCT). He is also involved in research and teaching and serves in many academic activities as an external examiner, reviewer in many scientific international journals, reviewer of funding applications, advisor in many scientific committees and research boards nationally and internationally. He is also a funded researcher who leads the Obesity and Diabetes Therapeutics Research Group at NWU and has published both nationally and internationally in reputable journals.

Emmanuel Mutungi is a Lecturer at Kyambogo University, Uganda. He is the Head of Department Industrial Art and Design and teaches graduate students. He is a Committee member of the Network of African Designers and a member of Academy of Management. His research interests are in material culture and indigenous knowledge. He believes that sustainable development can be achieved by utilizing local resources, knowledge, and skills available in the community before applying those that communities do not have or control. He has carried out several community projects in the areas of health, governance, and education using art as a tool, and has written articles and book chapters in the field of cultural entrepreneurship.

Shiphrah Mutungi is a Director of Morning Star Program—Viable Support to Transition and Stability—Juba, South Sudan. She has wide experience in processes for social development projects with emphasis in strategy development, implementation, monitoring, and evaluation. She has skills and experience in conflict transformation and peace building, trauma awareness and resilience building, organization development programs, HIV/AIDS, health programs, and gender institutionalization and advocacy. She has wide experience in using participatory and facilitation approaches that enhance ownership for sustainability.

Osikhuemhe O. Okwilagwe is currently a doctoral candidate in Strategy at Bournemouth University Business School, UK. Her research interests include policies for economic development, private sector development, collaboration, and public-private partnerships as well as strategic relationship management.

Henrietta Onwuegbuzie leads sessions in Entrepreneurship in the MBA and Executive programs at Lagos Business School (LBS), Pan-Atlantic University, Nigeria. She is currently the Academic Director for the Owner-Manager Programme and Project Director for the Impact Investing policy initiative at LBS. She has an MSc in Economics and Business Administration from the University of Navarre, Spain; an MBA from Lagos Business School; and a PhD in Entrepreneurship from Lancaster University, UK. She is currently a member of the editorial board of the *African Journal of Management*. Her areas of research interest include indigenous entrepreneurship, strategies for entrepreneurial growth, and sustainable development in emerging economies, as well as low-cost, high-impact business models that can be applied to both small and large-scale businesses.

Index